PRAISE FOR
ANATOMY *of a* GENOCIDE

"Furnishes well-lit imagination, though shaded with sadness, beneficial for the communities trapped into mutual impairment in various parts of the world."

—*New York Journal of Books*

"The result is breathtaking, painful, and astonishing . . ."

—*The Spectator*

"Masterfully researched and hauntingly rendered . . . nothing short of astonishing."

—*Providence Journal*

"A work of forensic, gripping, original, appalling brilliance."

—Philippe Sands, author of *East West Street: On the Origins of "Genocide" and "Crimes Against Humanity"*

"A brilliant book by a master historian."

—Jan T. Gross, author of *Neighbors: The Destruction of the Jewish Community in Jedwabne, Poland*

"Gripping, challenging, and masterfully written . . . A powerful warning against bigotry everywhere at any time."

—Tom Segev, author of *The Seventh Million: The Israelis and the Holocaust*

"Exemplifies the very best in current Holocaust history writing."

—Christopher R. Browning, author of *Ordinary Men: Reserve Police Battalion 101 and the Final Solution in Poland*

"Thoroughly researched and beautifully written . . . an exemplary microhistory of the Holocaust, a model for future research."

—Saul Friedlander, author of *Nazi Germany and the Jews*

ALSO BY OMER BARTOV

*Erased: Vanishing Traces of Jewish Galicia
in Present-Day Ukraine*

*Hitler's Army: Soldiers, Nazis, and War
in the Third Reich*

*Germany's War and the Holocaust:
Disputed Histories*

*The Eastern Front, 1941–45: German Troops
and the Barbaristation of Warfare*

ANATOMY

of a

GENOCIDE

The Life and Death of a Town Called Buczacz

OMER BARTOV

SIMON & SCHUSTER PAPERBACKS
New York London Toronto Sydney New Delhi

Simon & Schuster Paperbacks
An Imprint of Simon & Schuster, Inc.
1230 Avenue of the Americas
New York, NY 10020

First Simon & Schuster trade paperback edition January 2019

For information about special discounts for bulk purchases, please contact Simon & Schuster Special Sales at 1-866-506-1949 or business@simonandschuster.com.

The Simon & Schuster Speakers Bureau can bring authors to your live event. For more information or to book an event, contact the Simon & Schuster Speakers Bureau at 1-866-248-3049 or visit our website at www.simonspeakers.com.

Interior design by Lewelin Polanco

Manufactured in the United States of America

10 9 8 7 6 5 4 3 2 1

Library of Congress Cataloging-in-Publication Data is available.

ISBN 978-1-4516-8453-7
ISBN 978-1-4516-8454-4 (pbk)
ISBN 978-1-4516-8455-1 (ebook)

To my family

Wai-yee, Raz, Shira, and Rom
The rock of my existence and the fountain of my soul

And in memoriam

Yehudit (Szimer) Bartov, 1924–1998
Hanoch (Helfgott) Bartov, 1926–2016

I closed my eyes, so that I would not see the deaths of my brothers, my fellow townsmen, because of my bad habit to see my city and its slain, how they are tortured by their tormentors and how they are killed in wicked and cruel ways. And I closed my eyes for yet another reason, because when I close my eyes I become as it were master of the universe and see what I wish to see. And so I closed my eyes and called upon my city to stand before me, with all its inhabitants, with all its houses of prayer. I put every man in the place where he used to sit and where he studied and where his sons and sons-in-law and grandsons sat—for in my city everyone came to prayer.

—SHMUEL YOSEF AGNON, *THE CITY WHOLE*, 1973

Contents

Polish-Lithuanian
Commonwealth, 1569

Baltic Sea

Moscow•

MUSCOVY

Berlin
•

HOLY
ROMAN
EMPIRE

Warsaw•

Dnieper River

Kiev•

Habsburg Domains

•Buczacz

Vienna•

Dniester River

OTTOMAN EMPIRE

0   MILES   200
0   KM   200

Black Sea

Eastern Europe, 1914

SWEDEN

RUSSIAN EMPIRE

Baltic Sea

Moscow•

GERMANY

Wilno•
Minsk•

Berlin•

POLAND

Warsaw•

UKRAINE

Vienna•

GALICIA

•Buczacz

AUSTRIA-HUNGARY

SERBIA   ROMANIA

Black Sea

0   MILES   200
0   KM   200

Note on Place and Personal Names

The region discussed in this book was populated by several ethnic groups and ruled over time by different regimes. As a result, the names of places and individuals may differ substantially depending on the language and time period. For the sake of consistency, I have generally used the Polish version of place names, since they were also officially used for most of the period covered by this book, while providing in parentheses the alternative (usually Ukrainian, at times German) version when first mentioned, and keeping the original version when citing documents. For this reason I have generally kept the name of Buczacz (Ukrainian: *Buchach*) in its Polish spelling. But where there exists a conventional English spelling for known places, such as Warsaw, I have preferred that to the Polish *Warszawa*. Many Ukrainian individuals appear in Polish documents with the Polish version of their names, but whenever the Ukrainian name was known I have chosen to use it. Words in Russian, Ukrainian, Yiddish, and Hebrew are transliterated more or less according to conventional transliteration rules, apart from those names and terms already known in English spelling. Thus Moscow and not *Moskva*, Kiev rather than *Kyiv*, Dniester instead of *Dnister* or *Dnestr*, and Dnieper rather than *Dnepr* or *Dnipro*. I have normally transliterated the guttural equivalent of "ch" in the Scottish word "loch" as "kh" for all these languages apart from where other conventions already apply. Thus Pinchas rather than *Pinkhas*, and cheder rather than *kheder*. I have left out the soft signs from transliterations of Ukrainian and Russian for ease of reading. With a few exceptions, titles of books and articles written in languages not using Roman letters have been translated.

The author's mother, grandmother, and sister in Tel Aviv, 1979.

MEMORIES OF CHILDHOOD

The author's mother as a child in Buczacz, late 1920s.

"Tell me about your childhood," I said.

We were standing in my mother's kitchen in Tel Aviv. She was wearing a simple dress under a large apron. A diminutive, energetic woman, her still-ample curly hair dyed brownish-red, her face lined from the strong Middle Eastern sun and years of hardship. She was in her element in the large kitchen, the most important space in an apartment to which my parents had moved a quarter of a century earlier, just a couple of years before I left home and joined the army.

It was summer 1995, and she was making chicken soup. My seven-year-old son was playing next to us. Up to that day, I had never asked

1

about her life in Eastern Poland, before her parents moved the family to Palestine in 1935. She was seventy-one. I was forty-one. I had only a vague idea of her youth. I turned on the tape recorder.

I was born in Kośmierzyn [Ukrainian: Kosmyryn], a little village on the banks of the Dniester River in Polish Podolia, which is now in Ukraine. All the inhabitants of the village were Ukrainian. My father's father managed the estate of Graf [Count] Potocki's widow there. He lived on the estate. There was a rather large house there. I don't know how old I was at the time, perhaps four or five, so to me it appeared huge. It was a two-story house, and the grafina [countess], as she was called, lived there, along with the graf's sister and their sons. There was a huge courtyard, horse stables, cowsheds, and a large barn. My grandfather lived in a single-story house. There were Grandfather and Grandmother and the sons. I was born in the village. Soon thereafter we moved to Potok Złoty. Then we moved to Buczacz.

Today Buczacz (pronounced "Buchach") is a shabby post-Soviet backwater. Poor, derelict, depressed. In 1919 it had about thirteen thousand inhabitants. It currently has the same number. But its setting is enchanting: perched on several hills and intersected by a winding stream. Back when my mother lived there it was a quaint little town, and that's how she remembered it. She retained only fragments of her past, not unlike the bits and pieces of languages from that world she had kept somewhere in her head—Yiddish, Polish, Ukrainian, German, and the Russian in which she would sing to me as a child. She gently pulled little strands of recollections and affectionately wove them into her own fabric of childhood. She had been a teacher for decades. She had a good, strong voice and enunciated every word clearly.

We all lived in one house with Grandfather. The house had two units; we lived in one unit, on the right, and in the left unit lived Grandfather and Grandmother and my father's sister, who later married. The house was on a hill and was linked to the street by a stone staircase. And I remember the street—it led to the train station.

2

She never alluded to the fact that the street on which her house was located soon witnessed the deportation of thousands of the city's Jews, who were led along it, humiliated and beaten, to that very same train station, whence they were transported in inhumanly crowded cattle cars to the Bełżec extermination camp. Of the family that stayed behind, both hers and my father's, not a single member survived—all of them murdered. That too she didn't speak about in such terms. But our conversation must have evoked deeply suppressed memories in her because not long after, my mother began speaking about taking a trip back to Buczacz.

It never happened. She died three years later.

That conversation with my mother made me want to learn more about my ancestors—how they lived and how they died. So I spent the next two decades searching. I traveled across three continents and nine

Note from the Buczacz local branch of the Jewish Organization to the main office in Lwów on sending documents for immigration certificates for three men from Buczacz, including Izrael Szimer, the author's grandfather. *Source: Tsentralnyi derzhavnyi istorychnyi arkhiv, m. Lviv (Central State Historical Archives of Ukraine in Lviv, hereafter TsDIAL), fond 338, op. 1, spr. 240, p. 12, March 12, 1935.*

countries. I dug through countless archives. At one in Lviv, I found a note from March 1935 concerning three men from Buczacz requesting permission to enter Palestine. One of the three names is that of Izrael Szimer, my maternal grandfather.

I also discovered that the ship on which my mother and her family sailed to Palestine was launched in Glasgow in 1910. By the time it was scrapped in 1939, the *Polonia* had made 123 voyages between the Romanian port of Constanța and Palestine, bringing thousands of Jews.[1]

But I didn't find much more than that. I had set out on my quest too late. The people who could remember further back than my mother could were all dead. Some of the few remaining family photographs are inscribed and dated on the back, and at times I can identify a family resemblance, but no one is left to tell me anything about them. The moment to tap into the memories of the few who knew is long past.

Over those two decades, however, I did learn a great deal about the history of Buczacz and the catastrophe that befell it in World War II. I found a great many documents, mostly untouched since they were first deposited in dozens of archival collections, libraries, and other research institutions. I also identified scores of living survivors, as well as hundreds of written, audiotaped, and videotaped testimonies whose collection began even before the war ended and continued well into the 1990s. Personal diaries, eyewitness reports, judicial depositions, recorded testimonies, published and unpublished memoirs—all reflecting the manner in which each side understood itself and perceived others.

By letting those who lived that history lend their own words to the telling of it and providing accompanying photos, this book attempts to reconstruct the life of Buczacz in all its complexity and depict how the Polish, Ukrainian, and Jewish inhabitants of the town lived side by side for several centuries—weaving their separate tales of the past, articulating their distinctive understanding of the present, and making widely diverging plans for the future. Life in towns such as Buczacz was premised on constant interaction between different religious and ethnic communities. The Jews did not live segregated from the Christian population; the entire notion of a shtetl existing in some sort of splendid (or sordid) isolation is merely a figment of the Jewish literary and folk-loristic imagination. That integration was what made the existence of such towns possible. It was also what made the genocide there, when it occurred, a communal event both cruel and intimate, filled with gratuitous violence and betrayal as well as flashes of altruism and kindness.

If I have learned anything from the story of Buczacz, it is that we are all merely one link in that fragile yet astonishingly resilient chain of generations, of fate and struggle, of which history's relentless unfolding of events is made. Who we are, what we remember, how we raise our children, what we say and believe in and cherish and despise—these are the combined consequence of haphazard chance and human action, taken for reasons good and bad, deliberate and thoughtless, by us and by our ancestors. I may not have found out much about my family, but in a certain sense all history is family history. We all carry within us a deeply embedded fragment of memory, transmitted from one generation to the next, of those long centuries lived for better or for worse in what my mother called in Yiddish *ek velt*, that end of nowhere whence we came, like the fading echoes of a lost yet never entirely forgotten childhood.

The author's mother (front row on the left) about to board the ship to Palestine, 1935.

Chapter 1

THE GATHERING STORM

Election rally in Buczacz, 1907. Jewish candidate Natan Birnbaum at center front; Shmuel Yosef Agnon wearing a white fedora in the crowd on the right. *Source: The Nathan & Solomon Birnbaum Archives, Toronto.*

Buczacz first appears in the chronicles of medieval Poland in 1260 as an estate belonging to the noble Buczacki clan, noted defenders of Poland's eastern borderlands. In their prime, these early owners of Buczacz built a palatial wooden castle on a hill overlooking the village and river in the valley below. The sweeping landscapes of what the Poles call the *kresy*, or frontiers, have lodged themselves deep in the Polish romantic imagination. (The name of the ruling family, and hence the town's name, was probably derived from the surrounding beech forests, or *buczyny*.) In 1882 Sadok Barącz, a Polish Dominican monk of Armenian origins who spent his entire life in the region, published a colorful history of Buczacz that has become a rich source of local fables and legends.

Buczacz, he wrote, was situated "on the frontiers of Podolia and Red Russia," also known as Rus or Ruthenia, in "a green valley on a rocky base, divided into two parts by the narrow stream of the Strypa River. It is one of several charming, beautiful valleys in the region, richly endowed with capricious nature. The gloomy, ancient forests, the clear lakes, the wooded hills, the rich pastures, God's holy might splendidly spread out: all can powerfully harness the Slavic soul seeking freedom and security." The town was also directly on "the path of the Tatars," but the warriors of that "brave family from Buczacz" defended it "with their own bodies" against raids by these "wild oppressors." The Buczackis, Barącz assures us, "set an example to the knights of Rus and Podolia" by building "a defensive fort to protect the successful development of the town," motivated by "the holy flame of love for the land and for their ancestors." Whenever they heard "the terrifying sound of the enemy coming up from the dark valley," these "military units materialized on their brave steeds—known throughout Poland—as if they

Buczacz in the early twentieth century. *Source: Österreichisches Staatsarchiv, Vienna (hereafter AT-OeSt) / Kriegsarchiv (hereafter KA), BS I WK Fronten Galizien, 5839.*

had sprung out of the earth." Horses from this region were "highly sought after, and one pointed at them with pride: Look! This is a horse raised in Buczacz."[1]

The Nobel Prize–winning writer Shmuel Yosef Agnon, who was born in Buczacz in 1887, also associated the town's splendid physical setting with divine grace. In his posthumously published history of the town, *The City Whole*, he described Buczacz as "a city to which God has seemingly loaned some of His own land's glory." He envisioned it as a region of paradise, "situated upon mountains and hills," surrounded by "forests thick with trees and bushes," and nourished by a river that "flows within and around" it, by streams that "feed reeds and bushes and trees," and by "good springs" that "abound with fresh water." In Agnon's telling of it, his city was founded by a caravan of Jews, whose "pure hearts yearned to go to the Land of Israel" but who found themselves instead in a place of "endless forests, filled with birds and animals and beasts." There they encountered a band of "great and important noblemen," who were "so astonished by their wisdom and their well spoken manner" that they invited the newcomers "to dwell with them." Once the nobles "recognized that the Jews were their blessing," they told them, "The whole land is wide open to you. . . . Dwell where you wish, and if you want to trade in it so much the better, for there is no one in this land who knows how to trade goods." And so the Jews stayed; they "struck roots into the land, and built houses, and the nobility of the land liked and supported them, and the women were pregnant or with babies, and some had become exhausted and weak, and the elderly had aged a great deal and the journey would be hard for them." There they "lacked for nothing in learning of the Torah and the knowledge of God and were secure in their wealth and honor and their faith and righteousness."[2]

The events described in Agnon's mythical account fit the historical context, for the creation of the Polish-Lithuanian Commonwealth in 1569 had facilitated the takeover of vast tracts of Eastern Europe and Ukraine. As Poland expanded to the east, the nobility invited Jews to develop towns, commerce, and manufacturing, offering them favorable leases and privileges. The oldest tombstone in Buczacz's Jewish cemetery has been dated to 1587.

In 1612 the city was taken over by Stefan Potocki and remained the private property of this vastly rich and powerful Polish clan for a century and a half. Stefan had the foresight to convert the old wooden fortress into a formidable stone castle, protected by a complex of ramparts and trenches that enveloped the whole city. His son Jan, who inherited the city in 1631, saw the strength of the fortress repeatedly tested during the second half of the century.

By the mid-seventeenth century the 450,000 Jews of Poland constituted the single largest Jewish population in the world. But the colonization of these lands also caused mounting resentment among the local peasants and gentry, setting the background for the massive Cossack and peasant uprising of 1648. The destruction of Jewish communities was vividly described in Nathan Hanover's eyewitness account, *The Book of the Deep Mire (Sefer yeven metsula)*. Descriptions are so gory as to stretch credulity, yet they came to feature in people's imagination as identifying marks of the past and as threats or models for the future. As Hanover

View of the castle in the early twentieth century. *Source: ÖSA-KA.AT-OeStA/KA BS I WK Fronten Galizien, 5840.*

wrote, the Jews "were martyred in strange and cruel and bitter deaths. . . . Some were skinned alive and their flesh was thrown to the dogs; some had their hands and feet chopped off, and were then thrown on the high-way to be trampled by wagons and crushed by horses," and "many were buried alive." The most ghastly violence was directed at the most defense-less: "Infants were butchered in their mothers' laps. Many children were torn apart like fish; they slashed the bellies of pregnant women and took out the fetus and struck their faces with it. They tore open the bellies of some women and placed live cats in them," then "sewed up their bellies and cut off their hands so they would not be able to remove the live cats from their bellies." In other cases they "skewered some children and roasted them over fire and brought them to their mothers to eat."

Hanover recounts several instances in which the Poles betrayed the Jews and handed them over to the rebels to save their own skin. In other instances, Jews fought shoulder to shoulder with Poles on city walls, yet even then their own townsmen at times eventually betrayed them. Hanover wrote, "We wandered from place to place in the towns and villages and we lay on the open streets and even there we could not find rest. We were robbed and crushed, despised and reviled." In October 1648, having swelled with Jewish refugees from the east, Buczacz also came under siege by the Cossacks: "All the nobles and the Jews stood against them and shot at them with big guns and killed large numbers of the rabble and they could not conquer them." But "thousands upon thousands of Jews fell victim" to "great epidemics and famine" in the region caused by the war.

Overall, anywhere between twenty thousand and fifty thousand Jews were slaughtered, a substantial percentage of the Jewish popu-lation in the eastern part of the Polish-Lithuanian Commonwealth. The uprising ended in summer 1649 with the creation of a Cossack state from which Poles, Jews, and Jesuits were driven out; five years later the new state was merged with Muscovy, the rising power that became the Russian Empire.[3]

Buczacz was peaceful for the next couple of decades. The German tourist Ulrich von Werdum visited in February 1672. "This is a large

A melted seventeenth-century cannon in the Buczacz castle photographed in the early twentieth century. *Source: ÖST-KA.AT-OeStA/KA BS I WK Fronten Galizien, 5502.*

and very amusing town, situated on mountains and valleys" and "surrounded by a stone wall," he wrote. The city had "rather good houses, as well as three Roman Catholic churches, and a Russian monastery, now in the hands of the Dominicans. The Armenians also have a church there, and the Jews have a synagogue, as well as a beautiful cemetery, surrounded by a peculiar wall and planted with tall gay trees. The castle is built of stone as are its fortifications. It is situated on a mountain, below which the Strypa River flows, whose waters drive ten or twelve watermills that stand next to each other." "This picturesque town," continued von Werdum, "belongs to Lord Potocki" and "was completely burned down at the beginning of the Cossack uprising." But "it has now been largely rebuilt, especially by the Jews, who are very numerous in this town, as they are in all of Podolia and Rus."

Only a few months after von Werdum's visit, a vast Ottoman army besieged Buczacz. Since the lord of the city, Jan Potocki, was away fighting the Ottomans elsewhere, the city submitted to the invaders after only a brief defense. All of Poland followed soon after. In October 1672 King Michał Wiśniowiecki and Sultan Mehmed IV met in Buczacz and signed a treaty in which Poland was forced to surrender much of its eastern territories to the Turks and pay a hefty yearly tribute to the sultan.[4]

In 1675 the Ottomans stormed Buczacz once more, despite preparations by Jan Potocki, who even invited representatives of the Jewish community to discuss the defense of Buczacz and appointed a special superintendent charged with defending the Jewish quarter. The Ottoman general Ibrahim Shyshman, also known as Abraham the Fat, swiftly overcame these defenses and torched the city. While the nobles and some city dwellers escaped into the castle, the Jewish inhabitants were stranded in front of the locked gates and, in Agnon's words, "were slaughtered by the Turks like rams and sheep and their corpses found their graves in the bellies of wild animals and birds of prey."

The castle managed to hold out until the arrival of an army commanded by King Jan III Sobieski of Poland. But the following year, defended this time by Stefan Potocki, Jan's successor, the castle was finally seized. François-Paulin Dalairac, a French courtier of Sobieski's, observed that the Ottoman troops had "accomplished a lasting destruction" of the town, "so severe that only debris remained from the walls and the towers, and from the buildings almost nothing could pass for more than a ruin." As Stanisław Kowalski, a Polish author who lived in Buczacz during the interwar period, recalled in his memoirs, well over two centuries later local legend still maintained that the mighty castle had fallen only because of "the treachery of a woman." Her ghost, it was said, "appears in the gate of the castle on Resurrection Day, weeping and repenting her sin of betrayal."[5]

For the next few years, the Strypa River intersecting Buczacz served as the border between Poland and the Ottomans. But in 1683 King Sobieski finally liberated Buczacz. Writing his impressions of a visit the following year, Dalairac remarked that Buczacz, "once built of stone and surrounded from all sides by quadrilateral towers," now contained mostly "ruined and partly burned buildings, and only a few wooden taverns with thatched roofs." Once "a very considerable and well defended city" of such "vital strategic importance" that "the Sultan Mehmed IV himself came to its siege," Buczacz had become a mere shadow of its former proud self. As for its inhabitants, Dalairac noted that "round the city a large number of orchards are situated next to a great many springs," and "the peasants build their huts in accordance with the old Polish custom, next to the gate of the city and under the guns of the castle. Inside the city," he stressed, "live only Jews and some Poles."

Three centuries later Agnon observed that when they "returned to Buczacz" after the Turkish wars, the Jews "found the city desolate and their homes partly destroyed and partly occupied by gentiles. The synagogues and study houses had been uprooted and plowed and one could not tell where they had been." But Potocki, the lord of Buczacz, gave them land to build a new synagogue "so that they would dwell in his city and be satisfied with their residence, because it was the tradition since the days of his earliest ancestors in Poland that any place where the Jews dwelled saw life."

In 1699 Potocki reaffirmed and expanded the privileges granted by his predecessors to the Buczacz Jewish community, thereby creating the basis for Jewish life in the city until the Austrian annexation seven decades later. Jews were allowed to reside and pursue trade and commerce in Buczacz, to produce and sell alcoholic beverages, and to buy Christian homes; they were also protected from municipal courts by Potocki's assertion of his role as sole arbiter in "petty and major crimes" by Jews, whereas internal community disputes were handled by the rabbinical court; and while market days on the Jewish Sabbath were prohibited, Jews were allowed to "use the path leading from the walls of the church and the house of the priest to their synagogue on the banks of the Strypa River."[6]

In 1728 a massive stone edifice replaced the wooden synagogue on the riverbank. As was typical of "fortress synagogues" in this region, the building was designed to serve as a refuge for the community in times of war and violence, with walls up to fifteen feet thick; in order to prevent it from towering over nearby churches, its floor was dug well below street level. For Agnon it was the beating heart of the community: "As long as Buczacz existed, prayer in it never ceased." Its opulently decorated interior was illuminated by twelve opaque windows and four bronze chandeliers, shedding light on the murals of flowers and angels, the two iron rams topped by metal palms on either side of the Torah ark, the marble *bimah*, or reader's platform, at the center of the hall, and an array of other precious objects.

The Great Synagogue and
the Study House in 1921–22.
*Source: Beit Hatfutsot, Tel Aviv
(Museum of the Jewish People,
hereafter BH), 30544, 31266.*

The town's most spectacular edifices were built by Stefan's maverick son, Mikołaj Potocki, who started ruling in 1733. He funded the construction of the rococo city hall, the Basilian monastery, an adjacent two-story school, and a monastery church. Even more important, in 1754 Potocki provided an endowment for the Buczacz Collegium, the first secondary school in the city, which also provided housing, meals, and clothing to the students. Within fifteen years the school boasted 343 Greek Catholic and Roman Catholic students studying such fields as theology, history, geography, physics, Latin, and Greek. Jewish students were extremely rare, despite the growing presence of Jews in the city, who numbered over a thousand in 1765.[7]

Early twentieth-century views of the Basilian monastery and the city hall. *Source: AT-OeStA/KA BS I WK Fronten Galizien, 5492, 5541.*

✡ ✡

On October 3, 1772, as Barącz describes it, Mikołaj Potocki "watched sadly" as the Austrian "armed forces marched" into "his Buczacz." The humiliation of occupation made the magnate "completely lose heart," and the following year he handed over the ownership of Buczacz to his relative Jan Potocki. By the time Mikołaj died a decade later, the newly named province of Galicia, torn off from southeastern Poland and annexed by the Habsburg Empire, had undergone a radical transformation.[8]

With a total population of 2.6 million, the province was made up predominantly of serfs, along with 300,000 Christian town dwellers, 200,000 Jews, and 100,000 nobles. Buczacz was now located in Eastern Galicia, where Ruthenians formed the majority.

The new Austrian rulers sought to restrict the number of Jews in Galicia by imposing a "toleration tax" in 1773, which caused the deportation to Poland of those unable to pay it, as well as by demanding the payment of a fee for official permission to marry. But the authorities also believed that assimilated Jews could act as agents of Germanization; for this purpose, as of 1787 all Jews had to take German family names and the authority of Jewish religious leadership was subjected to centralized government control. The Austrians also tried to transform the socioeconomic condition of Galician Jews from a heavy concentration in trade and handicrafts to farming and agriculture by forbidding those not directly engaged in work on the land from leasing estates, mills, inns, taverns, and breweries. As a result, a third of the Jews in

Nationalities of the Habsburg Empire. *Source: A.J.P. Taylor, The Habsburg Monarchy, 1809–1918 (Harmond Sworth, UK, 1985), 36–37.*

Galicia lost their livelihood and were compelled to move into towns and cities; this only increased Jewish poverty and highlighted their profile as inhabiting a narrow economic niche.

Under the impact of the French Revolution, the Austrian government granted the Jews "the privileges and rights of other subjects," but while Jews were allowed to practice their religion and restrictions on marriage were lifted, they were still subjected to the "toleration" and "meat" taxes, to which a tax on candles, essential for Jewish religious rites, was added. Most troubling for Orthodox Jews was the imposition of military service, since recruits could not practice their religious customs. Still, in the long run, thanks partly to evasion of taxes and restrictions, and partly because of greater consideration by the authorities, the dynamic toward equal status for Jews led to substantial improvement in their status.[9]

The governmental effort to bring the Jews into the modern world was particularly visible in education. In 1787 Naftali Herz Homberg, a *maskil* (supporter of the Haskalah, or Jewish Enlightenment) from Bohemia, was appointed superintendent of all German-Jewish schools in Galicia. Homberg established 107 "normal" public schools throughout the province, including the Jewish boys' school in Buczacz that opened its doors in 1788. This radical educational reform aimed at creating a new generation of Jews, fluent in German and in proper Hebrew grammar, morally cultivated, and effectively trained to take up a productive trade. Attendance at the school in Buczacz increased from twenty-eight students in 1788 to two hundred in 1790, a clear sign of growing enthusiasm reflected in Galicia as a whole, where the number of students rose from six thousand to thirty thousand in the same two years.

The majority of Orthodox Jews in Galicia vehemently opposed this initiative, and Homberg's educational system was eventually abolished; the school in Buczacz closed down in 1806. But advocacy for Jewish educational reform continued. The moderate Galician *maskilim* Mendel Lefin and his disciple Joseph Perl, for instance, envisioned adaptation of Jewish customs, laws, and identity to the changing world around them. In 1814 Perl founded his Israelite Free School in Tarnopol (Ukrainian: Ternopil), forty miles north of Buczacz, which provided elementary education to boys and girls, combining Jewish and general subjects taught in "purified German." Perl's proposals to institute vocational training were also rejected, and his call to eradicate Hasidic mysticism and obscurantism similarly fell on deaf ears. Perl concluded in 1838 that the popular belief that a Jew "engaged in any kind of non-Jewish knowledge abandons both the Torah and the commandments" caused the ignorant to "hate and pursue" reformed Jews "almost to their deaths."[10]

In 1850 the *maskil* Moriz Bernstein published a pamphlet in Vienna ascribing Galician Jewry's "dearth of culture," "fanaticism," "dogmatism," "prejudices," and "spiritual stunting" to their children's education. At home, he wrote, children were told that religion was the product of "an endless series of forefathers," creating in them "a slave mentality" that "dragged human liberty to the grave" and made for the "stark religious barriers that divide people into enemy neighbors and separate humanity into numerous species." In the traditional cheder, the "filth and uncleanliness" of the classroom had a "most detrimental impact on the physical condition of the child." The teachers, who "had no knowledge of the world, no social tact, and no understanding of life," would "doggedly hammer the assigned weekly Biblical chapter into the poor child" and were "often very harsh." Such schooling was the cause of "all the mental lethargy, all the nonsense and muddled faith, and often all the spiritual ossification, which then accompanied the youth into adult life." Educated in this manner, lamented Bernstein, the ordinary Galician Jew was still "marked by his long caftan" and "grating jargon," making "the circle of his cultivated neighbors almost inaccessible" to him. Only by learning "the language of the land" would the Jews of Galicia "feel reconciled with their nationality at home," build "peaceful relations and even friendships with their neighbors," and "gradually tear down the partition that separates them."

Bernstein believed that the conundrum of the Jew's existence "as a tolerated person" and a "foreigner," who could naturally "have but little taste for any nation," would be resolved by granting the Jews equal rights. Once they could engage in other professions, Bernstein argued, Jews would no longer have to face "the bitter, offensive allegations and vituperative slurs that heartlessly insult" their "sense of morality and rights" and "injure the Jew within them." After all, "it is not the Jew who is a swindler, a usurer, as he is often called," but the legal restrictions that compel him to become that "profit-seeking salesman" detested by his neighbors.[11]

Emancipation would finally come in 1867, with Emperor Franz Josef's "constitution." Jews were labeled a community of faith rather than one of the empire's ethnic peoples; hence they could not declare Yiddish their "language of daily use," since language determined nationality. Instead Jews had to declare another language and were counted as members of the nationality that spoke it. Initially the Austrians had hoped this would increase the number of Germans in Galicia, but by 1910 almost all Jews registered as speaking Polish.[12]

Emancipation fundamentally changed relations between Jews and their neighbors. In 1848, reeling from the impact of revolutions that swept across Europe, the Habsburg Empire had abolished serfdom in Galicia, and over the next two decades a new nation would emerge in the larger, more populous eastern part of the crown land. Early stirrings of Ruthenian nationalism had preceded the revolution of 1848, led by small groups of priests, seminarians, students, and intellectuals, but before abolition they could not count on popular support. In the aftermath of the revolution, and especially following further reforms in the 1860s, the peasant masses, as the saying went, awoke from their slumber.

Most of the former serfs remained wretchedly poor, illiterate, and the target of ruthless exploitation by landowners. Ruthenian peasants associated their landlords with Poles and associated merchants, traders, shopkeepers, and tavern owners with Jews. The Ukrainophiles—Narodovtsi, or populists—who propagated the notion of a distinct Ruthenian-Ukrainian nationality and language, articulated best the political implications of these socioeconomic realities; they also reached growing numbers of people as literacy gradually spread with the introduction of village schools and peasants began reading newspapers. Helped by the Habsburg Empire's tolerant attitude toward nationalism, and by speaking directly to the peasants' concerns in their own words, the Narodovtsi became increasingly dominant.

Emancipation's lifting of restrictions on occupation and residence enabled Jews to return to the countryside just as rural Ruthenians were being nationalized through reading clubs and political rhetoric. Accompanied by the shift of the feudal system to a money economy, the growing presence and economic role of Jews in the villages created a popular sense of material exploitation and cultural decimation. Jewish moneylenders, shop and tavern keepers, cattle dealers, estate and mill leasers or owners were all presented as fleecing the ignorant peasants, tricking them into alcohol and tobacco addiction, lending them money at cutthroat rates, and retarding the development of a healthy Ruthenian nation. Indeed anti-Jewish comments in the new Ruthenian press soon surpassed attacks on Polish landlords.[13]

The Ruthenian newspaper *Batkivshchyna* (Fatherland), launched in 1879 by the national-populist Prosvita (Enlightenment) society, reflected such sentiments in a special section dedicated to reports by local activists in Galician villages and towns. One report spoke of "villages where out of a hundred households it is hard to find a single landed peasant who is not in debt—to the Jews, of course." Another report asserted that once a peasant borrows money from a Jew he "can't get the Jew off his back; he pays and works off the debt, but still ends up losing his land." This also meant, one correspondent wrote, that "our own Ruthenian way of life is dying out; in its place, bad customs from the outside are being introduced." The American etcher, lithographer, and writer Joseph Pennell shared the view that the Jews were destroying rural cultures, concluding from his European travels in 1892 that "the average Jew all over the southeastern part of the Continent is doing his best to crush out all artistic sense in the peasants by supplanting their really good handiwork with the vilest machine-made trash that he can procure."[14]

The fact that in 1900 only 20,000 Ukrainians, compared to 280,000 Jews, were employed (or dependents of those employed) in commerce certainly played into the argument that, as one correspondent wrote, "in our land Jews have taken over commerce to such an extent that it seems no one else can have a store or state concession, only a Jew." Rare reports of Ruthenian-owned businesses were a source of national pride; one peasant wrote gleefully that when a Jew entered a shop "and saw images of the saints on the walls, he became so frightened that he immediately fled."

But the starkest symbol of alleged Jewish venality was the village tavern, perceived by Polish and Ukrainian nationalists as the cause of the peasants' chronic alcoholism, indebtedness, and transfer of property to the Jews. Temperance movements often incorporated anti-Semitic rhetoric, and peasants learned to blame their own drunkenness on the Jews. One correspondent wrote, "You go into the tavern for tobacco, and the Jew . . . begins to praise his liquor and make fun of sobriety. . . . Before you know it, you've had one drink, then another." Finally, the peasant "sells his boots for his liquor and pays double for whatever he drinks," while "Iudka just puts his hands in his pockets, jingles his money, laughs and makes fun of the drunk."

Traditional peasant perceptions of Jews were more ambivalent. Jews could be seen as the embodiment of the alien precisely because they were so omnipresent. And since they provided the link between the agricultural producers and the marketplace, Jews were also perceived as mediators between the insular rural environment and the treacherous external sphere beyond it, the realm of death and the devil, with whom Jews were often associated: both were believed to be essential if malign presences in the cycle of life. Since the peasants were also deeply religious, they simultaneously internalized the Christian view of the Jews as damned for having murdered Christ and blessed as the sole witnesses of the Passion. Similarly, while Galician peasants might share popular Jewish faith in the magical healing powers of wonder-rabbis and *tzaddiks*, they also feared the menacing aspect that such powers could allegedly assume.[15]

This complexity of the Jewish presence in the Galician peasant imagination was radically transformed under the impact of nationalism. As the very first issue of *Batkivshchyna* succinctly put it, Ruthenians in Galicia faced "two terrible enemies: one of them is the clever Jew, who sucks our blood and gnaws our flesh; the other is the haughty Pole, who is after both our body and soul." Subsequent issues of the newspaper repeatedly resorted to anti-Semitic tropes, describing Jewish taverns as "a festering wound, which poisons and destroys our body; they corrupt the . . . soul of our village people . . . take away their property and drive them to criminality." The solution was not pogroms, but a boycott of Jewish businesses: "Then we will not have to drive out the Jews, they will leave us of their own volition." Similar sentiments were expressed by other newspapers; the Russophile *Russkaya Rada* warned that the influx of Jews would continue until "they have wrapped their spider's web around the entire village" and using "vodka and money push the peasants off their ancestral land. . . . Once we were masters of our land, but today the Jew says: I am master here, this is my land!"[16]

Emancipation was replete with ironies. With serfdom abolished, the peasants could sell their property, but their farms were small to begin with, and as they kept dividing them among their heirs, they could no longer live from the land. In contrast, once emancipated, the Jews sought economic opportunities outside the crowded and wretchedly poor ghettos, and those who made good could now buy land from peasants whose only option was to sell their plot and seek other occupations. By 1902 some fifteen thousand Jews owned farms or estates in Galicia, not a high figure for a Jewish population of close to a million but much higher than ever before and especially jarring to Ruthenian nationalists, who saw this as amounting to a Jewish takeover of the province. On the eve of World War I Jews owned over 10 percent of the estates, constituted 20 percent of the landowners, and made up more than 50 percent of the property leaseholders in Galicia.[17]

As estate owners and agricultural managers, Jews conformed neither to the stereotype of shtetl dwellers nor to that of rootless revolutionaries or Zionist separatists; they often identified with Poland, a sentiment that was not fully or consistently reciprocated. Unfamiliar to most urban Jews, the universe of Jewish landowners resembled in some ways that of the Polish landlords. But there were striking differences as well. Jewish estates also provided ample opportunities for contacts with gentile farmworkers and villagers.

This forgotten way of life prior to World War I was recalled decades later by Oskar Kofler, born in 1897 on his family estate of Petlikowce

(Ukrainian: Petlykivtsi), some ten miles north of Buczacz. Kofler's great-grandfather had obtained the right to own land as early as 1837 in recognition of his services as a court Jew (*Hofjude*); his grandfather already owned a mansion in nearby Mogielnica (Ukrainian: Mohylnytsia), and his father, Salomon, bought the estate and manor house of Petlikowce. An efficient manager, Salomon also had good relations with the estate's laborers and the Polish and Ukrainian villagers. But the staff on the estate "was almost exclusively" Jewish, and many other agricultural occupations, such as cattle and horse trading, as well as the grain market, were also "a near Jewish monopoly." Kofler recalled spending his childhood playing with farm animals and reading German classics; he attended Polish-language public schools in Drohobycz (Ukrainian: Drohobych), while at home the family spoke Yiddish and Polish and communicated with villagers in Ruthenian. He described his father as both "areligious" and "fluent in Hebrew and thoroughly conversant with Jewish scriptures and rituals"; his mother kept a kosher kitchen, lit candles on the Sabbath and the holidays, and said all the blessings. On Passover his father "headed the prescribed Seder," and on Yom Kippur he wore a white prayer shawl and yarmulke.[18]

Kofler took after his father and became similarly "areligious." And while politically his family "had no doubt as to their 'Polishness,'" he had fond memories of Ruthenian farmworkers. Generally his memoir depicts an ethnically mixed but quite harmonious social environment before 1914, not least "because the entire population spoke Ukrainian, mixed marriages were abundant, and no attention was paid whether one went to the Catholic or Greek Catholic church," the custom being that "male children from mixed marriages were educated in the father's denomination, the daughters in the mother's." To be sure, in retrospect Kofler was aware that "the animosity between the Poles and Ruthenians, which smoldered already since the end of the nineteenth century, became even more pronounced some years before the war." But open conflict "erupted mainly in the larger cities, particularly in Lwów," and "barely intruded into the more distant villages."

Kofler also disagreed that all manor laborers lived "in wretchedness

23

and degradation," insisting that this "depended on the personality of the employer and his attitude toward people." On Polish estates he did see a fair amount of hostility between farm laborers and landowners, not least because the latter did not maintain "permanent and direct contact with the people," preferring to spend their time away in cities and spas. Conversely, his father's relationship with the peasants was "exceptionally friendly" thanks to "his consideration, equanimity, fair treatment of anyone irrespective of his position, and his profound sense of justice." With hindsight Kofler wondered how this "was really possible," considering that "all these people knew very well that father was a Jew"; they must have been influenced by "prejudices picked up in church on the harmful role of Jewish leaseholders, which was supposedly the cause of all the peasantry's calamities." In part, perhaps, this had to do with his father's "unusual personal qualities" as well as his "general outward appearance," which was not "regarded as 'typically Jewish.'" But Kofler also remembered that villagers helped a fellow Jewish farmer who looked like "a prototype of the conservative Jew" simply because they saw him as "a decent man." Ultimately Kofler ascribed this behavior to the "incomparably higher moral standard of the people at the time" and to the fact that "generally there did not exist such deep-seated anti-Semitism" in prewar Eastern Galicia.

All this was wiped out in World War I, as Kofler was drafted and his parents were compelled to abandon the estate and move to Vienna. Anti-Jewish Polish land reform policies made sure they never got the estate back; his father died in 1927, wrote Kofler, "suffering and enduring the ruin of his life's work." In 1939 Kofler was called up again, this time to the Polish Army, and was soon taken prisoner by the Germans. His granddaughter, Ewa Koźmińska-Frejlak, who edited and introduced his memoir, comments acerbically, "The years he spent in captivity," partly in the so-called *Judenbarak* (Jewish compound), "would require a separate discussion." Kofler's first wife and son as well as his mother and sister were murdered in 1942; his nephew died during deportation by the Soviets in 1941. After the war Kofler changed his name to the Polish-sounding Koźmiński and worked for two decades at the Polish Ministry of Shipping and Foreign Trade. There were always those, observes his granddaughter, who liked to "remind him of, and reproach him for, both his 'Jewish' and 'class' origins."[19]

✡ ✡

The three decades that followed the destruction and erasure of pre-1914 Galician society belonged to the nationalists and ideologues, fanatics and zealots of a new breed, more willing to shed blood than to seek compromise, more determined to assert their hegemony than to preserve coexistence: impatient men with guns and bombs, often led by the half-educated and thirsting for a fight. But things did not start that way; before nationalism began to hate, it was also about education and enlightenment, material improvement, collective responsibility, and group identity. The path toward violence was neither foreseen nor inevitable.

Enlightenment meant different things to different people. The attempt to establish a Hebrew school in 1906–07 foundered when hostility from conservative religious circles compelled its director, Baruch Berkovich, to leave Buczacz after merely five years there. Jewish youths seeking public secondary education also faced many hurdles. Naftali Menatseach (originally Naftale Hertz Siegman) described being compelled to take the entrance examination for the gymnasium on the Jewish Sabbath, when Jews are not allowed to write, and, once accepted, having "to put on the 'gentile' uniform of the gymnasium and to cut off my short sidelocks"; he was also "fated to struggle with anti-Semitic teachers." Raised in an isolated village with only a handful of Jewish families, Menatseach recalled his father reading to him a newspaper article about the First Zionist Congress of 1897, as well as the great impression a booklet from Odessa titled *Chovevei Zion* (Lovers of Zion) had made on him. He devoured many of the popular Zionist historical novels of the time and avidly followed the literary magazine *Sifrei Sha'ashuim* (Books of Delight), edited in Buczacz by Yitzhak Fernhof. Initially homeschooled by his father, Menatseach subsequently attended the modern elementary Jewish Baron Hirsch School before being admitted to the gymnasium.[20]

The percentage of Jewish students at the gymnasium rose from one-fifth in 1900 to one-third of the five hundred students in 1914. Over the same time, the number of Greek Catholics declined from one-third to one-fourth, and the Roman Catholic student body was only marginally larger than that of the Jews. The gymnasium's pre-1914 annual reports contain many names of youths who sat side by side in the same classroom or passed each other in the school's corridors before setting out on radically different, at times antagonistic paths: the historian and chronicler of the Warsaw Ghetto, Emanuel Ringelblum, denounced and murdered with his son in 1944; members of the "Nazi hunter" Simon Wiesenthal's family; future *Judenrat* (Jewish council) member Bernhard Seifer, and future physician Max Anderman. There is something unsettling about seeing the normality of a school report composed three or four decades before so many of these families were murdered, deported, or dispersed. Yet this list of names hardly reflects the Polish and Roman Catholic gymnasium leadership's perception of its pedagogical and political mission.[21]

Established and supported by the Austro-Hungarian regime in what turned out to have been its waning years, the school boasted a curriculum that exemplified the ideals of a classical humanistic education. Yet from its very inception, and despite the glaring fact that a growing proportion of the students were Jews and Ruthenians, this public institution viewed itself as a bastion of Polish nationalism. The vast majority of the teaching staff was Polish. In 1901, out of seventeen teachers only one was Ruthenian and one Jewish. Even in 1914, with a total faculty of twenty-eight, there were perhaps five Jewish and even fewer Ukrainian teachers, all the rest being Roman Catholic ethnic Poles.

The tone was already set during the consecration of the new public gymnasium in 1899. Numerous dignitaries attended the event, including the Polish governor of Galicia, the local landowner Count Emil Potocki, the Roman Catholic prelate Stanisław Gromnicki, the Greek Catholic parish priest Telakowski, and the town's Jewish mayor, Bernard Stern. However, there was no Jewish religious representative. Following a service led by Gromnicki and a call by the governor for the gymnasium to "always produce brave people, who will act for the benefit of society and nation," the gymnasium's newly appointed director, Franciszek Zych, took the podium. Zych admonished his young audience

The Buczacz gymnasium with the Basilian monastery and the ruins of the castle in the background during World War I. *Source: AT-OeStA/KA BS I WK Fronten Galizien, 5534.*

"to repay the country" for their privileged education, resist "the world's enticing amusements and entertainments," and reject the "destructive doctrines of the era of materialism and the wild theories of revolution." The students' task was to bring "pride to your homeland," which must be able to "count on more brave members and citizens ready to make sacrifices." This homeland was made up of "our fraternal Polish and Ruthenian nations," and the students had to remember that they were "sons of the same land" and not to "pay heed to false counselors who try to plant the venom of hatred into your young hearts."

Zych's idea of the homeland, then, was "historic" Poland, and the fraternity he advocated implied the submission of Galician Ruthenians to Polish rule; it was a vision that left no room for a separate Ukrainian state. As for the seventy-five Jewish students present in the audience, they merited not a single mention in the director's speech and were not expected to share in the fraternity of nations he invoked.[22]

Not all Polish teachers bought into this hypernationalism. In an essay he wrote for the school's annual report of 1906, the teacher Leon Kieroński forcefully argued that students should be taught to be open minded and clear eyed; the goal of education was to encourage curiosity, tolerance, rationality, and objectivity. The popular social Darwinist view of life as "a ruthless struggle for survival" should have "no place in a school that educates people in the spirit of humanitarianism." The choice was stark: "Either we assume that society is right to be humanitarian," or we "devise means of exterminating one another in the easiest possible way." For that reason the greatest threat to the humanitarian ideal was the concept of a "national education" precisely because it transformed "this noble term" into "empty platitudes or chauvinism," which merely "exacerbates national differences and causes strife and conflict." Only education "in the spirit of humanitarianism" would allow patriotism to "blossom and yield noble, not wild, fruits." Ultimately teachers should strive to educate their students in a spirit of "pure harmony" that eventually "leads to the same objective as the Christian idea."[23]

The harmony Kieroński strove for was hardly reflected on the ground. Teofil Ostapowicz, who spent most of the first decade of the twentieth century as a student at the gymnasium, recalled that all five dormitories set up for poor students coming from the countryside were determined by denomination: Polish students were accommodated at the Głowacki and Mickiewicz dormitories; Ruthenians could apply for support from the "peasants' stipend" or the "Ruthenian (Russophile) stipend"; and Jewish students were eligible for a "Jewish stipend" that paid full board and provided academic assistance to those struggling in class.[24] For each of these groups, the school did serve as an incubator of future national elites, but its own orientation was exclusively Polish.

Most Jewish children still received only rudimentary schooling. Absenteeism and dropout rates remained very high, not least because of economic distress. While Jews were relatively better off than the peasants, and notwithstanding anti-Jewish claims to the contrary, apart from a thin crust of relatively affluent families, the vast majority of the Jews in Buczacz, as in the rest of Galicia, were poor; many of them left during those years in search of a better living across the Atlantic. Soon after arriving, the new immigrants set up self-help associations. The First Buczacz Benevolent Association, incorporated in 1892 in New York City, was established "to afford substantial assistance" to its members "and their families in cases of sickness and distress," as well as to promote their "social, mental and moral welfare." Seven years later this association was replaced by the Independent Buczaczer Congregation and Benevolent Association of the City of New York, two-thirds of whose principal members were already U.S. citizens. Two more associations of immigrants from Buczacz were founded in 1901 and 1904, both dedicated to helping the sick and the needy.

It took until 1911 for these immigrants to feel sufficiently secure economically to begin helping the community back in Buczacz. That year the Buczacz Relief Society of America was formed with the explicit "purpose of doing charity and relieving the distresses of the natives of the City of Buczacz" and helping "the students of the native schools whether in the City of Buczacz, Kingdom of Austria or any other place or country." Helping others was a sign not just of growing economic security but also of integration into American society. In October 1918, eighteen months after the United States entered World War I, the new American Buczaczer Relief Society would announce proudly that all signatories of its application for registration were U.S. citizens and pledged that it would be "rendering financial aid and assistance to American citizens of Austrian birth who are now in the Naval or Military service of the United States Government."[25] The old Buczaczers had become patriotic Americans.

✡ ✡

Most of those who left never came back. But some did. They brought with them a hint of the outside world and the possibilities of a different existence, as well as books, newspaper subscriptions, ideas, and opinions. But they also found themselves irretrievably trapped in the drudgery and tedium of provincial life. Their children, growing up among those books and magazines, ideas and disillusionments, at times decided to act where the fathers had not: to transform not just their hometown but the entire world. Some became adventurous, reckless, and tragic figures: their high hopes were irreparably dashed, their firm beliefs betrayed, the world of their youth wiped out, and the one that replaced it turned out to be infinitely more cruel and cynical.

Fabius Nacht and his sons are a good example. Born in 1848 in a well-to-do religious family that had already come under the influence of the Haskalah, Fabius spoke German at home and attended the state gymnasium in Stanisławów (Ukrainian: Stanyslaviv), where the language of instruction was Polish. He had hoped to study mathematics at the University of Vienna, but since Jews were barred from teaching that subject, he chose medicine instead. Returning to Buczacz in 1879 as one of a handful of locals with a university degree, he established a private medical practice, dedicated himself wholeheartedly to his profession, and for a long time was the most prominent medical authority in Buczacz. His expertise was sorely needed: in 1894 the dismal hygienic conditions caused a cholera epidemic that claimed a thousand lives in the Buczacz district; twelve years later the local Yiddish-language weekly, *Der jüdische Wecker* (The Jewish Awakener), again warned that "typhus, German measles, diphtheria, and whooping cough" were "showing signs of becoming epidemics" in the city, and proposed "to clean the streets every morning, and not just once a week."

In 1891 Fabius was appointed medical director of a newly built, modern hospital, a position he held until his retirement in 1925. Even after his retirement he maintained his private practice until his death in 1937. An obituary published in the Polish Socialist Party's weekly the following year hailed Dr. Nacht for having "retained his passionate enthusiasm for the ideals of freedom, equality and fraternity throughout his life"; it also noted that his "desk was overflowing with piles of socialist newspapers and magazines of all shades and languages." As his son Max explained decades later, in response to his encounter with "the reactionary, church-ridden Vienna regime," Fabius had became a socialist.[26]

Nacht's sons, Max and Siegfried, were raised as members of the first activist socialist generation in Buczacz. Agnon, who belonged to the same age group, recalled those heady early days of social mobilization. "An explosive new word is making the rounds in Buczacz and it is 'socialism,'" he wrote. Suddenly people's servants were declaring that "every person is his own master and does not belong to anyone else"; previously they "used to work from daybreak to midnight," but now they "stop

The Jewish hospital before World War I. *Source: Postcard in author's possession.*

working after eight hours." In the countryside "the socialists incited" the agricultural laborers to strike to demand "wages instead of being treated as beasts of burden." In response "the government sent in soldiers to bring the workers back to the fields, but the socialists came and talked to the army until the government began to fear that the poison of socialism would also penetrate the soldiers' hearts." Many of these socialists, commented Agnon, were Jewish "sons of the wealthy who appeared not to lack for anything," yet now every father feared that his son's activism "would land him in prison or that he would marry the daughter of a worker." Those who had thought that "Zionism is the worst of all upheavals in the world," quipped Agnon, now "discovered that there are even greater upheavals" since Buczacz had become "a city of socialists."[27]

Of course Buczacz never actually became "a city of socialists." But for a while the Nacht home was a hub of political ferment, "the meeting point for socialist youths of all nationalities," as the doctor's obituary put it. Siegfried Nacht, a volatile, restless youth, had been expelled in quick succession from the gymnasium in Buczacz and then from its equivalent in nearby Brzeżany (Ukrainian: Berezhany) for underground political activities, finally matriculating at his father's alma mater in Stanisławów in 1895. With a degree in electrical engineering from the

31

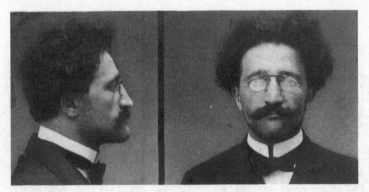

Siegfried Nacht, 1903. *Source: Schweizerisches Bundesarchiv BAR, Bern, E21#1000/131#9249.*

Technical University in Vienna, Siegfried's Jewish background, socialist politics, and hot temper stood in the way of his finding a position. By the end of the century he had denounced Zionism, renounced his membership in the Jewish community of Vienna, turned against Austrian Social Democracy as nationalist and anti-Semitic, embraced anarchism, and moved to Berlin. But he did not stay there for long; he appears to have spent the next few years traveling, mostly on foot, from one revolutionary cell to another. In April 1903 Siegfried crossed into Gibraltar and was promptly arrested on suspicion of plotting to assassinate King Edward VII during his visit to the British territory. The fact that he carried a pistol did not help matters.

The arrest made Siegfried a cause célèbre across the continent, igniting protests by the "Polish colony" in Paris and Ruthenian socialists in Vienna and prompting the establishment of a committee in London with such prominent members as the Russian anarchist Peter Kropotkin and the English philosopher Herbert Spencer. In Buczacz the news of Siegfried's arrest and subsequent release for lack of evidence on May 5 transformed him, in the sarcastic words of his brother, from "the disgrace of the town" into "a national hero, the fame and pride of the place." Depicted in the Polish press as "an engineer" and "an author" defended by "a former minister, a real countess," and "an actual prince," Siegfried was seen in Buczacz as a veritable "eighth wonder of the world, who had fortunately eluded the gallows." Agnon also vividly recalled Siegfried's triumphant, albeit ephemeral, return to his hometown, as he marched down the street "holding his head high like a prince, a black cape over his shoulders with its hem flowing down below his knees, a black hat on his head slightly tilted to one side, his moustache rolled upward and his beard descending in the shape of a half Star of David." Accompanied by "beautiful maidens from the best families" and with "all the officials making way for him," Siegfried "was walking as if" the whole city "belonged to him." This must have been the best day of Siegfried's life. In 1912 he emigrated to the United States, where his life does not seem to have amounted to much. But to this day he is remembered in anarchist circles as the author of the German-language pamphlet *The Social General Strike*, published under the pseudonym Arnold Roller in 1905.[28]

✿ ✿

By that time, such Jews as the Nacht brothers—active within the fold of radical politics, anarchism, and socialism—might no longer have been thought of as Jews, but as the cunning of history would have it, the very socialism that had facilitated their transformation came to be seen by other nationalists as a Jewish conspiracy. Nor did Jewish nationalism fare any better. Edward Dubanowicz's study of the 1907 national parliamentary election campaign in Galicia sought to explain the troubling coalitions between Jews and Ukrainians against Polish candidates. In the past, he noted, "our traditional Polish attitude did not allow us to remind foreigners of their foreign origin"; now one had to concede that "Jewish separatism" had "acquired serious political significance." As Dubanowicz saw it, in 1907 the Zionists had simply made "a cold and sly political calculation" intended "to inflame and feed the hatred of both allied parties," namely the Jews and the Ukrainians, "for their alleged mutual oppressor, the Polish nation," and to "wrest their co-religionist masses from Polish influence" in order "to gather their votes under the banner of Jewish identity."

From a Polish perspective, all this meant was that while the Zionists were "elected by Ruthenian votes," their presence in Parliament "weakened the numerical strength of the Polish representation in Vienna" and "increased the number of those who are presently the Polish nation's most implacable enemies," the Ruthenian nationalists. The naïve belief, concluded Dubanowicz acerbically, "that since it owes so much to the Polish nation . . . the vast majority of the Jewish population would be a loyal and sympathetic element within national politics, can no longer be sustained." Instead "the idea of a separate Jewish political identity" had won over "the Jewish masses" and "directly positioned" them "against the Polish political interest."[29] In other words, Poland had been betrayed by its Jews and would never again be able to trust them to defend its national cause.

In fact the "Jewish masses" in Galicia had little reason to sympathize with Polish nationalism, which offered no solution to their main concern: the grinding poverty in which they were mired. Close to two-thirds of the Austro-Hungarian Empire's Jews lived in Galicia, mostly in the eastern part, the vast majority of them in congested ghettos, with increasingly scarce economic resources. The tremendous obstacles faced by the Vienna-based Relief Association for the Destitute Jewish Population of Eastern Galicia, founded in 1901 and usually referred to as the Hilfsverein (Relief Association), in its attempts to alleviate this desperate economic situation, illustrate the sheer scale of the problem.

Lacking sufficient resources to establish an industrial base in Galicia, the Hilfsverein focused on training Jewish craftsmen in modern industrial technology. But the relatively few graduates of such courses in Vienna tended to "emigrate to America or to remain in western countries." An attempt to create a network of cottage industries in Galicia, many based on specialized training for women, faltered when it was realized that it was necessary to "enable the student after a short period of training to make a living" with her newly acquired skills, "since the main goal is to deal with the hunger of the poverty-stricken population." The plan to set up agricultural training also had to be revised when a study commissioned by the association in 1904 concluded that directing "many Jews to land cultivation could stimulate anti-Semitism because of the existing land hunger among Galician peasants."[30]

The Ruthenian population in the Galician countryside was of course even poorer and, to the despair of Ukrainian nationalists, also suffered from an abysmally low literacy rate. In the Buczacz district in 1880, out of a total population of 50,000 people only 2,500 men and 1,400 women could read. In the villages, where the majority of Ruthenians as well as many Poles lived, things were far worse. Those seeking to gauge the sense of national identity among villagers therefore had to rely on parish priests as informants. This was especially the case with Ruthenians, since village teachers tended to be Polish. A questionnaire distributed in 1911 to several communities in the Buczacz district suggested that Polish cultural, political, and educational hegemony, as well as emigration by Ruthenians and colonization by Poles, had set off a process of Polonization at the turn of the century. At the same time, the very fact that such surveys were being conducted demonstrated that in a region where the majority still spoke Ruthenian (including many Roman Catholics possibly of Ruthenian ancestry), this dynamic was being reversed by Ukrainian nationalist activists.[31]

With the exception of the peasant strikes of 1902, which had more to do with economic grievances, national mobilization in the Buczacz district was quite peaceful. Kofler found it was mostly in the larger cities that ethnic tensions occasionally erupted into open conflict, as happened, for instance, during a demonstration by Ruthenian students over the use of Ukrainian at the University of Lemberg (Polish: Lwów; Ukrainian: Lviv) in 1907.[32] But the potential for massive Polish-Ukrainian violence, which eventually erupted in the wake of World War I, was still lurking under the surface, suspended between conflicting narratives of past massacres and schemes for future radical "solutions."

The Polish elite still hoped to assimilate Ruthenians into a future greater Poland, whereas the Ruthenians were too weak to push their own national agenda. The "Jewish question" appeared more amenable to a "solution," not least because it was the only issue on which nationalist Poles and Ukrainians could agree. In a sense, the Jews clarified matters where they remained murky as far as conflict between their neighbors was concerned: where it was difficult to distinguish between Poles and

Ukrainians, both agreed that the Jews were clearly different, and while Poles and Ukrainians might struggle over ownership of the land, both agreed that the Jews had no business owning it. In this sense, the Jews served as a perfect foil against which one could easily identify oneself.

Between 1848 and 1914 new opportunities for self-realization and collective liberation appeared to first open up and then to progressively close down again: the period began with the revolutions of 1848, known as "the spring of nations," and ended up with mass death in World War I. History, as it subsequently happened, was not predetermined. The citizens of Buczacz, like those of many other towns in Galicia, had more choices than ever before or after. A new world was emerging, and the constraints of the old were falling away; tradition had weakened, religious faith was waning, authority was loosening its grip on family and society. Travel became easier, and people could go farther, change identities more easily, aspire to previously unthinkable goals, and embrace radical, exciting new worldviews. But as people began identifying themselves nationally and ideologically, they also looked at others through different eyes, distinguishing them not only by religion and ethnicity but also by whether their history gave them the right to continue living where they were. By the same token, those who bought into the nationalist discourse constrained their own horizons by determining who they were and where they belonged and what they could and should hope and struggle for. In this brave new world vast collectives were being transformed into communities of fate, whose history and future were determined by national affiliation; it was a fate from which others were excluded by definition, and yet one from whose repercussions there was no escape.

And so, in the last years before the war, all three ethnoreligious groups were turning inward, not only as they had done before, by simply ignoring each other, but in a more aggressive, resentful, accusatory manner, by perceiving their own hardships as a consequence of the other groups' conduct or success and by viewing the rights of others as necessarily restricting their own. This was not a viable recipe for continued coexistence. The trigger was finally pulled in 1914.

Chapter 2

ENEMIES AT THEIR PLEASURE

Bridge over the Strypa in World War I. *Source: AT-OeStA/KA BS I WK Fronten Galizien, 13936.*

I n retrospect it was thought that such vast multiethnic empires as Austria-Hungary were doomed to be torn asunder from within by the competing forces of opposing nationalists. Yet precisely because of its heterogeneous nature, the empire found ways to negotiate with national movements and to diffuse the radical nationalism that emerged fully only after its demise. In towns such as Buczacz before 1914, nationalists were often preoccupied with such seemingly non-militant projects as the promotion of literacy and education, economic progress and folklore, hygiene and athletics. To be sure, a growing accumulation of resentment, fear, and hatred, born of socioeconomic, ideological, and religious differences, simmered behind the façade of a well-regulated society and a prodigious, albeit unwieldy, bureaucracy. In different circumstances, such tensions might have been channeled toward nonviolent accommodation and adjustment. It was World War I that completely changed the rules of the game.

Most people know much more about the war on the Western Front than in the East. But the fighting between the Russian Empire and the German and Austro-Hungarian Empires was extraordinarily brutal and costly and devastated vast tracts of Eastern Europe. Following its declaration of war on Russia on August 6, 1914, Austria-Hungary tried to confront the numerically superior Russian Army by launching a preemptive offensive into Russian Poland. In return, the Russians invaded Galicia, pushing the Austrians all the way to the Carpathians by late September. For the next nine months the Russians occupied all of Eastern Galicia. These battles cost the Austrian Northern Army well over a third of its original 900,000 men, with the Russians losing a fourth of the one million troops who had marched into battle on that sector of the front. Ethnic tensions and demoralization were prevalent in both imperial armies fighting in Galicia, while the heavy casualties made discipline another major concern. Much of the brutalization of the troops on both sides can be ascribed to the opposing armies' weakened command systems, deficient training of recruits, and increasingly precarious logistics, quite apart from the horrendous bloodletting at the front.[1]

✡ ✡

Buczacz was swept into the carnage early on, when once again it found itself in the path of invading armies. Over the next six years it would be repeatedly conquered and occupied by one side or another, devastated by fighting, looting, wanton destruction, and ferocious violence. Eventually little was left of its former self but a memory of better times and mounting fear and rage, a lust for vengeance tempered only by the urge to return to an increasingly elusive normality.

We know about events in Buczacz throughout much of the war and its aftermath from the unpublished diary of Antoni Siewiński, the

Antoni Siewiński. *Source: "Pamiętniki buczacko-jazłowieckie z czasów wojny wszechświatowej od roku 1914 do roku 1920," Biblioteka Jagiellońska, Kraków, rkp. 7367.*

Polish principal of the boys' school in Buczacz prior to World War I. Siewiński, who was born in 1858, had set out to "note down every-thing that occurred in Buczacz and its surroundings" just "as soon as the world war began." And even though he lost and rewrote his diary twice during the war, it is a remarkable account by a perceptive though nationalist and anti-Semitic observer that reveals much about events in the city and about how they were viewed by the town's Polish intelli-gentsia at the time.[2]

Although Siewiński's school had catered to a mixed population of 180 Jewish and 120 Roman and Greek Catholic students before World War I, and despite the preponderance of Jews among the city popula-tion, the principal's view of Galicia as an inherently Polish land and of Buczacz as a bastion of Polish identity was unshakeable. Hence also his perception of the gymnasium, which all his sons had attended, as being charged with the task of forging "upright people and good patriots." And yet, as Siewiński unhappily conceded, prewar Buczacz was dominated by Jews, who owned all the handsome stone houses in the city center with their numerous well-stocked stores. Conversely, the houses of the Poles and Ruthenians "were hidden in the outskirts." Just as troubling was the fact that the Jews also controlled the local political scene: "the mayor of the city had always been a Jew," as were almost all his officials. "Even in the gymnasium," that fortress of patriotism, "there were several Jewish professors." Such Jewish hegemony meant that anyone blaming a Jew for misdeeds "was immediately berated as an anti-Semite," even when "everyone could see that the Jews had a hand in it."[3]

Like many other Polish nationalists of his generation, Siewiński perceived Jewish influence as both a cause and a consequence of Polish decline. The few "honest and honorable" Jews were merely "exceptions to the rule," and the fact that the Jews were "very concerned with their children's school training" merely highlighted the lamentable finding that since the Christian residents "care less about schooling," they spent much of their time in taverns, where they "drank away the entire city center, while the Jews became the owners of the nicest houses in the city." This was one reason for Siewiński's joy at the outbreak of war, in which, he was certain, "the entire Polish nation, oppressed for over one hundred and fifty years by the partition powers," namely Germany, Austria-Hungary, and Russia, which had partitioned Poland among themselves in the late eighteenth century, would finally be liberated by a new generation of youthful patriotic heroes. And indeed, he wrote, following the declaration of war, "whole trainloads of recruits from the west passed through Buczacz" on the way to the front. They "revealed no faintheartedness: 'Against the Muscovites,' they all called out." Other formations streamed through town on foot and horseback: "Hungarian Hussars in red pants and caps, infantry dressed in light blue uniforms," and "reserve units, made up exclusively of Poles and Ruthenians," who were served a warm lunch by the grateful citizens. "To us," Siewiński commented, "it first appeared to be a powerful army. Everyone thought that within three months they would knock down the entire Muscovite state and then the war would come to an end."[4]

On the Kofler estate in Petlikowce there was markedly less optimism. As Kofler recalled, "nearly all the stablemen were called up." Before leaving, "all of them turned up, without exception, on the farm, fed the horses and performed all the other tasks as on any other day." Then they "gathered in front of the storeroom," and "each of those who was about to leave restored his implements to the supervisor of the storeroom, then stepped forward to Father, kissed his hand and thanked him for his caring employment. Father embraced each of them, wished them God-speed and safe return (only very few ever returned alive). This was a heartbreaking scene. I did not cry aloud, but tears ran down my cheeks; others cried, too."[5]

But there was a vast difference between these Ruthenian peasants and such patriotic Poles as Siewiński and his sons. Józef, the eldest, was conscripted right away; the two younger boys, Zygmunt and Marian, joined a local paramilitary group of some two hundred Polish youths under the command of a seventeen-year-old gymnasium student named Władek Winiarski. Their plan was to join Polish leader Józef Piłsudski's newly established Polish Legions, but soon after marching out of town to prepare for war, they encountered the rigors of life in the forest, and many of them returned to their parents. The Jews in Buczacz also wanted to display their patriotism, which meant loyalty to the empire. As Siewiński recalled, in mid-August Mayor Stern invited the community to celebrate the emperor's birthday, and the Jews "put lights in all their windows and hoisted the black-and-yellow Austrian flag." Like many other nationalists, Siewiński perceived Austrian patriotism as anti-Polish. At a meeting he attended that evening, where "leading representatives" of the town's three ethnic communities were asked to discuss "the Jewish question," very little communal solidarity could be found. "The room was full of Jews," he wrote disdainfully, and "on the podium one kike [*żydek*] read from a book in Aramaic, and then delivered a speech in that language." (Obviously this was a Zionist who spoke Hebrew.) "Thankfully," continued Siewiński, "the next speaker, attorney Eisenberg, addressed the audience in Polish"; he asked the Poles and Ruthenians in the room to help the Jews create their own legion so that all citizens of Buczacz would "fight side-by-side . . . and thereby protect the common Fatherland." In response, the old Polish Professor Józef Chlebek, fondly remembered by some of the young Zionists from the prewar period, stood up and berated the Jews for not supporting the Polish cause.

Having profited to such an extent from Polish hospitality that they had become "the richest people in Poland," he exclaimed, the least the Jews could do was to "think like Poles and, despite their Jewish faith, to feel like Poles." Next the Ruthenian post office official Ostap Siyak stood up and "spoke to the Jews in Ukrainian in a similar vein," urging them to support the Ukrainian cause. Only a few days into the war, it appeared that the idea of a common fatherland had already expired.[6]

Beyond national loyalties, Siewiński found the very notion of Jewish soldiers entirely ludicrous. He described with relish encountering a group of "kikes" (żydy) marching in formation through the city a few days later, "each and every one of them as fat as a well-nourished ox, their snouts shining like lacquered lanterns." These "stupid Jews," he sneered, "thought they could accomplish in one day what Polish youth had been working their hearts out to achieve for many years." They obviously also lacked the required moral fiber; the moment "the Jews heard the first guns" in the distance, "the entire crew fled in all directions and on to Vienna, where they could finally breathe again." As for those who stayed behind, they hid "in some dungeons, from which they later emerged like rats and established a legion of dealers in stolen goods, traitors and denouncers, remaining always on the side of the most powerful."[7]

The truth of the matter, as Siewiński conceded elsewhere, was that upon hearing of the Russian invasion of Galicia "all the inhabitants" of Buczacz "were shaking with fear that they would be dragged away by the Cossacks," and "masses of people were fleeing from the city, in wagons, carriages, and on foot, carrying their baggage on their backs, while the dull echo of the guns in the east could already be heard in the city." Even the aspiring young legionnaires, lost in the countryside and finally discovered by a search party of reserve soldiers on bicycles, were urgently returned to Buczacz when Cossack units were spotted nearby. Meanwhile a steady stream of refugees from the East flooded the town, "a vast crowd of children, women, and elderly people." That they were "mostly Jews, screaming and panicked," indicated that they knew what to expect from the Russian Army. The train at the railroad station was packed; some "climbed on the roofs of the railcars," but most had to continue on foot to Monasterzyska (Ukrainian: Monastyryska). Fear, commented Siewiński, "is contagious, and there was such panic, that even the most serious people fled. Even many Catholics packed up their belongings and left the city."[8]

As these scenes were unfolding, the returning lads of the Buczacz Legion made hasty preparations to leave the city as a militarized formation. Some good people donated clothes, and several workshops were set up in the building of the Polish Sokół (Falcon) gymnastics society, where a cobbler made boots and a Jewish tailor sewed uniforms: since he was poor, the tailor was the only one "paid for his labor." Other youthful volunteers were arriving from the surrounding villages, while older members of the Sokół association gathered on the bridge over the Strypa "and deliberated what should be done with the youth"; some had heard "about the atrocious acts of the Muscovites" and expressed fear "that they would take all these youths captive and hang them." Late that night the Buczacz Legion, made up of sixty youths, including Siewiński's sons Marian and Zygmunt, marched out of the city. Only a few had weapons or any training with firearms, but they made up for that lack with patriotic zeal. Zygmunt declared to his weeping mother, "I must leave and protect another mother, who is mother to us all, our Mother Poland. She has now been resurrected and we have to support her. Why else would you have raised us as Poles?" His father was filled with pride. Still, as the young legionnaires marched in formation to the train station, singing patriotic songs, "the city brimmed with much sorrow and grief," wrote Siewiński. There was good reason to worry. The lads were not allowed by the authorities to board a train, so they marched on foot to a nearby Polish estate, where they spent the night. After that no more news about them reached Buczacz for many months.[9]

A few hours after the legionnaires left Buczacz in the early hours of August 23, the regular Austrian Army troops stationed around the city also pulled out; they were replaced by a formation of eight hundred reservists, all recruits from the Buczacz and Czortków (Ukrainian: Chortkiv) area. Many citizens invited them into their homes for lunch and made them gifts of extra bread and cigarettes. But what Siewiński remembered most vividly was that in the marketplace one Jewish woman struck a soldier in the face when he grabbed a handful of the melon seeds she was selling. The soldier did not react. But "the following day," Siewiński recorded gleefully, "the Jews would fare differently." On that day the soldiers took up positions outside Buczacz and "the city became as still as a gravestone; everyone was expecting something terrible." After several hours of shelling, the artillery ceased around 4:00 p.m., and people in the city could distinctly hear "the cry from thousands of throats: 'Hurrraaah!'" as the Russian infantry charged forward, accompanied by the rattle of machine guns. A unit of Hungarian cavalry could be seen "riding out of the forest and fleeing at great speed along the winding road, across the Black Bridge, through the Jewish quarter, and then further up the street to the village of Nagórzanka (Ukrainian: Nahiryanka)." They were followed by "automobiles filled with Hungarian officers," who were inexplicably shouting "Victory! Victory! Hail the emperor!" Finally the reservists abandoned their positions, crossed the Strypa, and headed westward through Buczacz under constant Russian fire. By 6:00 p.m. the shelling and gunfire died down and evening set in.[10]

That night the residents of Buczacz tried to absorb the shock of finding themselves directly on the front line of a vast military confrontation. Many women and girls who had lost contact with the rest of their family sought shelter in Siewiński's school, fearing rape. Later that night about a hundred wounded soldiers were brought to the Basilian monastery and the military hospital, headed by the gymnasium director Franciszek Zych. A doctor arrived only at midnight. The next morning, August 25, just before sunrise, Siewiński went to his school to fetch brine for the hospital. "Just as I was about to turn back," he wrote, "I found myself face-to-face with a Cossack." Up to that moment he had known of Cossacks "only from written accounts or woodcuts." This "was a big man, wearing a huge hat on his head, and holding a carbine in his hand." Then a formation of fifty-odd Cossacks rode down the path from Fedor Hill toward the city center. One of them, an older military doctor, greeted Siewiński. The Russian occupation appeared to begin in a friendly spirit.[11]

The Austrian military hospital in the school by the Sokół building across the Strypa during World War I. *Source: AT-OeStA/KA BS I WK Fronten Galizien, 5540.*

✿ ✿

That first impression did not last long. As violence quickly unfolded, observers such as Siewiński read into it the inherent nature of those involved. One instance occurred very soon after the Russians arrived, when three Austrian reservists, who had been left behind by their unit and spent the night in the city hall, woke up to find themselves surrounded by Cossacks. As such apocryphal tales would have it, the Jewish member of this trio "instantaneously took off his shirt, wrapped himself with an old blanket he grabbed from the wall, and walked out." The other two, a Pole and a Ruthenian, made their way to the hill where the ancient linden tree still stood, under which the "shameful peace" of 1672 was said to have been signed, and ambushed a squadron of Cossacks riding past. The two were swiftly caught, "horribly tortured," and executed; their mangled corpses were dumped on the street. Later they were buried in a common grave on Fedor Hill. "They were the first two warriors to be buried in this field. Unfortunately later there were thousands." In Siewiński's telling, none of them could have been Jews.[12]

The Cossacks were followed by the mass of the Imperial Russian Army. It took a single column of infantry and cavalry three hours to pass through Buczacz. Clad in oilskin, they "stank already from afar and soiled the entire city." Siewiński did not think much of the soldiers, but "their numbers were impressive" and their horses "gorgeous." He was not too troubled by the Austrian debacle: as far as Poles were concerned, "from the beginning of the war everyone thought about Poland's victory, not Austria's." In contrast, Kofler, who subsequently became a decorated combat officer, described "the shattering impact caused by the advance of Russian troops, barely a few weeks after the declaration of war." As the Russians, "preceded by frightening reports of acts of violence and murder, flooded all of Eastern Galicia," he noted, "the great majority of landowners and nearly all Jewish owners and leaseholders left their properties and went to Vienna or Hungary." The Koflers were among the very few who remained on their estate, although the Austrian military had recruited most of their farmhands and requisitioned many of their horses.[13]

From his isolated vantage point in Petlikowce, Kofler observed that for "three days and nights, without interruption, the masses of the military rolled over the main road from Tarnopol to Buczacz and on to the southwest: infantry divisions, cavalry of different descriptions, huge numbers of artillery and supply companies." Initially, he maintained, "Despite the monstrous rumors, it turned out that in the early months of the war the strictest discipline was maintained in the areas under Russian rule." At least as far as he could tell, "on all the settlements along the route and those nearby, no loitering or plunder occurred." But the Koflers also had a stroke of luck; early on in the occupation they were visited by "an observer from the Red Cross, whom we recognized as being Jewish. He was completely overjoyed at meeting coreligionists with whom he could talk." It was this man who shortly thereafter warded off the commander of a Don Cossack detachment demanding oats for his horses, thereby facilitating the Koflers' survival for a few more months. Elsewhere things were far worse, with arbitrary violence, plunder, and wanton destruction becoming increasingly common in villages around Buczacz. In the village of Zielona (Ukrainian: Zelena), for instance, a Cossack unit destroyed 105 beehives, looted the villagers, and set their houses on fire; those who tried to save their homes were shot, along with a twelve-year-old girl and a young pregnant woman. Siewiński remarked, "We quickly understood that with the Russians things would not proceed as smoothly and simply as it had initially appeared."[14]

Indeed Buczacz itself was subjected to endless acts of random violence and looting. Siewiński considered the Kuban Cossacks particularly unruly: "When they encountered anyone on the street, especially a Jew or a well-dressed Jewish woman, they robbed them right there and then." He concluded, "No one was safe and protected from such plundering." Sexual violence too was common. As Russian troops ransacked Jewish homes in the wealthier part of town, they "drove all the Jews out of the houses, leaving for themselves only the young and beautiful Jewish women," whom they subjected to a "most jovial" gang rape: "As soon as one group of soldiers left, another one arrived." Finally, following a military setback in nearby Monasterzyska, the Russians decided to torch Buczacz. The officer in charge of this operation, Lieutenant Majer, targeted especially the elegant houses in the city center, allowing residents half an hour to vacate their homes before they were set ablaze. "The soldiers were especially interested to know whether the houses belonged to a 'yevrey [Jew],'" in which case they were "burned down right away."[15]

The torching of the city center was accompanied by widespread looting, in which everyone seems to have participated: "Ukrainians drove and walked from the outskirts and nearby villages" and "plundered together with the Cossacks, and our Jews came with wagons and took whatever fell into their hands." Siewiński recalled stepping out of his home in the middle of the night and seeing "a vast sea of flames over the marketplace." The Russians let the fire burn for three weeks, while food in the city became ever scarcer. When Siewiński finally ventured out to a bakery, he encountered Lieutenant Majer, who suggested that he protect his own home by dousing its thatched roof with water. Clearly Poles and Ukrainians living on the outskirts were not targeted. As Siewiński and his neighbors clambered up on their roofs a Cossack horseman rode by calling, "Save your houses, drench them with water, we are burning down only the Jews!"[16]

The fires were finally extinguished only when they threatened to spread to the outskirts and after it was realized that munitions could no longer be safely taken on the main road through Buczacz. About 125 of the largest houses had been destroyed, including many public buildings, mills, stores, workshops, pharmacies, food storage facilities, breweries, and other economic enterprises. The local economy was in ruins, and the prewar social order had crumbled. On the streets of Buczacz Russian soldiers were selling pricy cigars and cigarettes, plundered from the tobacco factory in Monasterzyska, for a few kopeks. Now schoolchildren, "both Catholics and Jews . . . smoked thick cigars on the streets" and "laughed right in the faces of their old teachers, because they knew that in this environment center they could tell them nothing." The youth, exclaimed Siewiński, "had no shame any longer and [was] out of control, stealing whatever they could lay their hands on." While the Jews "bought the tobacco and cigarettes for rock-bottom prices and soon made golden business out of them," other "town residents flocked

Burned-out houses in Buczacz city center during World War I; Basilian monastery and Fedor Hill in background. *Source: AT-OeStA/KA BS I WK Fronten Galizien, 5841.*

to the fields to collect potatoes," regardless of "whose fields these were." After all, "since all the distilleries had burned down," no vodka could be produced, and once winter came the potatoes would in any case freeze in the ground. In this atmosphere of want and chaos, lamented the principal, "every Muscovite had a woman in the city and the outskirts" because "women whose husbands were at the front" now "threw themselves at the Muscovites with such zeal that even they spat at them."[17]

By mid-September, with the fires finally out, the city "looked terrible; everywhere blankets and pillows were scattered on the streets and in the gutters and one could take as many as one wanted. From several houses smoke was still rising; the whole city had been covered for weeks with a thick, black cloud of smoke which made your eyes tear up, and jackals in human form were roaming the streets in search of loot." A kind of order was eventually established by the commandant of the gendarmerie and district commissioner Captain Medyński; a Russified Pole married to a Polish woman, he made no effort to conceal his local mistress, whose own husband was serving at the front. Medyński's idea of order was to walk around "with a whip, and not a day went by without him punishing at least two Jews with it." Toward the end of September, Medyński paid a visit to the Petlikowce estate. Kofler remembered him as a "middle-aged Pole, graying, very good looking and tall." He greeted the family "very cordially, speaking all the time in Polish." It appeared that the Russian authorities wanted "to convey a feeling of security and safety" to estate owners so as to rebuild the local economy. Precisely because Medyński "knew that we were Jews," observed Kofler, "he wanted all the more to assure us of safeguarding our stability on the same level we had enjoyed heretofore." But moments later Kofler witnessed how this "graceful and well mannered gentleman became a wild beast," brutally lashing out in Russian at the village headman and the deacon of the church, whom he accused of redistributing land to the peasants. "This first acquaintance with the real face of Russian reality," wrote Kofler, "forever remained carved into my memory."[18]

The Russian district governor, a certain Szeptyłycz, whom Siewiński portrayed as a "very genial" and "fleshy man of considerable size, with a truly pleasant and agreeable face, always closely shaven," reigned over a deeply corrupt and often violent local occupational regime. Using various pretexts, the Russians imposed heavy fines on wealthy Jews, and whoever refused to pay "was immediately jailed and maltreated so badly" that he swiftly relented. Outright hooliganism was not uncommon: when the Jewish post office superintendent prepared his home for his daughter's wedding, the Russians plundered and wrecked it completely, bringing the best loot to·the governor's wife and their three daughters. Indeed the wives of Russian officials made it a habit to pick out choice fabrics for dresses from local merchants without ever bothering to pay. "The Muscovites," concluded Siewiński, "had a good life in Buczacz."[19]

Some attempts were made to care for the most needy. For instance, the Russians set up a soup kitchen in the building of the Sokół, demanding that the estate owners of the region deliver the supplies. The official opening, to which the city's intelligentsia was invited, included eloquent speeches by the police chief and the governor's wife. But what most "pained the hearts" of the Polish dignitaries was that a "huge red-blue-white flag" of Russia was hoisted over the Sokół where previously the Polish flag had flown.

As for Russian attitudes toward Jews, they acquired a certain ambiguity over time. On the one hand, during the harsh first wartime winter, as Siewiński reported, "the Russians put up a large samovar in the marketplace, where hot tea and a piece of bread were served day and night for the Jews." On the other hand, there were occasional outbursts of organized violence. One of the worst occurred in November 1914, when "the Muscovites drove the Jews out of their houses, and they fled to the Jewish cemetery, where they remained day and night. . . . The Cossacks came to the cemetery on horseback with their leather whips and ordered the Jews to leave the cemetery and cross the river to the left bank." The Strypa was on the other side of the cemetery hill overlooking Buczacz, where it flowed "in a wide but shallow stream," which could just be crossed on foot. "One can imagine the noise," recalled Siewiński, "as 4,000 people, mostly women and children, walked into the cold water, behind them the Cossacks shouting from their mounts and holding their leather whips." But "just as they crossed the stream, a Russian officer on the left bank ordered [the soldiers] to push them back to where they had come from." Since the Jews "could not change their clothes and were wet and cold, and as they could not warm themselves, many of them became ill, and many died."[20]

Anti-Jewish policies may have contributed to the cholera and typhus epidemics that struck the city. The authorities forced the Jews of Buczacz and other townships into a ghetto restricted to a couple of streets in the town center; wrote Siewiński, "These people were herded together like sardines in a can." Flight could be lethal; when fifty-three Jews were caught trying to get back to their hometown, "each of them was immediately given 59 strokes with the whip. Six Jews died on the spot during this action, the rest were driven back to Buczacz." By spring 1915 an epidemic was also raging in the field hospitals, "not to speak of the Jews, who lived in extremely filthy and crowded conditions. Every day numerous corpses were carried to the Jewish cemetery and buried there."[21]

Other measures targeting Jews included restrictions on movement, requiring special permission to travel from one village to another, which in turn called for bribes that only generated further extortion by local policemen. In contrast, fraternization between local Christian women and Russian soldiers was common, although frowned upon by Polish priests and patriots alike. Perhaps even more tellingly, men of Siewiński's status could enjoy enlightening conversations with educated Russian officers. One such encounter, he believed, was with none other than Grand Duke Nikolai Romanov, supreme commander of the Russian armies in the West, who was visiting Buczacz. Apocryphal or true, Siewiński's depiction of this conversation reflected one area of agreement between Poles and Russians, namely, that the latter "always made short shrift of dealing with" Jews. Those caught selling on the black market would be "brought right away to the district office and given fifteen strokes with a truncheon on the naked flesh, so that blood was drawn," a measure whose salutary consequence, in Siewiński's view, was that Jews "did their best to be at least a little honest." Another, less convenient result was that in their attempt to please the occupiers, the Jews "gave the entire city a Russian look" by hanging "over their stores huge signs and plaques in Russian script." Of course the Russians were not fooled and kept extorting money from wealthy Jews, not least by first arresting them and then demanding ransom for their release, a practice that became common throughout the territories occupied by Russia.[22]

Hooliganism was not directed only against Jews. In February 1915 Siewiński's school was taken over by a Russian unit returning from heavy fighting in the Carpathians: "Within a few days the beautiful school was unrecognizable, because the soldiers destroyed everything, plundered the bookcases and bookshelves, burned the school files in the oven, threw the school benches out to the yard, where they were taken apart and burnt in the oven," and "answered nature's call straight out of the windows." But after Siewiński's own home was also vandalized by a group of soldiers, they profusely apologized, saying they had thought it belonged to a Jew. In fact the Christian population of Buczacz, well aware of Russian attitudes "even before the Muscovites marched into the city," had "made every effort to distinguish themselves from the Jews by putting up icons in their homes." During the occupation, "every woman regularly wore a cross on her neck, not at all for religious reasons but in order to protect herself from violation by the Cossacks."[23]

✡ ✡

In summer 1915, as the front drew close again, Buczacz was visited for the first time in its history by an airplane. It "circled the city like a huge eagle" and dropped a few bombs on nearby Russian troop concentrations. Soon Buczacz became the site of "daily visits by Austrian airplanes." By then a daily stream of "thousands of automobiles and vehicles with ammunition drove through Buczacz," along with "thousands of cattle, horses, sheep and swine," as well as "entire caravans of trucks filled with furniture and various goods." It was, wrote Siewiński, akin to "a migration of nations from west to east."

The Russian retreat was accompanied by more destruction. A troop of Cossacks temporarily housed in the school library inflicted irreparable damage to its valuable collection, while a detachment from Kazan swiftly "liberated" the school "of all maps, pictures, clocks," indeed "anything not firmly screwed and nailed to the walls." Anyone traveling through the region, especially Jewish women, stood a good chance of being robbed "of their money, watches, rings, and furs" by the Cossacks, who did not desist from widespread armed robbery of private homes. In this "gigantic bedlam" there were no sanctions and "everything was allowed."[24]

It was also at that point that the Koflers' estate was finally destroyed. For several months they had survived "like an oasis in the desert," protected toward the end by two Russian soldiers, who turned out to be Jews from Warsaw; the two also helped them sell their remaining livestock before it was seized by the army. A third soldier, a Jewish Russian Hussar and former actor, later teamed up with the other two and defended the Koflers from the growing number of marauders roaming the region. But eventually this Jewish "protective squad" had to leave the estate and the Koflers were left to fend for themselves. In late summer 1915 they "got wind of the orders for total destruction of all properties"; the family "took shelter in the forest" and "watched at night as a sea of flames engulfed all the buildings." Shortly thereafter Oskar joined the Austro-Hungarian Army and his parents moved to Vienna. After the war, the new Polish authorities blocked the family from regaining their estate.[25]

By late August the fighting and killing in Buczacz and its environs were intensifying by the hour. Siewiński recalled that at one point eight hundred wounded soldiers were brought into his school: "There was not enough room, so they were placed in the school corridor, one next to the other, and as they were dying they called out 'Mama! Mama!' . . . This was a terrifying sight." He calculated that between August 1914 and September 1915 over a thousand men had died in his school, most of them Russian: "They were all young men, at the peak of their lives, of which they were robbed in the war." On Tuesday, August 24, the Russians confiscated all metal objects in Buczacz, mined its three bridges, and began evacuating the city. By Thursday they were gone, save for a few "marauding bands" that rode by, "certain that they could plunder without fear of punishment." That night, August 26–27, the Russians blew up the railroad bridge and tunnel. A last army column crossed the remaining bridges, and as they marched through the town the soldiers went on "damaging the houses along the road, breaking the windows with stones and then fleeing as fast as they could. Occasionally one could hear a cry of lamentation from a Jewish woman, but they did not kill anyone." The demolition squad charged with blowing up the bridge leading to Siewiński's school only partially destroyed it, and then threw down their guns and called out, "We have carried out our orders and now we will give ourselves up." Finally, on August 29, Siewiński ventured out and spotted several soldiers of the Polish 13th Infantry Company from Kraków on the street. After 372 days of Russian occupation, Buczacz had been liberated.[26]

✿ ✿

For Siewiński this joyous event was mingled with resentment toward the city's Jewish residents, who, "from one minute to the next," ensured that Buczacz would once again assume "a black-and-yellow look" by hoisting Austrian flags and putting up store signs in German. His indignation about this perceived false and misdirected patriotism was accentuated by his conviction that "while the Poles and Ukrainians were conscripted into the war and not a few of them came back as cripples, or were never to see again the soil of their homeland, these fat Jews laughed over the dumb Goyim, since they never got around to serving in the army."[27]

Facts rarely get in the way of prejudice. In reality, during World War I, 320,000 Jews, including 25,000 officers, served in the Austro-Hungarian Army. That the Jews of Galicia were generally *Kaisertreu*, or loyal to the Austrian emperor, was widely known and made perfect sense from their perspective, considering the alternatives. Jewish attempts to appease the Russians were in response to their abysmal maltreatment by the occupier, just as subsequent demonstrations of loyalty to Polish and Ukrainian rule were largely driven by fear of reprisals against an isolated and defenseless minority (although some Jews actively supported one national movement or another).[28]

Between 1914 and 1917 an estimated half a million to a million Jews were deported or expelled by the Russian authorities. These policies stimulated what one historian has called "the emergence of radical violence by Cossacks, soldiers, and local populations against Jews" throughout the Russian Empire. Up to a quarter of a million Jews fled to the West, with over seventy-seven thousand Jewish refugees counted in 1915 in Vienna alone. Buczacz itself remained too close to the front to take back any returning refugees following its first liberation. Many of its Jewish inhabitants had fled in August 1914, and some two thousand ended up in Vienna.[29]

However, far more people had stayed in Buczacz, some willingly, others for lack of an alternative. Mayor Stern, who was there throughout the Russian occupation, confirmed in a report to the Austrians shortly after their return that as soon as the Russians had occupied Buczacz, the city was subjected to widespread "plunder; women and girls were raped, even publicly on the street"; several factories "were set on fire," and then the entire "city burned from all sides." He claimed it was "only thanks to the urgent pleas and representations by the mayor to the city commandant" that "the fires and plunder were stopped and the city saved from total ruin."[30]

But precisely because Stern had managed to retain his position during Russian rule, once the Austrians returned, questions were raised about his conduct under enemy occupation. An anonymous denunciation blamed "state officials in Buczacz" for having "delivered to the Russians Jewish girls, who were then dishonored by the Cossacks." The investigation was apparently abandoned, likely because Stern still had sway with the Austrian authorities. When a Polish pastry shop owner was denounced by two Jewish residents for having "interacted with Russian officers and civil servants in a very friendly manner" and was indicted as an informant of the Okhrana, the Russian secret police, Stern vouched for him as "a loyal and politically irreproachable citizen," pointing out that "there was actually never an Okhrana office in

Main Street in Buczacz, September 1915. *Source: AT-OeStA/KA IBS I WK Fronten Galizien, 13867.*

Buczacz." The charges were finally dropped in June 1918, around the same time that Stern, who would have been in his seventies by then, also disappears from the historical record.[31] His time was up, and the world he represented was forever gone.

✡ ✡

Austrian-German rule in Eastern Galicia remained precarious. Siewiński recalled that throughout the months leading to the Russian offensive, "not a single night passed without a blaze" and "buildings were set on fire." As increasing numbers of Russian aircraft began to appear, "every night the sky was lit up by searchlights" and "one could hear the ceaseless rattle of rifles and machine guns." The first aerial bombing of Buczacz occurred in winter, killing "a destitute Jew carrying water across the market place." Over the next few months many more civilians were killed, often in their own homes. But in early May 1916, as soon as the Austrian officials who had occupied his school building evacuated it, Siewiński reopened the school to an impressive group of 614 boys and 546 girls, despite the total lack of desks, chairs, and even an air raid trench. The classrooms were still filled with barrels of vodka and rum: "The stench of the spirits was bearable only by keeping the windows open, but outdoors the sound of the artillery and gunfire was getting ever louder, on top of which almost every day Russian airplanes flew overhead and dropped bombs." Whenever the siren sounded, the entire school would run to hide in the nearby church of the Basilian monastery. Two anti-aircraft guns were positioned right next to the school, and some thirty bombs were dropped in its vicinity, but without causing major damage. Meanwhile increasing numbers of civilian air raid victims and soldiers wounded at the front only a few miles away were filling the town's military hospitals.

In the three days preceding the Russian offensive, the weather was foggy and Austrian reconnaissance aircraft could not take off. But on June 7, as the weather cleared, aerial observers reported that in the area of Dżuryn (Ukrainian: Dzhuryn), ten miles to the east, "a vast army was heading toward Buczacz." That same morning a visiting school inspector awarded Siewiński a medal for reopening the school. "At 5 p.m. we sent the children home from school. But the city was no longer protected as the soldiers were rapidly leaving it." Panic set in; Siewiński found his "entire apartment building in turmoil," and the city's "streets were jammed with wagons and automobiles, all fully packed with items from the field hospital and all ready to evacuate." The principal and his wife made a snap decision: "Under no circumstances did we want to stay with the Muscovites, since three of our sons were fighting against them, and the fourth was at the gymnasium in Stanisławów." Within ten minutes they set out for the train station, where they encountered "uncontrollable chaos." As "the fleeing and wailing Jews were pushing into the train cars," the "Germans were striking them with rods and batons and shouting, 'Go away, you damned Jews!'" According to Siewiński, the Jews protested their love for the emperor, but the Germans shouted back, "To hell with you and your love!" No Jews were allowed on the train. But Siewiński and several other fleeing dignitaries boarded one of the cars, where they were all served tea. At 11:00 p.m. the train finally left the station: "Through the windows we already saw the glow of the fires over

Jazłowiec (Ukrainian: Yazlovets) and the surrounding villages, and even as the train was moving we could hear the roar of the artillery."[32]

The capture of Buczacz was part of General Aleksei Brusilov's massive offensive, launched on June 4, 1916, along the entire three hundred miles of the Eastern Front's southern sector. This attempt to break the stalemate initially scored major gains in Galicia and Volhynia. But it came at a horrendous price, costing the Russians close to 2 million men while inflicting over 600,000 casualties on the Austrians. No wonder that within the larger historical context the Brusilov offensive is viewed as a Pyrrhic victory that hastened the end of the tsarist regime.[33]

The two Austrian infantry divisions defending Buczacz came under attack on June 8, and the next day the Russians streamed across the Strypa and captured Potok Złoty (Ukrainian: Zolotyi Potik). With Buczacz under a heavy-artillery barrage and in danger of being encircled, that night one of the Austrian divisions retreated west of the city. As dawn broke on June 10 the first Russian units entered Buczacz and took control of the bridges over the Strypa; later that morning the second Austrian division was pushed out of its positions on the eastern

A Russian position near Buczacz, 1916. *Source: Central State CinePhotoFono Archive of Ukraine, Kiev (hereafter TsDKFFA), O-184874.*

bank of the Strypa just north of the city. Buczacz was back in Russian hands, where it remained for over a year.[34]

✡ ✡

The fate of the Jews of Buczacz who could not flee once the Russians marched in was described by Aba Lev, a Jewish Russian soldier who followed the frontline units shortly after they had occupied the city. Lev kept a diary, written in Yiddish, throughout the war, a fragment of which, devoted largely to his experience in Buczacz, was published in a Russian translation in 1924. Returning from a mission in St. Petersburg to his unit in Czortków just after the start of the Brusilov offensive, Lev quickly learned from the local Jews "about the great calamity that had befallen Buczacz when our army entered it." He then "hastened to Buczacz," at whose outskirts he saw "a Jewish orphanage that the soldiers had set on fire in search of vodka." Several Jews were trying to put out the flames, but then "a drunken officer arrived and poured a bucket of water over the heads of the Jews and started beating them with the bucket." Lev went on to the town center. "When I entered the synagogue courtyard," he wrote, "I was stunned by the terrifying picture of destruction, vandalism, and cruelty." Once they recognized him as a fellow Jew, the traumatized survivors led him to a neighboring house, where he saw "a boy of ten, his hands broken; next to him lay his mother, her skull smashed and her legs cut off." In the next house was "a dead woman, who had been raped and then beaten so badly that she died the same day in terrible agony." Other houses were filled with "raped Jewish women" as well as "men with smashed heads and gouged eyes." In the hospice he "found five murdered people who had to be buried," while the man in charge recounted to him "the endless series of horrors which the human beasts had committed there." Lev was taken to see many other "Jewish houses with dead people who had been strangled, burned, and so on," while on the street he encountered numerous "injured people who had been beaten and raped."[35]

Lev quickly mobilized his Russian Jewish comrades and that very night brought a wagon full of food to the devastated community. Under

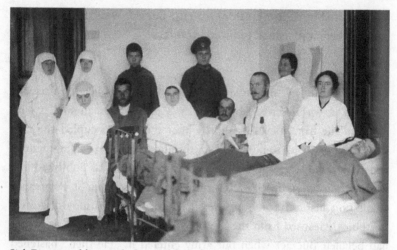

Sick Russian soldiers in the hospital for infectious disease in Buczacz, 1917. Dr. Etel Zeigermacher, a Russian Jew, is on the right; she immigrated to Melbourne, Australia, after the war. *Photo courtesy of her son. Hereafter: Zeigermacher photo collection.*

cover of darkness, the Jews "came out of their cellars to cry over their dead, who were soon taken to the cemetery." But the terror was not over. When Lev returned to the synagogue, he found the courtyard "full of half-naked women with infants in their arms; children in bundles and men with grim and lifeless eyes." Well into the second week of the occupation, he wrote, "the results of the Cossacks' exploits were felt everywhere." Lev and his comrades also collected 250 destroyed Torah scrolls and brought them to the Great Synagogue, "whose walls are as thick as those of a fortress." But all night "scores of strong Cossack arms were trying to break down the doors," hoping to loot the building. The following morning Lev reported to his unit's chief of staff "about what was happening in the city, where the defenseless Jews were at the disposal of drunken Cossacks." But the officer suggested that he "avoid getting mixed in this business," since only "two days earlier a Jew was caught making signals to the enemy from the high chimney of the brewery." Precisely because the city commandant and the general had "a good opinion about Jews, they were very concerned with this event," he said.[36] Thus yet another pogrom was justified by reference to imaginary espionage.

As it turned out, the real reason for the reluctance to enforce order was the zeal for loot. "Since most of the city dwellers had fled and abandoned their houses and shops," wrote Lev, the Russian "Seventh Army issued an order to requisition the goods that were left there," and the soldiers naturally "started looting on their own initiative." Within a few days, the city was flooded with Jewish refugees fleeing Russian Army violence in nearby towns. "They looked dreadful, and their stories about the calamities they had undergone were just as dreadful." The author S. Ansky, who visited the region the following winter, reported that "signs of war" could still "be seen at every step: parapets, torn fences, bullet holes, burned villages and ruins, endless ruins. The farther you travel the greater the devastation: destroyed, burned down, and erased cities and towns," remnants of "a terrible storm of destruction and devastation, of blood and madness." This illustrated "the very essence of the war's spirit, which swept through this place with blind fury." Finally reaching Buczacz late at night, Ansky drove through "scores of wide

Officers of the Russian 7th Army in Buczacz, 1916. *Source: TsDKFFA, O-184864.*

streets," all "destroyed and burned." The large electric lamps of the military hospitals "further magnified the tragic picture of this city." Many Jewish families were dwelling in cellars. Nor did the occupiers show any respect for the dead. An old man told Ansky the Russians also "destroyed the cemetery, broke and scattered the tombstones that had been there for six hundred years, and burned down the vaults of the greatest sages."[37]

Yet the Russian Army never managed to gain a firm hold in Galicia and Volhynia, and while sporadic fighting continued along the entire front, neither side made any major gains. Following the forced abdication of Tsar Nikolai II on March 15, 1917, the provisional government under Alexander Kerensky of the Socialist Revolutionary Party made one last effort to end the war on favorable terms. But the Kerensky offensive, launched on July 1 some forty miles northwest of Buczacz, quickly petered out, with Austrian-German formations driving the Russians all the way back to the old Austrian-Russian border along the Zbrucz (Ukrainian: Zbruch) River. On July 26, after fierce fighting along the Strypa, the Russians abandoned Buczacz and the Austrians marched in unopposed. They were to remain there for a little over a year.

A Russian battlefield position in the Strypa Valley near Buczacz, 1916. *Source: TsDKFFA, album 34, photo 54.*

The Russians leaving Buczacz, 1917. *Source: Zeigermacher photo collection.*

Things had changed in the course of the war and could no longer be reversed. As the official Austrian history conceded, "The longer the war lasted, the greater became the internal national tensions within the lands inhabited by Slavs, which constituted almost half of the Danube Empire." Within a month of the overthrow of the Russian provisional government in Petrograd by Vladimir Lenin's Bolsheviks on November 7, 1917, an armistice agreement was signed with the Central Powers, leading to the peace treaty of Brest-Litovsk in March 1918, in which the Bolshevik government recognized the independence of Ukraine.[38] Half a year later the Austro-Hungarian Empire ceased to exist and Galicia was once more up for grabs.

✿ ✿

The Austrians had reoccupied a devastated and depopulated land. In early 1918 an Austrian inspector reported from Buczacz that in view of "the plight of the population and the penury of the returning refugees," Mayor Stern had requested "the allocation of refugee support over the winter, at least until May 1919." For the moment, noted the official, the municipal administration had no income and was therefore unable to maintain even such "indispensable services" as public security and lavatories. Additionally the extensive damage to real estate during the fighting had caused a severe "shortage of housing and a rise in rental rates," which "hurts most immediately those who have a regular income," such as the civil servants, who urgently needed the restoration of municipal services. Indeed no fewer than 569 houses, a substantial share of the real estate in Buczacz, had been either totally or partially destroyed in the fighting.[39]

Siewiński returned to Buczacz in April 1918 and was immediately appointed director of the secondary school for girls, housed in the so-called barracks. The condition of the building was utterly lamentable: "Smashed windows and window frames, broken doors, everywhere filth and chaos, a few broken school desks." Even worse, to his mind, was the extent to which "the youth had been demoralized by the war." The girls "stole whatever they could put their hands on, even what passed for desks were not safe from them."[40] The state of the school and its students reflected the condition of the region as a whole. But the chaos was far from over.

On October 31, 1918, the Austro-Hungarian Empire was officially dissolved, and Polish nationalists perceived the defeat of the imperial army, in whose ranks many of them had fought, as an opportunity to resurrect Poland after well over a century of partition and foreign rule. For Galician Poles it seemed only natural that the former Austrian province would revert to its rightful place in the new Polish republic. But the very next day the West Ukrainian National Republic (Zakhidno-Ukrainska Narodna Respublika, ZUNR) was proclaimed and Buczacz again came under what Poles saw as foreign, or rather, rebellious peasant and bandit rule. Conversely, vast numbers of Ruthenians, who had increasingly come to think of themselves as members of the much larger Ukrainian nation, felt that for the first time since the fall of the Cossack state in the seventeenth century they were in control of their own land and destiny. The Great War was over. But the inhabitants of Galicia faced two more years of bitter fighting and bloody massacres, in which ideological conflict was often experienced as fraternal and communal violence.

Polish attitudes toward Jews in Galicia had also worsened, not least because of the widespread and not entirely vacuous belief that the Jews had preferred Austrian rule to the establishment of an independent Polish state. Popular rumors about Jewish wealth, allegedly accumulated through war profiteering, added fuel to anti-Jewish sentiments among Poles who refused to acknowledge the reality of Galician Jewry's utter destitution, even as they flaunted Polish heroism in fighting against Russia and for national independence. The ample evidence of Jewish participation in the fighting was either dismissed or presented as proof of Jewish support for the empire and opposition to Polish nationhood.

✡ ✡

For Siewiński the Ukrainian takeover of Buczacz on November 2, 1918, just half a year after his return to the city, had all the trappings of a dispute between old and well-acquainted, not always friendly neighbors. "At 10 a.m. on All Souls Day," he wrote, several local representatives of the newly declared West Ukrainian National Republic showed up at "the district offices and demanded that District Administrator Dniestrzański hand over the official documentation." Dniestrzański, it appears, "saw no alternative, and did as he was ordered," not least because "outside the window he could see many men with clubs and guns." All other civil servants followed his example, with similar scenes taking place at the district court and the post office. By and large, according to Siewiński, "the takeover of the municipal offices proceeded relatively calmly." But when the Polish railroad officials and operators refused to sign a declaration of loyalty to the ZUNR, they were removed from their posts and replaced by people who, Siewiński contemptuously remarked, "lacked higher professional training and had hardly a clue about operating the railroad." Similarly when "a crowd of people converged on the gendarmerie office and demanded to be given weapons," the policeman who tried to block them was "painfully thrashed."

Meanwhile, as more Ukrainians arrived from the surrounding

villages and were armed by the new authorities, these "peasants and farm laborers" began roaming the streets and "looting Jewish shops and Polish citizens." They were followed by "a dozen wagons filled with armed men," which arrived in the city as reinforcements, led by a village official who knew and greeted Siewiński. Up to this point, and despite the occasional violence, the Ukrainian takeover still seemed a fraternal affair. But in the afternoon a train pulled into Buczacz with three cars full of armed soldiers and two machine guns. Siewiński described the scene: "The soldiers disembarked, heroically positioned the two machine guns right next to the rails, and commenced firing at the defenseless and tranquil city." One of their targets was the gendarmerie building, "where there were only women and children. The bullets lodged into the window panes, tore up the roof, and sprayed all around the city, which was covered by a thick haze." This wild shooting came to an end only when "a brave woman holding a broom came out of one of the nearby shacks" and shouted at the soldiers to stop. The men then marched in formation to the market square, led by a former Buczacz gymnasium student and a classmate of one of Siewiński's sons. As darkness fell, the Ukrainians roamed the city, "shooting in the streets." Over the next few days, soldiers randomly stopped and brutalized people: "Every evening one could hear the shrieks of those who were beaten."

The men who took over the town were members of the local Ukrainian elite, including the new Buczacz district commissar, the attorney Ilarion Bochurkiv, and the engineer Viktor Luchkiv, appointed ataman (chief) of the district security forces. Not untypically for the region, both were married to Polish women. For Polish patriots such as Siewiński, it was bad enough that these "new rulers immediately introduced the Ukrainian language to all offices"; fortunately, in Buczacz "all Poles spoke that language perfectly." Much worse was that "this new pseudo-Ukrainian power completely banned the use of Polish in all offices and schools." The Poles, observed Siewiński, being "a cultivated people," had never banned Ukrainian. He conceded that "the local gymnasium had used Polish as the language of instruction," but that seemed natural, since Poles considered their language to be far more elevated. Now that Ukrainian was made the language of instruction, and all Poles refusing to sign a declaration of loyalty to the new state were ejected from the gymnasium, "only the Ukrainians and Jews remained" there. Siewiński was, of course, especially incensed with the Jews, who had all signed the required loyalty declaration in order to keep their jobs, save for one honorable professor, who "let it be known that although he belongs to the Mosaic faith he is a Pole."[41]

Within a week of taking over the district, Commissar Bochurkiv reported to the Ukrainian National Council in Lwów that he had already removed many local Polish officials and had established a militia that "provided perfect order." As a result of these measures, he asserted, "complete calm prevails in the district"; the Polish peasants even "display solidarity with the Ukrainian peasants," while "the Jewish population is loyal to the Ukrainian authority." Siewiński saw things rather differently, confiding to his diary that "all the grain stocks, as well as sugar, clothing, and money, were plundered from the district office and post office"; even a supply of new clothes for his teaching staff, which arrived from Lwów shortly before the Ukrainian takeover, had been requisitioned. Siewiński was especially scandalized when his own home was searched and plundered by a troop of Ukrainian soldiers headed by Ataman Luchkiv himself. The logic of separation between neighbors was already at work: when Siewiński's son Józef asked Luchkiv to give back the family correspondence, the latter responded dismissively, "We are enemies now." Siewiński, who had known Luchkiv as "an intelligent and cultivated man," concluded that he had finally "shown his true face." People who had been colleagues and acquaintances for many years suddenly "recognized" their essential difference; they no longer shared the same community, moral values, culture, or language.[42]

Following the example of the gymnasium faculty, all other Polish teachers in Buczacz declined to declare their loyalty to the Ukrainian state and were promptly dismissed and replaced by Ukrainians and Jews. In Siewiński's view, this made education a farce since "nothing sensible was taught in the schools, everything was politicized, and therefore there were often fights between the students." He was appalled to find that several Jewish teachers had remained on the staff, noting sarcastically that once the Jews signed the Ukrainian loyalty declaration, "they all promptly forgot how to speak Polish." But this was only the beginning. On December 26, barely two months into their rule, the Ukrainian authorities arrested sixty-seven members of the local Polish elite, including Siewiński and two of his sons back from military service in the defunct Austrian Army, and interned them in a monastery in nearby Jazłowiec for several weeks. Siewiński saw this as part of a larger pattern of lawlessness and criminality dressed up as law and order. The war, he observed, "had taught people to describe crimes and other rights violations with pretentious Latin terms" so that "simple robbery was called requisition," while "the expulsion of entire families from their homes, leading them to die of hunger and poverty," was called "evacuation," and "the arrest and incarceration of completely innocent people" was labeled "internment."[43]

But despite the growing violence between Poles and Ukrainians, Siewiński and many of his fellow Polish nationalists reserved greater animosity and disdain for the Jews. Even at the moment of their arrest, what bound this local Polish elite together was the surprising presence of a Jewish attorney in their midst, "who was as much use to us as a hound in church." His "desperate expression and terrified eyes," recalled Siewiński, "made us burst out with laughter," while his eagerness to sign the loyalty declaration so as to be released simply proved once more that "the Jews were real chameleons" who "would have hoisted the Chinese flag" for all they cared, "since their coat of arms is only gold." To Siewiński's mind, "the only salvation" for the Jews was "to convert to the Catholic faith, and thereby to become real sons of the soil on which they live." But he did not think that likely.

The Poles found greater affinity even with the Ukrainian guards who led them to the internment camp through the forest; once the arrested Poles began singing Polish and Ruthenian Christmas carols, "the severe faces of the soldiers lightened up": "They sang along with us and also made fun of Bochurkiv and Luchkiv and all the other idiots who had given orders to intern us." It would appear that at that point, just as it was often inconceivable that Jews could ever become part of either national group in Galicia, it was also still difficult to draw clear distinctions between Poles and Ukrainians. Yet both alleged essential differences and natural affinities could be causes of much violence. And, of course, whereas Poles and Ukrainians were claiming attachment to and competing over ownership of the same land, Jews were never seen as the "real sons of the soil on which they live."[44]

By late April 1919 the ZUNR was being threatened by the Poles from the west and the Bolsheviks from the east. In the ensuing chaos, the Ukrainian commandant in Buczacz ordered another round of requisitions from civilians, primarily from Jewish homes. People were even stopped on the street in broad daylight. Siewiński wrote, "Shoes were removed from the feet of pedestrians, clothes stolen, hats taken off the heads of people, and anyone who uttered but one word of protest would come into contact with a rifle butt." Items confiscated from Jews soon showed up among the local peasants. Young women coming into town from nearby villages were "all dressed up like dolls in lacquered shoes, with colorful kerchiefs on their heads and flashy skirts," all "presents from their admirers." Many other "impoverished citizens came into much property. Before the war they did not have enough sheets to cover their beds, now they can pile them up to the ceiling." Former paupers, snickered Siewiński, now "stroll down the avenues like respectable gentlemen," while village boys and girls were selling wares on the street for close to nothing: "No one asks where these things come from. This is war loot." And since Ukrainian troops were given leave to celebrate Easter with their families in the villages, and brought along their weapons, the incidence of armed robbery and murder also rose. "Even in Buczacz this kind of shooting went on, especially of Jews," wrote Siewiński, depicting in graphic detail the murder of two Jewish men on the street by a Ukrainian official and a soldier, carried out with total impunity. "That's how things were at that time, all thefts and murders went unpunished."[45]

As the front disintegrated and the Poles appeared poised to return, some Ukrainian soldiers rediscovered their Polish ancestors and relatives. The gendarmes of Buczacz, depicted by Siewiński as "a bunch of scatterbrains" and "good-for-nothing losers," who had previously "benefited from these times" by looting and evading frontline service, now melted back into the population. The brutalities went on. In early May a column of deportees was led through the city to the train station, "all in very bad shape, hungry, making a pitiful impression," some "close to death," many of them "Jews with anxious faces." But the Ukrainian Galician Army was falling apart: on May 23 Polish forces were reported in Stanisławów, forty miles southwest of Buczacz, and a column of two hundred carts carrying women and loot rolled through Buczacz on the way to Czortków, followed by trains filled with troops. As artillery fire could again be heard in the city, the looting and random violence also intensified. With enemies on both sides, it was not clear where the local Ukrainian leadership might flee. On May 30, 1919, seven months after the Ukrainian takeover, a Polish airplane flew low over the city, signaling the approaching end of Ukrainian rule.

By now public order was no longer maintained, and looting, robbery, and murder by peasants and soldiers became ever more prevalent throughout the region. In Buczacz itself, two Ukrainian workers were erroneously executed as "Poles and traitors," while Ukrainian troops arrested all young Polish men attending Sunday mass on June 1, although they were later released. The last Ukrainian Army patrol passed through the city a couple of days later; two stray soldiers randomly threw a grenade at a Jewish woman, severely wounding her, and robbed a passing Jew of his shoes; they were both shot dead by Luchkiv in a desperate attempt to restore his reputation just before the Poles arrived.[46]

✿ ✿

On June 4, 1919, after fighting their way through much of Western Ukraine, Polish troops captured Buczacz. The small military contingent that entered the city assembled in the marketplace, and Polish and Ruthenian women served the troops sausage, ham, roast beef, coffee, and tea. Luchkiv was promptly put under house arrest. The Jews, as Siewiński acerbically commented, quickly transformed the city, covering their businesses with signs in the Polish national colors of white and red, so that within minutes "the city had a Polish coat of paint and 5,000 new Poles. . . . A miracle had taken place! In an instant all the Jews forgot the Ruthenian language and began speaking only Polish." Yet this joy, whether genuine or pragmatic, was premature; four days later a Ukrainian counterattack brought Buczacz under artillery fire, and Siewiński fled to Lwów, fearful of what he called "the army of the Haidamaks" (the Cossack paramilitary rebels and brigands of the eighteenth century), which he depicted as "largely composed of bandits who acted arbitrarily and were responsible to no one, murdering with impunity not only Poles, but also Ruthenians."

The Ukrainians returned to Buczacz on June 12 and went on to push the Poles out of much of the territory they had occupied. Yet the second Ukrainian occupation lasted only three weeks, even though it was accompanied once again by a wave of violence, in which civilians and captured Polish soldiers were robbed, beaten, raped, and murdered. At the end of the month the Poles struck back, seizing Buczacz again on July 4, and finally driving the Ukrainian Galician Army across the Zbrucz River and out of Eastern Galicia altogether over the following two weeks. The Poles, for their part, emphasized fraternity with local Ruthenians in an effort to undermine the very notion of solidarity with Ukrainians across the border. As Siewiński saw it, the "uprising ended as quickly as it had broken out, and the population went back to work, especially the villagers, who had never dreamed of a West Ukraine." It had all been merely the product of cunning Austrian machinations intended to "sow discord between the Ruthenian nation, which comes from our blood, and the Poles," but "now love and reconciliation" would surely "prevail in the nation." In fact, however, the fighting had cost the lives of ten thousand Polish and fifteen thousand Ukrainian troops, not counting the mass violence against civilians and the substantial destruction and plunder of property, as well as several brutal pogroms by the Polish military against Jewish communities.[47]

Siewiński's own contribution to normalization was to reopen his school. Since the original "building overlooking the Strypa was totally destroyed," he went back to the alternative school "in the so-called bar-racks," which had also housed a military hospital, and could serve the purpose after some minor repairs. The bigger issue was the impact of the war on the children, many of whom had had little or no education for several years and had learned to "focus only on survival," having "watched numerous armies marching in and out of the city" and been exposed to "arbitrary plundering and unpunished robberies." Clearly, stressed Siewiński, "such youth could not be moral"; in fact the school became a site of "daily thefts." One student "even managed to remove a glass panel from the school window and bring it home, where the culprit was actually praised by his parents." Even after "the locksmith installed locks on the school's doors" and gave the keys only to the teachers, "within a quarter of an hour the keys were stolen." It was "under such conditions," concluded Siewiński, "that we taught school until mid-June 1920."[48]

During those early months quite a few complaints were lodged against fellow Poles who had not been punished for collaborating with the previous Ukrainian regime. But the need to establish stable rule in the city and the province as a whole made it imperative to avoid retribution against those who were willing and able to serve the Polish state, certainly if they happened to be ethnic Poles. The maintenance of law and order was handed over to Major Józef Wolgner, a local land-owner, who was appointed sector commander of the Buczacz district. This was hardly an impartial administration. As early as August 10, Wolgner chaired a patriotic rally in Buczacz, whose purpose was "to emphasize the indissolubility of Eastern Galicia with Poland." He also dealt aggressively with anything he perceived as anti-Polish agitation. "For some time now," he reported to Lwów on August 30, "secret and elusive groups of local Ukrainians and Jews have been observed, and rumors have spread regarding plans for an armed movement" aiming at "the seizure of this part of the country." Stating that "in the district and especially in Buczacz the Ukrainians announce openly and with impu-nity that armed Ukrainian troops will soon come to occupy Buczacz," Wolgner was adamant that in the face of this "vast Ukrainian-Jewish agitation" he needed substantial reinforcements in manpower and matériel. "It would be a complete disaster," he warned, "if the town of Buczacz were conquered by the Ukrainians, because they would massacre the Polish population."[49]

Such concerns only intensified with the approach of the defunct ZUNR's first anniversary. Consequently, when the Buczacz district command finally did receive reinforcements, it energetically set about removing any potential activists. By late October Wolgner could report that "public safety" had "greatly improved" after "about 400 former Ukrainian soldiers" were "interned and transferred to the concentration station for prisoners of war in Lwów." The Poles were now doing to Ukrainians precisely what the Ukrainians had done to them only a few months earlier. Much relieved, on November 1, the day of the anniversary, Wolgner confidently announced, "There is peace in the district and no visible signs of a planned armed revolt." Still, he warned, "knowing the relations in the district, we should note that pacification, which means first of all disarmament, may also result in several problems, since not a single peasant keeps weapons hidden at home but rather hides them somewhere in the woods, etc., so it is virtually impossible to find them."[50] Harassing the Ukrainian population, he observed, could increase its resentment and drive it underground, which is, in fact, precisely what eventually happened.

☆ ☆

In mid-August 1920, just over a year after Buczacz's takeover by the Poles, the war between Poland and Soviet Russia brought the city briefly under Bolshevik rule. But only a few weeks later the Polish counteroffensive, supported in Galicia by anti-Bolshevik Ukrainian forces, led to the city's final liberation. In October 1920 a Polish-Soviet truce was signed, leading to a peace agreement in 1921, which divided the entire territory between the two states. With this all hopes for Ukrainian independence were dashed, leaving a bitter legacy that would fester for the next two decades, before erupting into an even greater wave of violence in World War II. Especially in the former Pale of Settlement the

fighting had been accompanied by mass violence against Jewish populations, costing the lives of an estimated sixty thousand Jews, with many
more wounded and mutilated.[51]

Siewiński did not experience Bolshevik rule. As the Red Army
approached, he wrote, "we received orders that the teachers and civil
servants must head west, and so I had to flee for the third time." Board-
ing the train, he could already hear artillery fire from the east. But he
returned in October, remaining in the city throughout the interwar
period. In the early postwar years and before his retirement, Siewiński
did his best once more "to restore the school building, so that the youth
would not suffer." Even more important, he hoped to repair the psychological damage inflicted on youngsters who had little memory of
peace and order. "The youth," he observed, "was badly brought up,
which was hardly surprising, because for seven years all they had seen
was plunder, murder, slaughter and other immoral events." As he saw
it, "our task was to heal the youth as quickly as possible." Yet the legacy
of those war years remained etched in people's attitudes and mentalities
for decades thereafter.[52]

✡ ✡

As it was struggling to establish its rule over the multiethnic eastern
territories, Poland came under increasing international scrutiny for acts
of violence against its national and religious minorities. In June 1919,
under pressure from the Western powers, Poland signed a minorities
treaty intended to protect the rights of the approximately 40 percent
of its citizens who were not ethnic Poles. This attempt to address the
dilemma of a nation-state created in the wake of ethnic conflict, almost
half of whose citizens were perceived as not belonging to the majority
nation, ended up in failure. In certain ways the treaty may have even
exacerbated matters, since many ethnic Poles perceived it as imposing
limits on their new state's sovereignty through a combination of pressure from these minorities, especially the Jews, and Great Power politics, also allegedly orchestrated by international Jewish influence.[53]

The struggle between Poles and Ukrainians over Eastern Galicia highlighted the extent to which external and internal conflicts became inextricably linked in this era. This was well understood by foreign observers, even as both sides tried to put the best face on their own aspirations and actions and to paint the other side as criminally murderous in an effort to gain international recognition for their irreconcilable territorial and political claims. In the process the other major ethnic group in the region, the Jews, was cast in the role of a minority whose status could never be truly acceptable to either of the two major warring parties. Jews could be ignored, tolerated, or expelled, but by the nature of the nationalism that had evolved in this region, they could neither be recognized as a separate indigenous national group nor assimilated as ethnically kindred—the two options open to Polish Ukrainians. And as a supposedly protected and allegedly privileged minority group the Jews were seen as undermining the very core of Polish nationalism.[54]

Conditions in Eastern Galicia were of particular international concern in the immediate aftermath of World War I both because of the tense interethnic situation there and thanks to the region's position on the border of Soviet Russia. As early as July 1919, the secretary and the assistant military attaché at the American legation in Warsaw set out to visit the territory, which had just been taken over by the Polish Army. They quickly found that the local Polish administration was using the same methods to establish its rule and Polonize the province that the ZUNR had employed, rather less efficiently, before its demise. The Greek Catholic metropolitan of Lwów, Andrey Sheptytsky, told them that the Polish authorities had arrested two hundred Ukrainian priests, four of whom were "shot without trial by the troops." In Stanisławów the military hospital was "replacing the Ukrainian nurses and doctors with Polish nurses and doctors" and Ukrainian patients were being moved "to internment camps." In Buczacz the two Americans were told that 3,220 Ukrainian soldiers had been sent from the district "to places of internment," while in Tarnopol over a thousand mostly Ukrainian soldiers in a military hospital were lacking supplies and a typhus epidemic was decimating the city's largely Jewish population. The newly installed Polish governor of Galicia, Kazimierz Galecki, expressed few regrets about the "departure of a considerable number of Ruthenian inhabitants with the Ruthenian army."[55]

The British were also trying to better understand conditions in the region. In April 1920 Britain's vice consul in Lwów, Lieutenant-Colonel Wilfred James Whitehead, reported on a four-day tour he had recently undertaken in Eastern Galicia. The province's "certainly bad" economic situation, he concluded, was greatly exacerbated by the Jews, who sold on the black market surpluses of the aid supplies they received "from their own sources abroad" for exorbitant prices. Indeed much of the corruption and incompetence Whitehead detected everywhere could be traced back to the Jews, he believed, as well as to the inefficiency and lethargy of the local Polish administrators and to the fatalism of the "Ruthenian peasant." Additionally, the acute "scarcity of food and clothing" and the dearth of trained physicians also led to epidemics. As for "whether the animosity of the Ruthenian Population against the Poles is as bitter as is alleged," Whitehead insisted that the "Ruthenian peasant" was actually "a lazy fellow" who was "content with his lot." Having "lived about 700 years in harmony with the Poles," the peasant "desires to 'carry on' as before." "Of War he has had more than enough," whereas "his grievances" were largely material and could be easily addressed. It was rather with the "educated class of Ruthenians, such as School Teachers, Officials, and Clergy that one meets with discontent, and these form a very small minority indeed of the whole Ruthenian Population, but as usual they make the most noise."[56]

In fact Ruthenians had struggled to assert and maintain their national identity not only before but also during World War I, when they were subjected to concerted efforts to assimilate by the occupying tsarist regime. In May 1915 the president of the Ukraine parliamentary delegation in Austria strongly protested against the Russian assertion that Ukrainians were merely "Little Russians," and thus part of the "Great Russian" nation. Indeed, he contended, the Russians had been waging "a war of extermination against the language, customs, literature and culture of the Ukraine" since the seventeenth century. Portraying themselves as liberators, the Russians condemned Ukrainians "to national death," having "destroyed at one blow" the Ukrainian national renaissance: "The Ruthenian language has been forbidden," and "all the Ruthenian newspapers in Galicia have been suppressed, the libraries destroyed."[57]

By the time Whitehead reached the region, the Russians were long gone and Ukrainians were bitterly complaining about the new government's Polonization policies. Like the American representatives, Whitehead too heard that the numbers of Ruthenian public officials, state gymnasium teachers, and university professors and students had been starkly reduced despite Ukrainian demographic preponderance. Whitehead conceded, "The question of Ruthenian students continuing their studies is an important one and admits no delay in coming to an arrangement." It was from the ranks of a frustrated young generation of Ukrainians that a new, radical, and increasingly violent nationalist organization soon emerged.[58]

The official ownership of Eastern Galicia was not determined quickly. On June 25, 1919, the Supreme Council of the League of Nations empowered Poland to occupy the territory up to the Zbrucz River, but stressed that this did not determine its final status. Five months later, on November 21, the Supreme Council drafted a treaty giving Poland a mandate over Eastern Galicia for a period of twenty-five years, after which a plebiscite would be held. Vehement Polish objections led to the withdrawal of the mandate idea, and Galicia remained formally in the possession of the Entente Powers. Finally, on March 15, 1923, the Conference of Ambassadors, which had replaced the Supreme Council, handed Eastern Galicia to Poland, albeit with the proviso that "ethnographic conditions necessitate an autonomous regime in the Eastern part of Galicia." No such autonomy was ever granted.[59]

✿ ✿

The conflict over Eastern Galicia was conducted on the ground and also by means of a propaganda campaign intended to expose the brutality and inhumanity of the other side and thereby to undermine its claim to the territory. There was no dearth of atrocities to draw on;

looking through these materials one soon grasps the ferocity of this fraternal conflict, largely forgotten because of the even greater subsequent horrors of ethnic cleansing and genocide in World War II. It is also impossible to tell which group exceeded the other in the number of their victims and the heinousness of their crimes.

On July 29, 1919, representatives of the ZUNR wrote to Georges Clemenceau, president of the peace conference, in protest against the Supreme Council's decision to authorize the Polish occupation of Eastern Galicia. Besides claiming that this step "abolishes the principle of self-determination of peoples," the note asserted that the decision delivered Ukrainians "to the mercies of an unbridled Polish imperialism, to the horrors of a regime by Polish authorities, and to the brutalities of the Polish soldiery," which had already "committed innumerable acts of violence and terror." Providing a "long list of these abominable outrages" perpetrated by the Poles, the note dismissed as "wholly false or greatly exaggerated tales of cruelties practiced on the Poles by the Ukrainians." This was the start of a competition of atrocities in which there could only be losers. Polish crimes cited included mass arrests of "Ukrainian 'intelligentsia,' peasants, and artisans" and the internment of thousands in conditions of inhuman overcrowding and lack of food; numerous cases of shooting, hanging, beating, and flogging to death of captured soldiers and civilians, even children; gouging out eyes, public gang rape, and wanton destruction of villages, as well as torching or desecration of Greek Catholic churches and mass arrests and abuse of priests. Even "Jewish pogroms" were cited—clearly with the intention of drawing on sympathy for the fate of Jews and conveniently aligning it with Ukrainian claims of victimhood—along with the destruction of cultural treasures by pillaging and burning down libraries and archives and banning the Ukrainian language. The writers asserted, "The Ukrainian people in East Galicia find themselves in a hell, so to speak, and the persecutions to which they are subjected find no parallel in history." Elsewhere they argued that these atrocities were "on par with the barbarous cruelties perpetrated in the Balkans and Armenia."[60]

Only days after the Ukrainian report was sent, the Polish Foreign

From "Report on Ukrainian Cruelties Committed on the Polish Population of Eastern Galicia," August 1919, Department of Information. *Source: Archiwum akt nowych, Warsaw (hereafter AAN), Ministerstwo Spraw Zagranicznych (hereafter MSZ), zesp. 322, sygn. 9412a, end of booklet.*

Office issued its own "Report on Ukrainian Cruelties Committed on the Polish Population of Eastern Galicia." The two documents were largely mirror images of each other. But the Polish report also deprived Ruthenians of both intelligence and control over their own actions. Asserting that these crimes manifested "the brutalization and demoralization" of Ukrainians, described as "uninstructed and uncultured masses," the report presented them at the same time as victims of "provocative agitation carried out by foreigners," whose goal was to "preclude all understanding between the Poles and the Ukrainians." In other words, while Ukrainian nationalists condemned what they saw as Polish oppression, Polish nationalists argued that their Ruthenian brethren were merely manipulated by enemies of Poland, such as Russians, communists, and Jews. Although the report stressed that it was "not holding the whole Ukrainian population responsible," it accused the ZUNR of trying to excise the Polish presence from Eastern Galicia, not least by inciting popular resentment against Polish landowners and priests. This was followed by the same litany of murder, plunder, desecration, torture, and internment under deplorable and at times lethal conditions. In one camp alone over 2,600 deaths from typhus were claimed.[61]

This list of horrors, accompanied by a set of horrifying photographs, ultimately demonstrated not the greater bestiality of one side or the other but the cumulative effect of violence and dehumanization over several years of war, vicious propaganda, and fraternal conflict, which combined to unravel the moral fabric of society. We read of a Ukrainian ataman who established "a house of prostitution for the use of his soldiers, of young Polish girls," whom they "afterwards murdered"; women's "breasts having been cut off which the soldiers playfully threw from one to another"; a legionnaire "beaten with 'nahajki' (leaded whip), bastinadoed and thrown into a pond where he was shot at like a duck"; a priest "buried alive with his head downward"; a countess and her

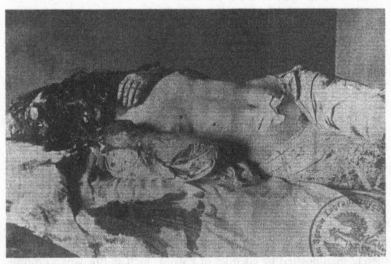

"The army nursing-sister Josephine Mroczkowska, who was wounded by a rifle-shot in the stomach and had the wound dressed by her colleagues, was taken prisoner by the Ukrainians and after seven hours of torture was murdered." *Source: "Report on Ukrainian Cruelties Committed on the Polish Population of Eastern Galicia," August 1919, Department of Information, AAN-MSZ, zesp. 322, sygn. 9412a, end of booklet.*

daughter who, "after cruel violation," were "literally torn in pieces by the teeth of the savage Ukrainian mob"; women and children "stripped naked" and forced into a pond, "then tied to the trees on the bank, so that they all froze"; a hospital where the "stomachs of wounded legion-naires were slit with scythes"; the inhabitants of an entire village locked inside a manor house and burned alive; strange tortures such as "tearing the skin off people's hands" and "winding the body from head to toe in barbed wire"; people being crucified and impaled.[62]

The report magnanimously concluded that despite "the immense total disaster which has been inflicted upon the Polish population by the savage Ukrainian hordes," the Poles were willing "to come to concil-iatory settlement," based on "the greatest tolerance and moderation," so that "a complete understanding might be arrived at and the two nations live together in peace." But that was merely another way of demanding Polish hegemony over a subservient Ukrainian population, rooted in the deeply entrenched notion of overall Polish superiority.[63] By then neither assertions of superiority nor offers of tolerance could undo the effects of fraternal violence: too much blood had been shed, and too many people were adopting extremism and intolerance. As for the Jews of Eastern Galicia, objectively they had little to do with this conflict. But both Poles and Ukrainians increasingly felt that the Jews were their enemy's friends, and since in reality this meant that the Jews had ever fewer friends, they grew increasingly vulnerable to a conflict in which most of them had no part. For the next twenty years, it was the Poles who dictated the terms of coexistence; once war broke out, the ghosts of the past returned with a vengeance.

Chapter 3
TOGETHER AND APART

Beis Yaakov students performing the play *Joseph and His Brothers*, Buczacz, 1934. U.S. Holocaust Memorial Museum (hereafter USHMM), photo 4959. Esther Rivka Wagner, second row, fifth from the right, b. 1924, daughter of Buczacz rabbi Shraga Feivel Willig, only survivor of her family, was interviewed by the author in December 2009. On Rabbi Feivel, see also S. Y. Agnon, *The City Whole* (Tel Aviv, 1973, in Hebrew), 650–52. Sarah Halpern, first row, first on the right, Mordechai Halpern's sister, was murdered aged seventeen. M. Halpern, *Family and Town* (Tel Aviv, 2003, in Hebrew), 71.

After six years of almost incessant violence and bloodshed, the killing finally came to an end with the liberation of the city from Bolshevik rule in Sepetember 1920. But even before that, following the end of World War I on November 11, 1918, some of the Jews who had fled Buczacz during the fighting began trickling back.

Jewish soldiers released from military service or POW camps were also returning. Many were exhausted, disoriented, impoverished, and traumatized. There was an acute need for new hope: perhaps no longer a Messiah, but at least a goal and a vision to lift the wretched out of their misery. The Balfour Declaration of November 1917, in which the British government promised to support the "establishment in Palestine of a national home for the Jewish people," was still reverberating throughout Eastern Europe. After the war, the young Zionist Zvi Heller called a meeting of Buczaczers in Vienna, urging the hundreds who attended to go to Palestine.

The Jews of Buczacz and the Tarnopol province (voivodeship) grew increasingly focused on Zionism and immigration to Palestine. Aliya, literally "ascent," to Eretz Israel was the very heart of the Zionist undertaking; its primary facilitator was the *hachshara*, or training camp,

Announcement of festive prayer in Buczacz on the tenth anniversary of the Balfour Declaration, 1927. *Source: Jewish National and University Library, Digitized Book Repository, JNUL/AMD – V 2001.*

which provided, in Heller's words, the "mental preparation and agricultural training" viewed as essential for the transition from small-town life in Galicia to collective farms, called kibbutzim, in Palestine.[1] There young men and women were expected to turn the Jewish occupational pyramid on its head and thereby transform the Jewish people from a nation of "wheelers and dealers" into a strong and proud race of farmers and warriors by conquering and settling the "wasteland" of Palestine and resurrecting the Promised Land of their biblical forefathers. This was a complex social, psychological, and political undertaking: its rhetoric of "normalizing Jewish existence" and forging "new Jews" borrowed generously from Polish and Ukrainian nationalist discourse. But it also had to be adapted both to the Judaic tradition of longing for Zion and to the unique socioeconomic circumstances of the Jews, by asserting the need to uproot the newly proclaimed nation from the foreign soil it had inhabited for centuries in order to recolonize a mythical and yet already populated ancestral homeland. Zionism has been grappling with the moral issues involved ever since. But at the time its sheer audacity was attractive to growing numbers of young men and women.

The first group of Buczacz pioneers (*chalutzim*), made up of members of the socialist Zionist youth organization Hashomer Hatza'ir (the Young Guard), went to Palestine as early as 1919. A second group, most of whose members were still gymnasium students, continued preparing for immigration by performing physical labor at a local stone quarry and cleaning barns on nearby farms. This made for friction with Polish nationalists disdainful of Zionists. On one occasion the Jewish pioneers were surrounded by young Polish Scouts (Harcerze) and a brawl ensued; as a consequence many of the Jewish students were expelled from the gymnasium and charged with treason. They were spared thanks to the brief Bolshevik occupation of Buczacz in 1920, during which Zionist activists destroyed the police records, so that once Polish rule was restored the charges were dismissed.

The youngsters from Buczacz who went to Palestine at that time were not employed in agriculture as they had expected; rather, like many other members of the Third Aliya that brought an estimated thirty-five thousand immigrants to Eretz Israel over the next four years, they were used for backbreaking road building and other public works. Many succumbed to dysentery, rheumatism, malaria, and other diseases caused by the harsh labor conditions, poor nutrition and hygiene, and the rigors of the climate. Their ultimate fate reflected that of most other young pioneers from Russia and Eastern Europe in the immediate aftermath of World War I. Some found their place in the emerging new Jewish society, while others "lost their Zionist faith" and returned to Buczacz within a few years.[2]

A chronic problem for the Zionists, whose accomplishments were measured by the number of members emigrating to Palestine, was that their very success deprived them periodically of their most enterprising and idealistic activists. They also suffered from lack of funds and so appealed to their communities to support their endeavor. One such group issued a pamphlet in Buczacz in 1924, demanding "the material means to go to Eretz Israel" from its fellow Jews: "We do not come to you as beggars and we do not stretch out our hand for charity." Instead, asserted these youngsters, their hand held "the key to the history and the future of the Jewish people." Zionism was a collective duty: "You too must take part in our national uprising and resurrection. Pay your debt!"[3]

Much of the funding for the Zionist project depended on the Jewish National Fund (Keren Kayemet LeYisrael, KKL), which relied not only on donations from the wealthy but also on contributions from all sectors of Jewish society by means of the famous "blue box" in every household, in which family members were expected to deposit their spare change. The presence of the box in a home symbolized the family's support for Jewish nationalism and the settlement of Palestine. In April 1930, for instance, the KKL Central Bureau in Lwów announced that since "the question of land now occupies the most important place in the work of Zionist realization and demands a quick solution," the organization had decided to use the occasion of Passover "to distribute in Eastern Galicia 10,000 new boxes and to receive commitments from the box owners that they would make a regular monthly donation."[4]

✡ ✡

Despite the hardship of preparation and emigration, for thousands of young Jewish men and women in Galicia this was a period of extraordinary ferment and hope, all the more keenly felt because of the surrounding misery and despair. David Cymand, a contemporary participant in these events and future Zionist activist, recalled many years later that during the mid-1920s educated Galician youths began veering increasingly toward Zionism and emigration. All this frantic "self-realization," he said, was the cause of endless ideological splits and disputes, as well as of tremendous youthful energy and solidarity. It was a decade of great hopes and looming threats that remained etched in the memories of all those who survived its immediate aftermath; many did not.[5]

Although these young pioneers could not know it at the time, the immigration certificates made the difference between life and death for many. But British concerns about Arab opposition to Jewish immigration, which culminated in the 1936 Arab uprising in Palestine, led to substantial restrictions on the number of available certificates. With growing pressure from those seeking Zionist "self-realization" and better job opportunities, squabbles over these increasingly scarce documents intensified and demoralization occasionally set in. In 1935 the Lwów center of Achwa (Fraternity), the youth movement of the moderate General Zionists established with the goal of attracting Jewish youths of modest means who might otherwise join more radical groups, reprimanded its Buczacz branch for poor fundraising. Expressing its "outrage and astonishment," the center warned that "such treatment of the essential affairs of our organization" would "lead to its ruin." However, the Buczacz branch felt that it had been sidelined in the matter of certificates and was not swayed by Lwów's assertion that it viewed every branch "as an integral part of the organization" and that "one cannot think in terms of 'us or them' on the issues of *hachshara* and *aliya*." The end result was that fewer young people joined the branch, which constrained its ability to demand more certificates. As the Lwów office bluntly stated in October 1936, "With such a small number of members we do not believe that you can be dominant in your town." The incentive to distribute more certificates was obviously lacking.[6]

All this meant that by the 1930s even the diminishing numbers of Zionist activists could expect ever fewer certificates, which further dampened their spirits. A cursory look may give the impression that interwar Buczacz was swarming with Zionist associations, but memberships often overlapped, and the total number of people engaged remained relatively small. One measure of commitment to Zionism was regular payment of the "shekel," a symbolic currency worth 1.5 złoty at the time. In 1933, for instance, only 769 people paid their dues to the local shekel committee in Buczacz, about a tenth of the Jewish population, although admittedly this was also an indication of the community's poverty.[7]

Many older and more prominent Zionist activists in Buczacz did not emigrate; they obviously had much more to lose. The community leader Mendel Reich and the industrialist Baruch Kramer had donated to the Zionist Federation as early as 1925, while the attorney Dr. Ludwik (Leyzer) Engelberg served as president of the Federation's Buczacz branch in the 1930s. They were still there when the Germans marched in. But the comments made by Engelberg in January 1939 are telling. Conceding a noticeable "passivity in the ranks of the Zionists in our town," he ascribed the local difficulties to a general "crisis of Zionism," a "depressed mood among the Jewish masses" in Galicia, and "the uncertain political situation in Eretz Israel," which had become "a cause for emigration" from Palestine. Most troubling, perhaps, to this veteran Zionist leader was "the lamentable fact that a large part of the Zionists turn out to be no longer deeply permeated with our ideas of [national] rebirth, and have in fact not even a shred of inner attachment to our movement and flag."[8] This general state of demoralization did not bode well for the future, as the community came under pressures of an entirely unprecedented nature.

✡ ✡

The majority of the Jews in Buczacz—as in Eastern Galicia as a whole—were not politically active; for them the interwar period was largely about recovering from the devastation of World War I and then making ends meet at a time of unremitting economic hardship and growing local and government hostility. The community's impoverishment was reflected in persistent requests for help from former residents now living overseas, which focused largely on caring for the dead and ensuring the future of the young. One of the postwar community's first appeals concerned the cemetery, a symbol of its centuries-long existence in Buczacz; as the author and diarist Ansky was told during his brief visit to Buczacz in winter 1917, the Russian occupiers had smashed many of the ancient tombstones. In asking for help to restore the site in 1921, community leaders expressed their confidence that "our *landsleute* [fellow countrymen] who live far away from Buczacz," would "have surely not forgotten their deceased parents and close relatives, who rest in our local graveyard." Repairing the damage was therefore a matter of both communal responsibility and filial respect; it would also preserve the historical record of continuous Jewish life in Buczacz since its early beginnings.[9]

More important than preserving the memory of the dead was educating the young. In 1920 the Talmud Torah Association in Buczacz, charged with the restoration and maintenance of this Jewish elementary school, appealed to a Jewish banker and philanthropist in New York for assistance. The school, which had "burned down during the invasion," had originally catered to the children of the poor, but now that "many middle class families have been ruined by the war," they too could no longer "afford to educate their children at home." Because of lack of funds, the association's ambitious plan for a modern Talmud Torah building that would accommodate up to 1,500 children was never realized; instead the old building was repaired, and elementary education, especially for underprivileged Jewish children, was resumed and maintained until the Soviet occupation in 1939.[10]

Many of the poor children were orphans, another tragic consequence of the war. In late 1919 the community established a shelter for children in a small house with two rooms, a kitchen, and an adjacent playground. As many as 130 orphans lived at the shelter in the early postwar years; just over half of them attended public schools, while the younger ones were educated at the shelter, which also provided them with food and, "if possible, clothing." Many of the children would sleep over at their remaining relatives' homes or with foster families. Two years later the shelter began a process of "transformation into an orphanage that would provide children with permanent accommodation and care." The importance placed on nurturing and educating children as a warranty for future Jewish life is indicated by the membership of the orphanage's executive board, which included some of the most prominent representatives of the community—many of them women of means and influence dedicated to improving the lot of the orphans.[11]

Malka Frenkel, born in Buczacz in 1913, lost her mother in the cholera epidemic toward the end of World War I and was among the first children admitted to the orphanage. She recalled that conditions were harsh. The children had to walk far every day to school, and the food was "neither varied nor particularly filling." Some of the children would bring food packages after spending the Sabbath at home, which they shared with those who had no homes to go to. Malka was fortunate because the director of the orphanage, Mrs. Pohorille, took a liking to her, and her elderly father visited often, at times waiting "for hours in the snow and the rain," always with a package of bread and fruit. The young girl naturally came under the influence of the mostly Zionist Jewish students who volunteered at the orphanage, "taught the wards, took them on excursions, and helped them overcome obstacles." She later joined the Chalutz movement and went to a training camp in Kraków, where she met her future husband, a member of another Zionist youth movement; in 1935 they married and emigrated to Palestine.[12]

The orphanage accommodated approximately fifty boys and girls between the ages of five and nineteen. The board tried to find positions or scholarships for orphan school graduates. Some clearly internalized the values they had been taught. One was killed fighting for the republic in the Spanish Civil War; another, remembered as an unruly child

The orphanage in Buczacz, early 1920s. *Source: Sprawozdanie Centralnego Komitetu Opieki nad Żydowskimi Sierotami w Lwowie, za lata 1923–1926 (Lwów, n.d.), 24.*

who had grown up among the villagers and "did not look at all like a Jew," chose to help fellow Jews during the German occupation, and "by saving the lives of others lost his own."[13]

Most of the graduates, even after further professional training, were unable to find jobs. Indeed young Jews in Poland were generally facing increasing difficulties in gaining entry into secondary schools and universities or finding employment. This was one reason for the establishment in 1927 of a Jewish gymnasium with Polish-language instruction in Buczacz, the first of its kind in the district. The director, Professor Izaak Palek, hoped to expand the first class of twenty-five mostly female students, but the few boys who came from impoverished families had to be subsidized by the school, which itself was funded by "people of good will" in the community, making the prospects for growth quite dim.[14]

The state gymnasium fared much better. By 1931 the school had been fully restored as a gymnasium for seven grade levels. But the numbers of minority teachers and students were progressively declining. In 1933 the school director, Tadeusz Poźniak, had a staff of fifteen teachers, of whom only two or three were Jewish and three Ukrainian. That year half of the 227 graduating students were Roman Catholic, well above their share in the local population; Jews and Ukrainians each made up only a quarter of the student body. Three years later, by now directed by Jan Szajter, the faculty had grown to seventeen, but the number of Jewish and Ukrainian teachers remained the same. As for the students, Jews and Ukrainians now each constituted only a fifth of the total. During that time, the gymnasium was also in the process of transitioning to a coed system, a topic of much discussion and debate in pedagogical circles, including in the school's annual report for 1932–33. But there was no discussion over the declining representation of ethnic minorities in the gymnasium; from the Polish national perspective, this issue, which had greatly exercised the school prior to World War I, seemed to be well on the way to a happy resolution.[15]

Polish students retained fond memories of the gymnasium in the interwar years. Stanisław Kowalski, born in 1921, described it in his postwar memoir as the town's "warm heart, pulsating with young lives eager for education, knowledge and the mysteries of the past, within which every young human being was to find his place among the people of his nation." For him this was literally the school of the nation, "where a new generation acquired the basics for development and the spiritual strength to overcome all possible future travails." Many of Kowalski's schoolmates ended up on the "endless Siberian routes, from the Urals to icy Kolyma," in "the Holy Land in the Middle East, the countryside of hospitable England," or "the battlefields of Monte Cassino, Falaise and Bredy." But all that time the "memories and feelings" of their youth still "stirred their Buczacz soul," and their vivid recollections of the gymnasium played an especially "great and important role." For Kowalski the gymnasium was the culmination of "efforts by the people of Buczacz to establish a school for all the town's ethnic groups, for the mutual benefit of future generations in the entire district." But that was more nostalgia than fact.

In reality the school had been conceived as the incubator of Polish nationalism. The teacher Julian Erdstein, who wrote an essay on the origins of the gymnasium for the last prewar issue of its annual report and was subsequently murdered by the Nazis as a Jew, proudly asserted, "From the very beginning of its existence up to this day the gymnasium was animated by Polish life and culture." Teofil Ostapowicz, who attended the gymnasium before 1914, recalled that the "youngsters' patriotic spirit was sustained by soirées enthusiastically organized at school" and often "patronized by one of the Polish teachers." They were all steeped in Polish Romantic poetry and fiction, reading and writing for nationalist magazines that "united young people and gave them hope for regaining Poland's independence." They also trained in the ranks of the Polish Scouts, which prepared them "for the struggle for independence."[16]

Kowalski recognized the continuity between that "image of student life in the first years of the Buczacz gymnasium's existence" and the "postwar period of independent Poland," which had "witnessed similar activities with perhaps even more intensive cultivation of Polish education and culture, instilling strong patriotic feelings in the youth." After so many school graduates had "sacrificed their lives for the great national cause" in World War I, the next generation strove "to reconstruct the homeland" and "build the sound and durable moral and material foundations that would ensure the nation's liberty." It was at that point, Kowalski conceded, that the gymnasium became explicitly "a Polish school with a Polish curriculum," even if he believed that it still maintained "the full rights of the Jewish and Ukrainian minority."

That was a matter of perspective; Kowalski remembered that after the war "classes were again filled with Polish, Jewish and Ukrainian youths" and that everyone had "equal opportunities to acquire an education and to create better living conditions for themselves and for the community at large." Yet the declining figures of minority students, the school's primary language of instruction, as well as its national-political orientation in general, all pointed in a very different direction. Still, the fact that Kowalski, who was entirely free of the anti-Jewish and anti-Ukrainian prejudices that motivated many of his colleagues, saw things in this manner testifies to the inability of members of one group, however well meaning, to understand the predicament of another, even at a great distance of time. For most Ukrainian and Jewish students, what seemed to Kowalski to be a unifying patriotic spirit merely meant that their own national identity was denied or dismissed and that they could either join the Polish nation by adopting its culture and religion or remain outsiders and aliens. And in the case of the Jews, even whole-hearted adoption of Polishness did not always suffice.[17]

Kowalski's role model in the gymnasium as the shaper of Polish patriotism was his mathematics and physics teacher Edward Pelc, who belonged to a postwar generation of educators engaged, as Kowalski described it, in "transforming the old Austrian system into a new Polish and more progressive one." Soon after arriving in Buczacz in 1929, Pelc's "name became synonymous with scouting," which he proceeded to make into "the center of the Polish youths' lives" to such an extent that "the patriotism of the borderlands became" their "leading theme." Another "patriot of the Polish borderlands" was the gymnasium chaplain, "whose moral and ethical rules and love for his homeland were a model to be followed by the young generation." For the chaplain "Poland was the central theme, and young people" served merely as "the human material that would consolidate and maintain its independence."[18]

Jewish gymnasium students could only interpret this Polish nationalism as aggressively exclusive, all the more so as their numbers continued to diminish. By 1936 there were only twelve Jews out of a total of eighty-two students in the two third-grade classes. One of them was thirteen-year-old Yitzhak (Izak Emanuel) Bauer, who recalled that he was one of only six Jews admitted to the school two years earlier. Among the students themselves, ethnic boundaries were not always rigid: Bauer's best friend in school was Roman Szajter, the director's son. But the Szajters had come from Silesia and were possibly of ethnic German origin. When Bauer was falsely accused of having shown disrespect to a photo of Marshal Piłsudski, Roman bravely took the blame on himself. During the German invasion in 1941 his friend tried to return home from Lwów, where he was studying; however, Bauer recalled, "the Ukrainians killed him on the way."

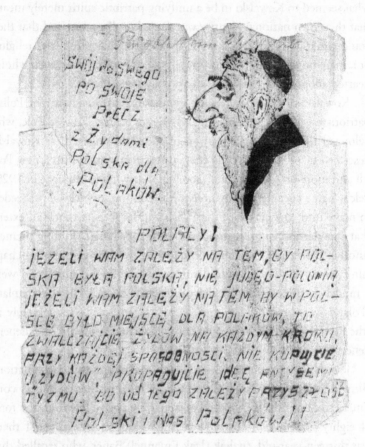

"Away with the Jews, Poland for the Poles! Poles! If you care about Poland being Poland rather than Judeo-Polonia . . . fight the Jews at every step, at every opportunity. Don't buy in Jewish shops, promote the idea of antisemitism, because that is what the future of Poland and Poles depends upon!!" Polish anti-Semitic pamphlet, interwar Buczacz. *Source: Maurice Wolfthal private collection, Phoenix, Arizona.*

Bauer's childhood memories were filled with instances of anti-Semitism. In the afternoon Jewish children went to cheder, but on the streets they had to fend for themselves. Bauer remembered going to bathe in the Strypa: "I would put rocks in my pockets, because the gentile kids would lie in wait for me." In public elementary school "the Christian teacher did not allow" Jewish children "to wear their yarmulkes"; one of his classmates "would run out as soon as the bell rang and put on a hat." This teacher was "an *Endek*," a supporter of the anti-Semitic National Democrats. Yet "whenever he met Grandmother or Mother," this old-fashioned gentleman "would take off his hat and greet them politely." In fact, Bauer pointed out, the teacher's "son and daughter would come to our house." But even seven decades later he could "never forget standing by the blackboard trying to solve some problem, with him facing me . . . our neighbor, and he says to me, 'Żydku ci nie ma pożytku,' meaning, 'Jew-boy, you are of no use to me.' To this day I am haunted by this phrase."[19]

☆ ☆

Most Jewish youths in Buczacz had no hope of attending the gymnasium and were condemned to eking out a wretched existence as a marginalized minority in a far-off corner of an aggressively nationalist and economically backward new state. The Great Depression and subsequent economic stagnation had a particularly detrimental effect on the Jews of Eastern Galicia, who had never quite recovered from the devastation of World War I and were increasingly impacted by Ukrainian economic boycotts and anti-Jewish government policies. In 1933 the prefect (*starosta*) of the Buczacz district noted that Jewish "economic activity" had come "to an almost complete standstill" because of "the general economic crisis and the resulting impoverishment of the population." The main engine of the local economy, "the Jewish merchants and industrialists," were "struck especially hard by the crisis" because "the fall in the prices of agricultural products and the consequent deterioration of the farmers' economic situation meant that commerce and trade, which are largely in the hands of the Jews, [had] lost their main customer, the peasant, who also found himself in a catastrophic situation." As the prefect pointed out, this led to "the bankruptcy of several substantial firms, and often the liquidation of entire enterprises," mostly Jewish owned and previously major providers of jobs in the area. These setbacks resulted in significantly "diminished activity" in Jewish "social life" and "cultural associations." Only organizations concerned with the welfare of the elderly, children, and adolescents were kept busy by "the enormous number of needy Jews in the district," but "because of the general impoverishment" in the region, they too were "able to provide only partial assistance."

Another consequence was that, apart from the Orthodox, only two major Jewish political organizations were still active: the Non-Party Jewish Economic Bloc, established in 1931 to represent middle-class professionals and artisans, and the Zionists. While the prefect believed the Economic Bloc had "a positive attitude toward the government," he predicted that even after uniting with the Orthodox it would lose the local community elections to the Zionists, which is indeed what happened, not least thanks to the increasingly anti-Jewish attitude of the government, while the Orthodox came to be represented by the Zionist religious Mizrahi party. The government's attitude also played a role in what the prefect described as "a rise in radical, indeed communist tendencies among the Jewish youth."[20]

Especially in the early 1930s there were still some issues over which Poles and Jews could unite. On July 6, 1932, for instance, the Jewish Economic Bloc and the Craftsmen's Union (Yad Charutzim) called an assembly in the Great Synagogue to protest "the violence against Jews residing in the German Reich." Among the five hundred who attended were Deputy Mayor Emanuel Meerengel and Count Artur Potocki, scion of the clan that had owned the city in the early modern era. Afterward the prefect reported, "All speeches expressed opposition to Germany, which was seeking revenge for its defeat in the world war, and therefore lashing out violently at other nations, especially the Jews." The assembly overwhelmingly passed a resolution condemning "the barbaric acts against the Jews by the German parties with Hitler at their head," called upon the Polish government to "stand on the side of international law and justice," and solemnly declared, "In case of violence and aggression by Germany, the Jewish population vows to stand by the Polish nation, willing to sacrifice blood and treasure for the threatened Fatherland."[21] But soon after Hitler was appointed Reich chancellor it became clear that Polish and Jewish priorities no longer coincided even on this issue.

Similarly, in the early 1930s many of the teachers, civil servants, and religious leaders listed by the Polish authorities as being "of Jewish nationality" were still labeled as "loyal to the government and the

The second-grade
Tarbut School certificate
of the eight-year-old
Jewish girl Mina Cohen,
Buczacz, 1930. *Source:
BH, 38870.*

state" and largely "uninvolved in politics." But growing poverty and political isolation gradually took their toll both on attitudes toward the state and on commitment to, or at least support for, Jewish causes. By 1935 fundraising for the Jewish National Fund in Buczacz had dropped significantly, not least, it appears, because fewer than a third of Jewish households could pay taxes. Two years later a third of the Jewish households were listed as indigent. Impoverishment obviously set limits on such private institutions as the six-grade Tarbut School, for instance, which could afford a staff of only three teachers and just 130 students, since it relied on donations and tuition. The enterprising principal, Israel Fernhof, sought to gain support for his school by opening the premises to the local branch of the Women's International Zionist Organization (WIZO), where he would also deliver lectures on topics of cultural and political interest. While WIZO filled an important gap especially in middle-class Jewish women's lives in the increasingly bleak atmosphere of the time, the hundred-odd members did their best to help Jewish education, support poor pregnant women, and raise funds for training women in handicrafts. Chaja Roll, one of the few members who survived the war, recalled that "on Saturday afternoons one could see women streaming from all corners of the city" to the WIZO home, where they attended lectures, public readings, and other events. "I believe it was the first time in the history of Buczacz," she wrote, "that women gathered on their own and lived their own lives. Not only young girls but also mothers and grandmothers got together and would attentively listen to an interesting lecture." But this was a small minority; most women had no time for such activities, and most families chose to send their children to the Polish public school, which was free.[22]

One symbol of the community's decline was the deterioration of the Jewish hospital, a proud accomplishment prior to 1914. Restored and modernized after the war with assistance from the American Jewish Joint Distribution Committee and local fundraising, during the economic crisis of the 1930s the hospital fell into a growing state of disrepair. Similarly, while the General Zionists claimed in 1935 to have become "the strongest group in our town," and the major Zionist sports associations Makabi (Maccabi) and Hapoel (the Worker) established branches in Buczacz, the reality on the ground for most Jews was of increasing desperation and hopelessness. The double bind of the last years before the outbreak of war presented diminishing economic opportunities in Poland, on the one hand, and increasingly restrictive policies on emigration to Palestine and the rest of the world, on the other.[23]

Under these circumstances, in 1936 Mendel Reich, president of the Talmud Torah School and an activist in the local Mizrahi party, appealed for help from Abraham Sommer, the financial secretary of the United Buczaczer Ladies Auxiliary in New York. The Jews of Buczacz, he wrote, were "condemned to wait as if on death row for an execution, without hope for better days to come," while "everyone around us, even the air we breathe, is conspiring to find a way to destroy us, to crush our existence, to make the lives of the Jews unbearable, and all we can think is 'from whence cometh my help?' " Where could they run? "The lands of immigration have shut their gates, and the Jews have no land of their own. Should we rise up to heaven and live there on air?" Trapped in their city, the Jews of Buczacz were "embittered and depressed"; having been "deprived of rights," they found themselves "defenseless, abandoned to the whims of the lowliest hooligan." At a time "when 'in the streets the sword will make them childless; in their homes terror will reign,' " stressed Reich, the Talmud Torah afterschool program had become "our last redoubt, when everything else has already burned to the ground." And yet, he added, "now we face the threat that the building, which we had built in better times, might be sold because we cannot even pay the interest on the loans to our lenders." If Jewish education were to be demolished, what hope would there be for the future?[24]

The paltry fifty dollars sent from America to help the Talmud Torah School sufficed for no more than some new clothes for the children. But the school hastened to assure the donors, "Our students are striving to progress with God's help in their studies and we can only hope that they will become scholars and good decent Jews. Many are already in Palestine, working as farmers, craftsmen, teachers and in other professions." The remaining 175 students were "being instructed spiritually and morally in the ancient and modern Jewish sense." But as Reich wrote privately to Sommer at the end of 1937, "the air" was "full of anti-Semitic sentiments." The Jews were being accused, first, of having "sent their God to heaven" and, second, of "not going themselves to heaven, to Mars, or at least to Madagascar, so long as one is rid of them." Having "lived together on the land for over a thousand years," Reich wrote in despair, the Poles perceived the Jews as "just an alien hump on their backs" and "each and every one of us as superfluous and an 'enemy.'" For all the "nice slogans" of fascism and socialism, Reich believed that "when translated into action," they both had "the scent of overt or covert anti-Semitism," whose "guiding principle is: everything that is Jewish means destruction. Jewish wisdom, Jewish art, culture, morals, even the Divine—if it only comes from a Jewish mind, a Jewish brain, it must be seen as a Jewish conspiracy." And because "anti-Semitism demands the annihilation of everything Jewish" at any price, it also empowers its adherents, since "in relationship to the Jew, every illiterate is a philosopher."[25]

It was for this reason that until the last moment many people did all they could to leave. Months and weeks before the war, some found themselves caught in limbo between the land of promise and their ancestral home, between hope and despair. Jacob Shapira had been frantically trying to join his child in the United States; his wife had died, and the boy was under the care of Abraham Sommer. In March 1939 Shapira was informed that his "slot in the quota" for an entry visa "would come up no sooner than July or August," although he had already booked passage on a ship sailing from Amsterdam to New York in early June. He begged Sommer to send him an affidavit to accelerate the process. "I will not be a burden to anyone," he promised. "I am a diligent and industrious man, have provided for myself until now with dignity and will make an honest living there for myself and my dearest child."[26] It is unlikely that Shapira was ever reunited with his son. No other information on him or his fate is available. All that is left of him is this letter, filed away for decades among Sommer's papers.

✡ ✡

Some members of the younger generation found it impossible to come to terms with the insufferable reality of political intolerance and economic distress. Portrayed as treasonous by the Polish authorities, they believed in their own heroic narrative at a time when idealism had become a worthless state-generated commodity. Their response was categorized by some as typically Jewish, seeking to erase religious and national differences by subverting the state. Eventually the best they could accomplish was to influence the manner and perhaps the subsequent meaning of their own destruction.

In summer 1931 three working-class Jewish men in their early twenties established a cell of the Komunistyczna Partia Zachodniej Ukrainy (KPZU, Communist Party of Western Ukraine) in Buczacz. Although the state police liquidated the cell within a year, communist activity in Buczacz continued under different guises throughout the second half of the interwar period. The activists were mostly Jewish men and women from Buczacz and its environs. While Zvi Heller later described these early young communists as coming "from the academic youth, especially those who had acquired this disposition at the University in Prague," contemporary Polish police reports stated that they were in fact "mostly Jewish working youth" of only rudimentary education. They were also singularly ineffective. Frequent police raids and arrests, facilitated in large part by a mole within the cell's executive committee, rendered them more of a specter that could be employed by the authorities for their own propaganda purposes than an actual threat. Attempts by this cell to appeal to the anti-Polish sentiments of Ukrainian nationalists also made no headway in view of the latter's vehement anticommunist and anti-Semitic ideology. As the regional state police office in Tarnopol pointed out in 1934, the fact that "communist activity in the entire region" had "declined considerably" was directly linked to "Ukrainian nationalist action in rural areas," which "paralyzes the work of the communists and deprives them of the influence they had previously had among the rural population." A couple of years later a senior Ukrainian communist from Stanisławów urged the cell to "focus on the workers" in town and to "prepare agricultural strikes" by the "agrarian laborers." But this was well beyond the capacities of the few remaining Jewish communists in Buczacz, who reportedly were increasingly fearful of the police, short of funds, and generally dejected by the second half of the 1930s. Aware of this problem, the KPZU leadership tried to dilute Jewish membership in the hope of changing the party's image. Ironically, by 1937 even the police in Buczacz distinguished between Polish communists, labeled loyal to the state, and Jewish party members considered hostile to it.[27]

Looked at from a different perspective, the youthful communists of Buczacz shared some similarities with their Zionist counterparts, especially in their rejection of current conditions and quest for a radical solution to what appeared to be an increasingly impossible predicament. From a still wider perspective, they also had much in common with young Ukrainians and to some extent also Poles, who similarly believed in and worked for a radical change in existing conditions. But despite these similarities, or perhaps precisely because of them, these groups found themselves vehemently opposed to each other; any weakening of the social order, let alone external military intervention, could and did trigger untold violence between them, greater than any of these idealistic youths could have ever imagined.

✧ ✧

The real internal threat to Polish rule in Eastern Galicia was posed by the increasingly disgruntled majority Ukrainian population. Especially troubling for the authorities were the radicalized nationalists, who were gaining support among the urban intelligentsia and making inroads with the rural masses. In the long run this conflict, whose roots dated back several centuries, culminated in catastrophe for Poles in the region, although that did not mean a Ukrainian triumph. Caught in the middle between these two rival groups, the Jews were often perceived by both as helping the other side, betraying their neighbors, or simply looking only after their own interests.

In 1931 two British members of Parliament, James Barr and Rhys Davies, reported to the House of Commons on their recent visit to Eastern Galicia. Seeking to verify reports "alleging harsh treatment of the population of this area by the Polish authorities" and to assess the condition of the Ukrainian population, "the largest minority now under alien rule in any country in Europe," they also inquired into the origins of the conflict. As Davies saw it, "the cause of all the trouble" was the refusal of the Poles to implement the guarantee of local autonomy given to the Ukrainians with the establishment of independent Poland. Promises made in 1925 to establish self-government in the three provinces of Lwów, Tarnopol, and Stanisławów, which now made up Eastern Galicia, formally known in the interwar period as Eastern Lesser Poland (Małopolska Wschodnia), were also not kept. It was for that reason, argued Davies, that among Ukrainians "vigorous nationalism and resentment ran riot in 1930 to such an extent that arson was committed on a fairly extensive scale." The violence, attributed largely to the underground and illegal nationalist Ukrainska Viiskova Orhanizatsiya (UVO, Ukrainian Military Organization), founded in 1920, and to its radical successor, the Orhanizatsiya Ukrainskykh Natsionalistiv (OUN, Organization of Ukrainian Nationalists), established in 1929, targeted mostly "the large landowners of Polish origin and descent living in eastern Galicia." In response the Polish government "swooped down on the guilty and innocent Ukrainian peasants alike without much mercy." In this "systematic attack," troops, "armed in some cases with machine-guns," surrounded "several hundred villages," with "villagers being dragged from their homes, stripped and most brutally beaten, sometimes to death," after which "heavy tribute was levied" and "hundreds if not thousands were imprisoned." Additionally "Ukrainian schools were closed down, Ukrainian reading-rooms, libraries and co-operative stores destroyed and other brutalities committed."

At the root of the violence were political aspirations but also widespread poverty. Davies was struck by "the abject conditions of the Ukrainian peasants," while the "very small proportion of the population who may be described as big landowners" were mostly Poles. As for "the landless man," commented Davies, he is "almost a beggar, and when he finds work his wages income is pitiful in the extreme." Such families survived on entirely inadequate nutrition; their children often "had only one piece of clothing to cover their nakedness," and "a large number of the population went bare-footed." The two MPs simply could not believe that "it would be our lot to find white people in any part of the world compelled to exist under such conditions of poverty." Things were further exacerbated by constant population growth, an almost total halt of emigration to North America, and state Polonization policies whereby "devious means are employed to sell all parcels of available land to Polish buyers in preference to Ukrainians." As Barr elaborated in his separate report, following the largely failed Land Reform Bills of 1919 and 1925, the lands of the few large estates that were divided ended up being distributed only to Polish peasants. Although the Ukrainian Cooperative Movement had made gains in exporting produce and training peasants, Barr was appalled by police interventions and restrictions and the authorities' handing over of Ukrainian monopolies to Polish cooperatives.

Other causes of resentment included job discrimination, whereby, for instance, seven thousand Ukrainian railway men were replaced with Poles; blatant political manipulation, with voter suppression and falsification of voter lists in the general election of 1928 causing the number of Ukrainian members of Parliament to fall from forty to sixteen; and attempted Polonization through biased educational policies. The act of 1924 had established bilingual schools in areas of mixed population on the basis of local plebiscites, but those were heavily skewed by the authorities, resulting in the number of Ukrainian schools declining from three thousand to seven hundred. In the bilingual schools Polish teachers predominated, so that the language of instruction was actually Polish, whereas many of the surviving Ukrainian schools were shut

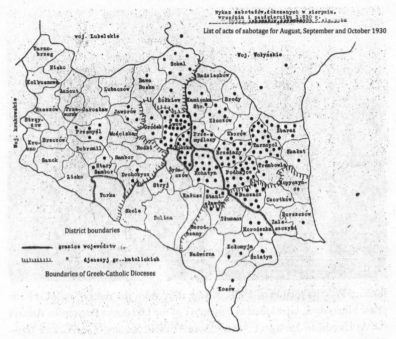

Ukrainian acts of sabotage in Galicia from August to October 1930. *Source: AAN-MSZ, 2257, p. 245.*

down during the "pacification" campaign of 1930. At the University of Lwów Ukrainian professors were required to teach in Polish, which also became the only official language in the law courts, the post office, and the railways. Barr concluded that, "so far, it cannot be said that a very hopeful report of progress" toward reconciliation could be offered.[28]

✿ ✿

The Ukrainian enlightenment society Prosvita was a main target of the Polish pacification campaign. In the Buczacz district, as throughout the region, World War I had taken a toll on the society, but by 1930 it had largely recovered, boasting forty-five reading clubs, thirty-two theater troupes, twelve choirs, and two orchestras. Intellectually its offerings remained limited, with just over a dozen lectures per year and a district

Buczacz Prosvita members, 1938. Sitting third from the right: Greek Catholic priest Hnatyshyn, later killed as a member of the Ukrainska Povstanska Armiya (UPA, Ukrainian Insurgent Army). *Source: Poshuk Archive, Lviv/Buczacz (hereafter PA).*

library of merely 740 volumes. The pacification actions that year almost led to the society's ruin: membership declined to only 141 people, many of them illiterate. But Polish repression also caused significant radicalization. A decade later, leading local Prosvita activists such as Tadei Kramarchuk ended up serving in the militias and police units that collaborated with the Germans.[29]

Prosvita closely monitored the senseless destruction of property and physical violence during the pacification campaign and over the following years leading to the war. Many of its members openly supported the political party Ukrainske natsionalno demokratychne obiednannia (UNDO, Ukrainian National Democratic Alliance), which advocated independence for Western Ukraine. They were also often suspected of being secret members of the OUN, which promoted the use of terrorist methods against the regime. On the eve of World War II, the Prosvita branch in Buczacz had grown to over four hundred members in close to sixty reading clubs throughout the district. Its leaders largely reflected the local Ukrainian elite and shared similar sentiments. But while the authorities perceived it as a threat to Polish hegemony, Prosvita's self-perception throughout the 1930s was of an association struggling both for funds and for greater support and loyalty from the people it hoped to enlighten. Father Vasyl Melnyk complained as early as 1930 that the general "decline and inertness of the reading clubs" reflected "the aversion shown by citizens and Prosvita members to popular education." Instead people preferred to indulge in reckless drinking. "A drunkard," thundered Melnyk, "while drinking alcohol, drinks in fact the tears and blood of his family, his relatives, and his nation." At a time when "there are no means available to revive Ukrainian cultural institutions, the Ukrainian people in Galicia squander their resources on drink."[30]

Many peasants did not appreciate being talked down to in this manner by the urban intelligentsia, not least because Prosvita

Meeting of a local Ukrainian peasant society in Buczacz, March 24, 1938. *Source: PA.*

officials rarely took the trouble to visit their villages. On one occasion, when Father Melnyk rebuked the reading club in Nagórzanka, on the outskirts of Buczacz, a member of the audience called out, "Nobody from the intelligentsia has visited us!" Indeed when forty members of the urban elite were invited to attend a meeting of the educational council at another village, only eight turned up. One village representative pointed out, "[This disregard] illustrated that the Buczacz intelligentsia is interested in educational matters only in their own city."

At the same time, Prosvita leaders feared that the very core of their mission, getting people to read, was in jeopardy: they had neither the resources to purchase enough books nor the means to persuade villagers to read them. In 1931 only five thousand books were available in Prosvita libraries for a population of seventy-two thousand Ukrainians, that is, one book for every fourteen people. Most reading club members chose not to read any books. Even the Ukrainian library in the city of Buczacz, which contained 628 volumes, had only twenty-five registered readers. Branch chairman Roman Slyuzbar expressed his concern about "the ignorance of our citizenry as compared to other peoples, even the Bolsheviks," and urged Ukrainians to learn from the Germans, who "despite losing the war catastrophically and thanks to their high culture, consciousness and discipline," had once more become the arbiters of war and peace in the world. Similarly, Prosvita's secretary, Volodymyr Koltsio, warned that Ukrainians, as a subjugated people, were undergoing "a moral crisis," to the extent that "in some villages the reading clubs" had become "nothing more than local taverns" that "spread demoralization." People had forgotten they could "overcome ignorance, gain consciousness, and become a civilized nation only through books and periodicals." What was to be done? Perhaps, suggested one board member, they should appeal "to the seminary and gymnasium graduates who are abundant in our villages and are not interested in anything." But many of these youths soon became attracted to more exciting activities than readings books and joined the ranks of the OUN. Some of them had likely studied with Viktor Petrykevych, a veteran of World War I

Viktor Petrykevych as an officer
in the Austro-Hungarian Army
in 1916. *Courtesy of his son
Bohdan Petrykevych.*

and the Polish-Ukrainian War, who began teaching at the Buczacz state gymnasium in 1929 and was an activist in Prosvita and a mentor of students associated with the OUN.[31]

It was thanks to the dedication of such men as Petrykevych that, despite all the obstacles, Prosvita played a crucial role in disseminating the message of Ukrainian nationalism in the interwar period. Celebrating its thirtieth anniversary in 1938, the Buczacz branch estimated a probably exaggerated total of thirty thousand supporters, which "proved just how much popularity and love Prosvita enjoys among our citizenry and how dear our educational appeals have been to them." With sixty-six thousand Ukrainians in the Buczacz district on the eve of the war, the local branch reported 1,150 registered and dues-paying members, along with an additional 8,000 members in fifty-six reading clubs throughout the district; it had also forged close links with numerous other associations, including forty-eight cooperatives of various kinds. Altogether Prosvita reading club members constituted 10 percent of

Galicia's Ukrainian population—no mean achievement considering the ubiquitous poverty and illiteracy. Ukrainian nationalism had become an established fact, even if many peasants had far more urgent issues to deal with in their daily lives.[32]

✧ ✧

Beyond widespread sympathy for Prosvita, the vast majority of Ukrainians supported the UNDO. In 1929 it was estimated that the party had secured 70 percent of the Ukrainian vote in the Buczacz district; this reflected the desire of the population for independence from Poland, but it did not necessarily mean agreement with the UNDO's rejection of violence as a means to attaining that goal. Although it is difficult to gauge how many UNDO voters also eventually supported the illegal OUN, which did advocate violence, the growth of other, increasingly militant associations indicates the progressive radicalization of Galician Ukrainians. These included especially the Ukrainian village sports association Sokil and the gymnastics and firefighting organiza-

Members of the Luh association, 110 boys and 30 girls, in Leszczańce (Ukrainian: Lishchantsi), Buczacz district, in military formation. *Source: PA.*

tion Luh, which largely served as a cover for the militant Sich Riflemen society, after it was banned by the Polish authorities in 1924. Active during the Ukrainian arson campaign of 1930, and despite being repeatedly targeted and harassed by the police, these associations only gained strength in the years that followed and clearly played a major role in stirring up popular feelings against Polish rule.[33]

By the mid-1930s, then, increasingly militant nationalism, cutting across age groups and social classes, had become the norm among urban Galician Ukrainians in such settings as Buczacz and other towns in its district. A tight-knit group of middle-aged professionals, businessmen, spiritual leaders, teachers, and other members of the local intelligentsia formed the core of a network of associations, cooperatives, societies, and clubs dedicated to promoting the cause of Ukrainian nationalism. Around them were wider circles of activists of all ages and social classes, supporters of the UNDO party, members of Prosvita, and potential operatives of the OUN who could be activated when the time came to realize their dreams of independence. In Buczacz they included a poorly educated farmer and cooperative inspector, a shoemaker and rally organizer, an attorney with a PhD, and a mining engineer and veteran Ukrainian Army officer. Younger activist men and women, mostly in their twenties, similarly ranged from laborers and unemployed gymnasium graduates to students of philosophy and law school graduates. And there was a group of teenage OUN activists in the state gymnasium.[34]

Certainly not everyone, likely not even a majority, supported the terrorist tactics of the OUN, but that was largely a question of the means rather than of the common goal of creating an independent Ukrainian state. However indifferent to nationalism many of the peasants may have remained, the efforts to nationalize the rural population were, it appears, bearing fruit, most especially among the young. Villagers surely disliked being patronized by bourgeois urbanites and were often too preoccupied with sheer material survival to contemplate a future Ukrainian state. But they were far more resentful of Polish rule and its local representatives, as well as of their marginally better-off

Members of the Orhanizatsiya Ukrainskykh Natsionalistiv (OUN, Organization of Ukrainian Nationalists) in Soroki, Buczacz district. *Source: PA.*

Jewish neighbors. On these matters there was not much indifference, but rather plenty of sullen accommodation and increasingly impatient anticipation of a radical, and possibly violent change.[35]

It should therefore come as no surprise that Polish fears and anxieties about ethnic minorities spanned the entire interwar period. Under the rubric of minorities, Jews were featured as an alien, inassimilable, and potentially subversive element, whereas Ukrainians were possibly susceptible to integration as fellow Slavs and Christians. And yet, both because of their numerical preponderance in the eastern territories and across the Soviet border and because of their long history of conflict with Polish rule, Ukrainians were simultaneously seen as presenting a direct threat to the integrity of the Polish state.

This history of conflict was intimately linked with the idea and memory of the *kresy*, Poland's historic eastern borderlands, which had once stretched far beyond the Dnieper and symbolized a moment of Polish greatness followed by a humiliating demise. A constitutive element in the collective national memory of many Poles, especially the educated elite, the nostalgia for the lost lands of the East was not necessarily confrontational; the underlying urge to return to those lands—or at least to hold on to the ethnically diverse regions of Galicia and Volhynia that had come under Polish rule in 1919—could be presented as part of Poland's traditional paternalistic role and civilizing mission, especially vis-à-vis the Ukrainians. But it obviously also contained a violent edge, because it reflected a genuine patriotic sentiment and conviction of historical and cultural rights beyond the exigencies of politics. Hence those who opposed Polish hegemony were by definition in the wrong and could not, indeed must not be argued with; they had to willingly consent to Poland's rule or be subdued into acceptance.[36]

Such views of the *kresy* as the heart and soul of historic Poland were held especially strongly by those whose own lives and worldviews were formed there. Bishop Piotr Mańkowski came to Buczacz as a refugee in 1920, having fled his bishopric of Kamieniec Podolski (Ukrainian: Kamyanets-Podilskyi), east of the Zbrucz River, from the advancing Bolshevik forces. Born and raised on his family's estate in Podolia, Mańkowski lamented that in agreeing on a new border with Soviet Russia, Poland had "renounced huge territories of the land that had once been within the Polish Republic," thereby "violating the history of several centuries." As he saw it, "We, the inhabitants of the eastern borderlands [*kresowcy wschodni*], were removed and rejected as unnecessary ballast in newly-constituted Poland." And because he feared that by losing those vast territories east of the Zbrucz, the Second Republic would be bereft of its very soul and sense of purpose, Mańkowski considered the remaining lands of the *kresy*, Galicia and Volhynia, as crucial components of the nation's patrimony.

To Mańkowski this was not merely a political position but at least as much a deep spiritual and cultural attachment. Coming to Galicia, he was struck by what he perceived as the quintessentially Polish character of his surroundings, as he and his retinue "enjoyed the fresh air, walked in woods full of wild strawberries, raspberries and mushrooms, and swam in the Koropiec River." Visiting the nearby town of Trembowla (Ukrainian: Terebovlya), they admired the ruins of the old castle but were repelled by "the Jewish houses" below; the debris of past Polish glory was more appealing to them than the detritus of a Jewish presence.

Jews generally made "a nasty impression" on Mańkowski; their inherently alien presence spoiled these authentic Polish lands. This was all the more disturbing when the bishop settled down in Buczacz, which looked "simply perfect from above and at a certain distance," but "from close range" appeared "just like any ordinary jerkwater Jewish town." He appreciated all the edifices built by the town's Polish owners and benefactors, such as "the ruins of the old castle" and "the beautiful eighteenth century baroque town hall," as well as "the large and grandiose parish church" and "the Basilian monastery with its school for boys." But like many other Polish observers, he seems to have never noticed the Great Synagogue.

Again like much of the rest of the Polish elite in Galicia, Mańkowski believed that the best path "for our eastern borderlanders" was reconciliation between Roman and Greek Catholicism and reintegration of Ukrainians into a Polish-ruled *kresy*. The refusal of Ukrainians to be co-opted into this Polish scheme made them appear intransigent and bellicose in the face of Polish acceptance and tolerance.

Mańkowski left Buczacz in 1925 and settled down in Włodzimierz, near Łódź, where he died in 1933. During those years this self-described "eastern borderlander" was tormented by "the neighboring Jewish houses" and the general "noise of the town" and pined for the "rural settlements," the "gently sloping spaces," and the "fresh air" of his beloved *kresy*.[37]

☆ ☆

Throughout the interwar period Polish politicians, administrators, patriotic associations, and social scientists were obsessed with population statistics, largely in order to demonstrate the progressive growth of Poland's hegemony in the eastern borderlands; they thereby also revealed a persistent demographic anxiety. This in turn led to increasing manipulation of figures and significant gerrymandering.

Statistics are notoriously malleable. In 1921, for instance, the town of Buczacz numbered 7,517 inhabitants, of whom just over 50 percent were Jews, 30 percent were Poles, and 20 percent were Greek Catholics. But when categorized according to self-declared nationality, Jews and Poles each constituted 40 percent of the population, indicating that a fair number of Jews chose to register their nationality as Polish. The countryside remained predominantly Ukrainian.[38]

The implications of the *kresy's* demographic realities for national politics had already been demonstrated in the parliamentary elections of 1922, considered "the only complete and free elections held in Poland until 1991." The country's political map was divided into three main electoral blocs: the center-left parties supporting Piłsudski; the coalition of right-wing parties around the nationalist and anti-Semitic Endecja party (National Democracy); and the National Minorities Bloc, combining most Jewish, Ukrainian, Belarusian, and German parties. The elections produced a draw between the left and the right, with the Minorities Bloc gaining a fifth of the seats in Parliament. Fearing an alliance between the left and the minorities over the choice of a president, who was elected by Parliament, the Endecja-led coalition unleashed a vicious anti-Semitic campaign against the Minorities Bloc, describing it as a Jewish party and an alien organization about to take over Poland. The atmosphere of incitement and riots led to the assassination of President Gabriel Narutowicz, depicted as a "Jewish" candidate, just four days after he was sworn into office.[39]

The National Minorities Bloc would have had greater impact on the elections had the nationalist Ukrainian parties not boycotted the polls in protest against what they saw as Poland's illegal occupation of their land. In Eastern Galicia this meant that fewer than half of eligible Ukrainian voters participated in the elections, thereby skewing the vote in favor of the Jewish electorate. As the prefect of the Buczacz district reported, "With few exceptions, the Ruthenian population and a certain part of the Polish population did not take part in the voting."

Consequently, although the East Galician Zionists, the largest Jewish political party in the region, won only 200,000 votes, they gained fifteen seats in the Sejm (the lower house) and became the largest faction of the "Jewish Club" in the national Parliament.[40]

In 1926 Piłsudski carried out a coup d'état, whose goal was to diminish the power of the anti-Semitic Endecja. But the elections of 1928 did not produce sufficient votes for Piłsudski's new Government Bloc to dominate Parliament. Ironically, this caused the regime to veer increasingly to the right, a trend that accelerated appreciably after Piłsudski's death in 1935. Thanks to its majority Jewish population, in the city of Buczacz the Galician Zionists won an overwhelming two-thirds of the vote in 1928. But Polish population statistics strove to obscure Jewish urban preponderance. The census of 1931 suggested that over the previous decade the total population of Buczacz had grown by almost 30 percent, to ten thousand people, but the share of Jews in the population had declined to 40 percent. A closer analysis reveals that these figures were reached by lumping together major Jewish centers such as Buczacz with smaller towns that had much larger relative Polish populations and by redistricting the town of Buczacz itself so as to include its predominantly Polish rural outskirts.[41]

Such voter manipulation was even more pronounced in the heavily rigged elections of 1930, in which the government in Warsaw resorted to undemocratic measures, disbanding Parliament and arresting the leaders of the opposition center-left coalition, as well as those of the national minorities parties. Yet although the Government Bloc managed to gain the majority of seats, its opponents on the extreme right, now grouped under the National Party (Stronnictwo Narodowe), also gained votes; this signaled where the winds of Polish popular opinion were blowing. With the end of parliamentary democracy in Poland, interethnic strife and violence would only intensify over the next decade.[42]

☆ ☆

The ongoing ethnic violence increasingly divided citizens at the local level. When eight thousand "people of all nationalities" convened in

Buczacz in 1930 to celebrate May 3, Polish Constitution Day, this national holiday was in fact organized as a purely Polish and Roman Catholic event, complete with an open-air mass and a sermon by an army brigade chaplain; a military parade of cavalry, police, members of the paramilitary Riflemen's Association, as well as fire brigade and Polish Youth Association units; and delegations of war invalids. Although services were also held in the Great Synagogue and the St. Nicholas Greek Catholic Church, the event included no representation of Ukrainian or Jewish associations. It was, in essence, a display of Polish hegemony.

Threats to that hegemony were confronted head-on. Jan Płachta, prefect of the Buczacz district, was particularly energetic in clamping down on local Ukrainian political activism; in this he was supported by the governor of the Tarnopol province, who dismissed complaints about Płachta's conduct as "baseless and unjust" and insisted on the need for the "security apparatus" to "put a stop" to the "unusual political activity" and separatist tendencies of the Ukrainians. The prefect was not engaged in "an attack on the Ruthenian national movement," asserted the governor, but rather was acting in conformity with "a policy of harmonious coexistence between all nationalities in the district." The problem was, of course, that Polish hegemony could not be democratically maintained in a region where Ukrainians were the majority, and in 1930 Poles made up only a third of the seventy thousand eligible voters in the Buczacz district. The declaration by the governor that the elections had "brought the defeat of the national minorities" therefore merely confirmed the success of state intimidation and manipulation.[43]

Polish hegemony was also maintained in the Buczacz district through employment and educational discrimination of the kind identified in the British parliamentary report on Eastern Galicia. For instance, in 1931 the entire district had only three Ukrainian judicial employees out of a total of thirty-eight (including one Jewish judge) and only one Ukrainian railway employee out of twenty-two. (There were no Jewish railway employees.) Where national minorities had to be employed, such as in schools, their political affiliations and activities were closely scrutinized. Most important, perhaps, teaching in Ukrainian was increasingly restricted. Since the primary language in bilingual schools was Polish, and the number of public Ukrainian schools had greatly diminished, the only way to preserve Ukrainian-language instruction was in private schools, supported by the Native School Society (Ridna Shkola); remarkably, by 1938 an extraordinary 40 percent of Ukrainian students were studying in such private secondary schools and colleges.[44]

Transforming Ukrainian schools into bilingual ones depended on plebiscites, in which parents declared their children's national-linguistic affiliation. But this process was open to government manipulation. In 1933 one such plebiscite was held in the Buczacz district, collecting 4,500 declarations of Ukrainian-language use from sixty-seven communes. Displeased with this outcome, the authorities pronounced almost half of the declarations invalid, leading the prefect to conclude that the plebiscite would not "affect Ruthenian society in any significant manner." Indeed he considered the entire undertaking "somewhat harmful, because this periodic raising of the Ruthenian population's awareness of the need for Ruthenian language instruction in the schools arouses some antagonism between the Polish and Ruthenian populations and makes it impossible for these two nations to coexist in harmony."[45]

Another way of overcoming demographic realities involved culture and biology. A Polish study published in 1931 argued that since a third of male and a quarter of female Roman Catholics married Greek Catholics in the Tarnopol province, the competition over national predominance was transformed into "conflicts within the family." Here, then, "victories depend on which party in mixed marriages more often transfers his or her nationality to their offspring." Unsurprisingly the study asserted that in this sphere too "Poland is the more victorious party." Polish self-deception about the progress of integrating Ruthenians appeared immune to factual evidence; even after the outbreak of war the exiled Polish Ministry of the Interior asserted that "the coexistence of Poles, Ruthenians, and Ukrainians had improved from year to year" during the 1930s. This was, pronounced the ministry, because "from the side of the government everything had been done to guarantee for the minorities, in accordance with the constitution, protection of life, freedom, and rights over property, equality before the law and access to public offices, the cultivation of language and of national minorities, the establishment of charitable, religious, and social associations, and schools with the right to use their own language." No wonder that "almost 50 percent of all marriages were mixed," that "there were no particularly hostile attitudes," and that "the two Catholic confessions regularly collaborated during the holidays."

This fantasy of interethnic harmony was not extended to the Jews, who were acerbically depicted as not feeling "tied to national and state matters, irrespective of which nationality they coexisted with in any given region." Instead Jews' "political action was determined by their egoistical striving to plunder the regions they inhabited and to exploit the labor performed in all those areas that promised the greatest material gain." Many others turned to subversion, as shown by the fact that "the Communist Party of Western Ukraine was made up mostly not of Ukrainians but of Jews," who sought "to fight against Jewish capitalists, and thereby cause harm to the Polish State." Hence, while in the case of Ukrainian-Polish relations there were purportedly "no problems that separated these two social groups from each other," the "coexistence of Poles as well as Ukrainians with the Jews was never distinguished by honesty and warmth, since the practice of merciless exploitation by the Jews had made it impossible to establish open relationships."[46]

Wartime rhetoric about past Polish-Ukrainian harmony notwithstanding, ethnic Poles retained firm control over Buczacz and other such cities throughout the interwar period. In 1936, for instance, the eleven thousand inhabitants of Buczacz, the majority of whom were Jews, were governed exclusively by Roman Catholic Poles. Jews held only subordinate positions, although many of the city's attorneys and physicians were Jewish. As for Ukrainians, there appears to have been little effort to appoint them to official posts and likely much to dissuade them; they were also far less well represented in white-collar occupations than either Jews or Poles.[47]

Assertions of religious harmony between Roman and Greek Catholics were similarly often and increasingly belied by events on the ground. In 1933, for instance, the Greek Catholic priest of the village of Medwedowce (Ukrainian: Medvedivtsi) allegedly incited three young Ukrainian women to paint the statue of St. Joseph in the center of the village with the yellow and blue Ukrainian colors, unleashing "great anger" among the Polish residents. Prefect Adam Fedorowicz urged his superiors to remove the priest from the village, warning that his presence might "incite serious feuds between the Polish and Ruthenian populations that may be detrimental to the interests of the state." In the village of Porchowa (Ukrainian: Porokhova) the Greek Catholic priest "condemned mixed Polish-Ukrainian marriages and threatened not to bless such marital unions." Going one step further, a priest in Nowostawce (Ukrainian: Novostavtsi) "condemned all signs of Ukrainian fraternization with Poles."[48]

These were all troubling signs that religion and nationalism were being fused together to produce an ideological and psychological climate ripe for widespread violence once the constraints on social order were removed or altered. By 1934 no Ukrainian organizations in the Buczacz district agreed to celebrate Polish Constitution Day, and many Greek Catholic priests even "neglected to say prayers for the state's success," while their congregations "went to the fields in the morning in order to avoid participation in the festivities." Members of "the Ukrainian intelligentsia and Greek Catholic clergy who had the courage" to organize interethnic events were said to "face the disdain of the general public, which condemns them and treats them as traitors to the nation." Even innocent socializing was sanctioned. In one instance, a Greek Catholic priest ejected two young women, a Ukrainian and a Pole, from a Prosvita-sponsored dance merely because they had spoken Polish with each other. As one parish priest near Jazłowiec put it, referring to the 1935 "normalization" accord between the UNDO and the government, "The Polish-Ukrainian agreement may exist in Warsaw, [but] there never was and never will be any agreement in the districts."[49]

Following the death of Piłsudski in 1935 and the disappearance of the last remnants of Polish democracy, and faced with an escalating international crisis over Nazi Germany's growing territorial demands, all political factions in the country were undergoing a process of progressive radicalization. By the late 1930s a "wave of extreme nationalism" permeated "a considerable part of the Ukrainian intelligentsia," which made up the bulk of "the UNDO party's local organizational cells," and began "washing over" all other "institutions influenced by the UNDO." This made for "numerous scuffles between the youth united in these institutions and Polish youth" and illustrated that the "idea of peaceful Polish-Ukrainian coexistence" was "sinking under the nationalist currents"; simultaneously, political radicalization led to "increasing anti-Jewish feelings in both Polish and Ukrainian society," as noted by officials in Tarnopol.[50] On one issue everyone seemed to agree, namely, that the Gordian knot of internal interethnic conflict and looming international war could be cut only with the sword.

In Polish political circles anti-Jewish feelings were running high in the last few years before the war. The replacement of the defunct Government Party with a new Camp of National Unity in 1937, intended to ward off the extreme nationalists, only led to a further tilt to the right of the entire political establishment. Officially opposed to anti-Jewish violence, the Camp of National Unity depicted Jewish citizens as a separate national group and insisted that the "Jewish question" could be solved only by emigration. From Buczacz the local police reported that the Jews "displayed an utterly negative response" to their depiction "as second-class citizens" or "complete outlaws" and protested that they "had done whatever Polish interests demanded, especially here in the borderlands." The police were also concerned that nationalist agitation had given rise to "some anti-Semitic feelings," which "could at any moment turn into hooliganism." At a rally of over two thousand supporters of the nationalist People's Party in Buczacz in March 1937, the party's leader demanded that Jewish "emigration to Palestine be facilitated."[51] The emerging consensus suggested that this minority should simply be removed from the country.

Talk of violence and removal was everywhere. If Jews were increasingly viewed as an unwanted burden and nuisance, Ukrainians were increasingly uniting around the urge to liberate themselves from Polish rule. As paramilitary organizations took on a transparently militant demeanor, countless meetings, rallies, and gymnastic-cum-military displays manifested Ukrainian strength and determination. In September 1937 seven hundred male and female Luh members from twenty-one branches converged on Buczacz. Marching into town in close formation, they began the day with a mass open-air religious service, then paraded through the town and performed gymnastic and military exercises, paying no heed to the massive police presence on the streets. Sympathetic observers "left the site with the firm conviction that the education of our village lads is on the right path." The prefect of Buczacz responded a few weeks later by banning three local Luh branches for "spreading hatred against people of Polish nationality and undermining the security and public order by assaults on the Polish population." But the rising tide of Ukrainian nationalist and militant sentiments could not be stemmed.[52]

A grim Polish assessment of Ukrainian nationalist organizations in the Tarnopol province on the eve of the war found that while 70 percent of the population still supported the UNDO, the real political influence and mobilizing capacity was in the hands of such associations as Prosvita, Luh, and Sokil, which together boasted hundreds of branches, subbranches, and reading clubs, as well as the "clandestine revolutionary-military organizations," of which the OUN was the most important. This elaborate network constituted a comprehensive effort "to completely engage Ruthenian society in every respect and to make it independent of the influences of Polish society and the Polish state," offering instead "a breeding ground for anti-state activities," the "propagation of separatist education," and "defense training for exclusively Ruthenian purposes."[53]

✡ ✡

Watching from the sidelines, some Germans tried to make sense of the tumultuous politics across their eastern border. In summer 1938 the German ambassador to Warsaw, Count Hans-Adolf von Moltke, reported to the newly appointed foreign minister in Berlin, Joachim von Ribbentrop, on the termination of the "normalization" agreement. The UNDO, he explained, had demanded territorial autonomy for the Ukrainian regions of Poland and recognition of Ukrainians as a separate nation under international law. The demands were modeled on those of the Sudeten German nationalists in Czechoslovakia, who claimed to be speaking "in the name of the seventy-million strong German bloc" in the Third Reich. But, noted the ambassador, since the Ukrainians did not have an equivalent foreign "protector," they could hardly expect their demands to be met, considering that even Polish opposition parties sided with their government on this issue. Hence Ukrainian leaders had acted "for tactical reasons," both "in view of public opinion among the Ukrainians themselves, and in the interest of keeping the Ukrainian question alive abroad." As German policymakers were keenly aware, Ukrainian nationalists were looking first and foremost to Hitler's Reich for political and military support.

With the German annexation of the Sudetenland in October, and the Hungarian takeover of southern Slovakia and Subcarpathian Rus the following month, a short-lived autonomous Carpatho-Ukraine came into being, whose very existence, as Moltke reported to Berlin, gave "the national consciousness of the Ukrainians a powerful boost." Interethnic tensions in Galicia were now running so high, he wrote, that the heavily attended religious services in Lwów, held to commemorate the twentieth anniversary of independent Ukraine, "were perceived by the Polish population as a provocation" and thus came under "planned and organized attacks by the Polish side against those attending church." In response "the Ukrainians established their own defense organization, which, however, did not limit itself to defending Ukrainian assemblies but also went on the attack against the Poles." Still, as a well-placed informant reported to Moltke, UNDO leaders "believe it would be impossible to resolve the Ukrainian question without foreign help" and had therefore decided to preserve their forces until "the emergence of a favorable foreign political constellation," namely, a German invasion. Meanwhile this Ukrainian "national awakening" was being met with what Hitler's ambassador to Stalin's Soviet Union called, without a hint of irony, "violent measures of all types geared to ruthlessly repress all yearnings for freedom."[54]

In late 1938 a German News Agency representative named Brandt reported to the German Foreign Ministry on a recent visit to Lwów. The Ukrainians' "ever more openly demonstrated irredentist sentiments," he wrote, had "unleashed measures by the Polish authorities that the Ukrainians described as 'Asiatic terror.'" These "terroristic" measures, in Brandt's words, included wanton destruction of property and mass arrests, often involving police brutality, along with bloody confrontations on city streets. In response Ukrainian villagers began torching police stations and Polish farms and hunting down all Polish speakers. This compelled the government to call in the army, which set out on a "punitive military expedition" to "pacify the countryside." Repressive measures included mass arbitrary arrests in the villages, in which women, children, and old people were at times chained to each other and paraded through their villages, as well as torture of prisoners by the police and abuse of women. The military also confiscated grain and livestock, and in several cases burned entire Ukrainian farms to the ground, all intended "to intimidate the Ukrainians, bludgeon the resistance movement and eradicate the irredentists." Instead, however, the repression drove the insurgents to carry out "innumerable acts of desperation," in which "Polish military personnel were also killed and wounded." Altogether, Brandt estimated, hundreds of activists and insurgents were killed between October and December 1938 and thirty thousand people were arrested, although no figures were reported publicly.

Brandt saw the OUN, "often also called the Ukrainian Fascist Secret Organization," as the main opposition to state repression. Insisting on "unconditional obedience" and the pledge of every activist to "give his blood and treasure to it," the OUN recruited members "from all existing Ukrainian organizations" and had "representatives all the way up to the leadership circles, not excluding the clergy." As "a secret military organization" it was dedicated to the "physical" struggle for independence, including "the establishment of terror groups and their effective deployment." Most important, it had taken up "the task of preparing a general insurgency movement" that "at the right moment" would "unleash the war of liberation." Spiritually, added Brandt, the OUN was motivated by "the ideologue Dr. [Dmytro] Dontsov," an avid student of all the dictators of that time, who identified racial purity as the distinguishing mark of master nations and envisioned an ethnically

OUN members and agents of
the Ukrainian Insurgent Army
in Buczacz district. *Source: PA.*

homogeneous future Ukraine. Aiming at the destruction of "the Muscovite-Jewish plague" and the "cleansing of Ukraine from the superfluous multiethnic elements," the OUN sought to unite all Ukrainian lands in a state stretching "from the Caucasus and the Caspian Sea" to the heart of Eastern Europe.

As Brandt saw it, the OUN's idea of freedom—clearly borrowed from the Nazi worldview—had to do with racial rather than political liberation. It was the task of the organization's youthful activists to disseminate this idea "from village to village, house to house," and "to always be prepared for the war of defense, to persevere despite the bloody punitive expeditions, and to hold fast to their hatred of the Poles." In this, Brandt believed, the OUN had clearly succeeded: "Today almost every Ukrainian, at least of the young generation, finds it shameful to speak Polish, to buy in Polish shops, to have intercourse with Poles and to be married to a Pole." In this accomplishment Ukrainian irredentists "have greatly benefitted" from "the numerous threads that run between the Reich and Polish Ukraine," threads that "strengthen the view of the Ukrainians that National Socialist Germany stands in support of the idea of freedom. Adolf Hitler," he concluded, "is seen by the Ukrainian peasants as the man who would bring them freedom."[55]

We may wonder what German officials in Berlin made of this Ukrainian attraction to the Olympians of National Socialism. Clearly in the grand scheme of things, the interethnic squabbles in Galicia and the hopes of Ukrainian nationalists for German help in establishing an independent state counted for little. The Reich was about to invade Poland and hand over its eastern territories, including their noisy ethnic minorities, to the Soviets; beyond that interim phase, Hitler had far greater plans to create a German "living space" in the East, and a Ukrainian state certainly had no place there.

War was about to break out just as the conflict between Poles and Ukrainians reached the boiling point. For Galicia and its people this meant that the armed confrontation would unleash fraternal violence on a scale and of a nature that even this region had never experienced before. That was of little concern to Hitler and Stalin, and might even prove amenable to their policies of deportation and genocide. But for the people on the ground this ethnic struggle took on a life of its own, related to but also independent of the larger war, shaping their conduct toward their neighbors, and determining their memories of those years long after the fighting died down and the map had been irreversibly changed.

Dr. Gebhard Seelos, posted as consul to the newly opened German consulate in Lwów merely five months before the outbreak of war, followed events in this ethnically convulsed region right up to its takeover by the Soviets. In late July 1939 he reported on "the bestial manner in which Polish police units operate without any reason against entire Ukrainian villages and do not abstain even from murder." In one case, a motorized and cavalry police formation numbering several hundred men surrounded a village, severely beat two dozen men and women, destroyed food stores, and paraded some sixty peasants through the village dressed in a manner meant to ridicule Ukrainian national pride. Many more similar cases were detailed by the consul, including one in which a Polish officer "forced people out of their homes with curses and destroyed national pictures," not least a portrait of the national poet Taras Shevchenko, exclaiming, "A Jew like that should hang in the outhouse."

Seelos's last report, sent in early August 1939, assessed the mood of the Ukrainian population and contemplated its potential response to the increasingly likely war between Germany and Poland. Fearing the future, the Poles had "resorted in the last few days to mass arrests," intended "to weaken the leadership echelons of the Ukrainians" and therefore "directed first and foremost at the clergy, doctors, attorneys, teachers and functionaries of economic institutions." This attempted destruction of the elites, later employed with devastating effect by the Soviets and the Nazis, would prove counterproductive since it removed those elements that might have exercised more control over the extremists. But Seelos had no doubt that "in case of an armed conflict between Germany and Poland, the Ukrainians" would "rise up as one man . . . take over the Polish estates and the isolated new Polish settlements in Eastern Galicia within a few days," and "drive out or slaughter the Poles." He predicted that "within one to two weeks following the outbreak of a general uprising in Galicia the entire land would be in Ukrainian hands, save for the overwhelmingly Polish towns and sites occupied with garrisons or border police barracks."[56] The writing was on the wall, but in Berlin no one was paying attention or cared much about the region. Even Seelos, who soon thereafter would desperately try to return to the Reich, could not anticipate the scale of the horror that was about to envelope Galicia.

Chapter 4
SOVIET POWER

ЗА НОВЕ ЖИТТЯ

Дитяча бібліотека імені Хнко Апера в Ереван (Вірменська РСР) має 30 тисяч книг на вірменській, російській і азербайджанській мовах. Бібліотеку відвідує коло семи тисяч юних читачів. За 1940 рік видано 126969 книг. Тут часто влаштовуються вечора—зустрічі з письменниками, артистами.

Юні орденоносець—поет Наірі Зар'ян (справа) читає свої твори молодим читачам.
Фото В. Єгорова.   Фото ТАРС.

Виборці Бучачського району в день виборів

The poet Nairi Zarian recites from his work to young readers in Buczacz, 1940.
Source: Derzhavnyi arkhiv Ternopilskoi oblasti (State Archive of Ternopil oblast): Za
Nove Zhyttia *(For a New Life), December 19, 1940, p.3. One thousand copies of this
Ukrainian-language newspaper were published daily and sold for fifty kopeks each by the
Buczacz District Committee of the Communist Party of Soviet Ukraine. The Armenian
Zarian (Hayastan Eghiazarian), born in 1900 near Van in the Ottoman Empire, was
the only member of his family to survive the genocide of 1915. He later moved to Russia;
long accused of denouncing fellow writers, he died in Yerevan in 1969.*

On September 1, 1939, Nazi Germany invaded Poland. Just over two weeks later, on September 17, in accordance with the secret clauses of the Molotov-Ribbentrop Pact between the Soviet Union and the Third Reich, the Red Army rolled into Eastern Poland. Izidor Hecht, nicknamed Junk and later known as Viktor Gekht, was eight years old at the time; he remembered that Red Army troops marching into Buczacz handed the children little red stars. Jadwiga-Wanda Turkowa recalled that the Soviets were "greeted with applause by a small group of Ukrainians and Jews." The teenager Witold Janda, like many other witnesses, was taken aback by the Soviet troops' response to the relative prosperity and modernity of Buczacz, as they stripped bare the shelves of the stores, covered their arms with wristwatches, and marveled at the miracle of running water and flush toilets.[1]

The Ukrainian gymnasium teacher Viktor Petrykevych, who was teaching at the time in Stanisławów, wrote in his diary that following the German invasion but before the Soviet intervention the Poles in the city were "in a very gloomy and resigned mood." Conversely the Ukrainians were exhibiting surprising "optimism," not least because "each and every one of us, whether educated or common men, has personally witnessed our [national] annihilation; and this experience stirs us to rejoice over the defeat" of the Polish state. But when the Red Army neared Stanisławów on the morning of September 19, the sight of "masses of people, mainly Jews, standing on both sides of the street and waiting for the Bolsheviks" clearly troubled Petrykevych. As the first tank drove into town, "the assembled Judeo-communists were overcome with triumphant emotions. The tank was covered with flowers and garlands," and when it stopped for a moment "some people leaped" on it and "began cheering the soldiers and kissing them," calling out, "Long live the USSR! Long live Stalin! Long live Soviet Ukraine!" This fervent welcome, wrote Petrykevych, "was performed mainly by the Jewish proletariat," although "now and then one could see a Ukrainian or a Pole." It was proof of "the power of the Jewish element in the cities," which included also "the Jewish bourgeoisie and plutocracy," who were soon "strolling down the streets, rejoicing that Hitler had not come to the city."[2]

Much of the Polish population in the region experienced this second invasion as a traumatic coup de grâce that put a definitive end to the Second Republic, and also as a sociopolitical upheaval that inverted the order of things. Foreign occupation was shocking enough, but in its immediate wake, those national minorities that had been under the thumb of the Polish authorities, the Ukrainians and even more so the Jews, now had the upper hand, as the Soviets used them to enforce their rule. It was indeed a world turned upside down. According to the construction engineer Stefan Szymula, in Buczacz "the leadership of the city administration was taken over by the Polish Jew Segal, who had spent several years in a Polish prison because of his communist views." The police too were initially "organized independently" of the Soviets and "recruited from local Ukrainians and Jews." Turkowa similarly remembered that "Segal—a Jew—was the town mayor, and his assistants and helpers of the NKVD [Soviet secret police] were Frost, a roofer, and Goldberg, a coachman, also Jews." She had no doubt that "local elements were informing" the Soviets "who should be arrested." Jan Biedroń, a district fire brigade instructor from Buczacz, claimed that as soon as the Soviets marched in, "the Jewish scum and criminals took over" and "immediately began to destroy everything Polish," even as they "incited the Soviets to carry out harassment and arrests." To his mind it was such "denunciations by the local population" that triggered the regime's "mass arrests of Poles" and the interrogations in which "false statements were extracted" from the victims, resulting in their families being "subjected to repressions of all kinds," including eviction from their home.[3]

The overwhelming sense of loss and resentment the Polish elites felt was articulated succinctly by Jadwiga Janicka, the wife of an army captain. "At the moment of the Red Army's invasion," she testified, "an indescribable depression dominated the Polish population. Conversely, there was lively enthusiasm among the Jews and the Ukrainians." As the district and city administration of Buczacz were taken over by "the local Jews—the greatest scum," arrests were also carried out by "local militiamen, recruited primarily from the Jews and Ukrainians." Janicka was appalled to discover that the new "head of the prison was a Jew, the coachman Goldberg." Stanisław Pawłowski, a former Polish state police detective superintendent, commented along precisely the same lines, emphasizing how disconcerting it was to find that "those in charge of all offices were communists who before the war had served time in prison." The brutal methods now employed in the prison were described by the grocer Wacław Mroczkowski, who noted that "interrogations were conducted with weapons and rubber truncheons in hand, mostly in the presence of three or four NKVD men and an officer. . . . They hit until they drew blood and broke bones; outside the prison they placed a generator, which was intended to drown out the screams of the prisoners." He too had no doubt that "the torture was done with the assistance of local communists and Jews." The Polish farmer Władysław Bożek said his house was regularly raided by local Ukrainians. Attempts at self-defense only brought police raids, arrests, and confiscations of weapons, so that "the Ukrainians could now act against the Poles with impunity," while police inspections, as the peasant Antoni Bodaj testified, were also "often followed by plundering and destruction," in which the Soviet authorities "were helped by Ukrainian militiamen."[4]

Reports from the rural areas surrounding the city of Buczacz contain many more accounts of Ukrainian violence just before and in the early phases of the Soviet occupation. Maria Bogusz, a twenty-four-year-old Polish settler from the village of Trościniec (Ukrainian: Trostyanets), related that as soon as the war broke out the Ukrainians "began to torment us and asserted that we are on their land." On August 28 they burned down the house of the teacher at the local Polish school, hoping that the fire "would kill all the Poles" since "on this street only Poles lived; but the wind changed direction and within two hours 160 houses burned down, homes of Poles and Ruthenians, and only ashes remained." Józef Flondro of the same village recalled that the Ukrainians also "murdered the estate owners . . . all civil servants, policemen, foresters . . . and even wealthy house owners. Power was taken over by the worst human element on earth, only bandits, thieves, and criminals." His neighbor, Canon Franciszek Bosowski, commented, "The NKVD officials called for a village meeting and asked the Ukrainians what they wanted, and they said that they wanted to take over the property of the colonizers and settlers."[5]

✡ ✡

Polish accounts of Ukrainian and Jewish collaboration often refused to acknowledge that these groups had good reasons to welcome the removal of Polish rule, even as they profoundly misunderstood the nature of Stalin's regime. Quickly forgetting their two-decades-long suppression of Ukrainian national aspirations and increasing anti-Jewish measures, Poles now felt they had been stabbed in the back by disloyal national minorities and associated their loss of independence and subsequent mass deportations by the Soviet authorities with Ukrainian nationalism and Jewish communism. The latter allegation, encapsulated in the Polish term *żydokomuna*, or Judeo-communism, was used during the war and in its immediate aftermath to explain popular Polish violence against Jews as a regrettable but understandable response to collective treason.

The early wave of fraternal killing evoked questions about the meaning and reality of interethnic relations, friendships, and communities, certainly among Poles and Ukrainians, who frequently intermarried, but also among Jews, who recalled many gentile friends and acquaintances. People repeatedly asked, Why did our neighbors, classmates, teachers, colleagues, friends, even family members turn their backs on us, betray us to the perpetrators, or join in the killing? The scale of the horror was such that survivors tended to paint an idyllic past of coexistence, even as they portrayed their victimizers as belonging to an essentially murderous or traitorous group, in a mirror image of how they were being perceived by their persecutors. The intimacy of friendships that served as a barrier to stereotypes was now transformed into an intimacy of violence that strove to eradicate personal qualms by inflicting gratuitous pain.

The Polish priest Ludwik Rutyna, born in Buczacz in 1917, conceded that while prewar Buczacz was "populated primarily by national minorities" nevertheless "the Polish side had the hegemony" and viewed itself as superior to Ukrainians, marginalizing them socially and professionally, and thereby creating "antagonism against the Poles." But he was also convinced that "certain circles of Jews and communists" had acted as "a fifth column," were "supported from abroad," and "prepared the local society for a future war." Furthermore, he insisted, not only was "commerce overwhelmingly in Jewish hands," but "their education in the synagogues and in certain circles was guided by the will to dominate their surroundings." This naturally led to the establishment of Polish "self-defense organizations" (*samoobrona*), intended "to finally get rid of Jewish hegemony" by way of boycotts of their businesses and professional services. Priests such as himself, observed Rutyna, had "understanding for the necessity of self-defense, but did not create feelings of animosity against Jews, or against Ukrainians," even if "it certainly did happen that a priest would warn his congregation to beware of being enslaved," all in the spirit of "self-defense aimed at enlightening people and raising their consciousness."

Rutyna was also convinced that Soviet rule in Buczacz was supported "mostly by Jews and Ukrainians," who "spontaneously organized

Father Ludwik Rutyna in the Roman Catholic church in Buczacz, 2007. *Photo by the author.*

and greeted the Soviets with flowers" when they arrived. Later, he recalled, they "used to say to us Poles: 'Your time is over, ours has arrived.'" Since the Soviets had no idea whom to arrest, "the local Jews took this task upon themselves, walked around and pointed at people"; "with communist armbands and rifles," he quipped, "they already were great warriors." He recollected the arrests with horror: "I saw how they threw their captives like cattle into the truck and sat on top of them with their rifles and took them away. These were teachers, people from the administration," whom "they unfortunately all later slowly murdered."

Rutyna's own opposition to physical violence was, in his words, practical, since "the enemy becomes a martyr through his suffering." It was an enemy he knew well, since he had visited the synagogue on numerous occasions and had Jewish friends; some even came to his home, where they "had a good time." One friend was his classmate Engelberg, whose father, a watermill owner, was a "progressive Jew, who already ate sausage and bacon with the peasants." Rutyna, who lived nearby, often went swimming with the younger Engelberg, but the lad was eventually "uncovered as a member of a communist association" and expelled from the gymnasium. Shortly after the Soviet takeover Rutyna encountered him again, this time as a Red Army officer; hearing that Rutyna was desperately trying to return to the theological seminary in Lwów, Engelberg swiftly arranged a travel permit for him.[6]

Władysław Hałkiewicz, born in 1914 and raised in Buczacz, worked in the local power plant from 1937 to 1944. Before the war he had good relations with members of the Jewish intelligentsia. But "the destitute Jews belonged to the communist party," and the local cell of the Communist Party of Western Ukraine constituted "a small group made up only of Jews." Conversely, "there was not a single Jew" in the government-controlled power plant. But when Hałkiewicz returned from the war in October 1939, everything had changed. Now the vice mayor was "Segal, a Jew and a communist," who had "been expelled from Israel," or rather Mandatory Palestine, "because of his communism." Segal asked Hałkiewicz to "restore order in the power plant," fearing that otherwise "those idiots [i.e., the Bolsheviks] will burn everything down." Now many of the workers in the plant were Jews: "They were pleased to see me arriving and together we restored order." Not only did Hałkiewicz find that "Jews are well-behaved people," but he also got along with the two Jewish plant directors; the first, he said, was "a very intelligent fellow" called Weinstock or Heller, while his replacement, also "a very decent fellow," was an engineer from Tarnopol named Cyzys. Noted Hałkiewicz, "During the Bolshevik period I was the only Pole working at the power plant in a managerial position; I was allowed to remain in this position because Jews helped me, since the official view was that I had 'erred.'"

At the same time, Hałkiewicz maintained, "the destitute Jews helped the Soviets," not least by denouncing Polish officers trying to flee across the border or pointing out family members who had stayed behind. Many Ukrainian peasants too denounced Poles, especially colonists, "because they wanted to rob them" of their property and to reclaim the land allocated to Poles by the previous Polish government.[7]

Jadwiga Kozarska-Dworska, who lived in Buczacz until 1941, had similarly ambivalent recollections. As a child she played with Jewish and Ukrainian classmates, and at the gymnasium, she insisted, "there was no differentiation between Ukrainians, Poles, and Jews." There were also Jewish teachers, such as Weingarten, "a wonderful man" who "taught physics and chemistry," and "Korngut, who taught Latin." The tolerant atmosphere at the gymnasium, she believed, was reflected in the school's practice of celebrating both Roman and Greek Catholic holidays; the Jews were simply "allowed not to come to school" during their holidays. In her view, "the problem of nationality did not exist for us"; it was primarily "the problem of social origins." From this perspective, Kozarska believed that Jewish children were "the best students" not only because they "had to read and write at preschool age" while attending cheder, but also because most of them "came from poor families" and had to excel in order to receive the state subsidy and to have better job prospects, considering that they had little likelihood of civil service positions reserved for ethnic Poles: "In Jewish families they used to say: 'You have to have something in your head.'" When her own father, who belonged to the landed gentry, "dropped out of the gymnasium in Tarnów," his father said, "'He can take the liberty of not completing it.'"

Kozarska conceded that in Buczacz the three ethnoreligious groups in fact "lived together and yet apart, especially with the Jews," and that her own "parents did not invite any Jews [to the house] and did not make friends with any Jewish families," even though in school "we spent every day with them." While she had "a very close Jewish girlfriend who used to invite me during the Holidays to taste their special cakes," her own family never reciprocated. Unlike the two Christian denominations, "the Jewish religion was completely different." It also provided an opportunity for childhood pranks. During the Jewish holiday of Sukkot (Tabernacles), for instance, the Jews would build booths, "cover the roof with branches, light candles, and pray in another language, swaying right and left." This was an opportunity for Kozarska and her friends to climb on the hill and "throw rocks" at such booths "from the top." But she insisted that "there was no aggression or condemnation in any of this."

As Kozarska saw it, in Poland's borderlands "we had to coexist whether we liked it or not, and therefore people reconciled themselves to that." But she admitted that toward the end of the 1930s "some animosity arose" between Poles and Ukrainians, especially over state support for the new Polish colonists' villages, while the "indigenous Ukrainian villages" were left mired in poverty. She also claimed that "the Jews certainly dominated the retail trade, small industry and the so called professional intelligentsia," such as physicians and attorneys. She specifically remembered one Pole whose new store in Buczacz quickly went out of business because "he was not capable of trading, he lacked that tradition"; such a person could easily "shift the responsibility" for his failure to a Jewish store owner who made good. But, she insisted, "this doesn't mean that he wanted to kill that Jew or that he hated him only because he was a Jew; no, he hated him because he was an obstacle to his career as a trader."

Thinking back about Soviet rule, Kozarska was willing to accept that Ukrainians "saw things quite differently" and "treated this as a unique opportunity to resolve their problem," not least because "Hitler had promised them to create a free Ukraine." And yet she could not desist from asking, "Did the Ukrainians already think at that time that they would stab us in the back?" Her most personal sense of betrayal was associated with her father's denunciation just hours after the Soviets marched into Buczacz. That very afternoon a group of armed soldiers, accompanied by a Jewish coachman—almost certainly the abovementioned Goldberg—broke into the family home and arrested her father. This same Goldberg, who used to drive her father home from the train station, had clearly denounced him. Perhaps, she tried to rationalize, the coachman had been "unaware of what he was doing" or had acted out of fear. She refused to collectively blame all Jews: "I don't know, I can't tell how many Jews agreed to collaborate." But she never quite forgave the Jewish coachman who had betrayed her father. Though he survived imprisonment, he never quite recovered.

Like almost all Poles, Kozarska asserted that while "the Polish intelligentsia suffered greatly" under the Soviet occupation, including from deportations, "not as many" Ukrainians were deported; she could not remember any Jews being deported and concluded that they had "benefited most" from the new regime, both because the Soviets "did not focus their policy of destruction" on them and because the Jews "thought they would achieve a better social status under the Soviets." Her younger brother maintained that the Jews "were the only informers." But Kozarska demurred: "We must not say what we have heard, we have to say what we saw with our own eyes, what we experienced."[8]

Witold Janda, who came with his mother and brother to spend the summer vacation of 1939 in Buczacz, recalled a warm relationship with the Ukrainian couple who initially hosted them in the suburb of Nagórzanka. Stranded in Buczacz when the war broke out, the family stayed in the city until May 1940. At the gymnasium he studied history with the same Edward Pelc who had served as a model of Polish borderland patriotism before the war. But now the teacher spoke "in a soft and broken voice"; he "discussed whatever the curriculum demanded of him, but at the end of his lesson he used to correct all historical distortions." One of the students must have denounced him, for "he was arrested by the vigilant NKVD just a few weeks into the school year and disappeared forever." His replacement, "a Jew from Kiev," was a "perfect ignoramus" who spoke "broken Polish" and "dressed in the same style as Papa Stalin, his most revered and highest superior." He also replaced the old headmaster, Jan Szajter, who was forced to serve as his deputy. His teaching was so appalling that even Janda's "Jewish friends agreed that something about it smelt bad."

Throughout this period Janda "never noticed any serious hostility between Poles and Ukrainians related to national origin." There were "numerous mixed marriages" between the Christian denominations, and all holidays "were jointly observed," while, thanks to the Jewish predominance in businesses, on "the Sabbath the majority of shops were closed." Precisely because of this "idyllic scene," Janda was horrified to find out a few years later from a former classmate "about his savagely murdered friends, male and female, who were also my friends." He also learned, "Our former congenial landlord from Nagórzanka was one of the 'commanders' of the UPA [Ukrainian Insurgent Army], and . . . many of my childhood playmates from that suburb of Buczacz had changed into bloodthirsty henchmen. And yet they had been so pleasant, congenial, amicable and hospitable during that beautiful summer of 1939." Janda could only understand this as the result of "a nationalist propaganda of hatred, which is nourished by the most base, beastly—surely not human—instincts!"[9]

✡ ✡

Soviet propaganda presented the invasion of Poland, agreed upon with Hitler and barely resisted by a Polish military already on the verge of collapse from the hammer blows of the Wehrmacht, as a "great task of liberation." A Soviet newsreel screened at the time declared, "The Red Army and Soviet Union bring freedom to all the working people of Western Ukraine and Western Belarus. . . . The Polish eagle—symbol of oppression and lawlessness—will never again fly over this land."[10]

The Ukrainian-language daily *Za Nove Zhyttia* (For a New Life), issued by the Buczacz District Committee of the Communist Party of

Soviet Ukraine, was a favorite venue for such propaganda on the local level. Even as the inhabitants of Buczacz were queuing for long hours in breadlines, and on the eve of the first mass deportation, the paper carried the triumphant headline on January 15, 1940, "A New Life Grows in the Liberated Land, Filled with the Joy and Happiness of the Workers." One reason for this joy: "The largest factory in our city is the technologically advanced mill with a turbine drum, in which 44 workers are employed." Although this "Stalin Mill," as the workers named it on "their own initiative," could allegedly "produce up to a wagon-full of flour every day," it clearly failed to satisfy the needs of the population. But its workers were apparently quite happy, having created for themselves an inn at their workplace, fondly referred to as the "Red Corner." They would reportedly "recover from work through cultural activities, listening to the radio, having newspapers read out to them, and sitting together." While many workers were illiterate, it was hoped that "the more familiar they become with the works of Marx, Engels, Lenin and Stalin, the more rapidly will their class consciousness grow." In the past they had labored under "inhuman working conditions," but "now, after the liberation of Western Ukraine from the repression of the lords, their work has become pleasant and full of joy."[11]

The plentiful flour produced by the "Stalin Mill" was efficiently made into bread thanks to "the nationalization of the four bakeries" in town, which provided ample amounts of loaves and rolls: "Thanks to improved mechanization, the work of the bakers has become greatly simplified," explained the paper; the bakers were also more motivated because "each of them works now no longer for a master and an exploiter, but for himself and for his Fatherland." Such cheerful productivity naturally also meant constant progress in the community's cultural life. As *Za Nove Zhyttia* reported, the Jewish theater club was preparing "a production of a comedy by Sholem Aleichem," a vast improvement over "the time of Polish rule," when "Jews were not allowed to play on stage" and, in fact, "had no rights at all." Now "Soviet power has finally allowed culture to blossom once again, artistic in form and socialist in content"; this facilitated the genuine self-expression of the "liberated people of Western Ukraine" by way of "a whole array of cultural associations" throughout "the small towns and villages of the district," where "self-organized art clubs and groups engage in political enlightenment." At the center of it all was the Stalin Club in Buczacz, located in the former Sokół building, whose eager members could join "theater, singing, music, and chess clubs."[12]

Education was another source of propagandistic pride in socialist progress. "Now," declared an article about the state gymnasium published in *Za Nove Zhyttia* in late January 1940, "all have the opportunity to attend school and to learn," whereas under the Poles most students "were children of the rich, or of those who worked for the authorities." In the past, the school was "the site of great animosity between the nationalities," but under the town's progressive Soviet rule, the total number of students had doubled to 650. Moreover "the level of the school" was "higher than before, since the students exert themselves to acquire good preparation in each discipline," knowing that this would enable

"Under the Banner of Marx, Engels, Lenin and Stalin, Forward to the Victory of Communism!," *Za Nove Zhyttya, May 1, 1940.*

141

them to attend university, which in the past "only the rich" could expect. But a crucial part of youth education was political mobilization, accomplished by the Komsomol, the communist youth organization. Four new recruits in early 1940 were publicly celebrated as "the avant-garde of the youth in the Buczacz district." The young men had joined this "famous" organization "in order to fight for the honor of Lenin and Stalin under Stalin's banner," thankful for having been liberated from "living without rights and being subjected to persecution in lordly Poland." Now their hearts were "filled with thanks to the Red Army and Soviet power and above all to comrade Stalin for their new, joyful, and happy life, for the rights of nationality and education—for their right to a just life."[13]

✡ ✡

The officials on the ground, however, had to distinguish between the fiction and the reality of Soviet rule, which was vastly different from its propagandistic depiction. In early January 1940, for instance, the Tarnopol Oblast (Province) Committee observed that "despite the organization of new cooperatives, the opening of new stores, cafeterias, and restaurants, and the significant growth in the circulation of goods by the consumer unions, the state of commerce" in the districts of Czortków and Buczacz remained "unsatisfactory." This too was an understatement. As the report elaborated: "The stores are dirty; the premises for commerce are ill-equipped; bread is sold by the loaf and not by weight, which violates the rules of Soviet trade; on some occasions consumer goods are held in storage but not available at the stores." This dismal situation was attributed in part to the fact that the responsible administrative apparatuses were "not adequately controlled and not up to their task" and that "the preparatory work for unifying the cooperatives" was "proceeding poorly."

The head of the provincial consumer union, Comrade Maslachenko, was therefore ordered to ensure the redistribution of such staples as bread, salt, and cheese by January 20; to determine store opening hours and ensure their cleanliness; to provide "the district consumer unions and the village committees with honest and vetted cadres"; and to arrange training courses for "the rank-and-file working contingent of the cooperatives." The problem extended to agriculture, since only two-thirds of the cereal grain had been threshed by the first day of 1940, leading to an eventual shortage of essential food for the population. This too was the result of local incompetence and negligence, and the district authorities were warned that it was "their personal responsibility" to improve matters rapidly. But it was probably too late to prevent severe damage to the food supply, which in turn caused long breadlines and a flourishing black market.[14]

As for transportation facilities, the Buczacz railroad station was found to be in an "unsanitary state," offering no "civilized conditions for passengers," and the railroad tracks were unlit at night. Similarly road repair and construction had been "conducted very sluggishly." Instructions were issued from Tarnopol to bring about "a significant improvement of the work at the Buczacz station" and to accelerate road building, as well as to undertake "an especially thorough study" of how "to achieve, on the basis of widespread socialist competition," a better work ethic and higher productivity.[15] But none of that happened.

As for the educational accomplishments of the new regime, in May 1941 the aptly named Polish-language organ of the Tarnopol oblast, *Bolshevik Truth*, boasted that Soviet power was doing "its utmost to create the best possible conditions for the youth's education, work, and rest" by way of a growing number of schools provided with "perfectly furnished libraries, laboratories and classrooms." Under the new Soviet system, all "formerly tyrannized and debilitated nations were given the opportunity to develop their national cultures according to socialist form and content," ensuring that "the young generation" would be "armed with the most revolutionary Marxist-Leninist theory." In return the grateful students were expected to "repay Stalin for his fatherly care with the highest number of excellent grades and a high degree of discipline." But this, conceded the paper, was not always the case, not least because headmasters—clearly fearful of official censure—had tried to meet these standards of excellence by administering intentionally easy exams. For this, assured the paper, they would be punished. Behind the façade of joyfully fulfilling "their honorary obligation" to "the great friend of the youth—comrade Stalin," there lurked deep layers of terror and resentment.[16] Before long some of these youngsters would be conscripted into the Red Army; many others were destined to join the German security apparatus, go underground, or be targeted for mass murder.

✡ ✡

As part of their attempt to legitimize and consolidate control over the newly annexed territories, the Soviets staged a series of elections; in practice, this only heightened interethnic tensions. The first elections, on October 22, 1939, which produced the National Assemblies of Western Ukraine and Western Belarus, left the strongest impression on the population. Participation was compulsory, and there was only one list of candidates, all appointed or approved by the authorities. On the face of it, the vast majority of eligible voters participated and almost all candidates were elected; in fact the entire undertaking was rigged. Rather than being an exercise in democracy, the election campaign provided the authorities with an opportunity to educate the population in the workings of the Soviet system through a combination of massive propaganda and blatant terror. In Western Ukraine 93 percent of those eligible cast a vote, and 91 percent chose the official candidates (1,484 out of a total of 1,495). Most of the new deputies were Ukrainian; only twenty Jews were elected. In the immediate wake of the elections the National Assemblies of Western Ukraine and Western Belarus requested, and were granted, formal incorporation into the Ukrainian and Belarusian Soviet republics of the USSR.[17]

Most Poles in the city and district of Buczacz experienced the elections as nothing more than an exercise in coercion, in which Soviet power flaunted its capacity to monitor and control everyone under its rule. The attorney Leopold Fenerstoin recalled, "Mass propaganda events began already in September; people were compelled to take part in these events, where the Soviet constitution was read out." In order to ensure participation, "the communist youth went from house to house," threatening "arrest and other measures" to anyone not attending. It was also "generally known that not voting would result in arrest." Fenerstoin, who "pretended to be sick," was "visited by the communist youth several times in order to check why [he] had not shown up at the polling station." He was finally arrested and deported in March 1940, followed by his family shortly thereafter. The fire brigade instructor Biedroń said people were enticed to the polling stations by "a free cold buffet and a banquet," courtesy of the authorities: "The voters were given cards with two names and were instructed to cross out whichever they liked less, and were then politely led to the buffet and the music." Those who were or pretended to be sick "were brought to the polling station under police escort." Biedroń was "escorted at 9 p.m. from a restaurant to the polling station": "On the way I was scolded for my disloyal attitude."[18]

The near-universal Polish aversion to the elections is reflected in numerous surviving accounts from Buczacz. The carpenter Józef Thieberger testified that "people were forced to join any kind of association," simply because each of them "had its own agitators, who praised the entire Soviet system." On Election Day "vast posters were plastered on the houses," and "a whole array of voters were carted" to the polling stations. Similarly Turkowa remembered that election officials either brought ballot boxes to the homes of the sick and the handicapped or "carted the people to the polling station." As the attorney Teodor Daniłow explained, refusal to vote "was considered a hostile action against the Soviet rulers." Nothing was left to chance. According to Mroczkowski, not only were "the critically ill and the very old carted to polling stations," but they were also handed "envelopes with instructions to throw them into the ballot box." Anyone who refused was interrogated by the NKVD, "and the same night that person was already in jail and his entire property confiscated, while the rest of the family were left to fend for themselves and later deported to Russia."[19]

Most people had little doubt that the whole undertaking was a farcical sham. The engineer Szymula concluded that the insistence on universal voting "had nothing to do with the number of the voting slips inserted into the polling box, which no one bothered to count, but with the number of voters that one could strike off the eligible voters' list." The merchant Leon Szydłowski from the village of Pyszkowcy (Ukrainian: Pyshkivtsi) on the outskirts of Buczacz recalled, "The election card was thrown into the polling box inside an envelope; I don't know what was written on the card." But the teacher Maria Wołkowa of Koropiec (Ukrainian: Koropets) said that "the election committee, which was made up of the local population, reported that almost all voting slips were crossed out" or scribbled over with "the worst invectives."[20]

Some Poles believed the elections were a Jewish and Ukrainian conspiracy. Szymula found it especially "tasteless and bitter" that "Ukrainian and Jewish agitators went from house to house," urging people to vote, and that "the elections committee was made up only of Jews and Ukrainians, without a single Pole." In Podzameczek (Ukrainian: Pidzamochok), as reported by Szymin Siwy, "the Ukrainian Ivan Bereshovskiy" chaired the elections committee, and other committee members "were confidants of the Soviets, especially Jews, Ukrainians and political functionaries of the NKVD." Similarly the shoemaker Stefan Medyński reported that in Barysz (Ukrainian: Barysh) the election committee was made up only of Jews and Ukrainians, the latter being mostly people "who had just come out of prison, only bandits and thieves, or those who were opposed to the Polish regime." And the peasant Flondro stated, "The polling lists were put together by communists and the NKVD, especially Ukrainians up to age 30 and Jews, who worked to the detriment of the Poles." Some observers recognized the pattern of Soviet policies. The law student Zbigniew Waruszyński of Monasterzyska remarked, "The Bolsheviks followed the principle of 'divide and rule' by using all the national-Ukrainian and communist-Jewish elements in order to strengthen the terror even more."[21]

If the elections were both humiliating and absurd, the terror of unpredictable arrests and mass deportations was experienced as a personal and material catastrophe and a collective national trauma. And although early assertions that up to a million people were deported and almost half a million arrested were widely exaggerated, the current estimate of 315,000 Polish citizens deported to Kazakhstan, Siberia, and the far north of the USSR, and of 110,000 arrested, all within the space of twenty-one months, is still quite staggering.[22]

Deportations occurred in four main waves: about 140,000 were deported in February 1940; 61,000 in April 1940; 75,000 in June and July 1940, and 36,000 in May and June 1941. Here too Poles were an absolute majority of close to 60 percent; Jews, who made up about 10 percent of the population, were proportionately overrepresented at 22 percent of deportations, followed by over 10 percent of Ukrainians and under 8 percent of Belarusians.

The focus of deportations shifted from Poles in the early waves to Jews in June 1940 and Ukrainians in April and May 1941. Fatalities among deportees, while considerably lower than traditional Polish estimates, were nevertheless appalling, perhaps as many as fifteen thousand by mid-1941. In hindsight only Jews could view themselves as "lucky" for having been deported, considering the well over 90 percent death rate of Jews who remained under the German occupation.[23]

On February 10, 1940, the Soviets deported thirty-two thousand people from the Tarnopol province to Siberia, including three thousand inhabitants of the Buczacz district. When Witold Janda went to school that day, over a dozen students were missing from his classroom; "overcome with despair," and despite the intense cold, he and his classmates headed off to the train station. "A tight cordon of NKVD men and police did not allow anyone access to the platform, where a long freight train was standing. The cries of numerous small children and the shrill wailing of women echoed from the carriages. When a few female friends attempted to force their way through the cordon," they were warded off with "brutal blows." The children from the school dormitory were not allowed to join their parents on the train: "They were forced to stay behind, alone on the streets of Buczacz, deprived of any means of survival."

The remaining Polish students and families organized charities to support the abandoned children and to send parcels of food to the deported. Janda's despised classmate Klajnfisz, a "chubby-cheeked Jew" and "the richest person in our class," brought "a lot of supplies pilfered from his mother's well stocked pantry." Janda was surprised that some Ukrainian students also "participated in these collections." But then came the devastating second deportation, in April, which "primarily affected the residents of Buczacz," including "the families of a few of our professors." A void opened up in the community. "Only half of the original number of students in my class remained," testified Janda, among whom "Jews and Ukrainians predominated."

Two months later Janda's family moved to Lwów, hoping to reunite with his father in German-occupied Poland. But they were swept up in the third deportation, of June 1940, and sent to Arkhangelsk. Janda eventually fought in the Soviet-organized Polish Berling Army, ending the war as an artillery officer in the Battle of Berlin.[24]

Thirteen-year-old Barbara Piotrowska-Dubik, whose father had been taken prisoner by the Germans, vividly remembered her family's deportation from Barysz during an ice storm on April 13, 1940: "Early in the morning an NKVD officer came to our house, along with two soldiers with rifles as well as a Ukrainian from Barysz and a Jew we knew with a red armband on his arm, who was quite jolly and amused. The NKVD officer sat at the table and said: 'Helena Piotrowska Kazimirowna and the three children, wake up and get dressed!'" Barbara "could not grasp why we should be so terribly punished." Six families were brought to an assembly point in the village. "Some wept, others lamented, still others sat quite still, or cursed. The Jew had fulfilled his mission. He extended his hand to my mother, but she did not respond, and he said to us: Goodbye." At 8:00 a.m. they were taken on wagons under guard to Buczacz. "At the railroad station there was a big crowd and much hue and cry. Our train had 62 freight cars." They were "shoved and pushed" inside. "No consideration, not even toward the women, the aged and the children. The railroad car [was] dark and crowded." Among the deportees was a young Ukrainian woman with her children, several Polish families, and a Jewish couple with their child. "Altogether we were 38 people in the car. . . . The doors are bolted with heavy locks.

We stand at the station for a long time; what was all the rush for? It is frightfully cold; we have nothing warm to drink. The train departs from Buczacz the following day, Sunday morning, after waiting for an entire day." The journey lasted two weeks; on April 28 they arrived at their destination, a *kolkhoz* (collective farm) in Kazakhstan, 2,500 miles from their home.[25]

Even those spared deportation faced the harsh realities of Soviet rule, often after their families had been shipped to the East. Jan Bojnowski's parents had come as colonists to the village of Czarnokońce Wielkie (Ukrainian: Velyki Chronokinski), forty miles east of Buczacz, in 1938. As a teenager working at a restaurant in nearby Borszczów (Ukrainian: Borshchiv), Bojnowski recalled that all the Polish officials there were swiftly arrested and deported. In the surrounding countryside many Polish farmers, including some of the seventeen settler families in his village, were "killed with knives and scythes" by their Ukrainian neighbors. Bojnowski's parents and younger sister were deported in February 1940 and died in exile; he watched the endless "column of sledges loaded with elderly people, adults and children, even babies, wrapped in blankets and down quilts, holding bundles . . . all covered with frost and huddled in horror." In Borszczów there was a rash of denunciations. "It was enough to be angry with somebody or to say something stupid in the wrong place—and the bloke was dead."[26]

✿ ✿

Ukrainian perceptions of these events differed dramatically. Petro Pasichnyk, born in 1923, attended the gymnasium in Buczacz under Soviet rule; he had no doubt that during that time things were much worse than under the Germans. The Soviets, he said, "behaved like Asiatics." As far as he could recall, they victimized exclusively Ukrainians: "I remember only that our people were arrested, our intelligentsia—lawyers, doctors." He vividly recalled, "They would take students straight out of the classroom!" The principal, a Ukrainian historian "linked to the NKVD," would come into the classroom, "whisper a few words to the teacher, and then say: 'Such and such, collect your books and prepare to leave.' The student would go and never come back. Nobody would ask about him, everyone was too afraid." Four of those students were subsequently shot. Later, when they were withdrawing, the Soviets executed the inmates in the Czortków prison: "It was not enough to just shoot them. . . . But to commit such atrocities—to tear out people's tongues, gouge out their eyes . . . it was horrible. They were such sadists." He assumed the Soviets "didn't touch" the Poles; as for the Jews, of whom "there were plenty" before the war, they simply "collaborated" with the Soviets.[27]

Like many other Ukrainians, Viktor Petrykevych's son Bohdan, who was a young teenager at the time, shared Pasichnyk's view that under Soviet rule "the Ukrainians suffered the worst." Although he was willing to concede that the Soviets "also arrested Poles," including "officers, anybody who was in the police," and "colonists from inner Poland," he saw this as just punishment because "they had been colonizing Ukrainian lands." In any case, he believed, none of these actions could be compared to Soviet crimes against Ukrainians; his own uncle, for instance, was arrested: "He was a very good doctor, a surgeon." The man's wife pleaded with the authorities to let him go; after he was deported to Siberia she committed suicide, and their baby daughter died of neglect. "People said that the Jews had denounced him, or the Poles," concluded Bohdan by way of indicating who was guilty of this tragedy.[28]

Many Jews had an ambivalent response to Soviet rule, both because of their prewar experience in Poland and because of what they knew about Nazi Germany; their experiences also depended a great deal on their social class, politics, and age. For the middle-aged Zionist activist Emanuel Worman (Bazan), the new regime meant liquidation of his bookstore and interrogation "by a Jewish NKVD lieutenant," to whom he pledged to disavow his former convictions. For the rest of the Soviet occupation he lived "in terror that they would knock on my door at night and take me back to the NKVD and no longer release me." He later found out that his name had been on "a list of all the Zionist leaders of Buczacz who were to be deported in early July 1941 to the far north of Russia." Ironically, he was spared that fate by the German invasion.[29]

Mina Rosner, the recently married daughter of a well-to-do businessman, saw her elderly father lose his business and be reduced to manual labor; she moved with her husband and baby to another town for fear of being identified as class enemies of the state. The teenager Etunia Bauer, also from a wealthy family, recalled that their estate was nationalized, most synagogues were closed down, and the study of Hebrew was prohibited. They now all had to work "for a minimal salary, barely enough to buy a loaf of bread once a week." Members of her family who had escaped to Buczacz from the German occupation zone "were pulled from their beds, loaded into trucks, and sent to Yakutsk in Siberia," where some perished. One could be arrested "for any number of crimes real or fabricated," but unlike under the Germans, "at least they could walk on the streets legally and not in fear of death."[30]

For fifteen-year-old Aliza Reinisch (Nir) the occupation began with looting by Ukrainian neighbors: "They forced their way into every store, they took all the merchandise from the Jews; the Russians said that these were rich people who had exploited the workers so now the Ukrainians could do what they liked." She remembered "one Ukrainian, who was a good friend of Father's," saying to him, "Now the good times are over for you, now we can no longer be friends, now it's our time." Her uncle was denounced and deported to Siberia, where he died. Hilda Miller (Weitz) was haunted by the thought that had her father not succeeded in saving her uncle and his family from deportation they might have survived the war. Izidor Hecht, whose next-door neighbors were also deported, expressed the same sentiment: "Many of those people who were sent away somehow survived," whereas "had they stayed in Buczacz, all of them would have certainly been murdered. I still have mixed feelings about all these facts."[31]

For working-class lads who had little to lose, as well as for communists, things were different. Mordechai Halpern claimed the Red Army "was welcomed with joy and kisses by the local communists, most of whom were Jews, sons and daughters of families from the religious middle class," like his own. This reception "enraged quite a few Poles who had lost their independence, as well as the Ukrainians who had been waiting for the Germans." But Jewish enthusiasm "did not last long," and even some of the local "communists discovered that this was a false prophet." Still, "most of them" were initially given "positions in the new administration as senior officials or policemen." Although Halpern's father became an agricultural laborer, as a teenager he himself benefited from the new order and gained admission to the gymnasium. Similarly, ten-year-old Pesach Anderman, who remembered that before the war children in school would chant "Jews, go to Palestine," commented that when the Red Army invaded "we were happy, because we had been told that in Russia there was no hatred of Jews." But that very day he witnessed a brutal gang rape by Red Army troops, and although "the anti-Semitic taunts ceased" in school, he was aware that "the old communist faithful in town managed to seize positions of power."[32]

Gershon (George) Gross, a young man from a working-class family, also recalled that before the war "the gentile kids didn't like us" and "the teachers called us names." Conversely, while under the Soviets "the rich people feared that they'd be taken to Siberia," the authorities "did nothing to us." Indeed, he maintained, "it was better than under Polish rule" since "the Jews had jobs from the Russians: police, militia." Simcha Tischler, another young manual worker, agreed that the Soviets "were greeted with joy," and "most Jewish communists, or even just leftists, as well as those without party affiliations, began working for the Russians. We accepted their rule, it wasn't anything special." Unlike Polish times, when "there were rich and poor people," under Soviet rule "we were all the same." Still, his father lost his carpentry shop, and the Zionist youth movement to which he had belonged was "eliminated."[33]

As the roofer Jakub Szechner put it, the Soviets "kept a tight rein on everyone," but "there was no peace." He saw it as a time of unremitting fear and suspicion: "Poles denounced Poles, Ukrainians denounced Ukrainians, and Jews [also] denounced." Victimization was about class, he believed, not ethnicity: "those who suffered most" at the time "were all members of the intelligentsia: Jews, Ukrainians, and Poles—everybody." But not everyone shared this view. The young workers Dawid (Ducio) Friedlender, Natan Dunajer, and other young communist activists "hastened to volunteer to help the Soviet authorities in their persecution of Ukrainian nationalists." Dawid's younger brother Yehoshua (Ozio) stated, "After the German invasion Ducio regretted that initiative, since at that time the Ukrainian police excused its murderous treatment of the Jews as revenge for the role those Jewish communists had voluntarily played in the deportation of nationalists to Siberia."[34]

While most Poles and Ukrainians perceived the Jews as beneficiaries of Soviet rule, many Jews recalled it as a period of oppression, denial of rights, loss of property, and profound uncertainty about the future. To be sure, for some Jews and Ukrainians it also initially appeared to be a time of opportunity and empowerment, however fleeting, especially when compared to their treatment by their former oppressors. This view of victimhood and victimization is in many ways typical of all three major groups: all saw themselves as the main victims of various configurations of the Soviet and German occupations, and each perceived the persecution of the other two groups as at least partly justified. Many Poles and Ukrainians had no trouble coming up with reasons for punishing Jews; Poles also overwhelmingly supported actions against Ukrainian "bandits"; Ukrainians enthusiastically approved the deportation of Polish colonists. For their part, few Jews in such towns as Buczacz mourned the demise of Poland; subsequently they fervently wished for vengeance against Ukrainian collaborators with the Nazis. Each group's conviction in the uniqueness of its own victimhood thus went hand in hand with a desire to punish those associated with its suffering; this was, in essence, the same kind of reasoning employed so successfully by the Nazis, who consistently presented themselves as victims of those they murdered.[35]

An anonymous report sent in late 1940 from Western Ukraine to the Polish government in exile epitomized the extent to which certain views remained unchanged despite the dissolution of the state. In their quest "to destroy the Polish nation," asserted the report, the Soviets were using "the dregs of society"; specifically "excelling in the oppression of the Poles were the Ukrainians and Bolshevized Jews," in a process whereby initial "lawlessness was replaced by organized terror." The

Soviets had initially targeted Polish elites, along with "those whom the Jews suspected of anti-Semitism." In the face of what the report described as Ukrainian, and even more so Jewish complicity and duplicity, the Polish victims were said to "bear these atrocities heroically . . . singing the national anthem and sacred hymns as they leave their homeland," accompanied by thousands of priests who "bring solace to those wretched people." The merely "several hundred Ukrainian nationalists" deported by the Soviets were apparently targeted on the reasonable grounds that "they posed a threat to Soviet actions." Only "a few dozen rich Jews, mostly Zionists, and therefore also Jewish nationalists," were deported, once again for what appeared to be a sound cause. This could hardly compare to the alleged 400,000 Polish deportees—and according to "some sources much higher numbers"—of whom "about 20 percent died." The competition for victimhood that began with the outbreak of the war and continues to this day was certainly making its mark on these distorted figures and accounts. Significantly, the report made a clear distinction between the deportation of Ukrainians and Jews, which was said to have been "of a clearly political and preventive nature," and that of Poles, which "was aimed at the destruction of the nation's substance." In other words, the Poles were targets of genocide, whereas Soviet actions against Jews and Ukrainians were at worst political persecution and at best security-oriented measures.[36]

Indeed the report found it difficult to concede that Ukrainians and Jews were victims of Soviet repression at all. "The Ukrainian issue," it insisted, "is strictly connected with the German action against Poland. Ukrainian terrorists, armed and trained by the German military and paid German money, played the role of a fifth column during the Polish-German War in September 1939." Moreover, since Ukrainians kept hoping "that Hitler would create for them a Ukrainian state," they had already begun "infiltrating all organs of the Soviet administration, pretending to be ardent Bolsheviks"; they were even helping the Soviet State Political Police (GPU) "draw up lists of people to be relocated," in which "they listed only Poles," clearly "with the aim of destroying the Polish element" and thereby clearing the way for a Ukrainian nation-state.

At the same time, the report granted that Ukrainians were also being "victimized by Moscow" because "Ukrainian armed groups," especially members of the OUN, "attacked Bolshevik leaders, soldiers, even Soviet patrols, often killing some of them." All this led to the bizarre conclusion, clearly the product of wishful thinking rather than hard data, that among "the non-political part of Ukrainians, the conviction has come to predominate . . . that the Ukrainian issue should be solved in a way that would locate the territories of mixed Polish-Ukrainian population within the Polish State." As a result of such "coexistence of Poles and Ukrainians," Ukrainians "would be gradually assimilated through cultural influence and well-functioning public services into the Polish State." Signs of ethnic solidarity had allegedly been observed in the Buczacz district, where "Ukrainians even put up guards to prevent the deportation of Poles," indicating, to the report writer's satisfaction, that "even though they did not always express this openly, the lower classes of Ukrainians now definitely missed the previous Polish regime."[37]

This renewed articulation of the old pipe dream of Polish nationalists, who viewed their Ukrainian counterparts as traitors and terrorists but the Ukrainian "masses" as potential Poles, merely demonstrated how removed from reality some observers on the ground and certainly politicians in exile had become. As for the Jews, the old prejudices were now given a major boost by allegations of collaboration with the Soviets. As the report underlined, "The Jewish population in general exhibits a hostile attitude toward the Poles, many of them take an active part in the persecution of Poles, and huge numbers of Jews enter the ranks of the Soviet administration." This was nothing new. "All Poles remember the collaboration of the Jews with the Bolsheviks against the Poles during the Polish-German war in September 1939," stressed the report's author, blithely ignoring the service of 100,000 Jews in the Polish Army; hence "their present attitude toward the Poles arouses a great deal of hatred among the Polish population." Fortunately the Ukrainians too were "dissatisfied with the actions of the Jews," not least because of "their activities on various levels of the Soviet administration." Astonishingly this circumstance only evoked "nostalgic memories of the good old Polish times," since the Ukrainians now said to themselves, "I thought this was Ukraine, but it turns out to be Palestine." Consequently, despite the conflicts between Poles and Ukrainians, "sometimes the Poles become reconciled with the Ukrainians over their mutual agreement in evaluating the behavior of the Jews." Here, then, was an agenda for Polish-Ukrainian reconciliation.[38]

These Polish nationalist attitudes toward Jews had a history that dated to the nineteenth century and persisted beyond the Holocaust; the very notion that under the Soviet occupation Jews were given more or less equal opportunities, albeit within the framework of an oppressive and brutal system, obviously played into the Polish understanding of the reality on the ground, a perception so powerful that even after the vast majority of Jews were murdered it allowed for further Polish outbursts of anti-Jewish violence in the early postwar years.

✿ ✿

Officially, of course, Germany and the Soviet Union were still allies. But within a year of the Molotov-Ribbentrop Pact on the partition of Poland, as it became clear that an invasion of Britain would not be feasible, Hitler turned his gaze to the East. For that purpose, Ukrainian nationalists—trained, funded, and armed in the Reich—proved a useful tool in the takeover of Eastern Galicia and the early phases of mass murder. Meanwhile, as they peered across the border into the newly occupied Soviet territories, the Germans could identify a fair degree of overlap between the policies and practices of the two regimes. Here Soviet Jewish policies were of particular interest. That Jews had entered the ranks of the police and administration under Soviet rule surely fit perfectly into the Nazi worldview of Judeo-Bolshevism. But that Jews would also be deported en masse by the allegedly Jewish-dominated Kremlin and NKVD was both odd and a source of glee, without having any effect on their overall perception of Soviet Russia.

In May 1940 the chief of the Gestapo, Heinrich Müller, wrote the German embassy in Moscow regarding requests by "Jews in former East Poland" for passports and other travel documents. "In principle," commented Müller, "I have no interest in the emigration of Jews who had been resettled to Poland and subsequently moved to the Soviet sphere of influence, since their further emigration will diminish even more the already very limited emigration possibilities for Jews from the territory of the Reich." But he nevertheless wanted to know "whether perhaps for internal political reasons the embassy considers the removal of these Jews from the Russian area necessary. In this case," he promised, "if available, passports could be sent to the embassy expeditiously." One can only imagine the anxiety of those applying for the documents, caught as they were between Nazi persecution and looming deportation by the Soviets. One of the applicants was Rosa Pohoryles of Buczacz, who indicated her desire to "travel to Warsaw, and from there via Italy to the United States to her husband in New York." The ambassador to the Soviet Union, Friedrich-Werner Graf von der Schulenburg, responded only in late June, visibly annoyed by this as yet unresolved situation: "The embassy would welcome it if a principled decision were reached regarding the treatment of the Jews living in and traveling to Eastern Poland, who are applying in large numbers to the embassy for passports." From his perspective, it did not matter whether they would all be completely "stripped of their citizenship" (*ausbürgert*) or would "be issued more or less short-term German travel passports." However, noted Schulenburg, "the embassy does not consider the removal of these Jews from the Soviet region to be necessary for internal political reasons, since as a result of the unique political situation, and the circumstances here, the Jews in the Soviet Union are more isolated from the rest of the world than in any other country."[39] They were, so to speak, ripe for the picking: no one would know, and no one would care.

Chapter 5

Skat and schnapps, 1942 (l. to r.): Buczacz Landkommissar Richard Lissberg, rail-road administrator Ewald Herzig, post office director, and labor office director. *Source: Generallandesarchiv Karlsruhe (hereafter GLA-K) 309, Zug. 2001-42/877-158.*

Strolling through Buczacz on July 4, 1941, roughly two weeks after the German invasion of the Soviet Union had begun, on June 22, Viktor Petrykevych observed everywhere signs of devastation and anarchy: "The stores have been smashed and plundered," while "the poor and the peasants are milling around in small groups, hoping to find something to loot." In one case, "a soldier shot a fellow who was carrying two military overcoats." The atmosphere of lawlessness,

Petrykevych heard, had prompted the Jews to send "a delegation to the Basilian monastery superior, asking him to influence the population and restrain it from attacking the Jews." There was reason for anxiety, since "leaflets inciting against the Poles and the Jews" were reported. That same day, around noon, the Red Army blew up the railroad bridge and tunnel leading to the city, a Galician engineering marvel and the only one of its kind in the province. The following day, July 5, Petrykevych wrote, "At about 9:45 p.m., Soviet time, horrible . . ." The rest of this entry is missing; we can only speculate what he had seen. In the mid-1950s, when the KGB dropped in for an unannounced visit after his father's death, Bohdan Petrykevych tore out a section of the diary. He subsequently explained that these pages depicted the welcome given to the Germans by the Ukrainian population. The last word, *horrible*, may have referred to anti-Jewish violence by fellow Ukrainians.[1]

That same day, at 12:30 p.m., the Wehrmacht's 101st Light Infantry Division reported that it had captured Buczacz, although heavy

The demolished railroad bridge in Buczacz. *Source: GLA-K 309 Zug. 2001-42/878-106.*

fighting was still going on in the vicinity of the city. On the following day the 228th Infantry Regiment established its forward command post in the city. Severely damaged by German bombing raids and Soviet demolition, Buczacz was initially occupied by a succession of German and allied Slovak military formations, while much of the area north of the Dniester was temporarily taken over by Hungarian troops. As these formations rolled farther east, reports started coming in of "murders of inhabitants (Ukrainians) in the prisons of Buczacz and Czortków." At the same time Germany's 52nd Army Corps reported that in Buczacz "a Ukrainian militia took over security duties until the arrival of German troops in order to prevent plundering." This militia, called "Sich" as a gesture to the Legion of Ukrainian Sich Riflemen of World War I, was in fact a major source of violence during the hiatus between Soviet and German rule.[2]

The self-proclaimed Buczacz Sich was rapidly recruited from OUN militants in the district. On June 26 the OUN district commander, Volodymyr Lutsiv, called a meeting at the village hall in Nagórzanka and organized a thirty-man platoon. This was followed several days later by a second platoon, formed in the village of Przewłoka (Ukrainian: Perevoloka) and armed with weapons looted from a Soviet Army camp they had raided. As one of the men recalled, on the night of July 4–5 they "liquidated 18 secret operatives, who included many Jews"; they also seized the prison in Buczacz, only to find that all the inmates had been murdered. The next morning these paramilitaries attacked the retreating Soviets. Although they met with fierce resistance, they captured several Soviet soldiers and arrested a number of Ukrainian Soviet activists. A few Ukrainian fighters were killed and wounded in the fighting, but by late morning "the city was in our hands and our guards were posted everywhere. On the houses the blue-yellow flag was hoisted." When Lutsiv "proclaimed the Independent Ukrainian State" in Buczacz, "many people came to the gathering, even Poles. In the afternoon German units entered the city." Soon thereafter a unified Sich for the Buczacz district was formed under the command of the former Prosvita activist Tadei Kramarchuk and Andriy Dankovych.

Snapshots of a parade of the "Ukrainian Army" and its local supporters in Buczacz on July 20, 1941. *Source: PA.*

Numbering over one hundred men, this unit engaged in hunting down the remaining Soviet troops and sympathizers. Eventually many of these men were transformed into policemen under German control, but Lutsiv, the local OUN chief, went underground to prepare the local struggle for independence.[3]

On July 20 the new administration in Buczacz demonstrated its strength and organization by staging a parade of the "Ukrainian Army" and its local supporters. Led by a well-equipped infantry unit from

Koropiec, the procession also featured a mounted squadron in traditional garb, as well as several scores of young women dressed in Ukrainian blouses and skirts and carrying blue-and-yellow banners and tridents decorated with garlands and local embroidery. As these men and women marched past an elevated platform in the market square where German officials framed by swastika flags greeted them with the Nazi salute, the identity of the real holders of power could not be mistaken.[4]

During those early weeks the Ukrainian militia carried out widespread acts of violence and vengeance against real and perceived local enemies. In one instance, militiamen arrested and summarily shot the Soviet activist Anton Nezhynskyi, the teacher Fedir Shukhevych, and a former member of the communist executive committee in Buczacz, Mikhailo Hrynkiv. The chairman of the village club in Nagórzanka was repeatedly beaten during his incarceration in Buczacz without ever being interrogated or charged, and a former Communist Party member of the same village, sent home after being severely tortured, was assassinated a few weeks later by unknown assailants. Altogether the Buczacz Sich abused about one hundred people before the German security apparatus was firmly established.

Apart from hunting down former Soviet officials, the Sich also enforced local patriotism and harassed Jews and Poles. Villagers recalled being pressured "to attend an assembly of Ukrainian nationalists and to sign a declaration calling for the release of [Stepan] Bandera," the nationalist leader arrested by the Germans on July 5 after declaring Ukrainian independence. Along with extensive raids on Polish homes in search of weapons and ammunition, the Sich engaged in forcible recruitment of Jewish labor. In one case local OUN leaders forced Jews from Buczacz to build a "memorial mound for the heroes of the Ukrainian revolution" in the adjacent village of Nagórzanka; Jews were also likely forced to erect the memorial mound on Fedor Hill, where later much of the Jewish community was shot and buried. Such arbitrary arrests and abuse demonstrated to the population that one could do as one pleased with Jews.

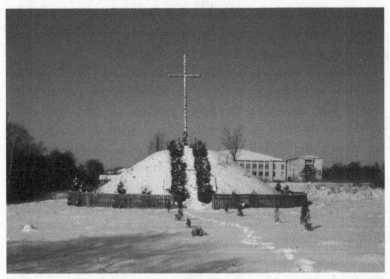

OUN memorial mound on Fedor Hill, Buczacz, 2006. *Photo courtesy of Sofia Grachova.*

Toward the end of July, the Germans asserted control over security in the region. Kramarchuk, the leader of the district militia, was replaced by the more compliant Volodymyr Kaznovskyi, a thirty-seven-year-old district attorney. The son of a Greek Catholic priest, Kaznovskyi, a fluent German speaker, had excellent relations with the occupiers and remained in the newly defined position of Ukrainian district police chief until the end of German rule.[5] He too had plenty of local scores to settle. One Ukrainian recalled being called to Kaznovskyi's office, where he "began shouting at me for having joined the Komsomol" and "punched me twice in the face." Another man related, "Kaznovskyi screamed at me that I was a communist and that he would stamp my forehead with a Soviet star. Since I had already been beaten, I could not stand calmly and erect in front of Kaznovskyi. Kaznovskyi grabbed me by the hair and slammed my head against the wall, so that I lost consciousness and was then brought back into the prison cell."[6]

In early August 1941 the Germans released about two-thirds of the prisoners incarcerated by the militia in the Buczacz prison; the remaining thirty-three were executed. The killing set the pattern for what soon became mass shootings of Jews on a far larger scale.

During the early weeks of the German invasion, "Jewish policies" in Galicia were handled mostly by the *Einsatzgruppen*, the task forces charged with eliminating the Reich's political and racial foes. Made up of three thousand men recruited from a variety of German police agencies and the SS, and supported by numerous other regular police battalions, Waffen-SS units, Wehrmacht formations, and local militias and auxiliaries, the four *Einsatzgruppen* sent into the Soviet Union directly behind the Wehrmacht murdered about 1.5 million people, the vast majority of them Jews, in less than a year, mostly by shooting. But as these mobile killing squads moved deeper into Soviet territory, they were replaced by Security Police outposts, whose primary goal was to murder the Jews in the areas under their control, deporting some to extermination camps—usually Bełżec in the case of Eastern Galicia—and shooting others in situ. The most intense killing was carried out between spring and summer 1942 and summer 1943; however, surviving Jews, whether still employed by the Germans or in hiding, were being hunted down and massacred by the Germans, their collaborators, independent local elements, bandits, and peasants, until the return of the Red Army the following year.[7]

On August 15 a district command was established in Buczacz, but the following month it was moved to Czortków, where the district administrative office was also located. Crucially, in the first month of the occupation Buczacz was under control of the Security Police, known by its acronym, "Sipo," in Tarnopol, but in September 1941 the city was subordinated to the Sipo outpost at Czortków.[8] It was the men from Tarnopol who carried out the first killings. As Kaznovskyi testified, the operation began when a dozen Gestapo officials from Tarnopol drove into Buczacz in early August: "The three officers [in charge] . . . entered my office and said they would be carrying out an execution and that a site for it had to be found and a mass grave needed to be dug." Kaznovskyi assigned several policemen to this task, who then "drove

Volodymyr Kaznovskyi after the war in a Soviet camp. *Source: Haluzevyi derzhavnyi arkhiv Sluzhba bezpeki Ukraïny (State Archives Department of the Security Service of Ukraine, hereafter HDA SBU), Ternopil branch, spr. 30466: 1957 indictment of Volodymyr Kaznovskyi.*

together with the three Gestapo men in their vehicle to the outskirts of the city, in order to select a site for the shooting of the prisoners." Leaving the Ukrainian policemen to dig the pit, the Gestapo officers returned to Kaznovskyi's office and presented him "with a list of those selected to be shot." One of the inmates recalled, "Kaznovskyi came into our cell with another policeman" and called out names of inmates from a list, ordering them "to step out of the cell"; these men, he said, "never came back." Kaznovskyi stated, "The Germans instructed me to choose a group of policemen who would escort the condemned and take part in the shooting." The prisoners "formed a column, and the Gestapo men, along with the selected policemen, walked with the convoy through the city to the execution site. I was not at this site," insisted Kaznovskyi.

The policeman Mykhailo Huzar explained that the prisoners were told they were being transferred to the town of Jazłowiec by way of a shortcut, but in fact they were led toward the forest in the direction of the village of Żyznomierz (Ukrainian: Zhyznomyr). "The wives of the prisoners were running behind the column and crying." As they reached the forest, "a vehicle arrived from which numerous Gestapo men climbed out and joined us. After walking for two-thirds of a mile through the forest, we arrived at a meadow guarded by the Germans. The prisoners were told to sit down at the edge of the meadow, and the [Ukrainian] policemen watched over them. The Germans took one or two men at a time from the group of the prisoners and led them into the forest, where a grave had already been prepared, and shot them there." When the shooting was over, "the grave with the corpses was covered up by the policemen."

Many of these policemen knew their victims personally. This too set a pattern, whereby the Jews of Buczacz were later rounded up and at times killed by men who had known them as neighbors, colleagues, classmates, or parents of their children's friends. Sofia Pelatiuk, the wife of Nagórzanka's village council chairman Vasyl Pelatiuk, recalled that in July the policeman Danylo Slipenkyi came to their house: "[He] ordered my husband to get dressed and come with him, saying to my husband: 'Don't worry, Mr. Pelatiuk, you'll be back home in two or

Vasyl Pelatiuk. *Source: HDA SBU, Ternopil, spr. 30466, appendices.*

three days.'" Pelatiuk remained incarcerated in the Buczacz prison for weeks, where Sofia brought him food every day. One afternoon, just as she arrived, she saw the prisoners being led away. "I walked behind the convoy with the other wives of the prisoners and saw where they were leading them," but they were forced by the policemen to turn back. Later the women "went into the forest to look for the bodies. We found the site where they had been shot and the pit into which the bodies had been dumped."[9]

✡ ✡

The early days of the German invasion were filled with terror for the Jews. One witness reported that even "before the Germans occupied our town," Kaznovskyi became "head of a band that took the law into its own hands" and "shot many Jews, Poles, and other people." Another testified that the Ukrainians "broke into our homes, destroyed our businesses and plundered whatever fell into their hands." The radio technician Moshe Wizinger vividly described the terror of seeing the blue and yellow Ukrainian flag flying next to the Nazi swastika from the city hall on July 5. In the evening Mordechai Halpern watched German Army units calmly roll into Buczacz; there was even "one unit on bicycles." It was, he wrote, "as if they had come on vacation." But shortly thereafter he saw a captured Red Army soldier denounced by his own comrades as a Jew and shot out of hand by the Germans.[10]

Violence was swift and ubiquitous. According to Wizinger, on the first night of the occupation "German soldiers, led by the Ukrainian dregs, broke into Jewish houses and raped young Jewish girls." The businessman Isidor Gelbart saw women being "hauled out of Jewish homes for cleaning work and mishandled" by the Ukrainian policemen. Subsequently, others reported, hundreds of Jews were forced every day to "sweep streets, remove debris," and "clean the public latrine pits," while being subjected to "severe beatings" as they worked. Orthodox Jews were a favorite target; Germans and Ukrainians chased them through the streets, "beat them, shaved their beards, tortured them, burned their religious symbols, etc."[11]

There were some exceptions to the mayhem and murder. Shmuel Rosen was given a loaf of bread by a German Army cook, who said, "Who knows, maybe one day my children too will be begging for bread." Gelbart described Ivan Bobyk, the newly appointed Ukrainian city mayor, as "a kind, decent, and unprejudiced man, who tried to help the Jews as much as he could." Gelbart believed that "compared to other cities, the Christian population of Buczacz was (objectively perceived to be) tolerant," at least as long as one "did not have particular enemies" among the gentiles. But most Jews recalled those early weeks as being filled with sporadic and at times murderous violence by Ukrainian activists, local hooligans, and unruly Wehrmacht troops. Jews were also targeted in the initial wave of settling political accounts. For instance, Wizinger told of armed Ukrainians breaking into the "houses of former communist activists" and hauling them out: "A few days later their bodies were found terribly mutilated, usually outside the city in some pit or swamp." The population was terrorized and "people could not sleep at night" since "no one knew whether he would be the next victim." A delegation of Jewish community leaders appealed to the respected Ukrainian optometrist Volodymyr Hamerskyi, who assured them, "The Ukrainian intelligentsia does not support the murder of the Jews." Unfortunately, he added, "those who are ruling now are the leaders of the previously secret Ukrainian bands," i.e., the OUN. Hamerskyi hoped "that once the Germans took over power, the atmosphere in town would return to normal." But as the Germans monopolized violence, they also systematized the killing.[12]

The old Ukrainian elite did intervene after "the Great Synagogue was gutted, the furnishings inside destroyed, the silver candelabras looted and many of the holy books thrown on the floor." The hooligans carried the Torah scrolls to the bridge leading to the Basilian monastery, where they "were unbound with one end attached to the top of the bridge and the other reaching almost all the way down to the water." This sacrilege "provoked a harsh protest by the Ukrainian priests, who demanded categorically from the leader of the Ukrainian bands, Dankovych, to stop profaning holy sites." The Greek Catholic abbot even "proposed to the Jews to bring the scrolls to the monastery where they would be safe." This was not the only time that local Christian leaders intervened to save Jewish religious items. In spring 1943 Samuel Rosental with several other Jews brought forty-five Torah scrolls and other objects to the Basilian monastery for safekeeping, and a couple of months later they hid the remaining twenty scrolls with the local Roman Catholic priest. Even as the community was massacred, many of these scrolls survived.[13]

☼ ☼

As the Germans tightened their grip on the city in August 1941, they imposed the wearing of white armbands with a blue Star of David, banned Jews from walking on the main streets, and ordered them to take off their hats whenever encountering a German, all on pain of death. They also demonstrated their predilection for extortion, arresting Jewish community leaders and threatening to kill them unless paid a ransom of one million rubles. Once the money was paid, the community was ordered to establish a Judenrat and *Ordnungsdienst* (OD, Jewish police).[14] Judenrat members, who represented a cross-section of the local Jewish elite, served their oppressors exceedingly well, even as they tried, in different ways, to save at least part of their community. Some of them illustrated the capacity of genocide to soil and implicate all too many of those who come into contact with it. The Judenrat's enforcement agency, the Ordnungsdienst, which numbered up to thirty men, had a particularly bad reputation. Many survivors never forgave those who collaborated with the Germans; others saw redeeming features in individual Judenrat and OD men. Some changed their opinions over time; in published accounts the most incriminating details about certain individuals and actions were often left out by the witnesses or expunged by the editors.

Working with the enemy, even if with the avowed intention of helping the community, presented those in positions of relative authority with impossible choices. Isidor Gelbart asserted that, "compared to other Jewish councils," the Buczacz Judenrat "was considered very good, because within the constraints of its powers it took care of the public's welfare." The teenager Izaak Szwarc saw it as "a kind of 'labor office,' to which all German demands for workers were directed," and hence a great improvement over the haphazard seizure of Jews for work by the Germans and the Ukrainian police. He praised it for its efforts to provide housing for the "thousands of Jews evicted from Subcarpathia," who "inundated Buczacz" in summer 1941, shortly before being murdered in Kamieniec Podolski. But he asserted that the Judenrat members "did not see, at least not at the beginning, that they would ultimately become a tool of the Gestapo."[15] Indeed, while he agreed that "collaboration by the Buczacz Judenrat was far more limited than that of many other Jewish councils," Szwarc concluded that it would be "better not to speak about it, especially during the period in which Baruch Kramer presided over it." He was even more disgusted with "the disgraceful actions of the Ordnungsdienst, which at the height of

Jews deported to Buczacz from the surrounding communities. *Source: GLA-K 309 Zug. 2001-42/878-53d.*

its degeneration and depravity was under command of M.A. [Mojżesz Albrecht]." In his first testimony, given in 1945, Szwarc was even more scathing, stressing that from the very beginning, "the wealthy, helped by the Judenrat, were able to buy their release" from serving in the murderous forced labor camps of Kamionki, Borki Wielkie, and Hłuboczek Wielki (Ukrainian: Kamyanky, Velyki Birky, Velykyi Hlybochok), and "instead of them, the Judenrat chose the poor."[16]

Over time the composition of the Judenrat also changed for the worse. Mendel Reich, the first chairman, was described as "a good Jew, an intelligent and honest man," nominated to his position by the town's venerable rabbi, Shraga Feivel Willig. But neither he nor his two immediate successors could withstand the pressure for long and either resigned or fled. The last chairman, Baruch Kramer, was described as "more a collaborator than a Jew." As Shmuel Rosen put it, Kramer was "a veritable bandit," a former Hasid who "shaved his beard under the Germans and became their servant" to such an extent that "during roundups he would walk around with a hatchet and betray the hiding places of the Jews." He also reportedly "amused himself with the Germans and forced young Jewish women to come to such amusements."[17]

Rosen described Dr. Bernhard Seifer, another prominent member of the community, as the "number two bandit" on the Judenrat. He represented one more example of the tension between seeking to help the community and relentless self-preservation, making the most of the tenuous but also critical authority given the Judenrat by the Germans— even as it became ever clearer that the occupiers' ultimate goal was total extermination. Halpern also claimed that Seifer had "played a particularly disgraceful role" precisely because, "in his capacity as physician, his job was to determine the medical condition of Jewish workers." He therefore "extorted vast sums of money from Jews by promising to release them from the most dangerous assignments," while "the sick were actually sent to the most difficult labor where, unable to withstand the heavy burden, they perished." Halpern found it an outrage that in 1948 Seifer was "still alive and liv[ing] abroad," one of only two Judenrat members who survived the war. According to Wizinger, in spring 1943 Seifer and Kramer took exorbitant bribes to allow surviving Jews to enter the newly erected labor camp in Buczacz, considered the last remaining safe haven in the city: "In this manner the two-hundred richest Jewish families found their way into the camp," while the rest of the population were deported to other towns and either "slain on the way" or murdered shortly after their arrival. Rosen concluded that because Seifer had "traded with people" in this manner, by the time Buczacz was liberated for the first time, in March 1944, "apart from a handful of decent people, only the dregs survived: policemen and informers"; most of these people were also murdered after the Germans retook the city in April.[18]

Seifer was spotted after the war in Łódź and was subsequently rumored to be living in Paris, England, South America, or Australia. In June 1946 he wrote to Abraham Sommer in New York to provide his own version of events: "People react in different ways to human wickedness, which has no limits, but I owe you an explanation, since you are my friend." Seifer was making no apologies. The day after the Germans appointed Mendel Reich as head of the Judenrat, he wrote, they ordered Reich "to supplement the list with the name of a doctor," who would direct the Jewish hospital. "As M. Reich was my friend, he gave my name without asking for my permission and I started organizing the hospital." Even Seifer's harshest critics, such as Wizinger, conceded that he had "managed, under the most difficult circumstances, to gather a very professional team and to acquire medicines that were officially banned." As for the systematic corruption of internal Jewish rule, Seifer put the blame on Reich, otherwise "a wonderful man," because of his naïve belief that he could "win over at least the local Germans by offering them some gifts." Since "the demands of the Germans were insatiable," the Judenrat had no choice but "to impose taxes" whose revenues would allow it to "buy those items from the Jews" and deliver them to the Germans. This was at best only partly true, since the Jewish police often forcibly confiscated whatever it wished.[19]

Seifer claimed that early on he had heard from one of his German patients "that Hitler had undoubtedly condemned us to death"; Seifer consequently demanded from the Judenrat that it "allow young people to go to the forest" and "to buy weapons," believing that "it was better to be killed fighting than simply to wait." But, he asserted, "no one else wanted to believe that such a cruel sentence could be carried out." At the same time, he also heaped praise on Baruch Kramer, whom he described as "a very brave man," and generally depicted the Judenrat of Buczacz as "the best" of its kind throughout the region, "the only oasis in Poland where there was no ghetto at all" and "where the mayor disclosed the time of the roundups" in advance, as did the "chief of the gendarmerie." No wonder, he concluded, that "Jews from all other areas kept coming to Buczacz." Much of this was untrue: all other accounts presented Seifer as a strong opponent of the resistance; a ghetto was in fact created in Buczacz, although, as was common in the area, it was "open" in the sense of not being surrounded by a fence; and while Seifer may have been told in advance of roundups thanks to his good connections with local Germans, that information did not reach much of the community.[20]

As hospital director, Seifer "had to examine and approve every man referred to labor" and "could not exempt everyone"; hence "whoever was referred became my enemy." He admitted that the Judenrat had been "deluding itself into thinking that as long as the Jews were working they were useful" to the Germans and "therefore safe." But he insisted that despite the "tragedy" of June 1943, when the last remaining Jews of Buczacz were murdered, "the work of Reich and Kramer was not quite in vain," since at the first liberation "over 1,000 human shadows emerged from the forests," making it into "the only town in Europe which could boast such a number of survivors." Consequently, he exclaimed, one "could not possibly have any reason to be ashamed" of having belonged to the Judenrat. "I knew those people and their work," and "no one should sling mud" at them. Such accusations had to do with a certain postwar "psychosis in Europe, mostly provoked by the

Jews in Palestine and those who were in Russia during the war, which claimed that every Jew in Europe who survived had obviously collaborated with the Germans." That was just "a downright lie."

In the immediate postwar context Seifer had little hope of convincing anyone of his version; others attributed the initially high survival rate of Buczacz's Jews to the resistance, which Seifer had opposed, and certainly not to the Judenrat. He concluded his letter with these somber words: "Under the present circumstances, since we shall probably never meet again in this life, please attach these pages to the book on Buczacz that should spring forth from amongst you, as fully worthy of credence, coming from a man whose life is over and who craves only death, in the face of which I am sending you this explanation. What else can I add? I make no excuses, because I have a clean conscience."[21] He then vanished from sight. His letter was never included in any publication on Buczacz; it was a self-serving statement filled with distortions, half-truths, and blatant lies, and lacked any hint of remorse. But it did reveal something about how decent men in dark times can become useful instruments in the realization of genocide.

There were also instances of personal courage. Wizinger declared that Jakob Ebenstein, "who, during his few months at the Judenrat, had become hated by everyone and was branded an agent of the Gestapo, died a hero's death." During the roundup on November 1942 Ebenstein was ordered to help the Germans

Shmuel Rosen as a lad in Buczacz.
Source: Yad Vashem, Jerusalem (hereafter YVA), 3592/3.

search for bunkers, but when they began "demolishing one of them," he "said that he would guarantee with his own head that searching there was useless." Once the German "started pulling the Jews out of there, Ebenstein figured that his end had come, [so he] grabbed a hatchet and tried to strike the Gestapo man. At the same moment another soldier shot him." According to Emanuel Worman, Ebenstein's own family was hiding in the bunker, which was why he had "vowed with his life that no one was there." In any case, Ebenstein "had risked his life to save others: This is a fact that people should know."[22]

Jakob Ebenstein during the German occupation. *Source: GLA-K 309 Zug. 2001- 42/878-98.*

✿ ✿

Even more reviled than the Judenrat, the Jewish police (OD) attracted young men from the wealthier families in Buczacz since it was believed membership would improve one's chances of survival. Gelbart said that even before the first mass shooting of Jews in late August 1941, a number of "Jewish youths from the white collar professions, whose names I will not spell out here for obvious reasons (they are no longer alive), took control over their own Jews." That fall the Judenrat's procurement office, headed by the butcher Fiszel Szwarc, joined forces with the police, whose "hated commander" Albrecht reportedly "robbed the Jews" of their property. As Wizinger wrote, at the time OD members "were able to lead a very good life and to amass large sums of money." Those who "tried to hide their belongings were mercilessly beaten." During the winter of 1942–43, the Jewish police continued "robbing, killing, worse than the Germans." Albrecht, wrote Wizinger, "walks down the streets in an OD uniform. Like the

Germans, he is holding a whip in his hand and woe to whoever stands in his way." As conditions deteriorated, the butcher Szwarc joined the swelling ranks of the OD; it was a smart move, since he was one of several Jewish policemen who survived the war. Halpern remembered that "the Jewish police acted with particular cruelty in relieving the Jews of all they had left. Assaults and beatings of their brethren became a normal phenomenon." Additionally, as Eliasz Chalfen observed, in the winter of 1941–42 the OD was "especially active" in rounding up young men and women for forced labor.[23]

Most devastating was the involvement of the Jewish police in the roundups, deportations, and mass shootings. Rosental testified that during the first roundup, in October 1942, the Gestapo received "considerable assistance from the Jewish police," which was "armed with axes." Rosen reported that in the second roundup, the following month, "the Gestapo men were assisted by the Ukrainian and Jewish police." And during the third action, in February 1943, "there were horrible scenes when children escorted their parents to the pit. The policeman Anderman—a young boy—had to lead his own mother to the mass grave." Other "Ukrainian and Jewish policemen were posted as guards on all the roads leading to Buczacz, and arrested Jews who had escaped from the 'actions' in their towns and were seeking asylum in Buczacz. They were all killed."[24]

As the killing intensified and struck closer to home, the willingness of some Jewish policemen to collaborate began to waver. Yitzhak Bauer, who joined the Jewish police in the fall of 1941 at age eighteen, eventually became a member of the resistance. "The Ordnungsdienst in Buczacz," he testified in 1968, "numbered about 30 people"; it was located "in the building of the Judenrat," to which it was "administratively subordinated." But during roundups "we were put at the disposition of the . . . Gestapo or the local gendarmerie [regular German police]." In such cases, Jewish policemen operated alongside German perpetrators. "As an OD-man I was personally . . . involved in two roundups," he stated. In November 1942 "we were ordered to report to the Judenrat at daybreak" and assigned to different squads of Germans "heading toward the Jewish houses." Bauer's task was to "participate in the cleansing of the Jewish hospital on Mikołaja Street," alongside two armed Germans, one of whom was the Gestapo driver Albert Brettschneider. At the hospital, which contained "about one hundred patients . . . horrifying things took place. The patients who could not move were shot on the spot directly in their beds. Others were escorted to the railroad station, from which they, together with the other Jews . . . were loaded into the railroad cars and deported to be exterminated in Bełżec." Bauer witnessed the killings at very close quarters. "We entered a room with bed-ridden patients, who could not raise themselves out of bed. There were five to six persons." He was "standing by the door" and could clearly see Brettschneider and his partner "walk up to individual beds and shoot those patients" by "aiming at a spot between the eyes and the nose. They simply rested the weapon at that spot on the face of the victim. After each such shot, the victim showed no more signs of life." Having murdered at least four people in that room, Brettschneider commented to the other man, "It's time to get some food" (*Es ist schon Zeit zum Essen*). It was about 8:30 a.m.[25]

Bauer also witnessed the roundup of April 1943: "Already on the way to the Judenrat I saw the bodies of people who had been shot lying in the street." Not only did the local German gendarmes also participate in the killing, but "even Germans from the Baudienst [Labor Service] of the Todt Organization," Nazi Germany's vast labor and construction agency, "took part in this action." He saw Rothmann, the local chief of the Baudienst, shoot the Jewish woman Jancie Hirschhorn on a street near the hospital. Bauer's own mother was murdered that day. Two days later he and OD member Hersz Gross had to accompany SS Corporal Richard Pal, who was in charge of collecting "the remaining belongings" of "murdered or deported Jews." In one of the apartments they encountered the mother of OD member Dunajer, who was still packing her clothes. "Without asking a word," Bauer testified, "Pal drew his pistol and fired two shots [at her] in front of my eyes. I saw—I was standing

Richard Pal, undated photo. A Romanian ethnic German born in 1912, Pal joined the Waffen-SS in 1940, was charged with murder and sentenced to eight years in prison in 1974, but was acquitted in 1979. *Source: GLA-K 309 Zug. 2001-42/871-01, 883; Bundesarchiv ZB 7129, pp. 1–26; B162/5175, pp. 4265–300; 5176, pp. 4631–35; 14533, pp. 1–211.*

at a distance of 3 feet—how she toppled over, covered in blood, without any sign of life." Then they had "to load everything in the apartment onto the cart" waiting in the street.[26]

Interviewed in 2002, Bauer commented that following their mother's murder (their father had died earlier of typhus), he and his younger brother decided to go to the forest and "joined a group" of resisters. He did not mention that he had previously served as a policeman. We learn from his story that the transition from the Ordnungsdienst to the resistance was far more natural than might appear in hindsight.[27]

Others joined the resistance in June, when the Germans set out to liquidate all the remaining Jews in town, including those in the enclosed labor camp and the Jewish police, who were housed separately on the outskirts of town. It was there, as Eliasz Chalfen testified, that the Gestapo and the Ukrainian auxiliaries "met with armed resistance." This last-ditch fighting by the OD allowed some policemen and a fair number of other Jews to escape into the forest. Many of them were denounced and murdered in the ensuing months. But alongside the solidarity of victimhood, resentment against those perceived to have bought their survival at the price of others lingered on. A Polish underground report issued not long after the first liberation of Buczacz, in March 1944, noted, "About 800 Jews came out of their shelters and right away began settling scores among themselves. The poor accused the rich that they had robbed them and that they hid themselves while turning the poor over to the Gestapo." Allegations of Jewish passivity or spinelessness also quickly surfaced, and the Soviets reportedly "accused the Jews of being parasites and asked them why did they not go to the forest to fight the Germans, and instead hid themselves in holes like cowards."[28]

✡ ✡

The Germans accomplished the rapid destruction of the Jewish population by creating a local apparatus of Ukrainians and Jews who helped them organize and perpetrate mass murder and by swiftly decapitating the community so as to minimize organized resistance. Apart from setting up the Judenrat and Ordnungsdienst, in early August 1941 the local authorities effectively transformed the Ukrainian militia into a uniformed district police force under Kaznovskyi's command, subordinated to the local German gendarmerie. This reorganization facilitated the first mass shooting of several hundred Jews on Fedor Hill. The victims, including a few women and non-Jews, were first held in the cellar of the police building, then escorted the following morning to the killing site by Ukrainian policemen, who secured the perimeter. What came to be known as the "registration action" was itself a dress rehearsal for all subsequent, much larger mass execution and deportation operations in Buczacz. Kaznovskyi, however, suggested in his postwar investigation that he had nothing to do with the massacre. One afternoon in August 1941, he said, "I was sitting in my office in the building of the Ukrainian police station in Buczacz. From the window I could see policemen escorting a column of Jews" toward the station. "As I learned later, the Gestapo had selected the men on the basis of a registration." Once the Jews were "assembled in the court-yard" of the station, "the Gestapo locked the gate." The next day, as he "was walking to the police station, the Gestapo men led the prisoners out of the courtyard," and, along with "some [Ukrainian] policemen, who had guarded the Jews overnight," they "escorted the prisoners in the direction of Fedor Hill. There were about 200 prisoners. After the policemen returned, they said that the Gestapo had shot the entire group."

Further investigation soon established that prior to the shooting Kaznovskyi had in fact ordered a group of fifteen to eighteen Ukrainian policemen to dig a mass grave on Fedor Hill and "escort the 'Jewish in-tellectuals' to the execution site." The policemen instead delegated the digging to villagers from Nagórzanka, who were also expected to cover up the bodies but escaped upon seeing the shooting. For that reason, as Mykhailo Huzar testified, the pit was covered with only a thin layer of soil, and soon thereafter "the bodies began to decompose" and "an unpleasant smell spread over the city," until Huzar and a colleague were sent "to put further layers of soil over the pit."[29]

The registration action, in which hundreds of the city's most up-standing citizens were murdered, had the added benefit of demon-strating that Jews could simply be taken aside and killed without even the semblance of an excuse or formality. As Gelbart recalled it, the ac-tion began on August 25, when the male Jews of Buczacz were ordered to assemble on the market square at 5:00 p.m. for labor registration. Gelbart, who decided not to go, was watching from his window, as the hundreds of Jews gathered in the square were "surrounded from all sides and led in military style to the Ukrainian police" building. "The victims were then interrogated about their particulars and many crafts-men were released." Those who remained overnight were described as "predominantly educated people," "the best youth and working in-telligentsia," and "the crème-de-la-crème of the Jewish population." Jewish survivors' estimates of their numbers range between 350 and 800.[30]

The selection was supervised by Major (*Sturmbannführer*) Hermann Müller, chief of the Sipo outpost in Tarnopol. Once that was accomplished, the elderly Jewish witness Józef Kornblüh reported, the Gestapo men "left for a drinking bout at the apartment of the Ukrainian physician Dr. [Alexius] Banach, where they drank until 4 a.m." Markus Kleiner, who was in the prison, testified that at about 8:00 p.m. police chief Kaznovskyi "and several other Ukrainian policemen came in with batons and began to beat up their victims. Some of the victims had their arms broken. The horror and the cries of the tortured people cannot be described." Inmates were forced "to drink their own urin[e]." The Gestapo returned at daybreak and led the victims to Fedor Hill, where "big boxes had been prepared for them to deposit all their belongings, and afterward they were shot." Kleiner, who had managed "to escape from the prison on the night before the massacre," was hiding nearby. He watched as the victims were "executed completely naked," and he "could hear very well the cries of the victims and the machine gun fire of the executioners." The Ukrainian policemen then "brought the booty to town and changed the belongings of the unfortunate victims against [i.e., for] brandy and vodka and celebrated their easy victory with yelling 'Death for the Jews and Poles, long live independent Ucraina [Ukraine].'" In this manner, Gelbart noted, "Buczacz lost its most valuable Jewish element already in the opening phase" of the German occupation.[31]

From their house Wizinger and his brother watched the victims walking to Fedor Hill, "surrounded by a tight cordon of Ukrainian policemen. They were led barefoot, some only in their underwear. The car with the Germans and their inseparable machine guns was driving slowly behind." Soon thereafter they heard shots from the forest, which went on for quite a while, followed by the Ukrainian policemen marching back and chanting, "Death to the Jews." Wizinger recalled that "many of them were wearing pieces of clothing that had belonged to the murdered Jews." But many family members refused to believe that their loved ones were gone; when the Germans falsely promised to release them in return for a hefty ransom, the "wives and mothers of those who had been taken practically besieged the office of the Judenrat," begging it to pay the ransom. People brought in their gold jewelry all day. But that night Wizinger, the Judenrat member Dr. Ludwik Engelberg, and a local Polish doctor located the freshly dug mass grave in the forest; it was filled with bodies. The following morning, when the Judenrat presented Major Müller with the gold, he demanded that they sign a document describing the ransom as a fee for the execution of four hundred communists carried out by the authorities at the request of the Jews. As it later transpired, charging fees for executions was common practice. According to Samuel Rosental, Gestapo official sergeant Kurt Köllner and SS corporal Paul Thomanek "would come to the Judenrat after each action, and were paid 20 złoty for every bullet fired during the action. The amount paid was registered in the Judenrat's accounting books and Thomanek would be given a receipt."[32]

There were two known survivors. Abram Brandes ran off from the marching column and jumped into a well; he then persuaded a Ukrainian policeman, whom he knew, to let him escape. From his hiding place in the bushes he watched hundreds of his townsmen being shot. Brandes was denounced and murdered shortly before the liberation. A young lad called Mandel crawled out of the pit after the shooting was over. According to Rosen, the boy survived and was living in Poland after the war but would "tell no one about his experience" or reveal "his Jewish background," saying that he had become "a different person from the moment he had climbed out of the mass grave."[33]

✡ ✡

Beginning in the fall of 1941, the agency directly charged with the mass murder of the Jews of Buczacz was the Security Police outpost established in nearby Czortków. The twenty-odd German members of the outpost carried out their task with notable efficiency: assisted by

Map of the General Government, published in *Krakauer Zeitung*, October 26, 1941. *Source: Biblioteka Uniwersytecka we Wrocławiu (Wrocław University Library, hereafter BUW).*

three hundred Ukrainian policemen organized in a so-called *Schutzmannschaft* (Auxiliary Police) battalion, as well as by local German gendarmeries, Ukrainian police, and Jewish Ordnungsdienst forces in the smaller towns, they murdered approximately 60,000 Jews in the Czortków-Buczacz region during the three years of the outpost's

Top: Heinrich Peckmann, fourth chief of the outpost, with his wife and son in front of the Czortków Sipo building; bottom: the German grocery in Czortków. *Source: GLA-K 309 Zug. 2001-42/878-110, 871-28.*

existence; only 1,200 Jews are thought to have survived. In Buczacz most of the victims were killed in just nine months, between October 1942 and June 1943.[34]

The new order established by the Security Police in the Czortków-Buczacz region was almost exclusively dedicated to the exploitation and murder of the Jews. In implementing its genocidal objective, the outpost effectively engaged all other available German agencies and every element in the local population, in most cases by providing tangible incentives in the form of material benefits and status elevation; to the Jewish leadership and police it offered a temporary lease on life. Beyond the extraordinary bloodletting this undertaking entailed, perhaps its most scandalous aspect was the astonishing ease with which it was accomplished and the extent to which the killers, along with their spouses and children, lovers and colleagues, friends and parents, appear to have enjoyed their brief murderous sojourn in the region. For many of them, this was clearly the best time of their lives: they had almost unlimited access to food, liquor, tobacco, and sex, and, most important, they became supreme masters over life and death. And when they were done, they packed up and left, often returning to their previous occupations as if nothing had happened, merely taking along a few objects of sentimental or material value, as well as nostalgic photographs of the good old days, unearthed years later when some of them were finally brought to justice.[35]

The man most closely associated with the murder of the Jews in the Czortków-Buczacz region was Kurt Köllner.[36] Born in 1908 and raised in the town of Bad Dürrenberg in Saxony, Köllner began working as a mechanic and driver in 1926, later joining the management of an automotive company in his hometown and establishing a car rental business of his own; he was considered a reliable and socially respectable businessman. Although his father was a lifelong member of the Social Democratic Party and his parental home hosted various influential political personalities of diverse ideological affiliations, Köllner himself was politically neutral, preferring sports to politics and clinging to his Evangelical faith throughout the Nazi period. He married in a church ceremony in 1934, and his son was born shortly before the war.

Decades later the court that tried him for murder learned that, following Hitler's so-called seizure of power in 1933, Köllner concluded that it had become "necessary for him to take up an unequivocal political position," which meant joining the SS. Köllner explained this step as an attempt to protect his father from incarceration in a concentration camp. But he quickly became an active member of the SS motor school in Leipzig and strutted around town in his elegant black uniform. To the court he insisted that all along he had resisted the regime's anti-Semitic ideology and had maintained good social contacts with several Jewish families. He had even helped a Jewish acquaintance to emigrate by buying his property—likely for a quite competitive price—and had expressed disapproval of the Kristallnacht pogrom of November 1938, although no witnesses could verify that. Indeed contemporaries remembered that he was nicknamed Mäuschen, or "Little Mouse," suggesting something less than physical courage and moral fortitude.

In December 1939 Köllner was called up for military service, and after a few months of training was posted to the Security Police in Warsaw. In August 1941 he was transferred to Lemberg (Polish: Lwów), arriving in Czortków toward the end of the year. In late July 1942 he was appointed head of the *Judenreferat* (Jewish section), a position he held until the outpost was dismantled. After the war he spent five years in various East German camps and prisons; he then joined his family in West Germany, where he worked for a local firm until his arrest in 1958 on charges of multiple murders. Köllner's defense hinged on the argument that he had treated Jews well and had actually suffered as a consequence. Even his transfer from Galicia's capital to a posting in its backwoods, he argued, was a form of punishment for his protests against the maltreatment of Jewish workers building the infamous Thoroughfare IV from Lemberg to the Black Sea.[37] In fact his service in Czortków was anything but unpleasant, since shortly after arriving his wife and son joined him there; his wife even found employment with the outpost.

One reason for Köllner's success in implementing local genocide was his knack for getting to know his victims before organizing their murder. Rather than employing dehumanization and detachment, he used trust, familiarity, and false promises, which both made things much smoother and provided greater opportunities for personal enrichment. Shortly before the first mass deportation from Czortków on August 25–26, 1942, Köllner warned the local Judenrat of the impending

The Sipo and Kripo buildings in Czortków. *Source: GLA-K 309 Zug. 2001-42/878-57, 58.*

action and ordered it to be prepared to deliver the necessary quota of Jews. But as a gesture of sympathy he also offered to protect young, fit Jews from deportation by stamping their labor cards. In fact he was acting upon instructions from Lemberg, because Jewish labor was still needed to maintain the region's economy. But since the Judenrat had no way of knowing that, it compensated Köllner generously for his kindness with money and gold. Having won the Jewish leadership's trust,

Köllner then notified it, just hours before the roundup began, that no imminent action was expected, ensuring that the population would be caught off-guard. As a result, approximately three thousand Jews were deported to Bełżec that day, and another three hundred were shot in their homes or on the street; when no more people could be crammed into the railcars, the remaining Jews were incarcerated in the Czortków prison and deported sometime later.

This was the first of numerous deportation roundups and mass shooting actions throughout the region in which Köllner participated. But the court would find him guilty of first-degree murder only if it could be shown that he had personally and willfully carried out individual killings. The cases presented to the court demonstrated the license such men had to wantonly kill whomever they wished and the obvious pleasure they took in demonstrating their omnipotence. During the second roundup in Czortków, in October 1942, for instance, Köllner

Group photo of Czortków Sipo members: Kurt Köllner is fourth from the right; Albert Brettschneider is third from the left; their wives are directly in front of them. *Source: GLA-K 309 Zug. 2001-42/878-60.*

personally shot three Jews who could not keep up with those being deported, either because of old age, physical handicap, or illness. In March 1943 he had two patients dragged from their hospital beds in Buczacz and shot them in the garden. Two months later he shot the plumber Schorr, his wife, and their toddler at close range in front of their older child, and later shot the teenagers Emil Kitaj and Hania Adler point-blank in the head as they knelt in front of him and begged for their lives; on this occasion he was holding the pistol in one hand and his own five-year-old son's hand in the other.

Even after the main roundups were over, Köllner continued killing individuals. During the liquidation of the forced labor camp in the village of Nagórzanka near Jagielnica (Ukrainian: Yahilnytsya) in early August 1943, for instance, he chased the teenager Mojsze Waisman, who tried to flee from the barn where he had been hiding, and shot him dead. He then shot the girls Bina and Gisela Horowitz, who had also hidden in the barn, point-blank in the head, once more as they knelt in front of him, a method of execution that seems to have appealed to Köllner and several of his colleagues.[38] While these and other murders combined utter indifference to human life with outlandish cruelty, they were representative of the conduct of the Sipo outpost as a whole; in a relatively short time, the murder of Jews, often in the most gruesome manner, had become normalized as a routine and casual act.

Köllner attempted to defend himself by arguing that the Czortków Judenrat had been complicit in these crimes by willingly revealing to him the locations of hiding places. But even if true, this obviously did not alleviate his guilt. He also claimed that in May 1943 he had been investigated by the SS in Lemberg for favoring Jews, leading to a search of his apartment in Czortków. As it turned out, the search actually revealed that he had been hoarding Jewish bribes rather than dutifully handing them over to his superiors. A last effort by Köllner's wife to provide him with an alibi also backfired, when she brazenly asserted that she had "known nothing about the murders perpetrated in the Czortków district," especially after another German woman testified that they had discussed "how one could keep what was happening at

Frau Köllner (on the right) with two other wives of Sipo personnel and a child, out for a walk in Czortków. *Source: GLA-K 309 Zug. 2001-42/878-18.*

the time with the Jews from the children." Clearly Köllner was not worried at all about that.

In 1962 Köllner was found guilty of multiple murders and sentenced to life imprisonment. The court rejected his claim of having had "inner reservations," finding that "his entire attitude" proved "that he had no humane considerations as regards the treatment of the Jews," thereby demonstrating his "moral transformation and the hold of National Socialist ideology over him." The judges also dismissed Köllner's claim of superior orders, stressing that he "did not shy away from avoiding" such "orders when it suited him," but did not do so on the numerous occasions in which he participated in mass murder. Paradoxically, the judges also argued that Köllner had "recognized quite early the danger of National Socialism" and had "remained inwardly unmoved" by its "ideas and goals." Hence he "would have probably continued to lead an ordinary bourgeois existence, had he not increasingly succumbed to the temptations of National Socialist ideology" following Hitler's seizure of power. "In this sense," stated the judges, who must have been thinking about their own careers under Nazism, "he became—like many others—a victim in the wider sense of the circumstances of the time." The court therefore concluded that Köllner's "guilt consists in the fact that he sacrificed his previous moral and human restraints and that in an effort to promote his own advancement and profit as much as possible, he became a compliant and pliable instrument of the regime of the time, especially in the planned eradication of the Jews, even though, according to his own description, he knew very well 'that this is murder.'"

In other words, the judges convicted Köllner of murder not because he had internalized Nazi ideology but because he used it for his own purposes, and not for having efficiently organized local genocide but for having personally and needlessly killed individuals who would have otherwise been consigned to collective murder.

✡ ✡

Köllner's superior, the stern-faced professional policeman Heinrich Peckmann, joined the Nazi Party and the Gestapo in 1937 after a twelve-year career in the regular police force. Posted to Czortków in October 1941, he served as deputy and then as chief of the outpost between late 1942 and October 1943. Resuming his police career after the war, Peckmann was arrested in 1960 but acquitted two years later for insufficient evidence. A second attempt to bring him to justice was dropped in 1966 for similar reasons, despite several testimonies alleging that he had commanded a number of mass executions in the region.[39]

But the previously laconic Peckmann was much more expansive about the modus operandi of the outpost when called as a witness at another trial the following year. Officially, he said, "it was forbidden to shoot Jews privately outside of organized actions" or "to visit the Judenrat." But

Sipo chief Hans Velde and his deputy Heinrich Peckmann (on right) hunting in the woods near Czortków. *Source: GLA-K 309 Zug. 2001-42/878-64.*

"no one bothered with these restrictions. In practice you could . . . do whatever you wanted without being held accountable." SS-Sergeant Artur Rosenow, for instance, had unleashed his "private" dog against a Jewish man walking down the street in Czortków, which literally "stripped him naked," in defiance of regulations, and "paid no attention" to Peckmann's instructions not to bring the dog to roundups. On one occasion Rosenow walked into the "Jewish camp" in Czortków, "shot a Jewish woman" with his pistol, and killed her child by "striking its head against the wall." Because of such men as Rosenow, stressed Peckmann, "nobody had to be assigned to a Jew-action, because there were sufficient volunteers" more than willing to do the shooting. Indeed Peckmann believed that it was "thanks to the bad example set by the SS-leaders of our outpost" that "people like [the Gestapo driver Albert] Brettschneider and the SS guards" became "Jew-haters [*Judengegner*]. It made them feel so important, when they drove to the roundups with the SS-leaders and were allowed to shoot Jews." The second outpost chief, Karl Hildemann, had just such a

corrupting influence. Peckmann related one instance in which "Hildemann walked into the canteen and asked, 'Who wants to come along to
shoot some Jews?'" But while Peckmann claimed to have been outraged
by such conduct, he conceded that other outpost commanders who dis-
approved of "private Jew-shootings" nevertheless were "on principle in
agreement with the extermination of the Jews."[40]

SS Corporal Paul Thomanek represented precisely the kind of unambiguously brutal face of German genocide alluded to by Peckmann.
Raised in interwar Czechoslovakia as the son of an ethnic German coal
miner, Thomanek joined the German police after the outbreak of war
and transferred to the Waffen-SS in October 1941. Posted initially to
the forced labor camps of Kamionki and Hłuboczek Wielki near Tarnopol, in November 1942 he was appointed commandant of the labor
camp in Czortków and soon became the master of all other labor camps
in the region. He was given a car and a house and for a while hosted his
wife, son, and father there. He also brought with him a German (or

Sipo member Fritz Kallmeyer and his child with other outpost personnel in
Czortków. *Source: GLA-K 309 Zug. 2001-42/871-26.*

Austrian) Jew named Wolf as chief of his Ordnungsdienst. Thomanek was finally arrested by the German police in 1957.[41]

Called *der Erschiesser* (the Shooter) even before coming to Czortków, Thomanek quickly made friends with two other SS men, Rux and Rosenow, and the three became collectively known as the *Judenschlächter* (the slaughterers of Jews).[42] His multiple killings in the Czortków-Buczacz region demonstrated the complete impunity such men enjoyed in perpetrating random violence quite apart from organized massacres. Because he was in charge of relatively small camps, Thomanek also often personally knew the people he murdered. In May 1943, for instance, he murdered Sofia Wolf for speaking across the Czortków labor camp fence with her child's Polish caretaker. She just had time to call out, "Herr camp commandant, spare my life, I have a small child," before he shot her in the face with his submachine gun. The following month, during the liquidation of the camp, his personal barber "Papusch" asked Thomanek to spare him, only to be cut to pieces with a burst of submachine-gun bullets. He responded in the same fashion when a blond seventeen-year-old girl named Jäger begged him to let her live, and then he joined the shooters at the execution site.

A German eyewitness described this camp liquidation as "the most frightful and cruelest event I have ever experienced": "Among the heap of Jews who had been loaded on the truck, all in a crouching position, with their faces down, a blond Jewish girl was sitting upright, like an angel looking into another world. The road winding its way through Czortków was paved with stones and it looked like the vehicle was driving over a stream of blood." Among the guards escorting the truck "in open cars with fire-ready weapons" he saw "Thomanek, who was unmistakable with his red hair."[43]

Thomanek also kept a room in Buczacz, where he often ordered the Judenrat to supply him with "girls," booze, and food. In February 1943 he was one of several SS and Gestapo shooters on Fedor Hill, although at his trial he claimed he merely helped SS Corporal Richard Pal collect the victims' valuables. He added that on the drive back to Czortków he said to Pal, "Look at these beautiful flowers and yet so many people

Left to right: Leo Folkenfok; Ginsburg, a Jewish cook; Pepi, a Jewish construction site assistant; Mrs. Leo Folkenfok; and unknown, possibly the subsequent Ukrainian denouncer, at the entrance to the Folkenfolks' former inn and house. *Source: GLA-K 309 Zug. 2001-42/878-115.*

have to die," to which his colleague reassuringly replied, "We have nothing to say about this, orders are orders." In fact Thomanek killed on his own initiative in Buczacz too. In April 1943 he took Rux and a young Ukrainian woman in his car to an inn on the outskirts of Buczacz; the woman had apparently informed them that the family of her former employer at the inn, Leo Folkenfok, was still hiding there with several other Jews, including small children and a pregnant woman. The two SS men forced the Jews to hand over their valuables and shot them one by one. A German civilian who arrived at the scene before the killers left testified, "I heard one of them say to the other that in the future he should not use explosive bullets."[44]

Tall, fat, and red-haired, Thomanek was easily recognizable and greatly feared throughout the region; the cry "Thomanek is coming!" terrorized all who heard it. His visits to the smaller labor camps in the district were also often accompanied by killings.[45] Indeed the murders were so ubiquitous, and Thomanek's appearance so striking, that despite his vehement denials the court rejected all his pleas. The defendant, it concluded, could not resort to claims of superior orders since orders calling for a criminal undertaking could not be seen as binding. The judges also stressed that Thomanek was never in a situation where "he could only save himself from a threat to his own life and body by acting as he did"; in fact it had not been shown that any "SS-man who did not take part in shooting Jews faced a danger" of this kind. At worst, he might "have had to reckon with dismissal from his post and possibly being sent to the front." Moreover it was clear to the court that Thomanek had acted in "his own personal interest." Believing that the Nazi regime and the SS were "at that time in a certain sense 'masters of the world,'" Thomanek thought "he could share that power" as long as "he behaved in the manner required and expected of him by his superiors." And indeed "things went exceedingly well for him." Thomanek enjoyed such "privileges" only "because he excelled in the 'treatment' of the Jews," which gave him "a position of enormous power that had absolutely no correspondence to his rank" and preserved him from being "called up to the Wehrmacht and sent to a frontline unit." This "selfish motivation," concluded the judges, made him "a willing tool of the National Socialist authorities" and "a person whose name evoked fear and horror in the Jews" as "an arbitrary master over the life and death of these unfortunate people." But although Thomanek was found guilty and sentenced to life imprisonment, the court could not refrain from making almost the same statement made at the conclusion of Köllner's trial, namely, that since Thomanek did "not carry any responsibility for" the Nazi regime's "ideas and plans or for the transformation of the political circumstances and the war," it could also be said that "to this extent he became—like many others with him—in a wider sense also a victim of that time."[46]

✡ ✡

Alone among the few members of the Czortków Sipo outpost who eventually faced justice, the Gestapo driver Albert Brettschneider unwittingly exposed a small portion of that potent mix of prejudice, self-righteousness, and sense of inferiority that motivated and rationalized his brutality. Born in Lithuania to a German father and a Lithuanian mother, and married to an ethnic German, Brettschneider joined the Security Police in 1941, arriving with his wife in Czortków that fall; they remained there until the outpost was dismantled. Finally subjected to a judicial investigation in 1965, Brettschneider's case was partly dismissed for lack of evidence in 1971 and terminated altogether following his death two years later.[47]

At his investigation, even as he described the killings in graphic detail, Brettschneider also betrayed a degree of nostalgia for the "good old days" in the outpost. Despite his low rank, he had formed close relations with many more-senior Sipo members and local administrators. In these small, isolated German communities, joint complicity in mass murder nourished a grotesquely merry intimacy. He fondly recalled a restaurant in Czortków "which I and almost all other outpost members often patronized, because it served good beer." He also "very often went to drink beer together" with other members "of the Gestapo outpost" at the train station restaurant. In Buczacz there was yet another inn where Brettschneider "always socialized" with SS and Gestapo personnel. Indeed things were so good that even when an SS captain from Lemberg had an affair with his wife around Christmas 1942, Brettschneider did not request another posting, as some of his friends had advised.

Personally Brettschneider claimed to be constitutionally incapable of inflicting violence: "I could never in my life kill a woman or even a girl. I have always worshipped women." He would also never "have thought of beating or killing a child." Anyone testifying that they had seen him participating in mass shootings had to be lying, since such professed witnesses would have in fact been "the first to be shot. I saw this once myself," he noted, contradicting his assertion that he had never been present at a mass execution. At the same time, Brettschneider readily admitted that finding shooters was never a problem. "At least 30 men would have been" at the killing site, including the SS guards who "lurked around just to get the chance to participate in the shootings," while several of his Gestapo colleagues "shot Jews eagerly." As a matter of fact, "no one needed to be ordered to take part in the execution commando. There were always volunteers," and whenever one of the shooters "emptied his magazine, another one would be lying in wait for the right moment to step in." In his own testimony Peckmann pointed out that Brettschneider was in fact one of those eager shooters.

Brettschneider expressed profound contempt for his Jewish victims, whom he blamed for their own murder. Instead of joining the partisans, he exclaimed, "all the Jews stayed in the ghetto. The members of the Judenrat are guilty of this. They not only prevented their own people from fleeing, they even handed them over to the Gestapo in Czortków," while "the Jewish Ordnungsdienst, which guarded the ghetto exits, did not allow any Jew out." Similarly in Buczacz "the Jews themselves are to blame" for their annihilation, because "had the Judenrat not driven the

Jews out and betrayed their hiding places, we would not have gotten our hands on them so easily." He still could not understand why "the Jews went to the execution like sheep. . . . I shook my head over that at the time."

✡ ✡

This normalization of murder, the removal of the Jews as part of a day's work, as entertainment, as background noise to drinking bouts or amorous relationships, along with

Albert Brettschneider in 1952. *Source: GLA-K 309 Zug. 2001-42/871-6.*

puzzlement at the Jews' conduct mixed with anger at them for making it so easy to kill them—these were part and parcel of the German experience of genocide, rarely reflected in postwar representations and ruminations, let alone historiography. Different people responded to this reality, which was largely of their own making, differently. Richard Heinrich, a Gestapo official charged with supply and logistics at the outpost, testified, "Whenever I wanted something delivered in Czortków, for instance boots, I had to go to the *Judenreferent*," who "would then communicate with Thomanek" in order to have them made in the "Judenlager" (Jew camp).[48] Jewish slave labor was taken for granted: "female Jewish tailors would commonly go to the homes of the Gestapo in Czortków," where they worked for them "or for their wives." Many of the German personnel used Jewish dentists; Heinrich himself "had a dental bridge made by a Jewish dentist in the Czortków Ghetto," free of charge, of course.

And when the time came, men like Heinrich played a similarly casual role in mass murder. In February 1943, he testified, "all members of the Gestapo outpost in Czortków, including the ethnic German guards," altogether about thirty men, drove out to Buczacz at about 5:00 a.m. Heinrich positioned himself behind a desk, and all Jews seized in the city were escorted to him and had to "put their valuables on the table"; then the guards searched them "for hidden valuables, such as money sewn into their clothes." Heinrich ran a tidy operation: "On the spot I immediately registered the valuables taken from the Jews on a list," while a colleague "put the things in a cardboard box right away." There were "watches, rings, U.S. dollars, English pounds, złoty, and so forth. I listed and later brought to Lemberg valuables and money valued at 20,000 to 30,000 Reichsmarks." Because the desk was merely "100–130 feet from the execution pit," the Jews "had to undress" shortly after handing over their valuables. "I believe there was just one vast pit, which was empty at the beginning of the execution action." He personally witnessed that "several hundred Jewish men, women, and children were shot." Subsequently "the clothes of the Jews, who were shot naked in the action, were bundled up." Heinrich, who had taken care to prepare sufficient amounts of vodka and cigarettes for the shooters, recalled that on the way back "the men did not speak about the action in Buczacz." Perhaps they were tired, or drunk. The entire operation took some twelve hours.

✡ ✡

While the men from Czortków would sweep in, do their killing, and return to their base, it was the local uniformed police, usually referred to as gendarmes, who represented the daily face of German order in Buczacz. Established in August 1941, the gendarmerie post eventually numbered well over a dozen regular and reserve policemen.

Undoubtedly the most notorious gendarme in Buczacz was Sergeant Peter Pahl. Born in 1904 near Hamburg, Pahl joined the police at age twenty and spent his entire working life in uniform.[49] Married in 1930, he joined the Nazi Party in 1937, by which time he had fathered two girls. His superiors thought well of him. In August 1942 he was evaluated as a "skillful, industrious, absolutely reliable gendarme with above average intellectual capacities" and "exemplary leadership and service performance." He was awarded the Iron Cross, II Class, in April 1944 for bravery in antipartisan warfare. Briefly imprisoned at the end of the war, Pahl was back with the police soon thereafter, remaining in service until his retirement in 1964. At his judicial investigation, launched two years later, he maintained, "I am of the opinion that in the course of my life I had given my utmost." Since he suffered a stroke that left him partially paralyzed, most of Pahl's investigation was conducted in the hospital. Finally indicted for murder in 1970, Pahl died the following year, putting an end to all further judicial proceedings.

At his trial Pahl had fond memories of Buczacz and claimed to have been on good terms with everyone. He warmly recalled the Ukrainian Chorny family that often hosted him: "In the summertime I had my armchair there and often rested in the garden." He "frequently ate

Peter Pahl as policeman in Germany, likely in 1935. *Source: GLA-K 309 Zug. 2001-42/871-21.*

there in the evenings" and "played cards with the Chornys and their Ukrainian doctor acquaintance." On the weekends they would go together to the cinema, located next to the Ukrainian police station. Especially Mrs. Chorny, whose husband worked for the local German administration, "was a kindhearted friend to me, because she spoke extremely good German." Pahl denied that she was also his mistress: "I did not have a lover in the proper sense." It was a good life. At the tobacco factory in nearby Monasterzyska, where Pahl was often posted, "they gave us good liquor and vodka, as much as we wanted"; there were also cigars and "a little snack bar, where one could order garlic sausage and vodka and a kind of seltzer water. I went to this restaurant often in the evenings after work. The owner was Polish, his wife was Ukrainian."

Pahl was also, by his own account, a friend of the Jews, among whom he was "well known and respected." Described by one witness as the bloodthirsty terror of Buczacz, Pahl responded that if that were the case, the Judenrat "would not have regularly come to see me," along with "other Jews, who came to me whenever they were desperate." For instance, on his birthday in April 1942 Baruch Kramer and another Judenrat member brought him a cake: "We celebrated my birthday together in my room." Pahl also regularly visited Dr. Seifer's home, where he was "a welcome guest." The doctor's wife "would always offer me

Portuguese red wine and sardines in oil, that is, things that at the time could hardly be found." No wonder he responded with righteous indignation when the former Buczacz Landkommissar (county administrator), Walter Hoffer, stated that Pahl "did not have a good name in Buczacz regarding the handling of the Jewish population," and one of his own colleagues depicted him as a "Jew-hater." "That is incorrect," Pahl insisted. "I had very good acquaintances among the Jews." Why would a local Jewish shoemaker have made him "a pair of long sheepskin boots . . . as a present" if the man did not consider him a friend? The very notion that "the Jews feared" him was preposterous. After all, he had actually informed the Judenrat chairman about an impending roundup, and "in gratitude for my warning" the man "brought me at midnight a black garment cloth."

Pahl did concede that during that roundup of April 1943 he and the other gendarmes escorted the victims up Fedor Hill; they stopped about three hundred feet from the execution site in order to secure the area from "curious onlookers." This, he argued, proved that he "did not cooperate actively with the execution." In fact when he saw "the Jewish woman Helene," the gendarmerie station's own housemaid, "being led to the execution," he said, "I thought to myself, 'How vile.'" But despite the pleas of the gendarmerie commander, Lieutenant Johann Horak, the SS would not release her. "Inwardly," insisted Pahl, "I was very much against this. I believe that no member of the gendarmerie post would have gone along voluntarily." But although "it was entirely clear to me at the time that everything happening there was unjust," he reasoned, "had we declined to take part in an execution action ordered from above, the whole gendarmerie station would have been liquidated."

Despite such threats, Pahl declared, he tried to save Jewish lives. During the action of February 1943 he allegedly hid thirteen Jews in his room, and even served them soup prepared by the soon-to-be-murdered Helene. And although "the story leaked" and Squad Commander Willy Kießling "reproached me about it," Pahl hid yet another group of eleven

Jews in his room during the next execution action. As he saw it, he had behaved much better than the Jewish policemen, who guarded the ghetto armed with wooden clubs, "beat the Jews the most," and "hauled the Jews out of their houses." Pahl, for his part, never acted violently. "In my entire life I fired only three bullets," he insisted, and then only to kill animals when food was running low. All allegations that he had participated in mass shootings were contradictions in terms, because "had the witnesses actually been there, they . . . would have been shot with the others." Witness accusations were lies, he asserted, rooted in the ancient Jewish predilection to hurt gentiles: "The Jewish Bible contains the following literal verse: 'You should not lie to and cheat any man; [but] if he is a goy, lie to him and cheat him, so that you might harm him.'"

Jewish witnesses painted a starkly different picture. Wizinger recalled Pahl storming into a synagogue, where he "brutally and sadistically beat up the Jews who were praying there, and cut off all their beards. At the end he tore up the Torah." In winter 1942 Wizinger was one of "about fifty Jews, men and women," who were rounded up in "a street-action" led by Pahl, incarcerated in the local prison, "severely tortured," and "driven out to the prison yard naked," where they were "ordered to do gymnastics while [they] were being beaten. As a result of this abuse two people subsequently died." In February 1943, while escorting about thirty Jewish children to the killing site on Fedor Hill, Pahl encountered an elderly man on the street and ordered him to join the group. Wizinger watched as the man begged the gendarme to spare his life. "Pahl asked him: 'How old are you?' 'Fifty-years-old,' the Jew answered. Pahl laughed and said: 'Man, fifty years old and you want to go on living. Your life is already over.' Pahl then drew his pistol and shot the Jew in the back of the head." In June Wizinger was helping another older man on the street when the sergeant showed up: "Pahl asked me whether this was my father and when I said that he was not, he began joking with the Jew and suddenly drew his pistol and shot him in front of my eyes."[50]

German gendarmes with women and a child in front of the Buczacz gendarmerie building, date unknown. *Source: GLA-K 309 Zug. 2001-42/878-44.*

Rosalia Bauer was working in a pharmacy in February 1943 when she witnessed a woman she knew being escorted to the prison with her child on her shoulders: "Pahl came up from behind with a drawn weapon. . . . Suddenly I heard a shot and . . . saw how the girl . . . fell down covered in blood in front of the doors of the pharmacy." That same day she saw another group of Jews escorted to the prison; one man was carrying a five-year-old child in his arms. "Suddenly I saw . . . Pahl firing his weapon at the child, who . . . fell down and showed no signs of life." Many non-Jews too were appalled by Pahl's conduct. Adam Steiger, director of the district court in Buczacz, testified, "Practically everyone feared" Pahl, who "was known as the meanest and most brutal of the gendarmes taking part in the actions against the Jews." From the courthouse, located on the second floor of the Ukrainian police station, Steiger observed that Pahl "shot a Jew in the prison yard" as hundreds of Jews were escorted to the execution site on Fedor Hill in February 1943. That summer he watched a mass execution at the Jewish cemetery hill across town. From that distance he "could not quite identify the people, but the silhouettes were visible and one could hear the echo of the shots . . . all afternoon." He subsequently heard that Pahl had "shot Jews with his pistol from different distances as shooting practice."[51]

✡ ✡

Pahl was not the only gendarme who denied ever personally killing anyone. Bruno Grocholl, who was forty-three and the father of five children when he arrived in Buczacz, subsequently insisted that he had merely performed "general gendarmerie service." The only policeman who had anything to do with the Jews, he said, was the deputy post commander, Sergeant Georg Barg, nicknamed "Judenonkel" (Jew uncle) because "he was literally in charge of the Jews of Buczacz." Whenever Jews were required for work, "Barg would contact the Buczacz Judenrat," which would then "assemble the requested number of Jewish workers with the help of the Jewish Ordnungspolizei." Grocholl could "not believe that Barg would have beaten the Jews" and thought that generally they had little to fear from the local German policemen, since "at the time a truly comradely relationship had been established between the gendarmerie post and the Judenrat in Buczacz."[52]

But Wilhelm Eger, a thirty-eight-year-old reservist and father of two, suggested at Grocholl's investigation that his testimony was a pack of lies: "That swine Barg drank the whole time. He was a gross person. He would force the Jews coming to work to do military gymnastics and then make them stand at attention. He pounced on the Jews and did not desist from boxing their ears," for which purpose he would also "bring along his dog whip." When Barg "wanted something" from the Judenrat they "had to bring it to him" at his lodgings. Eger also entirely rejected the idea that Pahl could have hidden any Jews in his room, because "it was very dangerous" to do so. To be sure, Dr. Seifer, whom he considered "a fine Jew," did "often come to the police station" and would "occasionally ask us what did the Jews have to do with our war." In fact, Eger admitted, Seifer "got to me, because he said at the time

Bruno Grocholl (center) and Wilhelm Eger (right). *Source: GLA-K 309 Zug. 2001-42/878-121.*

that there would always remain some witnesses of our actions against the Jews." Perhaps that was why Eger helped Seifer escape one of the roundups, if we are to believe his testimony.[53]

Eger clearly correlated the occupiers' material comfort and their sheer lawlessness with impunity, stating that "whenever a new German came to Buczacz, he would be provided with Jewish furniture." Still, he too sought to distance the local police from direct participation in murder. The gendarmes merely had to "report to the Gestapo how many Jews were incarcerated in the prison," and "once a certain number was reached, the Gestapo issued instructions to the gendarmerie station by telephone that the Jewish prison inmates should be 'resettled' by the Ukrainian police." Hence, unlike mass executions, in which Jews were shot "by members of the Gestapo outpost in Czortków . . . when there were only a few Jews" in the prison they were killed "by the Ukrainian policemen." In both instances, he claimed, the local police merely had to "escort the Jews" to the "execution site." When asked specifically whether the gendarmes joined the Ukrainian police in small-scale executions, Eger responded that in summer 1943 "the Ukrainians had seized several Jews" and "agreed with the German gendarmerie station to execute" them on their own since "it was not worth the effort to bring the Gestapo from Czortków for the execution." The Germans and Ukrainians then jointly escorted the "ten to twelve Jewish men, women, and children" to the killing site. Eger knew this because he was one of the two German gendarmes at the site. But he maintained that he and his colleague played only "a supervisory role." Hence he could claim that although as German policemen they were in charge, they did not personally kill anyone.

After some initial denials, Eger admitted that the gendarmes participated in a series of roundups in Buczacz. He conceded that in one case, while searching "through Jewish houses together with a member of the Gestapo," they "found a wash basket, in which three small children were sitting. The Gestapo man ordered me to shoot the children. I said that I would not do that. He responded that he too could not do it. He then handed the children over to Jews who were just then being escorted on the street to the prison." Eger knew that those "delivered to the prison were shot shortly thereafter, if they had not already died from hunger or maltreatment by the Ukrainian police." He had in fact been to the prison during the roundup of February 1943: "What I saw there was simply unbelievable. In a single room of at most 300–400 square feet some 150 Jews were literally pressed together . . . small children and women and men." He finally admitted that he and his fellow gendarmes escorted these Jews to the execution site and observed as they undressed and were taken in groups of three or four to the pit, where they were killed with short bursts of submachine-gun fire by the Gestapo waiting there. "It went very quickly," Eger commented, "and one could observe that the Gestapo had experience in such matters."

In fact Eger had taken part in no fewer than three mass executions. One occurred near the town of Kopyczyńce (Ukrainian: Kopychyntsi), twenty-five miles east of Buczacz, likely in June 1943. While Eger claimed to have "held myself very much back," he also stated that "various gendarmes of the Czortków platoon went out of their way and were committed 150 percent" to the killing. He saw hundreds of Jewish "babies, toddlers, children and men and women. The process was very brutal and already while the Jews were being rounded up both the Sipo men and the gendarmes shot Jews." The victims were "escorted out of the town to the edge of the forest," where "many pits" had been dug; "gradually the first pit filled up with the corpses of the executed babies, children, and adults. For me," Eger commented, "the scene was so appalling that I still think about it today. The heads of the little children were in some cases completely blown off by the submachine gun salvos. Everywhere one could see spattered brains." The killing ended around noon. "We were served lunch," but Eger "could not swallow anything." Yet he saw no reason to feel guilty. "I cannot blame myself for anything," he insisted. "I took part in the action on explicit orders and within the framework of the gendarmerie platoon of Czortków, and during the action I neither mishandled nor killed Jewish people. I also took no initiative. On the contrary, I initially held myself back."

That same month Eger participated in a mass killing at the Jewish cemetery in Buczacz. Again "the German gendarmerie in Buczacz, along with the Ukrainian militia, escorted the Jews from the prison to the execution site," where "three or four members of the Gestapo" were already waiting. The gendarmes "guarded the perimeter on the top" of the hill, and "the execution pit was . . . about half way down the slope." But "whoever wanted . . . could easily go there. Several of us also did so. I personally," admitted Eger, "was only one time next to the pit." From up close he could observe how "the naked Jews had to lie on their stomachs in a row, and were then shot." The next batch "had to lie on top of the Jews who had been shot, and were shot in turn, and so on. Women and men had to lie on top of each other in the pit. Children had to jump into the pit." Eger identified Thomanek and Brettschneider among the shooters. The latter, "right after he fired, made the sign of the cross with his hand over the execution pit and said: 'May the Lord bless you!'"

A few days later Eger encountered Brettschneider on a Sunday stroll in Czortków "with his wife and two children." He recalled thinking, "Here he is still playing the family man and just a short time ago he shot innocent children and all manner of people." But as for himself, Eger was convinced that he had behaved as humanely as the circumstances warranted. He remembered that as he was walking up the hill, "a Jewish woman with a little girl ran behind me." When they reached the top, "she said to me: 'Can you please shoot my daughter, I think the Ukrainians shoot badly.' I said that I could not do this. The woman and the child ran further to the execution site and were shot." On another occasion, he was walking behind "a long row of Jews" being escorted to an execution, when he noticed "an old Jew who could not walk well. I helped him a bit, whereupon he said to me that I was a good man." In this inverted moral universe, even helping old men reach their own

Albert Brettschneider (on the left) and his wife. *Source: GLA-K 309 Zug. 2001-42/871-8.*

execution or herding little girls to their death rather than shooting them oneself could be recalled as acts of mercy.

Despite such gruesome events, or perhaps because of them, some of these men found solace in romance, or at least in a sexual liaison. Eger recalled that his colleague, the reserve gendarme Heinrich Knaack, had struck up a relationship with a Polish nurse named Iwana Kardasz, and even tried to take her with him when the Germans left Buczacz. The recently divorced thirty-eight-year-old father of a small child and veteran SA (*Sturmabteilung*) and Nazi Party member arrived in Buczacz after the deportations had already begun. In his own testimony he never mentioned Kardasz, but she remembered that on the retreat from Buczacz in 1944 he had warned her to run away because Pahl wanted to kill her. She had reason to believe this was no idle threat, since she recalled Knaack telling her that "during one action a beautiful blond Jewish pharmacist was caught with a child on her arm. Pahl told her to throw the child to the ground to save her life. The woman threw the child to the ground and Pahl immediately shot her. I think he also shot the child."[54]

Knaack did admit to taking part in three or four actions, noting that "the sequence of events was almost always the same." About twenty men "would come to Buczacz from Czortków in the early morning hours and organize these actions"; the gendarmes were "divided into teams," whose task was "to help the SD [*Sicherheitsdienst*, the SS Security Service] round up a certain number of Jews in the so-called Jewish quarter," which "was raided indiscriminately; all Jews who could be seized at that moment were rounded up," and then "mostly escorted right away to a designated site and shot there." Knaack made no attempt to conceal the horror of these events: "I saw and heard frightful things during these actions and can hardly reproduce them. Even children were not spared. They were shot along with the others." He described the killings at the Jewish cemetery in summer 1943 in terms very similar to Eger's. "I was standing about one hundred feet from the pit," he said, watching how "children and parents climbed down into the pit. The women carried their little children in their arms or hugged them and in this manner went to their death."

Staff of the Buczacz hospital, date unknown. Iwana Kardasz (née Ptasznyk) is sitting on the right in the front row. The man in the dark coat to her right is hospital secretary Ptasznyk (relation to her unknown); the woman to his right is possibly Sofia Kriegel. Other identified figures, on second row from the left: Dr. Voronka's widow; surgeon Dr. Witold Ratajski; hospital director Dr. Hamerskyi; internist Dr. Szczipaniak; Jewish pharmacist, perhaps Gisela Kleiner. Dr. Ratajski testified that in 1940–44 he "functioned as director and later as chief physician of the district hospital" in Buczacz, had seen many shootings on the city streets, and helped Jews who came to him with bullet wounds. *Source: GLA-K 309 Zug. 2001-42/878-99; BArch B162/20037, November 12, 1970, pp. 958–60.*

Like everyone else, Knaack insisted that "there was no option" to avoid participating in these murder operations. "The order was unequivocal: 'You go here and there and do this and that!' As far as I could tell, almost all available members of the Buczacz gendarmerie post participated in these actions." He also expressed a somewhat peculiar veneration for the victims he helped lead to their death: "I admired the

Jews, how calmly most of them climbed down into the pit. Some of them prayed, others sang. There were naturally also scenes that cannot be described. Before their turn came, the Jews had to wait for their end in close proximity to the pit. They could therefore see almost everything that occurred in front of and inside the pit." Clearly, like other colleagues, Knaack had availed himself of the opportunity to stand "close to the pit," where he could "see all the details of this tragic event." Yet he refused to denounce his colleagues and was careful not to incriminate himself: "In this action too I did not see members of the gendarmerie post of Buczacz killing Jewish people. The implementation of the execution was once more exclusively by the hands of the SD." And while there is no account of this by surviving Jews, he too claimed to have saved some of the condemned, twice escorting "a group of Jews" in the fall of 1943 to "the outskirts of Buczacz" so as "to facilitate their escape." Whether or not Knaack was telling the truth, he certainly belonged to the majority of security personnel who appear to have never

Members of the Buczacz gendarmerie station. *Source: GLA-K 309 Zug. 2001-42/878-155.*

suffered from a guilty conscience, however traumatized they may have been by what they had witnessed.

✡ ✡

German civilian administrators in Buczacz, while not directly involved in the killings, made up an important component of the occupation apparatus; they and their family members also constituted an intermediate link between the pretense of normality and the atrocity of mass murder. They often could, and did, live in denial of their complicity during and long after the event, and they were rarely mentioned either by the perpetrators or by the victims. But their perspective sheds light on how life was experienced and remembered by German civilians in a town that had become a site of genocide.

The first Landkommissar of Buczacz, Richard Lissberg, had all the makings of an ideal Nazi. Born in Essen in 1912, he joined the Nationalsozialistische Deutsche Arbeiterpartei (NSDAP, National Socialist German Workers' Party) in 1930, was a member of the SA, and attended elite Nazi Party training schools. In 1940 he was posted as Landkommissar to the district of Warsaw but was demoted to a minor position within the office of the commissar for Jewish affairs overseeing the Warsaw Ghetto in July 1941. A few weeks later Lissberg was appointed Landkommissar of Buczacz, charged with reviving the economic life of the city and county. But in spring 1942 he was dismissed once more and enlisted in the Wehrmacht. By the time the West German police finally questioned him in 1965, Lissberg had long been a respectable businessman in his hometown.[55]

Lissberg initially denied any participation in or knowledge of crimes committed in Buczacz. By the time he arrived, he claimed, "conditions there had already essentially normalized." The Jews "still lived in their houses," and while "they were already marked with the Jewish star" and "a Judenrat had been established," absolutely "no coercive measures against the Jews had yet been undertaken by anyone." He knew nothing "about the great Jewish execution-action" of August 1941, could remember almost no names of German officials in the region, and was

Richard Lissberg (in light-colored overcoat) with a hunting party near Brzeżany, likely in winter 1941–42. *Source: GLA-K 309 Zug. 2001-42/878-225.*

entirely oblivious of the Sipo outpost in Czortków. He did recall a few brief meetings with the Tarnopol Sipo chief Major Müller but knew "nothing about the actions that Müller undertook against the Jews."

Under further pressure Lissberg conceded that the Jews of Buczacz had in fact been moved to "a specific part of the city" known as "the Jewish quarter," but he claimed that this had happened before his arrival and that he had "absolutely no knowledge of who conducted this transfer." He also had no influence on the recruitment of Jewish workers, which, he maintained, was strictly the business of the labor office. He did now recall that a construction firm owned by Klaus Ackermann had been contracted to rebuild the railroad bridge and tunnel and that the owner's brother, Josef, was his third-floor neighbor and hunting partner. What Lissberg conveniently left out was that he had accidentally shot and killed Josef Ackermann during a hunting trip, which may well have contributed to his dismissal. No wonder he denied having "any photographs or notes that would be of interest for this investigation."

By the time he was questioned again three years later, Lissberg's memory had greatly improved, no doubt thanks to the additional evidence amassed by investigators, including the former Landkommissar's photo album. It now turned out that Major Müller had been Lissberg's classmate and neighbor in Essen, which explained their extensive socializing in Buczacz and Tarnopol. Lissberg now also vividly recalled "most members of the gendarmerie station in Buczacz," not least Pahl, whom he described as "a calm and businesslike man." The two of them, he said, "occasionally played skat" in the local "Ukrainian casino," and Pahl also often came to the Landkommissariat, where he again always "appeared very calm." The reason for this ongoing interaction was that the local police were in fact at Lissberg's disposal, as he now admitted, "to maintain order or secure the German service posts in Buczacz," although "generally" they reported to the Gestapo. Far from having no contacts with Jews, it transpired that Lissberg's own secretary was twenty-eight-year-old Julia Rabinowicz, and that he had been heavily engaged in the so-called fur collection, the mass confiscation of winter clothes from the Jews; now he even remembered that "in early 1942 the furs of the Jews collected for the Wehrmacht were stored in the building of the Landkommissariat," that is, in his own offices.

Lissberg's wife, Henriette, was far less parsimonious in providing information on his activities and on social life in Buczacz more generally. Although they divorced shortly after the war, as late as 1969 she staunchly defended her former husband as "Judenfreundlich" (friendly to Jews), insisting that this was why he lost his job in Warsaw. But her statements also unintentionally contradicted many of her husband's assertions. In stating that by the time she and their three little boys joined her husband in Buczacz in September 1941 he had already been there for a couple of months, Henriette gave reason for the court to believe that Lissberg had after all witnessed if not directly participated in the "registration action." She also clearly recalled that their third-floor neighbor Ackermann "was shot by my husband and died in the district hospital in Buczacz," just weeks before Lissberg's dismissal, which would appear to link the two events. Yet Henriette was adamant that "the Kreishauptmann [district chief] of Czortków sacked my husband" as Buczacz Landkommissar "because of his attitude toward the Jews."

Indeed according to Henriette, her husband was intensely involved with Jews. It was through him that she "got to know the Judenrat member Kramer" and the chairman Reich, since the two of them "occasionally came to my apartment to negotiate with my husband." She testified, "When it was necessary to shovel the snow in the Landkommissariat, my husband would call the Judenrat, which then sent Jews to clear the snow." Lissberg also stepped in when he perceived any signs of injustice among the Jews. On one occasion, after he had ordered the Jews to repave one of the streets in Buczacz, reported Henriette, he "found out that only the poor Jews . . . were working while the gentlemen of the Judenrat and their sons looked on." Lissberg was "so incensed" that he ordered the men of the Judenrat to immediately join the other workers. He obviously did not lack compassion; when "a young Jew was injured at work," Lissberg "personally brought him to Dr. Hamerskyi for treatment at the district hospital." But like most German administrators and civilians, he saw Jews as a cost-free and entirely dispensable labor force.

On Lissberg's efforts at urban improvement, the Ukrainian teacher Petrykevych had his own perspective, writing in April 1942, "Along the riverbank several multistoried houses have been destroyed"; these were all "Jewish houses," save for "one that belonged to the Ukrainian bank," which would "be given another house that had formerly belonged to the Jews." Finding that "the city now looks much better," Petrykevych displayed no concern about the fate of the inhabitants of those destroyed "Jewish houses." Indeed he recalled that at the beginning of German rule the Landkommissar had not allowed the Ukrainian district administration, of which Petrykevych was a member, "to issue a proclamation to the population that would have underscored the liberation of the people from Jewish exploitation"; now it appeared that Lissberg was finally moving in the right direction. But that was clearly not enough, and people in the city were complaining "that the Jews had again bribed some influential person, and that is why there is no ghetto here, and the Jews are free to go as they please."[56]

Henriette adopted the same attitude as her husband. Jewish women came to clean the apartments in her building two or three times a week: "We paid them with groceries. I still remember one Jewish woman named Klara and her sister Emma, who occasionally came to clean for me." At times "up to ten Jewish women would report to us for house-cleaning" in the morning "and wait to be assigned a job. The Jewish women liked coming to us because they could be sure that on that day they would be given food." To the German civilians it soon appeared not only self-evident that they should be served by eager, half-starved, and terrified Jewish women, but that by exploiting their labor the Germans were actually helping them out. This also meant that German civilians got to know many of the Jews before they were murdered. In early 1942, for instance, the Lissbergs hosted the governor of Galicia, Otto Wächter, for dinner. Henriette remembered that when he "saw a woodcut horse in our son Udo's room," he asked the boy "who had

Jewish houses along the Strypa River that were later torn down on Landkommissar Richard Lissberg's orders because they were "full of rats and vermin." *Source: GLA-K 309 Zug. 2001-42/878-213.*

made him such a beautiful horse." The boy whispered in the governor's ear that it was carved "by our Jew Reinstein, who was a cabinetmaker." Reinstein was shot shortly thereafter.[57]

Following Lissberg's recruitment to the Wehrmacht, Henriette moved to a villa near the Ukrainian police station, on the road leading to Fedor Hill. Klara and Emma also came "to clean [her] new house," which was renovated for her by "several Jews and Poles," as well as some Ukrainians. It was not a bad life; when "the Jew Friedländer replaced the Pole Stein as my houseboy," she said, he also "brought our horses, which my husband had purchased in the market in Buczacz, to the stable of the new house." Friedländer worked for her at least until the city was declared *Judenfrei* (free of Jews) in June 1943. "I do not know," she remarked, "how Friedländer survived the persecution of the Jews." But she did "warn Friedländer" of imminent danger because "it was always known in advance that a roundup was about to take place"; on such days "Friedländer did not have to come to me," and he "clearly also warned other Jews of the threat of a roundup. After the roundup was over the Jews would thank me and also bring me presents, such as once, for instance, a cake." In October 1943, while she was visiting her husband in Lemberg, someone broke into the villa and stole "various coats and so forth." For safety, Henriette and her children moved to an apartment located over the post office in the center of town. "My maid told me at the time that the break-in was by a Jew," obviously one of the few survivors still hiding in the area and in need of warm clothing. Henriette remained in the new apartment until March 1944, when Lissberg returned to evacuate his family just before the Red Army marched in.

Yet Henriette also had extensive contacts with the local German police, including Peter Pahl. Initially she claimed that he "was always polite to me" and that she was "unaware of rumors in Buczacz about Pahl's conduct toward the Jews." Confronted with testimony by her former servant Friedländer, Henriette recalled that she had in fact berated "several gendarmes in the German gendarmerie building that it was not necessary to shoot down the Jews" (*die Juden über den Haufen zu schießen*). Kießling, the squad commander, had agreed with her, "repeatedly" saying "that what was being done to the Jews was not right." But Pahl was in a very different state of mind. In fact, she admitted, he was "feared by the Jews in Buczacz"; her own "Jewish cleaning girls," she now remembered, "often told me about this Pahl," who "would strike Jews on the street or even Jews employed in the gendarmerie station with his whip." Once, when she hosted the gendarmes in her home, Kießling again "agreed with me that one should not persecute the Jews," while another gendarme argued that "had Hitler not persecuted the Jews, with their help the German Reich would have been larger than it had ever been." But Pahl insisted "that when a Jew did not work fast enough one had to step in and give him a beating."

Henriette's testimony gives us a glimpse into the surreal mix of horror and normality in German-ruled Buczacz. For close to three years it was the home of several German families, complete with wives and children, parents and lovers, catered to by a host of household servants and workers, many of them Jewish. These tidy German homes were an

Henriette Lissberg with Ukrainian policemen in the Buczacz police station's courtyard, date unknown. *Source: GLA-K 309 Zug. 2001-42/878-215.*

The bridge to the monastery and Fedor Hill overlooked by the Lissbergs' apartment (with balcony), date unknown. *Source: GLA-K 309 Zug. 2001-42/878-149, 224.*

island of normality floating on an ocean of blood; one could peer out of the window and watch the horror, or chat about the killings over coffee and cake, card games and beer. Henriette recalled that when still living with her husband in a first-floor apartment facing the Strypa, they had lively social exchanges with Nazi higher-ups. Hermann Müller, the

Gestapo chief from Tarnopol, was a welcome guest; after all, Henriette "too, just like my husband, had attended the same school" as Müller, who "came with his driver to visit us in Buczacz shortly after Christmas 1941–42" and again later "three or four times." The Lissbergs in turn "often went to Tarnopol," where Henriette "got to know several more Gestapo men." Of course she knew "for certain" that Müller had "conducted execution actions" in the region; she had heard this from "the chairman of the Judenrat in Buczacz, Reich." But none of that could dampen the renewed friendship between these old classmates.[58]

Having already been exposed to numerous acts of violence on the streets of Buczacz, Henriette said that when she visited her husband in his training camp, he "dissuaded me from watching any more round-ups." But in fact it was impossible not to witness the killings in the city. One winter's day, she testified, "my nursemaid Ursula Wolf came from the city and told me that a roundup was taking place, and that I should not let the children out of the house. One could also hear sporadic shots from the direction of the town." Later in the afternoon, "I could observe

View from the Lissbergs' balcony of the market square with the Jewish cemetery hill in the background. *Source: GLA-K 309 Zug. 2001-42/878-148.*

the Jews being escorted up the hill past the Ukrainian police station and my house. I was standing by my door about sixty feet from the column of Jews." The distance "to the actual execution site" was a mere "10–15 minute" walk "from my house." There were "men, women, and children of all ages." Once "the Jews reached the hill, one could hear shots." Later that day, Henriette's "maid noted that the tap water had a strange smell and appearance"; it turned out that "the water was polluted by the mass grave" on the hill, and residents were instructed "to use only soda water for the next few days." This was the third action, of February 1943.

In April that year Henriette woke up one morning to the sound of shots and decided to take her children to the home of her friend Dr. Hamerskyi, located "near the train station," so that "they would not hear anything." But on the way they encountered "uniformed people rounding up the Jews." There was "an old couple escorted by a Jewish policeman holding a kind of rubber truncheon in his hand," and "a very young lad in a green uniform escorting a Jewish family with three children down the stairs of the old pharmacy" with "a fire-ready weapon on his hip." Once again "the Jews were shot on the hill behind my new house next to the Ukrainian militia." A few weeks later, "my son Klaus came home around lunchtime and told me that he had seen a dead Jewish woman lying on the ground, who had already been in the same spot in the morning." She went back with him to the pedestrian bridge next to the Sokół building, where she found "the body of a dead Jewish woman, about 30–35 years old, lying on her back with open eyes. It was a frightful sight. . . . She had a bloody wound over her right ear. I hurried back to the house with my boy." Just then, as she looked out of the window, Henriette saw "a Jewish woman running through the park behind my house . . . pursued by men in uniform." Not long thereafter they were woken up by the sound of gunfire; it was reported to Henriette by a Polish neighbor that her tailor, Mrs. Reich, "who was about to make suits for my children" and "had a dress I had given her to alter," was being held in the Ukrainian police station. Henriette appealed "to the Gestapo official who was standing on the Strypa bridge," and he agreed to help her "look for my Jewish tailor." There were "some twenty Jews" in the prison, "men, women, and children," including

Top: Richard, Henriette, and Klaus Lissberg in their villa; the road is across the wooden fence. Bottom: The Ukrainian police station and the road leading to the Fedor Hill execution site. *Source: GLA-K 309 Zug. 2001-42/878-218, 214.*

Reich and others Henriette "also recognized." The tailor would not leave without "her sister, brother, and husband," and eventually the Gestapo official released them and several children and craftsmen. Henriette identified the official as Köllner, saying he had "a friendly face."

Some German civilians came to Buczacz neither as part of the security apparatus nor as members of the civilian administration. They too were witnesses of mass murder, even as they maintained social relations with the killers and became acquainted with many of the victims. Some of them were horrified by what they saw, others became willing spectators, and still others joined in. Most adapted to the routine of daily killings and resumed their normal lives after the war without further ado.

Ewald and Berta Herzig arrived in Buczacz with their baby girl in early 1942.[59] Their Jewish maid, a twenty-eight-year-old former hairdresser named Blond, also took care of their baby. They kept her for a while after domestic Jewish labor was forbidden, "because," as Herzig put it, "even

Left to right: Henriette Lissberg, Ewald Herzig, and Ursula Wolf skiing next to the railroad bridge construction site. *Source: GLA-K 309 Zug. 2001-42/878-217.*

the German gendarmerie station continued to employ Jews." When the roundups began in the fall of 1942, he "always sent her away so that she could hide." Herzig was well aware of the violence that surrounded their cozy bourgeois existence. Testifying in 1969, he vividly recalled Pahl, who "stood out" as "a bully" and "drank a great deal. I was afraid of this fellow myself," because "when he was drunk he brawled in the street and played the strongman." Pahl "took part in Jewish actions not only under orders but also voluntarily." In October 1942, as he set out for his office in the train station, Herzig witnessed the first deportation. After following a column of some seven hundred Jews escorted by armed Ukrainian and German policemen from the market square to the station, he watched as the Jews were "shoved . . . kicked and flogged into the railcars." It was said "that the Jews would be taken to Rawa-Ruska," where "there was a gassing facility." That was in fact the last stop before the Bełżec extermination camp. One harrowing scene was imprinted on his mind: "a light-blond, picture-pretty girl of about 16," was standing next to a family that had been "sorted out" and spared deportation because the father was a chemist. "The Gestapo men asked me whether she too belonged to that family," he testified, "but since the girl denied it, and although the railroad cars had already been sealed, she was thrown into a car that had been re-opened and was also deported." On other occasions Jews he knew simply disappeared: "In our casino in the Buczacz train station we had a Jewish woman named Steffi, who did the cleaning. One day I came to the casino and heard that . . . Steffi had been taken away by the Gestapo."

His wife, Berta, denied ever seeing a roundup in Buczacz, although their third-floor windows looked out onto the Ukrainian police station, the Basilian monastery, and Fedor Hill just beyond, an excellent vantage point to observe the killings. She also recalled taking walks with her husband and child in the "large open meadow" at the top of the road leading to the hill. But when told that "executions took place on these heights," she declared emphatically, "I know nothing about that." What she could report in some detail was the daily life of German civilians in Buczacz. She recalled frequently shopping at the butcher's on the ground floor and at the grocery across the street, and buying fresh

The Buczacz train station during the German occupation. *Source: GLA-K 309 Zug. 2001-42/878-140.*

vegetables, butter, and milk from a nearby farm and at the local dairy. On market days in town, Berta said, "I would take along our Jewish woman Blond because I could not understand the people there." She added, "When I left our apartment together with my husband, the Jewish woman Blond stayed . . . to take care of the child"; in fact Blond had "practically taken up the role of a nanny." Blond "also used to bring me milk from the dairy, which was a little outside town," and, not to be dismissed in a small town with limited services, "she also did my hair" as well as going "to Frau Lissberg as a hairdresser." Typically the maid "would come to our apartment at 8 a.m. and leave at about 2 p.m." The only inconvenience occurred when there were "roundups in Buczacz, during which she would hide." Even after it became "forbidden to employ Jewish women in the household," in July 1942, Blond still "came on an hourly basis to do my hair, bring me milk and also to take care of our child when I wanted to go out with my husband." But this free service could not last forever. Berta heard that "the Jewish woman Blond fled to Hamburg and was brought back and shot."

✧ ✧

Many German employees of the Ackermann construction firm, which exploited Jewish forced labor for work on the railroad tunnel and bridge, witnessed the mass killings in Buczacz. A number of them appear to have participated in one way or another in the roundups, whether by looting abandoned Jewish homes or by watching the killings at close range; some may have even made use of their weapons.[60]

To be sure, such eyewitnesses tended to admit their morbid curiosity only under pressure. Perhaps they were ashamed; more likely they feared prosecution. Matthias Schinagl initially denied categorically ever carrying a gun or witnessing any roundups.[61] Later he relented, admitting that he had not only carried a weapon but also participated "with my work comrades" in "military exercises" supervised by "the German gendarmerie." He then conceded that he had watched "a Jewish action" on the cemetery hill "from a distance of 1,500–2,000 feet," where "Jews were shot into" a trench. Asked whether he was "present at the Jewish

Berta Herzig having drinks with a German official in Buczacz. *Source: GLA-K 309 Zug. 2001-42/878-209.*

cemetery when a large-scale execution action took place there," Schinagl finally blurted out, "Yes, we were there once. I can remember. Jews were being shot. I cannot say precisely how many Jews were shot. I also cannot confirm the date. I don't know who shot the Jews. We did not stand that close. I don't know whether the Jews were shot into a trench. At the time the Jews at the cemetery were naked."

Adolf Eichmann famously said at his trial in Jerusalem, "Remorse is for little children." He promised instead to write a book that would explain the "final solution," but this project was cut short by his execution.[62] For those who had lived through a daily routine of genocide, observing from nearby the systematic murder of men, women, and children, partying with their killers, benefiting from their services, occasionally helping them out or even befriending them, at other times denouncing, robbing, or killing them, their capacity to emerge into the postwar era with a clean conscience was nothing short of astonishing.

In the face of the decades-long postwar silence, denial, and complete lack of remorse that characterized most German defendants and witnesses from the Czortków-Buczacz region, it bears reiterating the public and nonchalant nature of the killings and the perpetrators' sense of impunity and omnipotence, their absolute power over life and death. Karl Ritter, general director of the tobacco factory in Monasterzyska during most of the German occupation, recalled two decades later how one evening in July 1942 "an SS-Hauptsturmführer [captain] came to me and disclosed that tomorrow an action against the Jews would begin. He also asked me to participate in the action. I explained to him that the next day I had to take care of urgent business in Lemberg."[63] When Ritter returned the following evening the secretary of the Judenrat "came to ask me if I would give him vodka and cigarettes," which he needed "for the gentlemen who had unleashed the action." The cost of such items, explained Ritter, "was regularly paid for by the Judenrat." He had missed the killing. "Even the bodies had already been taken away. The Jews were in cattle cars at the train station and were roaring like animals. I saw that train myself. Later on there were many more actions against the Jews." Ritter vividly remembered Pahl: "He came to me one day and said that he had just killed his two-thousandth Jew."

Ritter's Polish employee and future wife, Sophie, also witnessed several pogroms, as she referred to them: "The Jews were hunted on the streets like rabbits. Fleeing Jews were shot on the spot. Those who let themselves be captured were brought into the ghetto." In summer 1942, as she drove into Buczacz in the tobacco factory's vehicle, they "had to dodge" the "numerous bodies on the street." Several months later she saw German gendarmes and Ukrainian policemen escorting Jews toward the Jewish cemetery in Monasterzyska. "Because I was curious I went up to the second floor of the factory and observed the cemetery with binoculars." The Jews "were being taken in pairs to the cemetery. A large trench had already been excavated there. They had to take off all their clothes and were then shot in the back of the head on the rim of the trench. They fell directly into the trench." One day Pahl, who commanded the gendarmes in Monasterzyska, came into the factory office where Sophie worked with another woman, named Jakubowski. "He held out his hand to Mrs. Jakubowski and said, 'Today I killed my 1,200th Jew.' "[64]

✡ ✡

While estimates vary considerably, it appears that in the course of two years well over 10,000 Jews were shot in Buczacz or deported to the Bełżec extermination camp. In the first major action, on October 17, 1942, approximately 1,600 Jews were taken to Bełżec and several hundred killed on the streets and in their homes. On November 27 another 2,000 Jews were deported to Bełżec or shot on the spot. The following month a ghetto was established; the crowded conditions and lack of sanitation, food, and medication led to a typhus epidemic that claimed an unknown number of lives. Killings included a "street action" in which Jews were shot in the ghetto or taken to Czortków, where many died. In the third action, on February 2, 1943, an additional 2,000 Jews were shot on Fedor Hill; 3,000 more were murdered at that site on April 15. The last two mass executions took place at the Jewish cemetery: the "liquidation action" of May 27 targeted the remaining population of the ghetto, and the "*Judenrein* [Jew-cleansing] action" of June 26 attempted to wipe out the inmates of the labor camp and the Jewish police. During the next few months those who survived were hunted down relentlessly. Most of the few hundred Jews who emerged from hiding when the Red Army briefly occupied Buczacz on March 23, 1944, were murdered following the town's reoccupation by the Wehrmacht on April 7. By the time the Soviets returned for good on July 21, fewer than a hundred Jews were still alive in the area.[65]

Most of the perpetrators managed to wriggle out of a leaky judicial system and died peacefully in their beds. As this most thoroughly investigated state-directed mass crime in history amply illustrates, perpetrators of genocide usually get away with murder. Especially since the late 1950s, West German courts have performed an exceedingly important service for history by investigating the crimes of thousands of former Nazi perpetrators; at the same time, however, they committed a no less remarkable miscarriage of justice, allowing the vast majority of those investigated, who were in any case just the tip of the iceberg, to get off without penalty. The documentary evidence the courts amassed made it possible to reconstruct the crime, but precisely in view of its scale and nature one cannot but be appalled by the vast gap between the crime and the punishment. Willi Dressen, former director of the Central Office of the State Justice Administration for the Investigation of National Socialist Crimes in Ludwigsburg, calculated that by 2005, 106,000 people had been investigated for Nazi crimes, of whom only 6,500 were sentenced and only 166 received life sentences. "Purely statistically," he wrote, this meant that "each murder cost ten minutes in prison."[66]

The most striking feature of the men who murdered the Jewish community of Buczacz was the seemingly unbridgeable discrepancy between their mundane prewar and postwar lives and the astonishing brutality, callousness, and disdain for humanity they displayed during the occupation. German courts tried to make sense of this moral abyss; they sought the seeds of these men's criminality in their parental and educational background, religious and political affiliations, ethnic identity, and traits of character. In order to convict them of first-degree murder, the judges had to be convinced that the defendants were capable of distinguishing between good and evil and had chosen to act criminally out of "base motives," such as sexual lust, greed, or ideologically driven hatred, especially anti-Semitism—that they had, that is, acted on their own initiative, beyond the murderous orders given them by their superiors. Much of the evidence for these crimes came from Jewish witnesses. In this case the courts had to be reassured that these survivors were not motivated by a desire for revenge and could dispassionately yet vividly recall the crimes to which they testified and which they had often experienced themselves. The surreal nature of these investigations and trials was therefore derived from the fact that even as they reconstructed events of the utmost cruelty and barbarism, they were conducted in an atmosphere of rigidly enforced detachment, imposing a suspension of the very human sensibilities that might have prevented the atrocity in the first place. This is why we must listen closely to the voices of the victims.

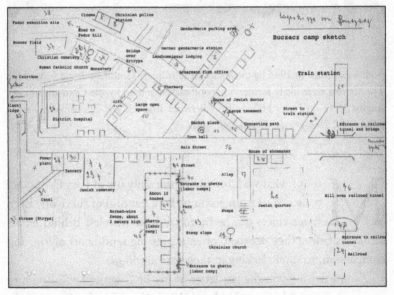

Schematic map of Buczacz in late spring 1943, as sketched for postwar German trials. *Source: GLA-K 309 Zug. 2001-42-869-Skizze.*

Chapter 6

Bodies exhumed in 1944 by the Soviet Extraordinary Commission on Fedor Hill. The victims were likely former Soviet officials executed by the Germans in early August 1941 on Fedor Hill, halfway between Buczacz and Żyznomierz. *Source: HDA SBU, Ternopil, spr. 30466, appendices.*

Most of what we know about the daily life of Jews in Buczacz comes to us from accounts by a handful of survivors. Even fewer voices can be heard of those who left behind letters or diaries before they perished, often expressing sentiments of love and compassion, so sorely lacking in their surroundings.

"I am writing you the last letter of my life," wrote Leon Rosen to his remaining children on October 4, 1943, "because after four months of squatting in a goat pen with three goats—it is impossible to stand up here—I must hand myself in to the Gestapo and ask them to shoot me, as I can . . . no longer endure these conditions. I have only suffered in the hope that I would perhaps still see you, but sadly I have no more strength."

In February that year the Rosen family was ordered into the ghetto of Buczacz and found room in the house of a former school director. "It was there that your beloved dear Mother was discovered and shot together with the Balin family in the hallway [of the house] on April 13, 1943," wrote Rosen. "The beloved Francia, your dear sister, was also discovered there and along with many hundreds of others was shot on the Fedor and thrown into a mass grave." Other friends and family members were murdered in quick succession: "Zosia Rosenman with her father and sister" were ordered to move to the town of Tłuste (Ukrainian: Tovste), twenty-five miles southeast of Buczacz, but "were killed on the way. Those who remained here in Buczacz were taken to the Fedor and shot," including "our beloved Frydzia Lipka and all her children." In September "the parents of the beloved Malka were found in a bunker in the city . . . and sadly shot, along with the beloved Lelka." As for Rosen himself, "I was in a forest and was robbed and stabbed by bandits, all I have left is the shirt I am wearing, without any other clothes, not a penny, I must go and report myself so as to put an end to my life. Dear children, stay healthy and many kisses, your Father, Leon."[1]

Children too found themselves isolated and alone. "Dear Daddy," wrote Duzio R. from his hiding place near Tłuste, "I am really surprised that you have not written me anything. . . . Must I add worries about you to my own misfortune and that awful wait for death?" It appears that the father was either in Buczacz or Czortków. Duzio was also taking care of his younger sister, Klara: "Our suffering is unbelievable. I cannot see any solution, and I have actually resigned myself to the thought that I will die. The only thing that breaks my heart is the thought that I may cause you trouble. Despite all my efforts, I have not been able to find any place for Klara. This girl is an angel. She begs me insistently to go to you. But my conscience will not allow me to leave her alone when she is in need." The children were hiding in a Polish village. "Yesterday there was much panic. Many militiamen came to Tłuste. We were sure there would be an action. We spent the night in the field and almost froze to death. I am ill. . . . My bones are aching terribly, but that's nothing. I cannot spend the night in the village, because the Poles themselves are afraid. Everyone is shattered. . . . I wish I could see you again." But the children likely never found their father. As their situation became increasingly desperate, Duzio reported, "Klara asks God to cut short our suffering." He too was losing hope. "I am begging you again," the boy wrote his father, "do **save us**." As the children fled to ever more remote villages, conditions kept deteriorating. "Here it's a real hell, indescribable dirt, hunger, poverty. There's no place to sleep, there's nothing to eat. . . . We are both begging for death. On top of all that misfortune, our guardian here," the peasant sheltering them, "demands money for keeping us. . . . If only I could find some place for Klara here. Please save me, otherwise I will die." Duzio and Klara were probably killed just days before the Red Army arrived. They were just two of thousands of Jewish children hunted down like animals, separated from their parents and desperately clinging to each other. In Duzio's possession was a letter from his friend Giza Hausner in Czortków: "I am here all alone, without Mama, without any money and belongings. Help me if you can. . . . We are waiting for the end at any moment. . . . You are my last hope. Do something for me if only you can."[2]

✡ ✡

Some parents sought safety for their children by handing them over to gentiles. Hiding with his wife, Malwina, near Buczacz in summer 1943, Aryeh Klonicki (previously known as Leon Klonymus) began feverishly writing an account of their life under German occupation. The roundups began just weeks after their baby, Adam, was born. Even then Klonicki was aware that the deported "would be burned in special crematoria," writing, "Every time I looked at my little child, so beautiful and full of life, I would imagine that I was seeing not a child but a box filled with ashes." He had witnessed multiple murders of children by the Germans, who found it easiest to fulfill their "task . . . in the hospitals and shelters for children. They would simply walk in and shoot the sick in their beds and throw the children out of the windows of the upper floors." At the execution sites "they no longer kill the children; they bury them alive (sparing bullets)." The Judenrat, on which Klonicki had served in an administrative position, as well as the Jewish police "made a fortune from the torments of the Jews and lived by the slogan: 'Eat and drink, for tomorrow we shall die!'" Appalled by the "many Jewish policemen who were renowned for their cruelty," who accepted "bribes from those taken to camps," and would "search through the clothes of the murdered and find dollars and valuables," he depicted this period as "a new chapter in our Golgotha: degrading Jewish morality to the lowest depths."

Once Buczacz was declared Judenrein, the remaining Jews sought "shelter in bunkers, among the Christians, in the fields. Had it not been for the hatred of the local inhabitants," insisted Klonicki, "it might have been possible to hide." Instead "every shepherd, every Christian child who sees a Jew, immediately reports him to the authorities and they go looking for him. Some Christians hide Jews for a lot of money and then rob their property and denounce them to the authorities." The Klonickis had given their possessions to a Christian woman in Buczacz in return for a hideout in her mother's village, but as soon as they arrived there they were robbed of all their remaining belongings. As a last resort they turned to Malwina's former Polish maid Franka Wąsik and her husband, Stanisław, who agreed to care for the baby, while Aryeh and Malwina hid in their cornfield. Crouching in the high corn, they could hear the men talking just a few feet from them "about peasants who made a fortune from Jews and are buying themselves the most expensive suits." On July 8 two dozen Jews were discovered in three different bunkers nearby and shot, and shortly thereafter the informer Nahajowski, who had "stepped up in his public stature to become a Jew-catcher," denounced several Jews hiding in the same village as the Klonickis. "Usually the work is done now by the Ukrainian policemen themselves," Aryeh noted. The Germans had "killed enough and do not go looking for Jews"; they depended on "such types as Nahajowski to bring them the prey."

On July 18 the Klonickis were spotted by a peasant and had to bribe him not to give them away. Fearing the worst, Malwina wrote her family, "I would like so much to raise my beloved child. . . . Perhaps you will be entrusted with raising him, and perhaps . . . the cruel hand of the murderers will reach him. . . . Will God have mercy on such a tiny and innocent being?" That same day Aryeh raged in his diary, "As if the hatred of an enemy such as Hitler were not enough, added to it is the hatred of the surrounding population, which knows no boundaries. Millions of Jews have been slaughtered and yet it is not satiated!" His last diary entry was dated July 22, 1943: "All night it rained and again in the morning . . . we were lying in a swamp." According to the Wąsiks, Aryeh and Malwina were murdered on January 18, 1944, most likely by Ukrainians. Before being evacuated to Poland, the Wąsiks handed Adam over to local Ukrainian nuns, who baptized him Taras; raised in an orphanage, the child's whereabouts could not be established for many years. But in 1962 Aryeh's brother in Israel received a letter from Western Ukraine. Taras, it tersely noted, "lives in the Lviv province, but . . . does not want his origin to be known. . . . He thinks of himself as Ukrainian, and is ashamed that his uncle lives in Israel. In my opinion, his uncle should give up the matter."[3]

Another rescued baby was Emil Skamene, subsequently a distinguished professor of medicine at McGill University in Canada, who spent the first twenty-seven years of his life believing he was the son of a Christian family from Prague. Shortly after coming to Harvard on a postdoctoral fellowship in 1968, Skamene received a letter informing him that in fact he was born in Buczacz, whence he was brought to Prague as a baby, together with "some material goods, like money and some gold and gifts," by a certain Rudolf Steiger. The letter was written by Steiger's recently widowed second wife, clearly in the hope of sharing some of the baby's inheritance. Having confirmed this story with his adoptive parents, Emil discovered that he was born in 1941 as the only child of Benio and Gisela Kleiner. His father, an accountant, had attended the Buczacz gymnasium, and his mother was a pharmacist.[4]

At the time of his rescue in early 1943, Emil and his parents were hiding in a Ukrainian peasant's cellar near Buczacz. Afraid that they might be denounced or killed, Benio wrote to his sister Frederika, who had studied medicine in Prague before the war and was living there with her husband, Richard Skamene, asking her "to do something to save" the baby. She in turn asked Steiger, an ethnic German who had "some function in the SS," to bring Emil to Prague for a fee that would be provided by the Kleiners. After two failed attempts Steiger managed to extract the baby from the cellar and take it all the way to Prague by train hidden in a backpack. Emil had been trained to keep silent; years later he recalled his father taping his mouth so that he could breathe only through his nose.

Raised as the Skamenes' natural son, Emil observed that throughout his childhood and youth Steiger "always appeared when something was happening to me" but "was always not introduced." Emil had no inkling of his Jewish origins: "I was even chasing Jewish boys on the street and I was yelling at them 'dirty Jew' as all of my other classmates [were doing] after the war." Later he found out that his mother "was celebrating all the high Jewish holidays in the synagogue in Prague," although "at home we were brought up as Christians." Even after he learned that his mother was Jewish, he was certain that his adoptive father "was a Christian" who had "helped my mother survive," which he "always thought was very heroic" and "an act of love." Only at the end of her husband's life did Frederika tell Emil that he too was a Jew.

Emil believed that although Steiger "originally did it for money," the act of rescuing a baby was such "an emotional and spiritual experience" that it became "important for him" to see the child "growing up and achieving something." This act also ended up benefiting Steiger in a more immediate manner. After the war, Emil pointed out, this former collaborator "would likely be killed by the Czechs" had it not been for "an affidavit from my parents" attesting that he had saved a Jewish baby. In that sense, Steiger had "lived his life basically in exchange for this unbelievable act of heroism." To be sure, he was also given all the money that came with the baby, except for a golden cigarette case that Emil's parents had "expressly wanted me to have as a memory of them." Ironically it was rumors about the riches that came with the baby that ultimately led Emil to discover his real identity. He also learned that his parents' fears were justified: they were apparently murdered by the Ukrainian peasant who hid them and wanted to put his hands on the rest of their money and the single fur coat they owned.[5]

Very few other babies and toddlers born in Buczacz and its vicinity are known to have survived. One of them was Jacob Neufeld, later an American historian and director of the U.S. Air Force Historical Studies Office. Jacob was born in 1940 as the son of the communist activist Natan Dunajer, who led a Jewish resistance group during the German occupation and was killed in April 1944. Jacob still recalled his father showing off his submachine gun when he visited the family's hiding place. Eventually they were denounced, and Jacob had nightmarish recollections of being a four-year-old running away from "wild shooting."[6]

Several small children survived with false identities and remained unknown to the rest of the Jews in Buczacz. In 1942, when Anita Karl was four years old, her mother, Mali, a fluent Polish speaker, took her, an older sister, and a baby girl out of the Lemberg ghetto, tore off their Jewish stars, and boarded the train to Buczacz. There Mali presented herself to the Roman Catholic priest as the wife of a Polish officer whose papers were lost in an aerial bombing. Having acquired false documents, they stayed in Buczacz for the next two years. Mali baked and peddled cakes, and with the income managed to bring her husband, Samuel, from the ghetto, though because of his accent and Jewish appearance he hid in their cellar. From their house, perched on a hill, the children could observe the killings all around them. During one action, a Jewish youth was discovered nearby. Anita recalled, "They shot him right in front of me. . . . The blood splattered all over the window and he died there." In summer 1943 a large bunker with scores of Jews was discovered in the vicinity of their home. Anita saw "how they pulled the people out through a hole by their hair, ripping it out in the process; the screams and shouts were horrible." Her mother was standing close by, and "one of the women pushed a little bundle toward her; it was a baby. As my mother bent down to pick it up, the Nazi [policeman] saw her and pulled out a gun and pointed it at her, saying that if she picked it up, he would shoot her. He took the baby out [of the bundle] and in front of everyone ripped it in half. The rest of the babies were beaten against the cement wall, and the adults were taken away and killed."

In March 1944 Mali and the girls were evacuated from Buczacz with the rest of the civilian population, leaving the father in the cellar. Seeking to save him, Mali returned a few hours later, claiming she needed warm clothes for the children. It was too late; Samuel had been discovered and was executed shortly thereafter. He was thirty-three years old.[7]

While children could evoke sympathy, they were just as often seen as a liability and were always vulnerable to deception, exploitation, and murder. Renia Tabak recalled hiding in a bunker in Buczacz in 1942; she was six and her sister was three. "Before long we heard screaming and shooting and dogs and looting in our house. First the Germans came, screaming, '*Juden, Juden raus, raus!*' . . . We knew, not a word, not a sneeze, not a cough, because then you could be heard and it would be instant death." Renia's cousin Danny "was not silent and complained. People said, 'Put a pillow on him and choke him,' and everyone agreed, there were eighty people there, and they began to put a pillow on him and he was smart and stopped crying." Once "the Germans were finished came the Ukrainians and the Poles, looting and taking everything out of the house and calling '*żyd, żyd!*' Then you came out and found a bloodbath in your house, outside the door, in the street, bodies everywhere." In one such roundup her aunt "ripped up the feather blanket and put the kids under the feathers, but they found one of her limbs sticking out and shot her and then found the kids and shot them too."

Because Jewish life was so cheap and readily available, perpetrators could afford to show gallantry in the midst of slaughter, especially toward elegant and well-educated young women. During one roundup

Renia successfully evaded the Gestapo and reached the bunker, but the rest of her family was caught. Shortly thereafter "my parents and sister arrived; due to Mother's perfect German she talked them out of [killing the family]. She said to them: 'You are going to get us sooner or later. My little daughter is gone. Let us live another day or two.'" Renia's mother, Sala, was "educated and classy," a graduate of the Buczacz gymnasium. In summer 1943 they were stopped again on the street in their hometown of Skala, forty miles southeast of Buczacz, this time by regular soldiers. "My mother asked them to let us go just for this day. And the German said, '*Gehen Sie, Gehen Sie*' [Go, go], and closed his eyes." As Renia saw it, whereas the Ukrainians "could tell who were the Jews . . . the ones who saved our lives were the Germans," because her "mother was a lady and would not throw herself at them but reason with them and this way she got us out."

At other times, none of this mattered. In summer 1943 Renia and her family were hiding in a field of tobacco when she woke to "terrible screaming and curses in Ukrainian." "The Ukrainian militia . . . were chasing the Jews with dogs and we heard this rampage and started running . . . blindly for our lives. . . . It was the scariest thing I can remember, we saw dismembered bodies, bodies without heads and . . . death all around us." They were saved by the locals, hidden in a pit under the barn of a Polish peasant who had worked for Renia's father before the war. "No one could stand up" in the pit and it was "full of rats and other vermin. . . . When the [farm] animals urinated the urine would spill into the hole." But for Renia "*stara pani*, the old Polish woman, was truly a saintly and wonderful human being who risked her life and that of her daughters." She gave them seven dumplings stuffed with potatoes or cabbage every Sunday and "very little in-between." It almost ended happily, but in April 1944, while escaping the German reoccupation of the region after a brief period of Soviet rule, Renia's little sister was killed by shrapnel. When she finally returned to her liberated hometown that summer, Renia had little room for pity. She remembered going "for our entertainment to the hangings . . . of collaborators in the municipality. . . . We saw them strung up and urinating and I'd be in heaven." For the rest of her life she suffered from neuroses, was terrified of the dark, disliked being surrounded by people, and would choose "to sit at the end [of a row of chairs], for a quick escape."[8]

In the immediate aftermath of the liberation surviving children were often still deeply traumatized. Interviewed in 1946, ten-year-old Genia Weksler recalled hiding in a bunker in Buczacz during a roundup: "I was suffering from German measles," and the others "wanted to strangle me because I was coughing." Later she was sheltered with her mother and four-year-old brother by a peasant "who hid us under a thatched roof and brought us food." Then the Germans arrived and "looked for grain" precisely "where we were hiding. I closed my eyes so that I would not see how the Germans beat me. But the Germans threw the whole thatched roof on me and did not find us." Throughout this time, she said, "I was very afraid of people; I always wanted to be alone. I dreamed of food. Oh, I envied Polish children: 'Why is God punishing us, for which sins,' I thought." At some point they tried to pass as Christians. "The Poles said that we were insane people. A German gave me bread and a blanket." Toward the end of the occupation Genia worked in a remote village. "I grazed cattle. I didn't like playing with children. I was afraid. I didn't speak Polish very well. In the house they often talked about Jews," saying " 'Jews are cheats.' . . . The children always played 'Germans and Jews' . . . and 'Jew hunt.' . . . I was often told that I have Jewish eyes, black Jewish hair. I answered that if 'you take a closer look it is possible that I'm completely Jewish.' " Two years after the liberation, Genia was still haunted by these events: "My daddy often appears in my dreams. I dream of the Germans, how they catch us, but we manage to escape."[9]

Children's extraordinary will to survive could also lead them to betray others. While hiding in a bunker, six-year-old Aliza Griffel heard a Jewish boy saying to a Ukrainian policeman, "I'll show you where there are Jews, will you let me live?" But most Jewish informers were killed along with those they turned in. Friendship often counted for little. When Aliza's father "knocked on his friend's window," the Ukrainian peasant said, "We cannot help you with anything." But they were taken in by complete strangers, Ivan and Paulina Kozak, "very poor" peasants who sheltered them for half a year and "treated us well," even teaching Aliza "how to cross myself like the Ukrainians" and "how to recite all their prayers." She slept with the peasants and their children in one large bed. Still, the constant threat of death took its toll, and Aliza remembered that one day she could not stop crying: "Mother held me in her arms and I looked at the Holy Mother, and I said to Mother that if I survived I wanted to be like her, to be Christian, I would never be Jewish."

Under such circumstances, love could lead to thoughts of homicide. When hiding in winter 1943 in the freezing attic of an abandoned Jewish house in Buczacz, Aliza, her older sister, Dvorah, and their mother were slowly dying. At some point, recalled Aliza, "Mother took me in her arms and said, 'Go to sleep, I'll press you very, very hard, and then you will not suffer cold and hunger any more, and you will be with . . . all the angels.'" But Aliza insisted, "I want to live!" recalling with horror, "She simply wanted to strangle me. . . . She probably could not bear to see me suffering."

They were rescued by a Polish couple in the nearby village of Wojciechówka (Ukrainian: Martynivka), where they stayed until the Soviets returned in March 1944. When Aliza's family went back to their home in Buczacz they found that the floor had been ripped out in search of hidden money. The only trace of the community was "a forest clearing" on Fedor Hill, "around which everything had grown, only the mass grave was barren." It was said that "the soil was too densely fertilized" with human remains. Aliza participated in the commemoration at the site, captured on camera: "I am in that photo, one of the children."[10]

Some children ended up entirely on their own in barely imaginable conditions. Ten-year-old Izidor Hecht (Viktor Gekht) hid during the first roundup, in October 1942, with his family in the hayloft of Ukrainian friends: "We could hear the screams of those who had been murdered, mostly the elderly, children, and the ill." During the second deportation action, in November, they hid "on an isolated farm, not

Survivors and the makeshift memorial on Fedor Hill, 1945. *Source: YVA, 10002/1.*

far from Buczacz," with a Polish-Ukrainian couple, Józef and Barbara Zarivny, whom Izidor remembered as "very kind and brave people." Later they were crammed into the ghetto, where they shared "a tiny second-floor hallway" with "a group of skinny, hungry, and worn out adults and children. Many of them had starvation-related edema, were crippled, and were lying on the floor. Many had typhus. There were multitudes of fleas and lice. There was barely any food or water. Almost all our belongings had been traded for food. It was also very cold, and I became sick very often." Trying to find food outside the ghetto, the boy's mother was stopped "by one of the local Ukrainian policemen" and shot when she tried to run away. During the third action they hid behind the staircase; "up to thirty Jews were standing jammed in that tiny space." Then "a young child started to cry," wrote Izidor. "Its mother was scared that because of its crying we would be discovered, so she placed a pillow over the baby's head." Later, when "she lifted the pillow, we all saw that the baby was dead. Everyone was quietly sobbing."

The experience of hiding in a cramped space with armed men

searching just inches away was deeply traumatizing. During the roundup of April 1943 Izidor hid "in complete darkness . . . lying motionlessly next to each other and barely breathing. Above our heads we could hear boots stamping, curses, yells and gunshots. . . . The feeling of death stomping right above your head is impossible to communicate. You wish you could turn into an ant, you close your eyes and try to hide somewhere deep in the ground. I felt my heart pounding like a great bell, and that people walking aboveground could hear it. It was impossible to believe that up there it was a sunny spring day. I felt that we would never get out of this place." Eventually Izidor fled Buczacz with his father "like hunted animals; we were hiding in the surrounding ravines, pits, wheat and rye fields, and forests. There was almost no food or water. I kept fainting. . . . I was almost constantly delirious." They had no choice but to return to the Zarivny family, where Izidor's maternal grandmother, Rosa Hirschhorn, his aunt, and her three-year-old daughter were already hiding. "We were all lying there in the dark almost motionlessly." But in 1944 the Ukrainian police raided the farm. Everyone was murdered, save for Izidor and his grandmother, who managed to reach the hayloft in time; from their vantage point, they "could hear the shots and our relatives' last screams." They were the only survivors of their family, thanks especially to the Zarivny couple, who "were constantly risking their own lives."[11]

During the chaotic Soviet evacuation of April 1944, when the Wehrmacht returned to Buczacz, Izidor and his grandmother fled to Skalat, where the boy was adopted by the Red Army. He was "extremely skinny, poorly dressed, practically barefoot and covered with lice." Taken in by a field hospital, he recalled how the nurses "cut my hair, bathed me, altered a military uniform to my size and even found a belt and small-sized boots for me." The boy was "transformed from a barely alive vagabond into the 'son of the regiment.'" But shortly thereafter the field hospital was relocated, and Izidor was separated from "the single close person I had [his grandmother]. . . . I never saw her again, and I felt guilty and suffered from that for the rest of my life." Educated in a Soviet orphanage, Izidor remained in the USSR. Only in 1999, at age sixty-eight, did he finally visit his relatives in Israel; his grandmother had long since passed, having lost any trace of him. All he could do was visit her grave.[12]

☆ ☆

Jewish accounts of the German occupation in the Buczacz district are invariably about rescue and betrayal by local gentiles. This is why testimonies are filled with mixed emotions of rage and vengeance, on the one hand, and gratitude and guilt, on the other—guilt not only for having survived when so many died but also for failing to acknowledge and thank those who made survival possible at enormous risk to themselves and their families. Yet the memory of goodness cannot erase the horrors enabled and perpetrated by the callous indifference, gratuitous violence, and homicidal avarice of neighbors, much of it lacking even the veneer of ideological motivation, however perverse and inhumane.

Anne Herzog experienced the consequences of betrayal as an eight-year-old in late 1942, when a gentile barber in Buczacz, who heard the sounds of digging under his shop, informed the Germans of the bunker where she and her parents, along with many other Jews, were hiding during a roundup. "About 90 percent of my family were taken out of that bunker" and shot, she testified. She still recalled the "screaming and shooting and gassing" inside the bunker, as she and her parents escaped into a roomful of people who had been "shot dead on their beds" and "hid under those beds, where the blood was dripping down." Eventually finding shelter with Ukrainian peasants in the countryside, Anne recalled that just "a few days before the liberation" the peasants who were hiding another Jewish family nearby "took them out to the bitter cold winter on the white snow in a remote area of the village and shot them." Anne and her parents were so close they "could hear" the shots. The peasants knew the Jew they had killed because "he had a store there," where he "used to sell bread and all kinds of things." Fearful of the repercussions, the peasants hiding Anne's family simply "threw us out, and we were just on the snow. . . . We were walking and saw a little house and we just had no other recourse, we went in, and there in that farm was such a poor farmer, he had nothing, he had no cows, he just had an empty stable, so he let us stay in that stable until we were liberated."[13]

At times the margin between rescue and abuse was very narrow. Rózia Brecher, thirteen years old, was hidden in the village of Myszkowce (Ukrainian: Myshkivtsi), near Buczacz, by the Polish Antosia Sztankowska, between May 1943 and March 1944. Shortly after the liberation Rózia recounted her physical and mental abuse by Hryń, Antosia's Ukrainian brother-in-law. In one instance, Hryń climbed to the hayloft where she was hiding: "He hugged me and began to ask whether I had ever been in German hands and faced death and whether I was a communist. He said he would go to town to take part in a roundup. At that moment I didn't want to live any longer. He continued to talk but I didn't know what was happening with me. He went down from the hayloft and I began to cry. Antosia came, but I didn't say anything." Another time she related, "I heard Hryń come into the stable with another guy and they drank. The other man left and Hryń climbed up to the hayloft. . . . He was very drunk and . . . he asked who was my father and what organization my parents belonged to and what they believed in." On yet another occasion, Hryń "climbed up to the hayloft and grabbed me by the neck but I managed to scream and begged him to let me go. He said, 'Give me 1,000 [złoty] and I will let you go, and if not I will denounce you.'" At that point his wife and Antosia arrived. "I climbed down from the attic in the dark and ran to the courtyard, to a hole where sugar beets were stowed, and I threw myself under them."[14]

Whether Rózia couldn't bring herself to admit to being raped or, considering her traumatic experiences, could not remember or recount the event, such incidents were hardly uncommon. Aliza Reinisch (Nir), who was seventeen when the Germans occupied Buczacz, recalled that "gentiles would come from the villages and go through the houses in the ghetto looking for a beautiful girl so they could hide her." Subsequently some of these women "returned to the ghetto pregnant"; others were taken "straight to the Gestapo after the man had used them as much as he could." And yet "the parents of such girls would say, 'go [with the gentile] just so that you survive.' It's inconceivable now, but this was the price of staying alive."[15]

The most striking feature to emerge from these accounts is the ambivalence of goodness: even those who took in Jews could at any point instruct them to leave or summon the authorities; even those who had initially hoped to enrich themselves from the Jews they sheltered could be moved at a certain point to risk their own and their family's lives without any thought of profit. Evil was less ambivalent: most of the perpetrators killed thoughtlessly and displayed no pangs of conscience either then or decades later. But occasionally, out of impulse, the pleasure of displaying their absolute power over life and death, or even a momentary recognition of the victim's humanity, individual perpetrators could spare lives in capricious acts of goodness in the midst of slaughter. For those spared, such haphazard decisions were a momentous event that determined the rest of their lives and were never forgotten, even if for the perpetrators they could be nothing more than a blur in an ocean of blood and horror. The single act of goodness cannot be said in any way to have diminished the evil of mass murder, but the choice not to pull the trigger, whether it emanated from a deep and never entirely extinguished sense of shared humanity or was performed as a grotesque display of gallantry, demonstrated that there always was a choice, a path taken by very few, and in even fewer cases for reasons we might associate with pure kindness.

Edzia Spielberg was saved more than once by gentile neighbors and strangers, as well as Germans, by the time she was liberated at the age of fourteen. In July 1941 she and her family were staying with Christian friends in her parents' ancestral village of Połowce (Ukrainian: Polivtsi), halfway between Czortków and Buczacz. One night a group of locals "went to our home and threw in a hand grenade." These were "neighbors; Ukrainian people who bowed and said good morning, good afternoon, and good evening . . . very polite . . . people that we literally knew." One of them was Edzia's female schoolteacher. Then the mob banged on their hosts' door and demanded that they hand over the Jews. "They were there with axes and guns. And I was in bed shaking."

When their Christian friends refused to open the door, the mob went to Edzia's uncle. "He went under the bed. His wife and two little boys panicked as she went to the door, and they just split their heads with axes, all three of them." They also "axed to death" another couple, two of their children, and the grandmother. The Germans had not yet arrived on the scene.

Both survival and destruction often depended on local intervention. As conditions under German rule deteriorated, and the family was slowly "dying from hunger," Edzia's mother sneaked out of the ghetto and walked to the village of their former Ukrainian maid to barter for food; instead the maid called in the Ukrainian police. "They were going to kill her right there." But the mother was accompanied by a German friend, the wife of "some kind of an executive" in Buczacz, who reportedly said, "I'm not going to come back without this lady," until the police relented. On another occasion, Edzia herself was arrested and brought before Ukrainian police chief Kaznovskyi. Although she reminded him that he knew her father, who was brewing alcohol for local consumption at the time, and gave him her mother's wedding ring, Kaznovskyi told the little girl, "You are going to be executed." When he finally let her go she was sure he would shoot her from behind. "This is something very difficult to describe. . . . You don't breathe and you wait for that bullet to kill you. He didn't. He let me go."

In early summer 1943 the family went into hiding on a farm; from now on their lives depended entirely on the goodwill of those sheltering them. Five other family members, including two children, were denounced by the peasant hiding them on a nearby farm. Edzia was subsequently told, "My uncle was pulling out his hair and begging the [Ukrainian] police, just don't kill the two little girls, let them live. . . . My little cousin who was five years old . . . was holding the policeman's hand. He just pushed her away and took the revolver and killed her first in front of the parents because she was annoying him, she was kissing his hand." But Edzia's family was kept for eight months in a hole dug under the cowshed by the Ukrainian Kafchuk family, "a poor farmer with a wife and four children." They were, recalled Edzia, "very kind, wonderful people." Kafchuk's wife assured them, "It doesn't matter how long it takes, we will share our bread and potatoes with you."

When the Germans recaptured Buczacz in April 1944, Edzia's father was caught on the street and executed, but the rest of the family managed to flee the city. Edzia, who looked "Aryan," found work "peeling potatoes, washing dishes" for a German Army unit, while her mother and little brother hid nearby. The local commander took a liking to the girl, but then her Ukrainian coworkers denounced her as a Jew. Rather than shooting her, the officer escorted Edzia, her mother, and her brother toward the front line, leaving them there with the words "I hope you all live well." A few hours later they were liberated. Edzia recalled being "very happy to get away from the Ukrainians" when they left for the West in late 1945, "because they had pogroms after the war. They were killing Jews." To her mind, "they were worse than the Germans. . . . I think my family was mostly killed . . . by Ukrainians who were our friends."[16]

Jacob Heiss, also born in 1930, remembered how the Germans arriving to carry out roundups would call out merrily, "*Spielzeit für die Kameraden*" (Playtime for the comrades), and the next day "you would get up in the morning and see hundreds of dead people every place you walked." Yet he insisted that "the Ukrainians were worse than the Germans," perhaps because before the war he had had "a lot of non-Jewish friends" in Buczacz. Early in the occupation a Ukrainian man barged into the synagogue "and tore the beard off one of the men . . . with the skin"; in the ghetto, Ukrainian policemen "used to beat you up" or "shoot you right there." On one occasion Jacob was caught fishing in the Strypa and was almost drowned by the police before his brother came to his rescue. They were always hungry; people ate "cats, dogs, horses, everything," and would even "kill each other" for food. The urge to live could overcome all moral compunctions; some Jews caught by the Germans during roundups sought to save themselves by disclosing the location of bunkers. And yet Jacob and his family survived thanks to acts of kindness; hiding in the sewers, they were given food by local Poles. Before the war one of their rescuers used to supply Jacob's father,

Jacob Heiss and his older brother shortly before the war. *Source: Photo courtesy of Jacob Heiss.*

a shoemaker, with leather; he was none other than the dogcatcher Kowalski, who had remade himself a Jew-catcher under the Germans.[17]

The often contradictory attitudes toward gentile locals and even Germans in survivor accounts are not indicative of witness inconsistency, forgetfulness, or irrationality, but rather of the fact that under extreme circumstances people behaved in unexpected and at times conflicting ways, motivated by factors that often contradicted each other: ideological conviction and prejudice, but also altruism and courage; greed and cowardice, as well as pity and compassion; callous indifference and righteous rage, along with fear of retribution and defiance.

Alicja Jurman, the same age as Spielberg and Heiss, faced the whole range of attitudes under German rule. Having already lost one brother to Soviet brutality, she lost another to Nazi forced labor, a third to local denunciation, and the youngest to a Ukrainian policeman. Her father was murdered early on in the registration action; her mother, denounced by a Polish neighbor, was shot in front of her eyes just before the end. Alicja herself was handed over to the Gestapo by her best friend's father, who had joined the Ukrainian police; she was hidden for a lengthy period by an eccentric elderly Polish nobleman living on the edge of a village, "a splendid, beautiful man," who defied all threats from local Ukrainians; she was denounced by a local peasant after escaping mass execution, but the soldier who spotted her told her to run, saying, "*Du bist ja unschuldig, Mädchen*" (You are an innocent girl, after all). Both her survival and the murder of many family members, then, were largely the result of choices made by neighbors and strangers.[18]

✡ ✡

Surviving on one's own as a young woman could be deeply traumatizing, even for those who had all the attributes necessary for blending into gentile society. By her own account, Fania Feldman "was blond . . . had braids" and "didn't look Jewish at all"; she also "spoke Ukrainian very well," so "they couldn't recognize me." Indeed, she remarked, "I was with Ukrainians all the time," but "as soon as I left they killed this one and they killed that one; so they were murderers, they were no good, I was just lucky, that's all." Any association with Jews drew hate and violence. She remembered how, early on, when she asked a neighbor for some milk for her sick father, he responded, "I'd rather give it to a pig than sell it to a Jew." Fleeing to the forest after her father's death, she was soon relegated to the status of a hunted animal, like so many other Jews at the time. "I was four days without food, I didn't know where to go" and "didn't have somebody to ask, to advise, nothing, just alone in the woods." She was "always afraid [of] what they would do to me," having heard that the Ukrainians "did terrible things, they take out the eyes, they cut the tongue, they took everything, whatever they wanted." A truck driver offered her a lift and then stopped the vehicle in the woods. "He says to me, you probably had a husband. And I was so afraid, I was pulling my hair, I was breaking my fingers, I was crying, I said no, I don't have a husband and I am very young, I said, maybe you have a daughter and somebody would do this to your daughter and what would you do?" In her recollection, the man then drove away; it is not unlikely that he first raped her. Feldman recalled her despair: "I only wished I would get a bullet in my back." She "used to envy the people that were already dead," and even "a dog that is free and not afraid."

Taken in for a while by a Ukrainian family that knew her before the war, Feldman soon heard that the local priest was warning his parishioners against hiding Jews. Not long thereafter the village was raided by a band of armed Ukrainians, and she barely managed to escape. On another occasion she witnessed seven of her relatives, four adults and three children, denounced by villagers and murdered by the local police: "The Ukrainians, they knew these people. . . . They told them . . . 'Just give us whatever you have, and we will let you go.' They gave them everything, and when they went out everyone separately got a bullet in the head. . . . I heard every shot." There were many other cases in which material gain easily trumped human lives. At one point two Jewish lads hiding with her in the forest tried to retrieve a sewing machine left with a gentile neighbor so as to barter it for food. Instead one of the boys was stoned to death, and the other, who later related this to Feldman, was left for dead. "This was the very good friends who kept their sewing machine, you trusted them. I couldn't trust nobody," she remarked. Although she largely owed her own survival to Ukrainians, Feldman insisted, "Nobody can tell me that there are some good Ukrainian people, maybe one or two, because I know best what they did, what murderers they were. When [the Jews] gave the money to Ukrainian people . . . they killed the person, put him in a sack, and threw it down in the water. . . . It could be the nicest neighbor."[19]

A number of surviving male teenagers and young men were critical of the Jewish elite and recalled Christian rescuers with respect and gratitude. Like many other survivors, Zev Anderman, born in 1927, described the Ukrainians as "terrible" and "a thousand times worse than the Germans." But he also depicted in detail how his family found shelter with several Polish and Ukrainian families in the nearby villages of Podzameczek, Medwedowce, and Piława (Ukrainian: Pylyava) during several actions. He spoke with derision about Judenrat chairman

Mendel Reich, who acceded to German demands for "furs, blankets, boots," and about the "young Jewish lads," the policemen who requisitioned them. Many members of Zev's family, including his mother, were murdered in October 1942, when "a Jewish girl" informed the Ukrainian police where their bunker was located in the hope that "they would spare her." Yet Zev could recognize the fact that "the will for life," perhaps especially among the young, "was enormous." He recalled having to exhume the victims of the February 1943 mass shooting that were polluting the town's water supply: "The soil was frozen. They stuck to each other. We worked there with pickaxes to separate one piece of flesh from another. . . . We did not cry. We were stronger than steel." Possibly it was that same will for life that motivated Zev's brother Janek to join the police. Zev never alluded to this directly, describing instead how in June 1943, just as he intended to join the partisans (like other Ordnungsdienst men), Janek tried to conceal a bunker sheltering his father and many other Jews; identified by the Germans, he drew his pistol and shot at them, upon which they beat him to death. Zev saw this as one of several Jewish actions that deterred denouncers by demonstrating "that Jews are shooting back," accounting for why "many Jews survived in Buczacz." These youngsters, he exclaimed, were "glorious heroes."[20]

At the time, Zev and his uncle were hiding in the village of Petlikowce Nowe (Ukrainian: Novi Petlykivtsi) with a Polish acquaintance, who used the first opportunity to rob them of all their belongings. Fortunately they were then taken in by the Ukrainian brothers Mykhailo and Ilko Baran of the same village, who were already hiding several other Jews; they stayed there until spring 1944. Zev described Mykhailo as "an angel." He fed them well, and his wife "would wash our shirts and underclothes." Ilko supplied the teenage Zev with books: "I put them in the bunker and that's what saved me, I read non-stop." Altogether the Baran brothers saved fifteen Jews; after the fall of the communist regime Zev sought out their sons, and they were recognized by Yad Vashem, the State of Israel's national institute for the memory and commemoration of the Holocaust. "Among the Christians, Poles and

Ukrainians, there were also human beings," concluded Zev. "We and history must not forget that."[21]

Shmuel Rosen, his brothers Henryk and Yehiel, and their mother spent much of 1943 in a hideout they built inside the Potocki family crypt at the Christian cemetery on the slope of Fedor Hill. In this they were helped by the Polish undertaker Marjan Świerszczak and his Ukrainian wife, Maryna. Despite interrogations and beatings by the Ukrainian police, Marjan never revealed their whereabouts. Shmuel admired the undertaker's courage, as opposed to the Judenrat officials he despised, especially Dr. Seifer, who had taken exorbitant bribes from "the 200 richest Jewish families" in Buczacz in order to allow them to enter the labor camp in spring 1943 while the rest of the population were murdered. But Moshe Wizinger, who had known Marjan since their youth, recalled that when he escaped to the cemetery in June 1943, Maryna had told him to leave right away because "the Germans might come to look here any day now and if they find you we might also be punished." She suggested that he follow the example of other Jews who "were giving themselves up to the Germans," since "sooner or later they are going to find you anyway." Wizinger, who eventually joined a local Polish resistance group, told his leader, known only as Edek, about this denial of shelter, and in response Edek raided the Świerszczaks' home and gave the wife a severe thrashing. He also warned the husband, "If you are afraid of repression by the Germans for helping Jews and partisans, I want you to know that we will punish loyalty to German orders with death. Remember this and tell the others."[22]

This episode encapsulates much of the complexity of rescue and betrayal: the same Świerszczak who was remembered as a "gorgeous man" by Henryk Rosen had also denied shelter to Wizinger, thereby betraying their friendship. Almost killed by a Polish resistance fighter for betraying the national honor, decades later Świerszczak was honored as a righteous gentile by Yad Vashem. Wizinger recalled a speech by Edek exhorting Jews to fight the Germans and greatly admired his fellow Polish fighters and the villagers who helped them; he was even prouder when he found out about the small Jewish bands led by Dawid

Friedlender and Natan Dunajer. The impact of Jewish resistance was marginal, but it gave these youngsters a sense of meaning and purpose in the midst of utter inhumanity. Still, by the time of the liberation, these local bands had been decimated and most of their leaders were dead. As Wizinger awaited the arrival of the Soviets with a few remaining young Jews, he thought victory had come too late: "I look at the others: they are the last of a dying nation."[23]

Yitzhak Bauer, who successfully transitioned from the police to the resistance, provided some insight into the capacity and purpose of armed Jewish bands. As he recalled, in the wake of the liquidation action of June 1943, "we organized a rather large group and went to the forest some twenty miles from Buczacz." After acquiring a pistol and a few rounds from Soviet partisans, Bauer and his brother, along with two other lads, decided to leave the vulnerable family camp that formed in the forest and returned to the vicinity of Buczacz. There they established contact with Dunajer, who was living in a cave with his wife, their four-year-old child, and two other men, also brothers. "We had one sawed-off shotgun and my Nagant [Russian service pistol] and

Natan Dunajer (left) and Dawid Friedlender (right) in the 1930s. *Source: Polish police file (Dunajer); Eyal Ziffer private collection (Friedlender).*

thought that we could fight the entire German empire," chuckled Bauer. They also made contact with Friedlender's group and took part in an attempt to assassinate a Polish denouncer.

Unlike his self-deprecating view of the resistance, Bauer was adamant that in the Buczacz area "the Ukrainians were relatively alright"; even police chief Kaznovskyi refrained from acting when he discovered that his own father had "hidden several Jews" after the ghetto was liquidated. The Bauer brothers relied on contacts with Ukrainian friends and acquaintances. When they went to visit their elderly prewar neighbor he called out to them, "'Children, my children,' in Ukrainian, '*dity moyi dity*.'" He "made a package of food for us, and said, 'I wish you manage to survive.'" Their friend Alpinski "would sit us at the table and make us an omelet whenever we came to him from the forest," and he helped find hideouts for other Jews. A man called Shenko stored some of their belongings, provided the Bauers with food, and hid three Jewish women in his barn; in early 1944 they were shocked when he joined the Ukrainian police, but he argued that "the alternative was to enlist for labor in Germany or join the SS-Division 'Galicia.'" According to Bauer, becoming a policeman did not help Shenko; his house was burned down when "they found Jews there." Much worse, their friend Alpinski was denounced and murdered along with his wife and younger daughter. For that reason Bauer found it important "to emphasize that there were among them people who were not evil, especially among the inhabitants of Buczacz. The villagers" were different, and "each time there was an action, they would come with sacks to plunder."[24]

Almost all of the more than two hundred testimonies by Jewish survivors of the German occupation of Buczacz and its environs reflect the same ambivalence about relations with gentile neighbors, ranging from gratitude and admiration to rage and desire for vengeance. Some older witnesses and parents of young children at times had greater insight into the cynicism, greed, and callousness that genocide can bring out in those not directly subjected to it; they may have recognized with greater clarity the rare cases of pure altruism as well. The saved were obviously more likely to have experienced that altruism than the far larger multitudes of the drowned, but even in their case, instances of unadulterated goodness appeared miraculous precisely because of their rarity.

Róża Dobrecka, a well-educated young woman from western Poland, who escaped from the Warsaw Ghetto with her five-year-old child, Seweryn, in summer 1942, arrived in Buczacz just before the massive action of February 1943. Her husband and mother escaped the ghetto later and joined them. They barely survived, hidden by Polish acquaintances. Speaking perfect Polish and equipped with false papers, the family's survival depended on posing as Poles whenever they left the confines of the ghetto. Things became even scarier when Dobrecka realized that she knew SS corporal and camp commandant Paul Thomanek's "Jewish Gestapo-man Wolf," with whom he frequently showed up in Buczacz, since he had been "often a guest in our house before the war." Now "all dressed up in leather," Wolf "was obviously pleased that the same people who" in the past "had wanted to have no contact with him, since he was a gambler and a seedy character, were now dependent on him." Throughout that spring Wolf and Thomanek spent much of their time in Buczacz "terrorizing the population. They orchestrated endless orgies, demanding to have young women brought to them." Invariably "their presence produced victims. Thomanek shot into crowds of Jews," and at times Wolf "would take Thomanek's revolver from his hand and shoot on his own."[25]

Dobrecka's own family was soon targeted. Her mother was denounced and shot on the way to see her other daughter, Hala, who was living as a Pole in a nearby town. Her younger brother, Olek, was sent to a labor camp as punishment for having "spoken ill of the vice-head of the *Judenrat*, Dr. Seifer." Even "on the edge of the abyss," observed Dobrecka, "the ghetto's leaders were blinded by ambition and vanity." After his release, Olek was arrested while visiting Hala; denounced as Jews, the two siblings were shot, and Hala's meager belongings were promptly stolen by her denouncers. Similarly, when Dobrecka and her husband emerged from their bunker after the action of April 1943, they "found nothing; our neighbors had cleaned out and taken away everything"; indeed she saw "one Buczacz resident walking around in my clothes from Warsaw." Following the "Judenrein action" in June, surviving Jews hid with "'their' so-called peasants," but as Dobrecka pointed out, "in many cases" they were quickly "robbed down to their shirts and thrown out." Finally she and her child simply boarded the train to Warsaw, where they eventually survived disguised as Poles. Her husband and remaining brother were murdered within days of her leaving Buczacz.[26]

Possibly the oldest Buczacz witness was Józef Kornblüh, already sixty-five at the time of these events. His survival, while remarkable for a man of that age, revealed the entire gamut of gentile engagement in Jewish fate, ranging from sheer exploitation to selfless rescue. Kornblüh had paid the Judenrat 2,000 złoty to allow him to stay in the ghetto after the mass execution action of April 1943, but in early June he wisely went into hiding with a local Polish municipal worker. This saved him from two rounds of killings later that month, but on June 28 he was asked to leave because the Germans were inspecting former Jewish homes (suggesting how his host came by his property). After a few wretched days in the open, Kornblüh was offered assistance by a young Pole who turned out to be a proper profiteer, handing Kornblüh from one person to another and charging him ever more money. Eventually, in November 1943, Kornblüh was ejected from his hideout with a Polish widow, who claimed that she had received no payment for her trouble, and found himself without any shelter at the height of winter: "I didn't know where to go. I knew there was no rescue for me and sat down at the edge of the woods. . . . The following morning an elderly beggar-woman spotted me. She saw at a glance that I was a Jew and asked me why I'd been sitting in a place where everybody could see me and hand me over to the police. I told her that I had been thrown out and that there was no place for me to go. She asked me if I was hungry. I told her that I didn't have any food." That afternoon the woman returned "and brought me coffee and food. I learned at that time that there also exist people who are willing to help without expecting anything in return." Eventually Kornblüh made it to the village of

Żnibrody (Ukrainian: Zhnyborody), twenty miles south of Buczacz, "where Poles helped me." He described his rescuers as "very proper and noble." When the Red Army reached the other bank of the Strypa, Kornblüh could not cross over since the bridge was heavily guarded; instead his Polish host's son "arranged to meet me at the river, undressed completely and carried me across the river. Thanks to this noble man I reached the Soviet side earlier and was liberated."[27]

✿ ✿

The last months of the German occupation were a period of unmitigated chaos, mayhem, and brutality, sprinkled with rare moments of altruism and grace. Many of the Jewish victims at that time were murdered not by the Germans but by an array of Ukrainian paramilitaries, local bandits, and brutalized peasants. Remarkably, most of the few survivors were saved by a German administrative official and a couple of Wehrmacht officers; it is thanks to the testimonies of those they rescued that we know anything about this world turned upside down, in which the handful who escaped systematic genocide were mercilessly hunted down, yet in recording their agony also preserved the memory of their saviors.

Eleven-year-old Samuel Eisen was an exception; rather than being saved by others, he became a fighter. In summer 1943 Samuel witnessed the murder of thousands of Jews in his hometown of Tłuste, including many inhabitants of Buczacz recently deported there: "They dug four deep pits in the cemetery, then put boards over them. Ten people, stripped naked, were ordered to stand on each board and a machinegun shot them into the pit; they were followed by another ten people." Surviving Jews related that "they had to go down into the pits and arrange the corpses one next to the other, packed like sardines, in order to squeeze in as many as possible. Children were thrown into the pits alive, and covered up with the corpses. A German would grab a child by the neck and shout: '*Nimm das dreck und schmeiss herein!* [Grab the filth and throw it in.]' The children were swimming in blood in those pits. Two girls managed to dig themselves out from under the corpses and came back to town but they had lost their minds and could not speak."

For a while, Samuel, his little brother, Jakób, and their father worked on an agricultural farm, but after six weeks the father was killed in a Ukrainian police raid. The boys found him "lying naked among all the other corpses; they had taken away everything. . . . My brother and I dug a hole and buried our father naked. We had no clothes for him." They then went into the forest. "We had no money, but many Poles lived in that village, they all knew us and were kind to us. They were afraid to hide us, but they always gave us food. We slept in the forest. . . . We washed our shirts in the river and dried them in the sun. We were only afraid of Ukrainians who might give us away." As winter approached, Samuel joined a Soviet partisan unit operating in the region; he left little Jakób with Ignacy Wiszniewski, giving the Pole "a gold watch" and promising to "give him everything" he had "after the war if he hid my brother." Samuel relished his service with the partisans. "I was with them for the entire year. . . . They taught me to ride on horseback . . . to hold the reins with our teeth so as to free our hands to load a submachine gun. . . . We were not afraid of anything. When we heard that the Ukrainian police were in the village, we went there, caught them and hanged them on trees in the forest." They also ambushed and destroyed a German unit, taking many prisoners. Samuel's partisan detachment welcomed the returning Red Army. "I was the youngest, so they gave me a red flag and I rode in the front between two officers." He then gave all his property to Wiszniewski and took back his brother; in May 1945 they were living in Kraków. "I only want to work in Palestine," Samuel wrote. "But when it comes to fighting again, I shall defend it, I shall know then what I am fighting for."[28]

One account illustrates the sheer horror of these final months of German rule in the region. Mojżesz Szpigiel, a forty-four-year-old former estate manager, survived the June 1943 mass shooting in Tłuste with several members of his family, including his father and fourteen-year-old son. They joined the labor camp in nearby Hołowczyńce (Ukrainian: Holovchyntsi), where the Polish work supervisor "extorted money from Jews" seeking to be certified as officially employed in the camp. Some of the wealthier Jews had gone "into hiding with Poles or Ukrainians" but "returned a few weeks later because the farmers had taken everything from them and thrown them out." In contrast, the German supervisor of all the camps in the area, "Vathie," as Szpigiel called him, "had a good relationship with the people" and "was tolerant." Yet the general situation of the Jews in the region was so utterly hopeless that even after the second mass killing in Tłuste, in mid-June, which cost the lives of another 1,800 people, "the few who had escaped began returning to the town because in the woods they were attacked and killed by the Ukrainians." In early July the camp laborers in Hołowczyńce were warned of a liquidation action and escaped to the forest, and "the local Ukrainians took advantage of this, went into the camp and took everything away from all those who still had something." Sometime later the camp was raided by the Germans. As the Jews fled into the forest, testified Szpigiel, "we were assailed by peasants. The Ukrainians began catching people, torturing them, and taking their money." That night Szpigiel's father and his two nephews were murdered by a Ukrainian who had worked for their family. Yet the few survivors had no choice but to return to the camp in the morning. Now "a reign of hunger and misery began" since "the people did not have clothes and underwear, because they had been robbed of everything," even their shoes, which led to a typhus outbreak and a mass shooting of the sick.

In January 1944 the camp was attacked by heavily armed Ukrainian militiamen; the slaughtered included Szpigiel's son. "It is important to state," he declared, "that this killing was not a German action, that it was performed by Ukrainian policemen and bandits." Apparently that day Vathie was on vacation. Still, Jews kept streaming into the camp, having been evicted from their hideouts by peasants fearful of bandit attacks. The camp was raided again on March 8; by Szpigiel's count approximately a hundred bandits massacred forty-six Jews with knives and pitchforks. Returning from the forest "in the morning, we saw a terrible scene. The child orphans were stacked up in a pile, ten children were butchered, one on top of the other. . . . Other victims were lying with open guts in different locations. We buried them, gathered the injured and took them on two horses and carts to the camp in Tłuste. Everybody said they would rather die from a German bullet than from a bandit's knife."

When Vathie left just a couple of days before the Soviets arrived, "the Jews earnestly cried," "afraid of this transition period." By now they "were no longer afraid of the Germans because the Gestapo was there no more"; rather they "were afraid of the Ukrainians." To their surprise, the new commandant of Tłuste, a young German Army officer, "who saw that we [felt] sorry about Vathie" leaving, announced to the surviving Jews, "As long as I am here, nothing will happen to you." He then "ordered [someone] to butcher a cow and to give us potatoes." He was not the only Wehrmacht officer to protect the Jews from armed militias. As Szpigiel testified, the following day a unit of Ukrainian policemen "came to the camp with their guns drawn," yelling, "Vodka or death!" Szpigiel managed to flee and alerted a German Army major, who "went there with his aide, hit one [Ukrainian] policeman on the head with his revolver, threw them out, and ordered them to leave the area immediately."

Soon thereafter the Red Army rolled in. They were finally liberated. However, seventeen-year-old Ester Nachtigal, who was recovering from wounds sustained during a Ukrainian attack, vividly recalled that just then "German planes arrived" and "strafed anyone who was running":

> I managed to get off my bed and reached the door and began to cry. . . . Until then we always thought only how to survive, always thinking quickly from one moment to the next how to avoid death. Now I understood that I was alone and had survived. But this was not yet the case, because suddenly everything was flying around me, I was already faint from hunger. I found myself in a half-destroyed hut. The other hut was burning. The wounded there died in the flames. I stood there alone without knowing what to do, all covered in blood.[29]

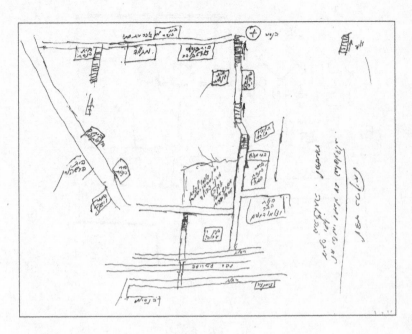

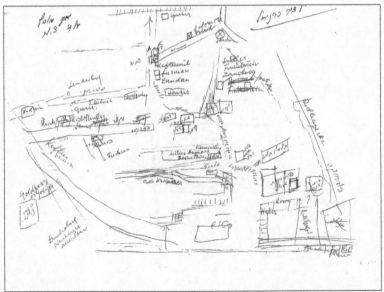

A survivor's sketches of Buczacz. *Source: Private document courtesy of Zvi Karniel.*

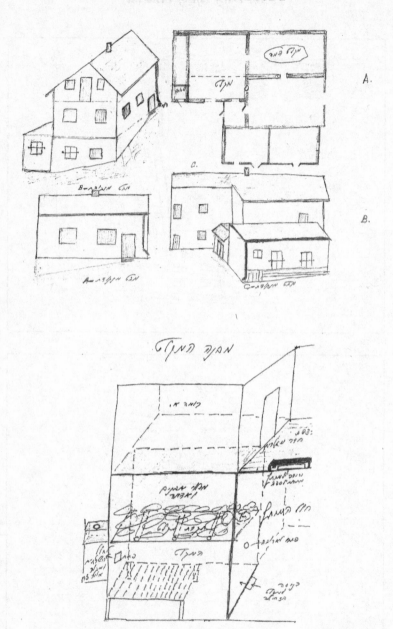

A survivor's sketches of a hideout. *Source: Private document courtesy of Zvi Karniel.*

Chapter 7
NEIGHBORS

OUN-UPA members in Uście Zielone (Ukrainian: Ustya Zelene), Buczacz district, 1942. *Source: PA, photo 4-1. See also O. Synenka, For the Homeland, for My People (Ternopil, 2002, in Ukrainian), 156–57.*

On the eve of 1944, Buczacz was, as Viktor Petrykevych described it in his diary, "a miserable sight," a town whose heart had been torn out and replaced by refuse: "Since the Jews, exterminated by the Germans, had previously inhabited numerous houses, many buildings stand empty. . . . The Christians—petty merchants, artisans, and workers—have moved into the better houses and keep them as well as they can. But the remaining empty houses, where nobody lives, are in ruins, the windows broken, the window frames torn out, the doors and stairs shattered . . . [rooms] full of garbage and dung. There is so much filth that it is hard to look at them." Under these circumstances, the old teacher was consumed by self-pity and resentment: "Our present existence is destitute; we live in unprecedented poverty." And yet, he added, "some of the people live well and comfortably; they make profits and buy everything still available. Certainly, the war destroys and ruins some, and gives too much to others, often undeservedly." The war, observed Petrykevych, had "caused a revolution in values." While the "civil servants and clerks are the poorest, and of them, teachers are probably the poorest of all," the local "merchants and artisans earn well," particularly because "now they have no Jewish competition" and can offer many "fancy goods," likely looted from murdered Jews, to trade in. Similarly, "professionals, doctors, veterinary surgeons, and dentists" also benefited from the disappearance of their Jewish colleagues. And in the villages many peasants were thriving by selling "home-brew alcohol," a product formerly associated with Jewish manufacturers. In other words, for some sectors of the population, the extermination of the Jews could only be described as a blessing. "Such people," grumbled Petrykevych, "fare well and do not feel the burden of the war."

These blessings of genocide were short-lived. In early January 1944 Petrykevych wrote, "This morning we could see for the first time refugees and exiles from the East. . . . The Ukrainians of Buczacz shake their heads and think: what will happen to us next?"[1]

As the Red Army advanced, the Ukrainian underground reported that the Wehrmacht was undergoing "demoralization on a scale never seen before," with German troops "raping young women and girls" and manifesting a growing "inclination to bribery" and a "complete lack of faith" in their cause, accompanied by "fear of partisans." At the same time, noted the OUN, "the Polish underground" was becoming "very actively engaged in anti-Ukrainian operations," and Polish peasants in mixed villages had taken to denouncing their Ukrainian neighbors.[2]

Accounts by Poles focused primarily on the destruction of Polish

Viktor Petrykevych in 1930. *Source: Petrykevych private papers, courtesy of Bohdan Petrykevych, Ivano-Frankivsk, Ukraine.*

existence in the eastern territories. This tragedy differed from the genocide of the Jews in that it had little to do with German policy; instead it was the result of a nationalist Ukrainian campaign to ethnically cleanse the lands for a future independent Ukraine. The radical wing of the Organization of Ukrainian Nationalists, known as OUN-B after the name of its leader, Stepan Bandera, whose followers were consequently called Banderites (Polish: *Banderowcy*; Ukrainian: *Benderivtsi*), was now in the process of transforming itself into the underground political wing of an insurgency against German rule and in preparation for the possible return of Soviet rule. In 1943 many Ukrainian policemen serving the German occupation authority abandoned their units and formed the new military arm of the OUN-B, the Ukrainska Povstanska Armiya (UPA, Ukrainian Insurgent Army). Operations by the UPA in Volhynia, the province northeast of Galicia, led to massive ethnic cleansing of the Polish population there. In early 1944, with most of the Jews gone, the UPA and the OUN increased their pressure on the Polish inhabitants of Galicia. The result was that next to the ongoing efforts by the Germans to exterminate the last remnants of the Jewish population, and the intensifying struggle between the Wehrmacht and the Red Army in Ukraine, a civil war between Ukrainian and Polish nationalists, largely organized by the Polish Home Army and local peasant formations, cost the lives of thousands of civilians and paramilitary combatants, quite independently of the German occupiers and their interests.

Altogether between 30,000 and 40,000 Poles and up to 5,000 Ukrainians were massacred in Eastern Galicia between 1943 and 1945, with an overall toll in the Polish-Ukrainian conflict of possibly as many as 100,000 Poles and 15,000 to 20,000 Ukrainians. The killings continued even after the Red Army returned to Eastern Galicia, although

"Crimes committed by Bandera OUN-UPA groups in Buczacz County." *Source: "Ludobójstwo i czystki etniczne: Zbrodnie banderowskich bojówek OUN-UPA w pow. Buczacz, woj. Tarnopolskie," Na Rubieży 4 (1995): 4.*

at that point the UPA turned its attention largely to resisting Soviet rule. Mobilizing some thirty thousand partisans and faced with tens of thousands of NKVD troops sent in to subdue the insurgency, the OUN-UPA kept up the fight until the early 1950s. By then Soviet punitive policies had led to the deportation of over 200,000 family members of insurgents to the interior of the USSR.[3]

To justify its activities, the OUN claimed it was under attack. In the district of Buczacz in particular, the local OUN leadership asserted that the Polish underground was directly involved in "physically eradicating our membership," while "the Polish population praises" such "terrorist activities." In Petrykevych's estimate, some three thousand partisans were now engaged in chaotic rural fighting throughout the region: "Polish partisans attack the Ukrainians; when Ukrainian partisans arrive, they punish the Poles for the murder or beating and looting of Ukrainians. What has been happening in remote villages of the district, on the edge of the forest, can only be described as anarchy." As the UPA moved into the area, and with the corresponding expansion to 3,500 armed fighters of the Buczacz district's Polish Peasants Battalions, loosely connected to the Polish Home Army, the interethnic struggle in the region was unleashed in earnest; there was only sporadic German intervention. And as sometimes happens in fraternal conflicts, according to Władysław Wołkowski, a member of the Polish underground, it was often difficult to tell the two sides apart. During the Ukrainian assault on Korościatyn (Ukrainian: Korostiatyn, now Krynytsya), fifteen miles west of Buczacz, in February 1944, for instance, the attackers sowed confusion in the Polish ranks by pretending to be Poles, so that "the Polish formation that arrived" on the scene "stood helplessly by for some time, because everyone was yelling in Polish not to shoot their countrymen."[4]

This clearly had to do with the tradition of Polish-Ukrainian intermarriage in this area, which went back many generations. Father Ludwik Rutyna explained that "there were many mixed families," in which the boys followed the father's religion, the girls followed the mother's, and families attended services together in both Roman and

Greek Catholic churches. For the nationalists on both sides, this was always perceived as a threat, especially when the fate of the region was once more hanging in the balance. In August 1943 the Polish Interior Ministry in exile observed that "the issue of so-called 'mixed' marriages" was increasingly "perceived as a serious danger" and "condemned by the Ukrainian press as the strongest factor of Polonization in the prewar period." By the end of the war, Rutyna recalled, there were "many [Greek Catholic] priests in the [Ukrainian] underground," and the Poles were running for their lives. "They didn't want to leave," but "when death grabs you by the throat, anyone who can will flee." Only some of "the mixed families stayed"; "many Ukrainian women married to Poles immigrated to Poland." The heavily mixed nature of families in the town of Koropiec, fifteen miles southwest of Buczacz, motivated an increasingly homicidal effort to tear them apart. In one case, the entire family of the Ukrainian Justyna Maćków, who had married a Pole and had three sons by him, was hanged. As related by Michał Sobków, the teenage child of a Polish father and a Ukrainian mother from Koropiec, "News spread that all Banderites with a Polish sister or mother should kill them, since this was the demand of patriotism." In Koropiec, he wrote, "the Poles feared the Banderites" and "the Ukrainians feared the Poles." Everywhere "grown men stood guard on the roads from evening to morning . . . armed with pitchforks, axes, scythes, and iron bars, whether Banderites or Poles."[5]

By late February 1944, even Petrykevych was willing to concede that Ukrainian insurgents were "driving the Poles out of their villages" in Volhynia and Galicia: "The Poles flee to the cities; those who stay behind in the villages do not sleep at night and stay on guard, armed. Murder, arson, and robbery are rife." While insisting that the massacre in Korościatyn that month, where Ukrainian "partisans burned down the village and killed over a hundred people with guns or hand grenades," was provoked by "a Polish ambush that shot dead one or two" Ukrainian fighters, he also observed, "The partisans are having a good time, [and thanks to] the latent thirst for revenge . . . human blood is flowing." On March 15 Petrykevych wrote, "Those who had enriched themselves have left the city." So did his wife and children, as the killings continued unabated. On March 20, three days before the Soviets arrived, "the Germans found nine Jews in a shelter and shot them on the Fedor." All the remaining Christian youngsters were being seized by the Germans for forced labor, while those "merchants, artisans, and other people, who lived in former Jewish houses" were "moving out . . . in view of the recent developments in the war. They anticipate Jewish revenge." This set off a frenzy of looting by the poor of previously plundered Jewish belongings. Finally, on the afternoon of March 24, "the first Bolshevik tank entered the city."[6]

☆ ☆

"The Poles were glad that finally the Soviet troops would return and put an end to the nightmare of the Banderites," wrote Michał Sobków. In spring 1944 the London-based Polish government in exile estimated that the number of Polish inhabitants in the Buczacz district, which had stood at 48,000 before the outbreak of war, had been halved. Adding to an estimated loss of 10,000 Ukrainians and the vast majority of the original 15,000 Jews, it appears that 50,000 people, over a third of the district's prewar population of 140,000, were lost through killing, deportation, expulsion, or flight.[7]

Suddenly, with the return of the Soviets, the situation was reversed; in summer 1944 seventeen-year-old Stanisław Kubasiewicz joined a locally recruited "destruction battalion," one of numerous such units established by the NKVD from mostly Polish local inhabitants to suppress the Ukrainian insurgency. They also participated in deporting suspected militants' families. "I felt quite uncomfortable after such actions," Kubasiewicz wrote, "which were usually accompanied by women's cries. I wasn't suitable for such a job; they were our enemies, and perhaps one of their husbands or sons had participated in murders of Poles in nearby villages, but I could not stir up any hatred in myself. After all, these people were not strangers to us."[8]

The Soviets proved particularly effective in mobilizing local elements to help them establish rule and root out their opponents. As the

OUN saw it, the NKVD "mostly relies on the Poles" for information and repression, treating "Ukrainian-Galicians as enemies" and assuming that "every Ukrainian is a Banderite." But Soviet rule did not entirely eliminate Ukrainian violence, as a gruesome massacre in Puźniki (Ukrainian: Puzhnyky) in February 1945 grimly illustrated. Indeed the recruitment of Polish men left their own villages vulnerable. Sobków recalled that "all young men from [Puźniki] had been conscripted into a 'destroyer battalion' stationed in Koropiec," about midway between Buczacz and Puźniki, of which he was also a member, and so the attacking Ukrainian force found only defenseless "women, children and the elderly." By the time Sobków's unit reached the village at daybreak, they discovered a scene of horrors: "Many women with hacked off breasts were howling in pain. Everywhere we encountered people with bleeding head wounds caused by axe strikes." One toddler's "skull had been smashed, the pieces held together with bread"; another baby's "mouth had been cut with a knife." Altogether 104 people were murdered in Puźniki; only fourteen Polish households remained.

In Sobków's view, the most traumatic aspect of this period was the transformation of his community from one enjoying interethnic harmony to one assaulted by ethnic butchery, and like so many other Poles, he perceived the main tragedy of the war as the loss of his homeland. At age seventeen, along with his mother and sister, a horse, and a cow, Sobków left Koropiec forever.[9]

The terrifying language of murderous threats, often followed by massive bloodshed, that characterized this internecine conflict was graphically presented in a leaflet distributed in June 1944 by a Ukrainian "self-defense" group to the inhabitants of Hnilcze (Ukrainian: Hnylche), a village located twenty miles northwest of Buczacz. "The Polish authorities and their followers have responded to our repeated efforts to appease Polish-Ukrainian relations," stated the pamphlet, "with terror, denunciation, murder and plunder"; rather than "fighting against the Muscovite or German occupation," the Poles were striving "to bring about the greatest annihilation of the Ukrainian people with their help. . . . Polish bullets have cut down hundreds of innocent victims, and many Ukrainian villages have been burned down and destroyed." But now "terror will be answered with terror!" Justice was on the side of "the Ukrainian people," which "possesses on its soil sufficient right and might to mow down the Polish leaders with their imperialist delusions." Hence the group vowed "our vengeance will be tenfold," and "the irresponsible Polish leaders who began the struggle between the Polish and Ukrainian people will have to bear the responsibility for that." As Petrykevych remarked at the time, reflecting the brutalization of popular imagery further exacerbated by exposure to systematic genocide, Ukrainians "say that just as the Jews went to Bełżec, so too the Poles should go to Auschwitz."[10]

What ultimately put an end to this fraternal conflict was the flight and subsequent deportation of the Polish population from Eastern Galicia. The Lublin agreement of September 9, 1944, between the Polish communist leadership and the Kremlin facilitated a vast Polish-Ukrainian population exchange. Between 1944 and 1947 an estimated 560,000 Poles were removed from Eastern Galicia, which became part of Soviet Ukraine; altogether up to 750,000 Poles were deported from the western regions of the newly expanded USSR, while over 500,000 Ukrainians were deported from Poland as it was reconstituted in its postwar borders.[11] By the end of the decade, then, as a result of genocide, ethnic cleansing, and population policies, these once multiethnic lands had become almost completely homogeneous.

Yet the Lublin agreement did not put an immediate end to the civil war in the region. While the Soviets had initially employed the Poles in their fight against Ukrainian nationalists, now they were busy deporting Poles from the region precisely in accord with Ukrainian nationalist aspirations. In this sense, the Soviet Union had accepted the logic of the nationalists of creating ethnically uniform regions so as to put an end to interethnic conflict. In October 1944 the OUN noted this change in Soviet policies, commenting that the authorities had begun conducting "arrests and raids in Polish villages": "At the latest meetings of village council heads arranged by the districts, the Bolshevik government discussed the issue of relocating the Poles from Western

Ukraine to Poland." The Poles would have to "leave their residences, abandoning their farms, households, and tools, because Ukrainians from Poland would be taking over their homes. News is circulating," remarked the OUN with some satisfaction, "that the Bolsheviks are doing this in order to put an end to the internecine conflict between the Poles and the Ukrainians and to ensure appropriate behavior by the Banderites toward the Bolsheviks when Galicia is populated exclusively by Ukrainians." Of course, stated the OUN derisively, the Poles "cannot get it into their heads that they would have to abandon their hearths in the rich land of Galicia, to which they have made unfounded claims from time immemorial. Today they are still dreaming of Poland on Ukrainian lands."[12] Ironically, then, the old dream of Ukrainian nationalists was about to be realized by their most hated enemy: an ethnically pure Western Ukraine created by Soviet population policies.

✿ ✿

In early 1945 the first secretary of the Buczacz district committee of the Communist Party of Ukraine, K. M. Rybachuk, described the conditions he had encountered when he first arrived in the district. The Germans, he wrote, had "looted and caused terrible devastation" everywhere. "The population was transported beyond the boundaries of the district, the fields were abandoned, and the absence of crops caused the economy of the district to decline even further." The Germans had destroyed numerous plants and food manufacturing facilities, mills, bridges, water-supply systems, electric and telephone networks, schools, the power station, the railroad station, and a hospital. Worst of all, "the Germans killed more than 10,000 civilians in the district and deported over 6,000 young people to slave labor. The town of Buczacz became desolate. Of the original 15,000–16,000 inhabitants, no one was left in Buczacz by Liberation Day"; six months later, the population had grown to merely 2,750 people.[13]

At the time of the report, the town still had more than nine hundred empty houses, some of which were partially destroyed. Much of the livestock in the district was gone; five thousand horses and a similar number of swine, ten thousand heads of cattle, fifty thousand hens, as well as five thousand tons of grain and "many other agricultural products and tools," had all been removed by the Germans. In return the Wehrmacht had sown 300,000 landmines in the pastures and fields. Rybachuk reported that during those first six months, much had been restored, including two distilleries, a bakery, the power station, the hospital, the printing press, a few agricultural machines, clothes and shoe manufacturing facilities, schools, the town club, and the movie theater; additionally 184,000 mines had been cleared.[14] But Buczacz was still in a wretched state, and would remain so for a long time thereafter.

The Soviets also dedicated considerable efforts to investigating the crimes committed during the German occupation. Already in late July

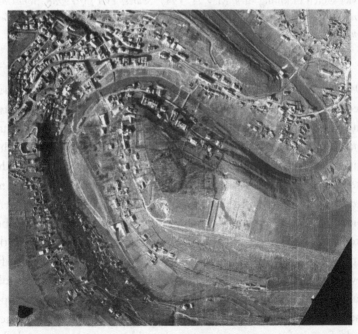

German aerial photo of Buczacz, April 1944. *Source: National Archives and Records Administration (NARA), RG 373: GX12125 SD, exps. 32, 33, 62, and 63 (combined).*

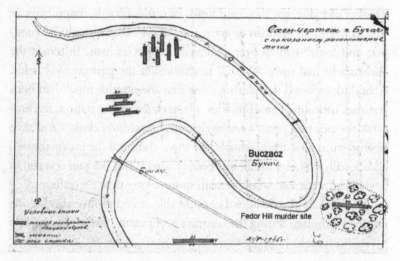

Soviet sketch of killing sites, May 21, 1945. *Source: YVA JM/19988, from Gosudarstvennyi Arkhiv Rossiiskoi Federazii (GARF) (State Archive of the Russian Federation), 7021-75-731.*

1944, an inquiry was launched into Nazi crimes in the recently liberated districts of Czortków, Zaleszczyki (Ukrainian: Zalishchyky), Tłuste, and Kopyczyńce. The report explicitly referred to German "mass executions ('pogroms') of the Jewish population," noting that "the entire Jewish population" of the town of Czortków "was annihilated." Many other details, such as the imposition of identifying armbands, ghettoization in the cities, practices of extortion and bribery, epidemics and starvation, and methods of mass execution, were elaborated. The report concluded with the cautious statement that in the entire Czortków district a total of "13,000 entirely innocent peaceful Soviet citizens" were murdered, but the bulk of the report left no doubt that the Jewish population was the main target of the German perpetrators, as well as of many, mostly Ukrainian "traitors to the Fatherland." Some of these men were mentioned by name, but most eluded justice.[15]

In early October 1944 local representatives of the Soviet Extraordinary Commission for the Investigation of Nazi Crimes launched a similar inquiry in Buczacz. The investigators exhumed mass graves and carried out forensic analysis, interviewed locals, and tried to obtain information from survivors. The commission also identified by name (although often misspelled or garbled) many Sipo men, gendarmes, Ukrainian policemen, and other local collaborators involved in the killings. An interim report issued in mid-October identified fourteen mass graves on Fedor Hill, containing altogether 13,670 victims; it was followed a few days later by a report on three mass graves found at the Jewish cemetery with an additional 5,000 victims. But the final report, submitted on November 5, concluded that "about 7,000 decomposed corpses" had been found, undressed and showing signs of firearm wounds to the back of the head, including "children aged under 15," some "with crushed skulls." This final version omitted all previous references to local collaborators, and while witness testimonies had unambiguously pointed out that the vast majority of the victims were Jews, the conclusion merely stated that these were "crimes against Soviet citizens."[16]

✿ ✿

For Ukrainians in Buczacz, the mass murder of the Jews had been both appalling and a cause for apology and self-justification. Like many others, Petrykevych was shocked by the roundups of winter and spring 1943, when he witnessed the Jews being "taken to the Fedor, where the Baudienst [labor service] had already prepared graves a few days earlier; they shoot them in the back of the head and throw them into the grave." But he insisted, "Our policemen let some of the Jews escape; our people are hiding them in barns and haystacks." At precisely the same time, hundreds of young Ukrainians in Buczacz were volunteering to serve in the Waffen-SS Division "Galicia," established in spring 1943 to symbolize Ukrainian participation in the German fight against the approaching Red Army.[17]

And yet, as Petrykevych noted, in the countryside the Germans were carrying out widespread requisitions of food from the peasants with such "draconian brutality" that the villages were filled with "wailing, groaning, and grief." German rule had become increasingly destructive, yet the prospects of Soviet occupation filled Ukrainians with dread. As Petrykevych observed in late September 1943, "some people have begun packing their possessions" for fear that the Soviets would "wreak ferocious revenge on those who collaborated with the Germans." Since the most damning witnesses of this collaboration were the few surviving Jews, this provoked a new wave of denunciations. "Every week, by chance or through denunciation, their bunkers are discovered; from there, they are taken to the police." Nonetheless Petrykevych was troubled by the fact that the Jews were "getting bolder. Carrying arms, some of them come in the evening to families that had been asked by other Jews to store their belongings, and demand to hand them back." And "if anyone refuses to return [the belongings], they declare that the Jews will punish them later."[18]

Other Ukrainian witnesses similarly combined empathy with denial. Maria Khvostenko, a teenager at the time, vividly recalled watching a terrifying scene from the window of the gymnasium facing the

Parade of volunteers for Waffen-SS Division "Galicia" in Buczacz, 1943. *Source: PA.*

town center: "In the middle of the main street a crowd was going around the city hall and toward the bridge over the Strypa. Gendarmes with dogs, Gestapo, and policemen with six-pointed stars surrounded the crowd and were hustling it toward the Fedor hill. What a horrible sight it was! There were women, men, old people and young—our schoolmates and friends. . . . They were our neighbors and strangers, but they were people!" This was only one of many horrors she encountered. "The killing machine worked methodically and without a hitch. From about the fall of 1942 to the end of 1943 they would hold execution actions, always on Fridays." Arriving "on Thursday evening," the Germans would "'act' or 'work' all night, and the next morning, as we were running to school, we could see the results of their work: corpses of women, men and children lying on the road. As for infants, they would throw them from balconies onto the paved road. They were lying in the mud with smashed heads and spattered brains." Near Fedor Hill "we could hear machine-gun fire accompanied by the drone of engines, which were intended to drown the sound of the shooting but instead only intensified it."

Khvostenko remembered that a Polish family living nearby had "tried to save their Jewish friends and were all shot," save for their daughter, who was her classmate. "She had been away on some errand and when she came back she found her family dead. She went mad and nobody saw her after that." There were several other stories of rescue: one Jewish woman was hidden in the Basilian monastery; another hid in the basement of the Roman Catholic church. But Khvostenko firmly believed that "our people respected the religious feeling of the Jews and never abused them" and that "there were no quarrels between neighbors, no slander or disrespect." While she indicated the presence of Jewish policemen "with six-pointed stars," she failed to mention the ubiquitous presence of armed Ukrainians at the killings and the rash of denunciations that cost the lives of so many Jews on the eve of liberation.[19]

Julija Trembach, who came from a Polish family but married a Ukrainian and remained in Buczacz after the war, was still troubled by memories of the German "crimes against Jewish people" even at the age of ninety-three. During the war she had a front-row view of how the Germans "buried them alive on Fedor Hill, and how those people dug their own graves. From the street where I lived, I could see how the ground was moving over the people who were still not dead. I will never forget the moans and cries of those people," who had "committed no crime." But she also insisted that although "the Germans forbade us to help Jews and to give them shelter" on pain of death, "our people, both Ukrainian and Polish, tried to help in any way they could. They made dugouts in the ground, and Jews hid there. Secretly people would bring food to those dugouts. And God only knows how much food I brought by myself." During one roundup, she recalled, a young woman "came running to me. She had a baby in her arms." The woman "was crying and exhausted. She whispered: 'Save us, hide us.' At my own risk I hid them in the hayloft. . . . I fed that little girl with my own breast, because I had a baby myself." She kept them at her house for several days, until a group of Jews took the mother and baby with them. Nor was this "the only case," declared Trembach. "We pitied those people, for they were beaten, always scared for their lives and never knew what would happen to them at any moment."[20]

✡ ✡

For some Poles, including sympathetic observers, the German murder of the Jews was associated with the alleged Jewish participation in the Soviet victimization of the Poles. The Buczacz power plant manager Władysław Hałkiewicz conceded that as far as the Jews were concerned, both Poles and Ukrainians "had an opportunity to help more but did not want to," largely because under Soviet rule "the poor Jews had collaborated with the Soviets, leading to the deportation of the Polish intelligentsia to Siberia," while "the Jewish intelligentsia" conveniently "assumed a neutral stance toward the Bolsheviks." Father Rutyna agreed decades later that the people of Buczacz had "suffered so much under the Jews, since the latter had bound themselves to the Soviets during the war with all their agitation and sympathies."[21]

But a few testimonies concerned primarily with the rescue of Jews give us a glimpse into the courage, ingenuity, and perseverance of Poles who chose to risk their lives to save others. One striking example is Mikołaj Szczyrba, who was raised and educated in Buczacz and was living with his wife, child, and parents on the farm he had purchased in the village of Grabowce (Ukrainian: Hrabivtsi), some eighty miles southeast of Buczacz, on the eve of the war. He described the local Ukrainian peasants as "generally hostile" to the many Jewish farmers, tradesmen, cattle dealers, and butchers living in the surrounding villages: "Very often windows in Jewish houses were smashed, their shops robbed and their apartments demolished." After the Soviets withdrew in summer 1941, large-scale violence erupted. In the village of Piłotkowice (Ukrainian: Pylatkivtsi), "the Ukrainians took all Jewish men (and boys) to the forest, where they had to dig a pit for themselves and were then killed." The remaining widows and orphans were driven out. In Zieliniec (Ukrainian: Zhylytsi) the Ukrainians "murdered the whole Jewish population—slashing everyone's throats: children, women, the elderly, and the men"—and threw the bodies into the river. Only in Łosiacz (Ukrainian: Losyach) did the local priest forbid the peasants from killing "any more Jews or Poles."

Szczyrba witnessed much more violence over the next two years, including the liquidation of the ghetto in Borszczów "by German gendarmes and Ukrainian police." Forced to bury the corpses, he saw that "the walls were covered with blood; fragments of human flesh and brains were everywhere on the streets." Notices warned people against hiding Jews and promised payment for handing them in. This sparked "many denunciations and informing on others by Ukrainians," resulting in additional murders of "hidden Jews as well as of the Polish families that had hidden them, while the traitors received a reward." Initially, Szczyrba testified, when asked by his "Jewish acquaintances" for help, he was "afraid and refused" because "there had been many cases in which Jews were interrogated under torture and disclosed the names of their protectors." But in May 1943 the twenty-seven-year-old farmer decided to help a group of sixteen Jews from Borszczów to hide in the forest; he provided them not only with food but also with weapons, left behind by Red Army troops he had helped escape in 1941. In time the number of those in hiding rose to thirty-two, "mainly young people and couples without children." With his instructions and tools they built a large and well-camouflaged underground bunker.

Three months later Szczyrba was denounced by suspicious Ukrainian neighbors and arrested. He spent seven weeks in prison in Czortków, was "interrogated, abused, beaten, and tortured," but refused to "confess anything." Released thanks to generous bribes by his friends, Szczyrba returned home to find that during that time in prison "my wife and my stepfather had taken food to the Jews in the woods every other day." Not long thereafter some of the Jews joined Soviet partisans, while others organized their own band, raided a German Army barracks for weapons, and managed to release scores of Jewish, Ukrainian, and Polish inmates from the prison in Borszczów. Tragically, in December the group was ambushed and most of its members were killed. Of those who had remained in the bunker, many also died in a German forest raid. But there were still six Jews being cared for by Szczyrba when the area was liberated. They remained in touch with him after the war, but as he testified, "Unfortunately they cannot help me at all because they themselves live in very hard material conditions; nevertheless they know best how I and my wife sacrificed ourselves to save their lives."[22]

In the immediate aftermath of the war, some Poles hoped to benefit from true or false claims of having saved Jews. In August 1947, for instance, Michał Boczar, formerly of Porchowa, a small village ten miles southeast of Buczacz, appealed for help from the Central Jewish Committee in Warsaw. Now living on "a dilapidated farm abandoned by German refugees" near Wrocław (German: Breslau), he claimed, "In 1943–44, I selflessly hid five Jews for ten months, risking my own life." His house was "close to the forest, where many Jews were hiding," and he regularly provided them with "hot meals, bread, and sometimes also clothes"; in winter they "occasionally spent several nights at my abode for fear of persecution by the Banderites." After the war those he had rescued were living outside Poland and could neither send him money nor furnish any proof of his good deeds. He thus requested "a single benefit amounting to 30,000 złoty" (roughly the equivalent of 200 U.S. dollars today) in order "to support three children, one of whom is disabled, a seven-year-old, and a daughter who is getting married soon."[23]

Two months later, Eugenia Czechowicz, living at the time in Szczecin, also appealed to the Central Committee. Beginning in the fall of 1942, she wrote, she had taken to hiding Jewish children in Buczacz whenever an action was expected; she even adopted an orphaned five-year-old boy "as my child." Thanks to her actions, she said, she was nicknamed "the wet nurse of the Jews." She had also sheltered adults, including Munio Altchiler (Maurycy Altschüler), who later "went abroad and has not been heard from since." In April 1944, when the Wehrmacht reoccupied Buczacz, Czechowicz was arrested and the Jews she was hiding, including her adopted son, were taken away. She herself was "beaten and tortured" for four weeks "in a concrete basement," then released. She ended up in Poland, having lost all her property and also her husband, a cavalry officer, who ran off with Anna Zilber, a Jewish woman they had hidden, "while I and my child were deprived of husband and caregiver." Feeling betrayed by the very people she had saved and suffering from failing health, Czechowicz asked for money to help her open a shop.[24]

It is impossible to tell whether these stories of rescue were true, but from numerous Jewish testimonies we know that most of those who survived were helped by Christian acquaintances or complete strangers, and that such help could and at times did come at a steep price for the rescuers. It is also true that some survivors began seeking their saviors only many years after the war, whereas others showed their gratitude as soon as they were able to. There were also, however, false claims, made by people who had never helped and by people who had sought to make a profit during the war and now hoped to gain a little more. Yet as Czechowicz's story indicates, assuming it was true, beyond the life-and-death struggle for existence, people caught in these events also experienced many other, more mundane but deeply painful tragedies, of love and passion and betrayal, which marked their lives for many years thereafter. In Czechowicz's case, what could be told as an unlikely romance between a Polish cavalry officer and a Jewish woman in hiding became the unjust consequence of an act of kindness and sacrifice.

✡ ✡

The October 1944 investigation of Nazi crimes in Buczacz was not much more than a sideshow in the effort to reestablish Soviet power in the region, dedicated primarily to crushing the Ukrainian insurgency and transforming the demography of an already devastated region. It was a herculean task. In August 1944 the first secretary of the Tarnopol regional committee, Ivan Kompanets, wrote the future Soviet leader Nikita Khrushchev, at the time first secretary of the Communist Party in Ukraine, about the dire conditions in the recently liberated territory. One's first impression, Kompanets pointed out, was that "the vast majority of the inhabitants . . . had been transported to Germany by the Nazis" and that the towns were "totally lifeless." Just as disconcerting was the fact that when the population began trickling back a few days later, "the vast majority" were Polish. As Kompanets explained, "from conversations with the people of the liberated towns and villages it became clear that before the German army retreated" it had "forced the inhabitants . . . to march to Germany in columns." One villager related how "the Germans chased every man like beasts" and then "took them away, no one knows where." Kompanets made no reference either to Poles fleeing Ukrainian terror or to Ukrainians fleeing anticipated Soviet and Jewish vengeance. Instead he triumphantly informed his boss, "The population of the Nazi-occupied regions, after experiencing the harsh German oppression, was greeting the Soviet representatives with open arms, telling them about all the Nazi atrocities, and volunteering to assist the local authorities in restoring what the Germans had destroyed." One peasant had allegedly exclaimed, "We and our offspring will hate them forever. Now we know how much we should appreciate Soviet power."[25]

This peasant's view was clearly not unanimously shared by the

Ukrainian population. Reporting again to Khrushchev in September, Kompanets noted that the Tarnopol region had been experiencing a "significant increase in bandit activity," so that "in July and August not a single day went by without the murder of a district officer, a village head, or a Soviet activist." Indeed, he stressed, "terrorist groups and even larger bandit formations have penetrated almost all districts in the region," and their activities "go practically unpunished." Kompanets was especially concerned about "the professional OUN leaders with their many years of underground experience," and the insurgents' supply of "portable radios and underground printing presses," with which they "disseminate propaganda literature to the population of the region." Simultaneously the UPA "had prepared a significant number of commanders and leaders" and had "considerably increased the number of their trained fighters." These "bandit gangs terrorize the local population, murder Soviet and village communist activists, stage raids on village councils, burn grain and threshing machines, rob cooperatives, storage silos, and butter plants, burn down Polish villages and kill Poles," and "organize daytime and nighttime ambushes on the highways, shoot at military vehicles and kill army troops." Kompanets thus asked for urgent military and NKVD assistance, additional weapons and ammunition, and "permission to deport the families of the bandits from the region."[26]

The response by the Soviet authorities was swift and brutal. In early October 1944 units of the NKVD began streaming into the region, and anti-insurgent operations, including massive deportations, greatly intensified. On October 14 the NKVD reported that "3,329 families of OUN members are scheduled for resettlement from the western regions of Ukraine, altogether 10,517 persons." Additional resources were needed for the "transfer of OUN-families" to Siberia, entailing "the resettlement of 5,000 families with 15,000 people, scheduled for October and November 1944." From the region of Tarnopol alone, 525 families, or 1,500 people, were scheduled for deportation, with another 245 families numbering 711 people already confirmed for resettlement. The deportations were carried out under appalling conditions. On November

18 even an NKVD officer expressed concern that "the families of OUN-members are being transported to Kiev in train cars unfitted for winter. Thus train number N-49339 is unheated; there are no windows in the railcars, and the stoves do not work. As a result there has been a high incidence of illness among these special resettlers, among them twelve dead children." But such petty complaints had no impact on the overall situation. By November 26 a total of 13,320 people had been deported from Western Ukraine, with many more awaiting their turn.[27]

Deportations of civilians went hand in hand with hunting down and eliminating the insurgents. In planning its operations in the Buczacz district for 1945, the NKVD identified a large number of underground groups and allotted forces for "annihilation actions" in numerous villages. For this purpose several "destruction battalions" were established, each numbering 180 men, and intelligence was gathered through recruitment of "internal agents" charged with "infiltrating the UPA organization as well as the OUN underground." Local officials were instructed to "intensify the repression against the families of bandits," as well as to "fill the ranks of combat units fighting the UPA" with "all those arrested during an operation" who might "express a desire to fight the bandits" rather than end up in a gulag. Finally, all adult district residents were registered, and families were warned that if "a person in hiding" did not "show up for registration in the city council, Soviet power will consider him a collaborator with the [insurgent] bands and will apply repression against his family."[28]

As a result of this system of raids, recruitment, and surveillance, by late fall 1946 the Buczacz district authorities had "liquidated" five "gangs," killed 188 and jailed 167 "bandits," arrested 254 OUN members, and deported 58 "families of bandits and their collaborators." The estimated overall number of nationalist fighters thus declined from 500 to 71.[29] By the end of 1946 the insurgency in the Tarnopol region was clearly on the wane, with over 200 insurgent groups liquidated, approximately 2,500 fighters killed, close to 6,000 fighters and underground members arrested, and 1,000 "families of bandits and their accomplices" deported. Less than a year later, the authorities in the Buczacz district concluded that the insurgency had diminished to a single OUN group of four fighters and "20 isolated bandits."[30] One estimate put the total number of nationalist victims of repression in the Buczacz district between 1944 and 1953 at 671 fighters killed, including 59 women, as well as 1,628 imprisoned or deported to Siberia, about half of whom were women. Meanwhile, as military operations were winding down, deportations were intensifying, with close to 350 families deported between July and October 1947. It was stated that "the vast majority of the poor and middle class people approve of and support" these deportations, whereas "the mainly rich villagers and relatives of the deported sympathize with them and are frightened." Clearly deportations entailed not only punishing the insurgents but also social engineering and buying off the much larger poor section of the peasantry with the property of the deported. As soon as the trains left for the East, the troops and local Soviet activists reportedly proceeded "with the inventory and removal of the deportees' belongings."[31]

☆ ☆

Even as the Soviets were hunting down insurgents and deporting their families to the East, they were simultaneously engaged in "repatriating" the remaining Polish population in the region to what became communist-ruled Poland and absorbing Ukrainians deported from Poland, as agreed in Lublin. In this the authorities were paradoxically helped by the OUN-UPA's ferocious attacks against Polish communities, which led to increasing pressure by local Poles to enable them to flee the region. As Secretary Kompanets reported from Tarnopol, in the first ten months of 1945 close to 80,000 Polish families, almost a quarter of a million people, had registered for repatriation, of whom 45,000 individuals had already left the region. During the same period 7,000 Ukrainian families with 23,000 people had arrived from Poland. The figures kept growing, despite various logistical difficulties and attacks by armed bandits on caravans trekking from one country to another. By late June 1946 the Czortków region had relocated to Poland 107,000 Polish citizens (including 1,852 Jews and 1,000 "others");

of the remaining 1,000 still slotted for repatriation, half preferred to stay where they were. The Buczacz district had relocated 12,000 Poles, leaving behind not a single registered Polish citizen. With this, declared the local official in charge, "the transfer of Polish citizens is basically complete."

By 1948 the Buczacz district's demography had been entirely transformed. The overall population had shrunk to 36,000, including merely 4,000 in the city of Buczacz. As the district authorities reported, these were "principally . . . Ukrainians," including close to 1,500 relocated persons from Poland. People were said to be "generally well disposed toward the Soviet authorities," largely thanks to financial investments and economic development in the district.[32]

Once the two main obstacles to a firm hold on the region—the interethnic conflict with the Poles and radical Ukrainian nationalism—were removed, the heavy shroud of Soviet power descended on the towns and villages of the Buczacz district. Promises of economic and educational progress, greater equality and the eradication of poverty, improved professional training, and employment prospects may well have appealed to a population desperately trying to recover from years of upheaval and oppression, shattered hopes, and drastic dislocation. But the system ended up choking the region, thanks to its own internal contradictions and because so many of the most enterprising and best-trained inhabitants had been murdered, expelled, or deported. Those who tried to fill the vast gaps torn in the fabric of society were ill prepared for these roles, coming into the desolate towns either from nearby backward villages or as deportees from remote rural locations in Poland.[33] By the time the curtain was raised in 1991, towns such as Buczacz had all the appearance of having remained stuck in a time warp, their shabby Soviet façades and dusty streets reflecting the hopelessness of their inhabitants, so many of whom still seemed, even decades later, to be grappling with the question of what urban life in a neglected borderland province should look like. Not a great deal has changed since then.

The Jewish cemetery in Buczacz, 2003. *Photo by the author.*

All three ethnic groups living in Buczacz and its district under-
went extreme suffering, although their agony peaked at different times and often at the hands of different perpetrators, just
as their propensity to collaborate with the occupiers depended on different factors and changing circumstances. And yet, at the time and long
after, each group sought to present itself as the main victim, both of the
occupying powers and of its neighbors. Poles and Ukrainians were particularly keen on highlighting their martyrdom, in part out of fear that

the Nazi genocide of the Jews would overshadow their own victimhood but also because in reality both groups had far greater room for accommodation with the Germans, even as they benefited from much more elaborate and effective underground organizations than were available to the Jews under the relentless German onslaught. Additionally widespread anti-Jewish prejudice and resentment, fueled by suspicions of Jewish collaboration with the Soviets and a common view of the Jews as not belonging to the land and not deserving any share in its future, combined to marginalize or dismiss the mass murder of the Jews, isolated expressions of sympathy and compassion notwithstanding.

The Ukrainian Petro Pasichnyk, born in the village of Zielona, six miles north of Buczacz, and a former member of the UPA, was haunted by wartime memories. Because of the "great animosity" between Poles and Ukrainians, he said, "our people destroyed" Polish villages; in return, after the Germans were driven out, "Poles in 'destroyer battalions'" helped the Soviets suppress the Ukrainian insurgency. In one case "they caught a female teacher" deployed as a messenger for the UPA "and just murdered her, just chopped her into pieces." He described the murder of the Jews, including some of his classmates, but found it somewhat mystifying. "I saw how they were driven into the forest to execution," he said, "but I just wonder: how could they go so passively?! They did not escape. Did they believe that this was their fate, or something else?" After all, he insisted, "there were only a couple of Germans" at the site. "It was a horror," he added. "It is indeed dreadful to see corpses lying [on the ground], murdered children." Pasichnyk had evidently observed some of the killings from close by, but he made no reference to the numerous Ukrainian policemen who rounded up the Jews and guarded the perimeter of the execution site. Indeed, when asked, he responded adamantly, "I did not see the police, I saw the SS. The SS would come, take [Jewish] children and throw them out of windows. You would go through the street and see bodies everywhere. But our people—I don't know, there could have been something somewhere, but I can't say anything because I know nothing."

Pasichnyk's insistence that this was a purely German action made it necessary to explain the alleged failure of the Jews to escape by invoking their predetermined fate or uncanny acceptance of massacre. It was also immediately relativized by reference to Ukrainian martyrdom, even if by a different regime: "Equally horrible was the time when the Soviets were executing our people. Every day . . . there were corpses, corpses, corpses. . . . They would bring them [to Buczacz]—and display them. . . . When they hanged someone, they would bring people to watch." And since Pasichnyk also energetically confirmed that "yes, of course, the Jews collaborated" with the Soviets, his account created a certain symmetry of horror between the somewhat mysterious eradication of the Jews and the heroic martyrdom of "our people." This was a version of the past that many Ukrainians of his generation in Western Ukraine had internalized and retained for decades thereafter. But it demanded a degree of selective recollection.[1]

According to Ihor Duda, the author of a guide to Buczacz published in 1985, Buczacz had experienced tremendous progress over the previous four decades of Soviet rule. (He did not know that the communists would soon be out of office.) It was also an idyllic site for tourists. Along the "picturesque banks" of the Strypa, he wrote, "various recreation areas have been laid out—parks, public gardens and a beach. The extraordinary beauty of the Strypa valley with its partially forested rocky slopes, narrow creeks and terraces, and deep ravines, is quite striking." Buczacz also "abounds in monuments of history and architecture," dating back to earlier centuries as well as "from the Soviet period." The latter included such delectable sites as "the house where the district Revolutionary Committee was situated in 1920 and the Provisional District Administration Board convened in 1939"; a Lenin monument; and an artillery gun along with a tractor "placed on pedestals as testimony to the glory of the Soviet people in war and labor." Additionally Buczacz benefited from new industrial undertakings, including factories for metal and tinned food, a mechanized bakery, a sugar refinery, a distillery, a mixed fodder plant, a cheese dairy, and a unit of mobile mechanized machinery. There were numerous schools as well, for agriculture, technology, motor transport, music, art, and sports, supported by fourteen libraries, two "palaces of culture," a cinema, and a museum of local history. Judging by this account, Buczacz was a veritable Western Ukrainian haven of the best Soviet civilization could offer. No wonder that, according to Duda, year by year the city was "becoming younger and nicer. It has a rich history and beautiful present."

Regarding that rich past, Soviet Buczacz was especially proud of its local history museum, opened in 1982 in the former city hall, which displayed such items as, on the first floor, "a model-reconstruction of the Buczacz castle, the interior of a peasant's hut," and "items of national costumes, ceramics and household objects," while the second floor was dedicated to more recent Soviet history. Here the eager tourist could find "photographs and personal belongings of the Western Ukrainian People's Council delegates," along with those of "other honored citizens, veterans of war and labor," and "many materials concerning the Great Patriotic War and the liberation of the city from the German-Fascist occupants." The museum had swiftly become, according to Duda, "a center of patriotic and internationalist education for the youth," who learned in this manner "about the high price paid for our beautiful present." Those youngsters privileged enough to study in the former gymnasium, now Secondary School No. 1 and named after the locally born Ukrainian ethnographer Volodymyr Hnatiuk, imbibed a regular communist educational diet that strictly avoided any information on such prewar students as Emanuel Ringelblum and Simon Wiesenthal, let alone anything about the author Shmuel Yosef Agnon or more generally on Jewish Buczacz. Leading his readers from one site to another, mostly Soviet schools, factories, and memorials, Duda ended his recommended walk through the city at "an observation spot" located on "top of the Baszty hill." From there, he wrote, "we can see almost all the routes we passed" while touring the city. Duda and his imaginary tourists would have been standing at that moment just feet away from the Jewish cemetery and its mass graves. But the guide made no mention of the Jews who lived and died in Buczacz.[2]

At a commemoration ceremony held in 2006 next to the OUN-UPA memorial on the slope of Fedor Hill, only a couple of dozen veterans attended. After the fall of the communist regime, the local administration officially recognized the veterans' sacrifice and provided them with a symbolic supplement to their pensions. Even more important, they now had a keeper of the flame, Oresta Synenka, a small elderly woman who directed the local branch of the Poshuk (Search) society in Lviv, served as chairperson of the Russian Memorial society's district affiliate, and was founder and director of the Museum of the Liberation Organizations, located in the former offices of the NKVD in Buczacz and dedicated to commemorating the victims of communism and the martyrs of Ukraine's struggle for independence.[3]

Oresta came to Buczacz as a twelve-year-old in 1945; she recalled that there were still two synagogues in the city at the time, "one at the place where now the yellow house stands, and the other right behind it." The former was the Study House, or *beit hamidrash*, a site that the author Agnon fondly invoked in many stories about his hometown.

The Buczacz Museum of the Liberation Organizations, 2006. *Photo courtesy of Sofia Grachova.*

The latter was the Great Synagogue. Oresta's father worked as a foreman in a construction and demolition brigade; he told her that since "the whole block of houses" in that location "had been bombarded," the crew decided that "there was no sense in repairing the synagogue, so they demolished it. They were done by 1950." It was said that the materials from the Great Synagogue were used to construct the new Soviet cinema that stands in the city to this day.

Oresta's interest in local veterans may have first been sparked when she met her future husband, Ivan Synenkyi, whose own succinct testimony she eventually recorded in 2004. Ivan, who was a teenager at the time, was deeply scarred by his wartime experiences. "I was witness to the events of the Holocaust," he stated, recalling that "before the war" Jews had lived in Buczacz "in peace with Ukrainians, Poles and other national minorities." Under German rule, "the Hitlerites carried out regular monthly actions against the Jews," during which "they would assemble 300–400" people and "shoot them all in the forest on the Fedor hill. . . . They would force the doomed to undress, take them to the edge of the pit and shoot them down." Among the victims he knew were "Lumcio Rosenbach, his wife and their twelve children." Only one son "survived by miracle; later he found himself in Russia, and now he lives in Israel." Asked whether people in the city could hear the executions of the Jews, he said, "Oh yes, we could hear that very well." Oresta, presumably reporting what her husband had told her, added, "Some guys would even go to see the shooting. They would climb on trees and watch." Ivan must have been one of the onlookers, since he too was puzzled by the victims' conduct: "The Jews would go to the execution site passively. They didn't resist, they only lamented." His wife explained, "They knew they were doomed. They had no help from anywhere. Ukrainians were not hostile, but they would be executed for helping a Jew." Still, some did help. "Ivan's brother-in-law saved a Jewish girl and baptized her. Later she married. She still lives in Rohatyn," not far from Buczacz.

Ivan insisted that while "the Nazis were merciless to Ukraine" as well, "the bloodiest trace they left in our city was the fate of the Jews." Describing the killing sites around Buczacz, he concluded, "There are

Memorial tombstone on Fedor Hill, 2003. *Photo by the author.*

almost no Jews left in the city, but the graves and the memory of the bloody terror of that time remain."[4] In fact contemporary Buczacz contains very few traces of the lives and mass murder of its Jews. The memorial tombstone on Fedor Hill is surrounded by a dense forest and barely accessible; a humble memorial at the Jewish cemetery, erected a decade ago, has been damaged and is hidden for much of the year under tall thorny bushes.

As for the Study House, the only original Jewish religious edifice in Buczacz, Ivan said, "The Germans turned it into a granary. It was still a granary in the 1990s, until it was pulled down." The event was witnessed by Ruhama Albag, an Israeli scholar of Hebrew literature, who happened to be visiting Buczacz on Agnon's birthday, August 8, in 2001. She recalled from Agnon's writing that "in the heart of the city there were two that had become one: The old Study House adjacent to the Great Synagogue." As they "approached the market square," she wrote, all that was left "were mounds of dirt, piles of stones and wooden beams. Deafening tractors had reduced . . . the old study house to ruins." What Agnon had considered to be the soul of his town was gone, replaced by a garish yellow shopping center.[5]

Demolition of the Study House, 2001. *Photo courtesy of Ruhama Albag.*

Writing about "the Holocaust in Buczacz" in a local newspaper in 2000, the Ukrainian journalist Tetiana Pavlyshyn may have been right to conclude that although "more than half a century has passed since that time . . . people's memories have not changed" and "are stamped with that horrible moment in our history."[6] Those fraught and traumatized memories contain as much forgetting as remembering. But selective as they are, they hold great elements of truth and pain despite the massive memory erasure imposed by the previous Soviet narrative of the war, whose effects still linger long after the fall of communism. An echo of that tale could be found in another essay in the same paper, published just a few weeks before Pavlyshyn's article and intended to enlighten readers about the events of World War II in the Buczacz area. In describing the crimes of the Germans, the author, Oksana Chorniy, simply noted, "Over seven thousand civilians were exterminated, and 1,839 young men and women were deported to Germany." The only brief reference to Jews in the entire essay came from the mouth of Hanna Muzyka, a Ukrainian woman who had worked in a German Army kitchen. One of the Germans, she was quoted as saying, "employed two Jewish girls as servants, and nobody denounced them. Later those girls thanked everybody for that."[7]

Fifteen years earlier, Duda's guide to Buczacz had provided a local version of the classic Soviet narrative of the Great Patriotic War. Although "about 7,500 civilians from the city and the district villages" were "exterminated" by "the Hitlerites," "the population did not submit to the fascists"; following the liberation "hundreds of Buczacz residents joined the ranks of the Red Army," and "over thirty of them fell in action fighting for their Motherland." This was not the same motherland for which the men and women of the OUN-UPA had fought. And just as the memory of the insurgents was expunged from the Soviet narrative, so too the memory of the Ukrainian nationalists' complicity in the genocide of the Jews and their direct engagement in the ethnic cleansing of the Poles was erased from their own postcommunist glorification. In the Buczacz district, these fighters included Mykola Ivantsiv ("Rosa"), an adherent of Prosvita and a loyal member of the OUN, who joined the UPA in Volhynia in 1943, "where he received his baptism of fire." Ivantsiv, who "continued to fight after returning home" to the Buczacz district, eventually "blew himself up with a hand grenade" rather than surrender to Soviet troops in 1947. Even more tellingly, Volodymyr Lutsiv ("Orel"), the leader of the local Sich that undertook "cleansing" operations following the withdrawal of the Soviets in 1941, joined the fight against the Poles and the Soviets in 1944 and was killed by NKVD troops in 1948. By then his parents had died in Soviet deportation; of his three brothers, one was deported, a second jailed and tortured, and a third killed in the ranks of the UPA. Lutsiv's wife, an OUN activist, was sentenced to twenty-five years in a gulag and died shortly after her release, while their daughter died of neglect at a young age. In 2003 Volodymyr and his daughter were reburied in a solemn ceremony in Buczacz, in a "holy grave for a son and a daughter of the Ukrainian nation."[8]

If the Poles described the Ukrainian insurgents as savages, and the

Jews saw them as "worse than the Germans," from their own point of view they were martyrs of a just and holy cause, the liberation of their land from foreign oppression: the goal justified the means, including massacres, ethnic cleansing, and genocide. Many of them died in battle, were executed by the NKVD, or spent long years in gulags. Others fled to the West, where they formed the nationalist hard core of the Ukrainian diaspora. Vilified by the communists as fascist collaborators, they emerged from obscurity and were celebrated as the harbingers of the nation after Ukrainian independence in 1991, especially in Western Ukraine. Two decades later, as a newly resurgent Russia sought to reassert its influence on Ukraine, the UPA again came to symbolize the country's historical struggle against its mighty eastern neighbor: in 2016 the black-and-red banner of the insurgent army was again fluttering from the remnants of the medieval Polish castle overlooking Buczacz. History was back to its old tricks.

UPA flag on top of the castle in Buczacz, 2016. *Photo by the author.*

Acknowledgments

This book has been long in the making. It spans two decades, three continents, nine countries and as many languages, and scores of archives. Most important, it was nourished by a network of support and wisdom, institutional and professional, as well as personal and emotional, so thick and dense and entirely indispensable that I would never be able to sufficiently thank and acknowledge it. At the same time, I must admit that I have been waiting for a long time to write these words, not only in order to express my profound gratitude, but also because they signify the completion of an undertaking which, at times, seemed to have taken on a life of its own and to have entirely taken over mine. By having brought it to completion I have had to accept that it is far from perfect, but also that perfection is unachievable and that we therefore always hover somewhere between what we can make and how we would like it to be. Bringing things to a close is both an accomplishment and a surrender to the constraints of time and ability. Halfway through writing this book I encountered the wonderful saying by Shmuel Yosef Agnon, the great biographer of Buczacz, who once described his vast, unfinished masterpiece on his hometown with the words: "I am building a city." The construction of living cities never ends; they are the products of all those who build them. Building a city of ghosts, or as Agnon called Buczacz decades before its destruction, "a city of the dead," is another matter. It is a very lonely project, but it cannot be accomplished alone. I am at a loss for words to thank those who led me on this path, and I apologize to them all for having taken so long to complete this book and for the multiple imperfections it contains. All I can say is that "for us, there is only the trying. The rest is not our business."

I owe this book first of all to my mother, who planted its seed and never lived to see it grow, and to my father, whose faith in this work sustained me throughout all these years, and who slipped away to a better world just as it was finished. May their memory be a blessing.

I would not have been able to research and write this book without the generous help of Rutgers University during the project's inception and the sustained and unstinting support of Brown University since my arrival in 2000. I have been fortunate to enjoy many research grants that allowed me periods of leave to concentrate on research and writing. I am especially grateful to the National Endowment for the Humanities, the Radcliffe Institute for Advanced Study at Harvard University, the John Simon Guggenheim Foundation, the Internationales Forschungszentrum Kulturwissenschaften in Vienna, the American Academy in Berlin, the Pembroke Center and the Cogut Institute for the Humanities at Brown University, the Center for Advanced Holocaust Studies of the United States Holocaust Memorial Museum, the Distinguished Visiting Professorship at National Taiwan University, the Institute for the History of Polish Jewry and Israel-Poland Relations at Tel Aviv University, the International Institute for Holocaust Research at Yad Vashem, and the Israel Institute for Advanced Studies at the Hebrew University of Jerusalem.

Along the way I have been helped by a large number of research assistants and translators, a number of whom also became close friends. I would like to especially thank Sofia Grachova, Frank Grelka, Anna Michalska, Joanna Michlic, and Naama Shik for many years of close collaboration, as well as Jane Zolot-Gassko, Eva Lutkiewicz, Oleg Majewski, Lars Nebelung, Eliezer Niborski, Kateryna Ruban, Vicki Shifriss, Taras Tsymbal, Rebecca Wolpe, and Evelyn Zegenhagen. Natalia Aleksiun remembered "my" Buczacz in archives and listened to me going on about the book. Dagmar Herzog was a source of continuous inspiration. Irit Halavy knew the soul of the book before I conceived it. Yoel Rappel shared his knowledge of the region and of many other matters. Shimon Redlich read drafts of several chapters and provided invaluable comments, as did Jonathan Beard. Uzi Vogelman joined me on the most recent journey to his father's hometown of Brzeżany (Ukrainian: Berezhany) and the potato cellar where he survived in the one-street village of Kuropatnyky. Roman Voronka linked me to his birth town and never gave up on me. Thomas Weiss took me on a virtual tour of Buczacz and, together with his sons, made the tombstones readable again. Maurice Wolfthal gave me a box full of treasures over breakfast at Phoenix, Arizona.

Many other friends and colleagues have provided advice and support over the years. I would like to thank especially Vadim Altskan, Tarik Cyril Amar, Israel Bartal, Ela Bauer, Delphine Bechtel, Doris Bergen, Ray Brandon, Suzanne Brown-Fleming, Jeffrey Burds, Marco Carynnyk, Alon Confino, Martin Dean, Havi Dreyfus, Sofia Dyak, David Engel, Dan Eshet, Ziva Galilee, Simone Gigliotti, Amos Goldberg, Nurit Govrin, Jan Grabowski, Jan Tomasz Gross, Atina Grossmann, Wolf Gruner, Geoffrey Hartman (z"l), John Paul Himka, Ariel Hirschfeld, Peter Holquist, Yaroslav Hrytsak, Zvi Karniel (z"l), Samuel Kassow, Mykola Kozak, Wendy Lower, Yaacov Lozowick, Paul Robert Magocsi, Dirk Moses, Norman Naimark, Boaz Neumann (z"l), Yohanan Petrovsky-Shtern, Antony Polonsky, Alexander Prusin, Elchanan Reiner, Grzegorz Rossoliński-Liebe, Per Anders Rudling, Raz Segal, Avner Shalev, Joshua Shanes, Paul Shapiro, Marci Shore, David Silberklang, Timothy Snyder, Stanisław Stępień, Adam Teller, Richard Tyndorf, Larry Warwaruk, Amir Weiner, Eric D. Weitz, Larry Wolff, and Boguslaw Zdzieblo. There were many more, from Caracas, Venezuela, to Melbourne, Australia.

I owe more than I can express here to my teacher Saul Friedländer, ever since those exhilarating days of study and debates at Tel Aviv University in the late 1970s, when the world of knowledge and understanding opened up and Facebook and Twitter were not even a little dark cloud on the horizon. In recent years I benefited tremendously from the knowledge, sensibilities, and friendship of Alan Mintz, who devastatingly passed away in the midst of his Herculean labors on Agnon's Buczacz and literary biography.

In bringing this book to see completion I was fortunate to be guided and helped by my agent, Don Fehr, my editor, Sean Manning, and my publisher, Jonathan Karp, who stepped in decisively just as I was reaching the depths of despair.

It is customary to thank one's family for having provided the indispensable circumstances for producing a book. In this case my family has spent so long with my book-in-being that it has become almost a way of life; they may not even recognize me as I exit my study. But I hope it is not too late to make it up to them. There are always more books to be written, but in truth, this book would have never seen the light of day without them.

—Omer Bartov

Notes

MEMORIES OF CHILDHOOD

1 The Ships List: http://www.theshipslist.com/ships/lines/balticam
.shtml; Haapalah/Aliyah Bet: http://www.wertheimer.info/family
/GRAMPS/Haapalah/plc/1/2/bc69f6d1a2c5c4e7a21.html; The Palestine Poster Project Archive: http://www.palestineposterproject.org
/poster/polonia; SS *Polonia*: http://pl.wikipedia.org/wiki/SS_Polonia
(all accessed August 29, 2016).

Chapter 1: THE GATHERING STORM

1 S. Barącz, *Pamiątki Buczackie* (Lwów, 1882), 3–4.
2 S. Y. Agnon, *The City Whole* (Tel Aviv, 1973, in Hebrew), dedication
page, 9–13. See the selective translation *A City in Its Fullness*, ed. A.
Mintz and J. Saks, multiple translators (New Milford, CT, 2016). All
translations of Agnon are my own. For local Ukrainian versions see Y.
Stotskyi, *The Basilian Monastery* (Lviv, 1997, in Ukrainian), 36–38,
48–49; I. Kladochnyi, *Brief Sketch of Buczacz* (private publication,
no city given, Canada, 1990, in Ukrainian), 1–3. See also Barącz,
Pamiątki Buczackie, 4–7, 48–52; S. J. Kowalski, *Powiat Buczacki i jego*

zabytki (Biały Dunajec, Poland, 2005), 25–26, 32–36, 42–43, 49–50, 54–55. For the larger historical context, see P. R. Magocsi, *Historical Atlas of East Central Europe* (Seattle, 1995), 10, 12, 15, 18–20, 31–33, 46, 48–53, 59–61; D. Stone, *The Polish-Lithuanian State, 1386–1795* (Seattle, 2001), 3–20, 36–66, 136–39, 147–48; P. R. Magocsi, *A History of Ukraine* (Seattle, 1996), 175–228; O. Subtelny, *Ukraine*, 3rd ed. (Toronto, 2000), 124, 127; J. Lukowski and H. Zawadzki, *A Concise History of Poland* (New York, 2001), 75–83.

3 M. Y. Brawer, "Buczacz: A Geographical Outline," and N. M. Gelber, "A History of the Jews in Buczacz," in *Sefer Buczacz* (The Book of Buczacz), ed. Y. Cohen (Tel Aviv, 1956, in Hebrew), 43 and 45–46, respectively, and citations therein; J. Tokarski, *Ilustrowany przewodnik po zabytkach kultury na Ukrainie* (Warsaw, 2000), 2:37; M. Nosonovsky, *Hebrew Epitaphs and Inscriptions from Ukraine and Former Soviet Union* (Washington, DC, 2006), 25, 107; A. Brawer, "Buczacz," *Encyclopaedia Judaica* (Jerusalem, 1978), 4:1037; B. D. Weinryb, *The Jews of Poland* (Philadelphia, 1972), 25, 27, 115–16, 151–52, 318; G. D. Hundert, *Jews in Poland-Lithuania in the Eighteenth Century* (Berkeley, 2004), 6, 14–15; M. J. Rosman, *The Lord's Jews* (Cambridge, MA, 1991), 37–40; I. Bartal and S. Ury, "Between Jews and their Neighbours," in *Polin*, vol. 24: *Jews and their Neighbours in Eastern Europe since 1750*, ed. I. Bartal, A. Polonsky, and Scott Ury (Oxford, 2012), 14–15, 17–20; J. Goldberg, "The Role of the Jewish Community in the Socio-Political Structure of the Polish-Lithuanian Commonwealth," in *Polin*, vol. 22: *Social and Cultural Boundaries in Pre-Modern Poland*, ed. A. Teller, M. Teter, and A. Polonsky (Oxford, 2010), 142—55; N. N. Hanover, *The Book of the Deep Mire* (Tel Aviv, 1944–45, in Hebrew), 31–32, 37–38, 40–43, 52, 56–57, 63 (my translation); N. N. Hanover, *Abyss of Despair*, trans. A. J. Mesch (New Brunswick, NJ, 1983 [1950]), 42–44, 50–51, 54–58, 68–69, 76–77, 86; S. Stampfer, "What Happened to the Jews of Ukraine in 1648?," *Jewish History* 17 (2003): 207–27; J. Raba, *Between Remembrance and Denial* (New York, 1995), 38, n. 128, 75, 98–99, 108, 367–434; F. Sysyn, "Ukrainian-Polish Relations in the 17th Century," in *Poland and Ukraine*, ed. P. J. Potichnyi

(Edmonton, 1980), 55–82; J. Pelenski, "The Cossack Insurrections in Jewish-Ukrainian Relations," and F. Sysyn, "The Jewish Factor in the Khmelnytsky Uprising," in *Ukrainian-Jewish Relations in Historical Perspective*, ed. P. J. Potichnyi and H. Aster (Edmonton, 1988), 35, 43–54. On subsequent communal violence see H. Abramson, *A Prayer for the Government* (Cambridge, MA, 1999), 109–40; chapters by S. Lambroza, P. Kenez, and H. Rogger in *Pogroms*, ed. J. D. Klier and S. Lambroza (Cambridge, UK, 2004); K. Lada, "The Ukrainian Topos of Oppression and the Volhynian Slaughter of Poles, 1841–1943/44" (PhD diss., Flinders University, 2012).

4 *Das Reisejournal des Ulrich von Werdum (1670–1677)*, ed. S. Cramer (Frankfurt/M., 1990), 210–11; Biblioteka Czartoryskich w Krakowie, Poland, man. 609, p. 89; A. Zamoyski, *The Polish Way* (New York, 2001), 185; Stone, *Polish-Lithuanian State*, 235–36.

5 Kowalski, *Powiat Buczacki*, 26–27, 37–38; Barącz, *Pamiątki Buczackie*, 6–7, 11–12, 53; F.-P. Dalairac, *Les Anecdotes de Pologne ou Memoires secrets du Règne de Jean Sobieski* (Paris, 1699), 230–31; Gelber, "The Jews in Buczacz," in *Sefer Buczacz*, 46–47; *Akta grodzkie i ziemskie* (Lwów, 1931), 24:380, Nr. 198, sections 2–3; Kladochnyi, *Brief Sketch of Buczacz*, 3; Agnon, *The City Whole*, 16; Magocsi, *Historical Atlas*, 60; Stone, *Polish-Lithuanian State*, 170–72, 174.

6 Gelber, "The Jews in Buczacz," in *Sefer Buczacz*, 48, 67–69, 72–73, citing Österreichisches Staatsarchiv, Vienna (hereafter AT-OeSt), MdI: IV T. 1777, X, and Ossolineum, Wrocław, man. 3636; Dalairac, *Anecdotes de Pologne*, 228–32, cited in Barącz, *Pamiątki Buczackie*, 10–13, and further in 14–16, 27, 54; Agnon, *The City Whole*, 14–15; Kowalski, *Powiat Buczacki*, 27–28, citing W. Urbański, *Buczacz i jego Powiat* (Buczacz, 1936), and further on 34, 49–50; A. Żarnowski, *Kresy Wschodnie II Rzeczypospolitej* (Kraków, 1992), 17; Stotskyi, *Basilian Monastery*, 39, 143; Kladochnyi, *Brief Sketch of Buczacz*, 4; "Bazylianie w Buczaczu," in *Oriens* 5/4 (1937): 155.

7 The wooden synagogue on the banks of the Strypa was built in 1685 after the old synagogue burned down. Mikołaj Potocki also built the Roman Catholic and the Greek Catholic St. Pokrova churches

in Buczacz. Kladochnyi, *Brief Sketch of Buczacz*, 4–7, 10–12; Agnon, *The City Whole*, 12, 18, 20, 25–27, 29–40, 43–56, 89–90, 233–38; S. Y. Agnon, *A Guest for the Night* (Tel Aviv, 1998 [1939], in Hebrew), 11-13; D. Neuman, "The Synagogues in the Town," and response by M. Rabinowitz, *Davar Supplement*, August 28 and September 9, 1938 (in Hebrew), cited in *Sefer Buczacz*, 89–92, and also Gelber, "The Jews in Buczacz," in *Sefer Buczacz*, 56, 53, n. 28, citing AT-OeSt, MdI, IV T 1, Carton 2582, Nr. 143, October 1812; Archives of the Lwów Episcopacy, Ukraine, *Directorium Divini Officii in Archidioecesi Leopoliensi* (Lwów, 1819), 73 and (1835), 68–69; *Schematismus Universi Venerabilis Cleri Archidioeceseos Metropolitanae Graeco Catholicae, Leopoliensis* (Lwów, 1832), 89; *Tygodnik Ilustrowany*, 1860, Nr. 24, Archiwum Państwowe w Krakowie (The National Archives in Kraków, hereafter APK), Teki Schneidera (the Schneider collection), file 227, pp. 665–68; Barącz, *Pamiątki Buczackie*, 33–34, 54–59; T. Kuznek, *Przewodnik po województwie tarnopolskiem* (Tarnopol, 1928), 222–23; "Bazylianie w Buczaczu," 155; Kowalski, *Powiat Buczacki*, 28–32, 35–37, 44–52, 45–46, 70–71; Żarnowski, *Kresy Wschodnie II Rzeczypospolitej*, 8, 15–17; Stotskyi, *Basilian Monastery*, 39–44; B. Voznytskyi, *Mykola Pototskyi, Bernard Meretyn, Ioan Heorhiy Pinzel* (Lviv, 2005, in Ukrainian).

8 Barącz, *Pamiątki Buczackie*, 34–35. In his 1833 masterpiece *The Undivine Comedy* (*Nie-Boska komedia*) the author Zygmunt Krasiński described Mikołaj Potocki as a ruler who "shot women on trees and baked Jews alive": https://wolnelektury.pl/media/book/pdf/nie-boska-komedia.pdf (accessed August 28, 2017), 51. See also C. Miłosz, *The History of Polish Literature*, 2nd ed. (Berkeley, 1983), 243–7, and L. Wolff, *The Idea of Galicia* (Stanford, 2010), 145, citing L. von Sacher-Masoch, *Graf Donski*, 2nd ed. (Schaffenhausen, 1864), 343. Others saw him as a great patron of the arts. See, e.g., *Słownik Biograficzny* 28 (Kraków, 1984–85), 113–14, also citing F. Karpiński, *Pamiętniki* (Warsaw, 1898), 18, 66, 74–76, and J. U. Niemcewicz, *Pamiętniki czasów moich* (Paris, 1948), 81–83; Lukowski and Zawadzki, *Concise History of Poland*, 88–96; Żarnowski, *Kresy Wschodnie II Rzeczypospolitej*, 8;

N. A. Feduschak, "A Prince, Philanthropist and Playboy," *Kyiv Post*, November 2, 2011, http://www.kyivpost.com/article/guide/people /a-prince-philanthropist-and-playboy-an-exciting-li-116186.html (accessed September 2, 2016).

9 A. J. Brawer, *Galizien: Wie es an Österreich kam* (Leipzig, 1910), 15–17, 22–29, 35–49; W. O. McCagg, *A History of Habsburg Jews* (Bloomington, IN, 1989), 27; N. Sinkoff, *Out of the Shtetl* (Providence, RI, 2004), 201–225; S. Grodziski, "The Jewish Question in Galicia," in *Polin*, vol. 12: *Focusing on Galicia*, ed. I. Bartal and A. Polonsky (London, 1999), 61–72.

10 R. van Luit, "Homberg, Herz," *YIVO Encyclopedia of Jews in Eastern Europe*, http://www.yivoencyclopedia.org/article.aspx/Homberg _Herz (accessed September 3, 2016); Tsentralnyi derzhavnyi istorychnyi arkhiv, m. Lviv (Central State Historical Archives of Ukraine in Lviv, hereafter TsDIAL), fond (record group) 146, opys (series, hereafter op.) 85, sprava (file, hereafter spr.) 1903: "K.k. Galizische Statthalterei, 1772–1854"; Sinkoff, *Out of the Shtetl*, 228–31, 269; N. M. Gelber, "The History of the Jews of Tarnopol," in *Encyclopaedia of the Jewish Diaspora, Poland Series, Tarnopol Volume*, ed. Ph. Korngruen (Tel Aviv, 1955), 46–51, 55–83; Gelber, "The Jews in Buczacz," in *Sefer Buczacz*, 55, on Rabbi Pinchas Eliyahu Horowitz, an early Orthodox reformer, who spent several years in Buczacz. See also J. Perl, *Sefer Megale Temirin*, ed. J. Meir (Jerusalem, 2013, in Hebrew).

11 M. Bernstein, *Einige Kulturhistorische Blicke über die Juden in Galizien* (Vienna, 1850), v, 11–12, 13–15, 17–18, 32–33, 39, 41–43. See also C. Thornhill, "Eastern Jews and the Sociology of Nationalism," in *Ghetto Writing*, ed. A. Fuchs and F. Krobb (Columbia, SC, 1999), 68–82; M. Wodziński, *Haskala and Hasidism in the Kingdom of Poland*, trans. S. Cozens (Portland, OR, 2009), 117, 159; S. W. Baron, "The Impact of the Revolution of 1848 on Jewish Emancipation," *Jewish Social Studies* (hereafter *JSS*) 11/3 (1949): 195–248, esp. 231; Y. Slezkine, *The Jewish Century* (Princeton, 2004), 4–39; S. J. Zipperstein, *Imagining Russian Jewry* (Seattle, 1999), 41–62.

12 J. Shanes, *Diaspora Nationalism and Jewish Identity in Habsburg Galicia* (New York, 2012), 31–37. In 1886 Buczacz numbered 1,920 Roman Catholics, 1,761 Greek Catholics, and 6,281 Jews; 2,551 people, presumably mostly Jews, declared German their language of daily use. By 1900 Buczacz had 3,078 Roman Catholics, 1,918 Greek Catholics, and 6,730 Jews; only 395 declared German, while 8,948 (of whom 5,000 were likely Jews) gave Polish as their common language. *Special Orts-Repertorien der im Oesterreichischen Reichsrathe vertretenen Königsreiche und Länder*, K. K. Statistische Central-Commission, vol. 12, *Galizien* (Vienna, 1886), 66; *Gemeindelexikon der im Reichsrate vertretenen Königsreiche und Länder*, K. K. Statistische Zentralkommission, vol. 12: *Galizien* (Vienna, 1907), 100.

13 A. S. Markovits and F. Sysyn, eds., *Nationbuilding and the Politics of Nationalism* (Cambridge, MA, 1982); J.-P. Himka, *Galician Villages and the Ukrainian National Movement in the Nineteenth Century* (London, 1988), 158–75; J.-P. Himka, *Religion and Nationality in Western Ukraine* (Montreal, 1999); P. R. Magocsi, *The Roots of Ukrainian Nationalism* (Toronto, 2002); C. Hann and P. R. Magocsi, eds., *Galicia* (Toronto, 2005); K. Struve, *Bauern und Nation in Galizien* (Göttingen, 2005), 384–433.

14 Himka, *Galician Villages*, xxv, 66–86, 163, 167; J. Pennell, *The Jew at Home* (New York, 1892), 56.

15 Himka, *Galician Villages*, 169–70, 173–74; Struve, *Bauern und Nation*, 386–401; K. Stauter-Halsted, *The Nation in the Village* (Ithaca, NY, 2001), 48–52, 116–17, 138–39.

16 J.-P. Himka, "Ukrainian-Jewish Antagonism in the Galician Countryside during the Late Nineteenth Century," in Potichnyi and Aster, *Ukrainian-Jewish Relations*, 12, citing issue 1, October 1, 1879, and 113, issue 3, June 1, 1881; Struve, *Bauern und Nation*, 394, citing issue 3, February 1, 1880, and 413, citing issue 5, March 1, 1876.

17 Struve, *Bauern und Nation*, 415–16; O. Kofler, *Żydowski dwory* (Warsaw, 1999), 8–9, citing T. Gąssowski, *Między gettem a światem* (Kraków, 1997), 48; S. Pawłowski, *Wielka własność w byłej Galicji Wschodniej* (Lwów, 1921), 12–13, 16. According to Himka, *Galician*

Villages, 158, in 1902 Jews owned 18.5 percent of the tabular land in private estates in Eastern Galicia. S. Gruiński, *Materiały do kwestyi żydowskiej w Galicyi* (Lwów, 1910), 27–29, notes that by 1902 over 25 percent of the landed properties in Galicia were in Jewish hands; Jews rarely possessed vast latifundia, but they owned almost 40 percent of medium-size land properties and paid 10 percent of all taxes received from landed property.

18 Kofler, *Żydowski dwory*, 240–45, 292–93. See also YIVO Institute for Jewish Research library, New York (hereafter YIVO), Nr. 77378A: O. Kofler, "Jewish Manors," undated typescript of the book's English translation, likely by the author himself, 136–39. Court Jews traditionally handled the finances of royalty and nobility in early modern Europe. In 1900 the estate of Petlikowce Stare (Old Petlikowce; Ukrainian: Stari Petlykivtsi) had a population of fifty-eight Roman Catholics, twelve Greek Catholics, and twenty-eight Jews; eighty-nine declared Polish their language of daily use, and nine spoke Ruthenian. *Gemeindelexikon von Galizien, bearbeitet auf Grund der Ergebnisse der Volkszählung vom 31. Dezember 1900*, ed. K. K. Statistische Zentralkommission (Vienna, 1907), 104.

19 Kofler, *Żydowski dwory*, 5–9, 15–21, 117–21, 128–29, 134–35, 248–72; Kofler, "Jewish Manors," 1–4, 57–60, 64–65, 68–69, 140–54.

20 Z. Heller, "My Memories"; N. Menatseach, "My Youth"; B. Berkowitz, "The First Hebrew School in Buczacz," in *Sefer Buczacz*, 145, 167–70, and 174–78, respectively. Y. Fernhof, an early influence on Agnon, was born in Buczacz in 1866 and died of typhus in Stanisławów in 1919. Y. Cohen, "Yitzhak Fernhof," in *Sefer Buczacz*, 122–27.

21 *II. Sprawozdanie dyrekcyi C. K. Gimnazyum w Buczaczu za rok szkolny 1901* (Lwów, 1901), 36–39; *III. Sprawozdanie . . . za rok szkolny 1902* (Lwów, 1902), 17, 52, 54; *VI. Sprawozdanie . . . za rok szkolny 1905* (Buczacz, 1905), 79, 81–82, 85; *X. Sprawozdanie . . . za rok szkolny 1909* (Buczacz, 1909), 65, 68–69; *XII. Sprawozdanie . . . za rok szkolny 1911* (Buczacz, 1911), 67; *XIII. Sprawozdanie . . . za rok szkolny 1912* (Buczacz, 1912), 85–86, 88, 92; *XIV. Sprawozdanie . . . za rok szkolny 1913* (Buczacz, 1913), 98–100; *XV. Sprawozdanie . . . za rok szkolny*

1914 (Buczacz, 1914), 89–92, 94–96. Biblioteka Jagiellońska, Kraków (hereafter BJ), Mf. 11712.

22 *I. Sprawozdanie dyrekcyi c. k. Gimnazyum w Buczaczu za rok szkolny 1900* (Stanisławów, 1900), 3–10.

23 *VII. Sprawozdanie dyrekcyi c. k. Gimnazyum w Buczaczu za rok szkolny 1906* (Buczacz, 1906), 3–5, 16–18, 24–26.

24 Teofil Ostapowicz, "Wspomnienia wychowanka buczackiego gimnazjum z lat 1901–1909 i trochę historii tegoż z lat poprzednich od roku 1754," vols. 1 and 2, Biblioteka Zakładu Narodowego im. Ossolińskich (Library of the Ossolineum National Institute, Wrocław, hereafter BOss.), sygnatura (file, hereafter sygn.), 15396/II, pp. 49–51; Żarnowski, *Kresy Wschodnie II Rzeczypospolitej*, 21. Gymnasium graduates included Mieczysław Gębarowicz, director of the Ossolineum National Institute in Lwów; Władysław Ostrowski, interwar parliamentary representative of the Polish Peasant Party; and Władysław Kalkus, the last commander of Poland's air force in 1939. See P. Czartoryski-Sziler, "Wielcy zapomniani: Mieczysław Gębarowicz," *Nasz Dziennik*, October 1–2, 2005, http://lwow.home.pl/naszdziennik /gebarowicz.html; "Polish Air Force Order of Battle 01.09.1939," *Axis History Forum*, http://forum.axishistory.com/viewtopic.php ?f=111&t=179631 (both accessed September 9, 2016).

25 All incorporation certificates of Buczacz associations in New York City are on microfilm at the American Jewish Historical Society.

26 W. Portmann, *Die wilden Schafe* (Münster, 2008), 12–17, 18–19, citing *Tydzień Robotnika* (Warsaw, Lemberg edition), no. 6, February 6, 1938; M. Nomad, *Dreamers, Dynamiters and Demagogues* (New York, 1964); *Das Österreichische Sanitätswesen*, ed. J. Daimer et al. (Vienna, 1894), 733; M. Bałaban, "Buchach," *Yevreyskaya Entsyklopedya*, ed. L. Katznelson and D. G. Ginzburg (St. Petersburg, Russia, 1906–13, in Russian), 5:135–36; S. Hryniuk, *Peasants with Promise* (Edmonton, 1991), 171–92. And see Zvi L-L, "From the Jewish World," *The Jewish Awakener*, Nr. 42, Buczacz, August 10, 1906; Menatseach, "My Youth," noting that the paper, established by Eliezer Rokach and co-edited by Agnon, appeared in 1906–1908; C. Roll, "The Hospital and

the Home for the Elderly," and D. D. P., "Memorable Women," all in
Sefer Buczacz, 104–5, 171, 180–82, and 222, respectively.

27 Agnon, *The City Whole*, 644–46.

28 Portmann, *Die wilden Schafe*, 55–58, and citing M. Nacht, "Anarchis-
tenjagd," *Neues Leben*, Nr. 23 (June 6, 1903) and Nr. 24 (June 13,
1903); Agnon, *A Guest for the Night*, 236–37, 323–25. The news of
Siegfried's release arrived on the same day by telegram: Buczacz had
a telegraph office since 1863. Kladochnyi, *Brief Sketch of Buczacz*,
13; Stotskyi, *Basilian Monastery*, 42. See also, e.g., *Robert Graham's
Anarchism Weblog*, https://robertgraham.wordpress.com/2010/09/10
/siegfried-nacht-the-social-general-strike-1905/ (accessed February 17,
2017).

29 E. Dubanowicz, *Stanowisko ludności żydowskiej w Galicyi wobec Wy-
borów do parlamentu wiedeńskiego w r. 1907* (Lwów, 1907), 6, 8–12,
16–17, 22–24, 34–35, 39–40, and table, 41. Paradoxically, while Jews
had a plurality in the city of Buczacz, the candidate of the Jewish National Party, Natan Birnbaum, lost the election because most Ruthenians preferred the Polish candidate. Conversely, in the rural Buczacz
district, although Greek Catholics made up two-thirds of the population, the Jewish candidate won thanks to an agreement between the
Ruthenians and the Jews, becoming one of only four Jewish National
Party representatives in the Austrian Parliament. *Wiadomości statystyczne o stosunkach krajowych wydawany*, ed. T. Pilat, vol. 23, pt. 1: *Wy-
bory do Sejmu krajowego z r. 1908 i lat dawniejszych*, ed. M. Nabodnik,
Krajowe Biuro Statystyczne (Lwów, 1910), 10, 14–15, 23–24, 28, 31,
34–35; vol. 24, pt. III: *Materiały statystyczne do reformy sejmowej ordy-
nacie wyborczej*, ed. M. Nadobnik, Krajowe Biuro Statystyczne (Lwów,
1912), 8, 14, 17–18, 24; *Oesterreichische Statistik*, vol. 84, Nr. 2: *Die
Ergebnisse der Reichsratswahlen . . . im Jahre 1907*, ed. K. K. Statistische Zentralkommission (Vienna, 1908), 86–87. Shanes, *Diaspora
Nationalism*, 266, 270, 275, has a somewhat different interpretation.
Dubanowicz became a professor of law at Lwów University and a
member of the Polish Parliament as an affiliate of the anti-Semitic National Democratic Party. G. J. Lerski, *Historical Dictionary of Poland*,

966–1945 (Westport, CT, 1996), 119; J. Faryś et al., *Edward Dubano-wicz, 1881–1943* (Szczecin, Poland, 1994).

30 Gruiński, *Materiały do kwestyi żydowskiej*, 20–21, 35, 46, 49–50. The Jewish Colonization Association (Ika) in Galicia also trained poten-tial immigrants in agriculture and settled them "as farmers in extra-European countries," especially Argentina, but also Canada, Cyprus, Palestine, Asia Minor, and Brazil, and in cooperation with the Jewish Agricultural and Industrial Aid Society, also in the United States, no-tably in New Jersey (52–53). Pilat, *Wiadomości statystyczne*, vol. 23, pt. 3: *Podatki bezpośrednie w Galicyi przypisane na r. 1910*, ed. M. Nabod-nik, Krajowe Biuro Statystyczne (Lwów, 1910), 12, 17; *Bericht über die Tätigkeit des Hilfsvereins für die notleidende jüdische Bevölkerung in Galizien während des Jahres 1905* (Vienna, 1905), 4–10, 21–22.

31 TsDIAL, fond 309, op. 1, spr. 2547, pp. 44–45, 47–50. The question-naire was distributed by the Shevchenko Scientific Society, founded in Lwów in 1873 to promote the Ukrainian language, and later a schol-arly institute led by the historian Mykhailo Hrushevsky with significant input by the author Ivan Franko. See the Shevchenko Scientific Society's website, http://www.shevchenko.org (accessed September 9, 2016).

32 "Students Wreck University," *New York Times*, January 24, 1907, http://query.nytimes.com/mem/archive-free/pdf?res=9907E6D8153EE 033A25757C2A9679C946697D6CF (accessed September 9, 2016).

Chapter 2: ENEMIES AT THEIR PLEASURE

1 *Österreich-Ungarns letzter Krieg 1914–1918*, ed. E. Glaise-Horstenau et al., vol. 1: *Das Kriegsjahr 1914*, 2nd ed. (Vienna, 1931), 37–47, 155–338, esp. 305, 319–20, 595, 599; *Österreich-Ungarns letzter Krieg*, vol. 2: *Das Kriegsjahr 1915*, pt. 1 (Vienna, 1931), 176–77. See also N. Stone, *The Eastern Front, 1914–1917* (London, 1975); H. H. Herwig, *The First World War* (London, 1997); J. A. Sandborn, *Draft-ing the Russian Nation* (DeKalb, IL, 2003).

2 Antoni Siewiński, "Pamiętniki buczacko-jazłowieckie z czasów wojny wszechświatowej od roku 1914 do roku 1920: pamiętnik rodzinny,"

BJ, rkp. 7367 II, 4–6. Siewiński appears as temporary director of the four-grade public boys' school in Buczacz in *Szematyzm nauczycielski wraz z kalendaryum na rok 1911* (Lwów, 1910), 123. See also W. Maćkowicz, *Wspomnienia polskiego nauczyciela Pogranicza (1893–1976)*, ed. J. Zdrenka (Toruń, Poland, 2005), the diary of a younger Polish teacher who attended the Buczacz gymnasium before World War I.

3 Siewiński, "Pamiętniki," 8–10.

4 Ibid., 10–11, 13–15, 22.

5 Kofler, *Żydowski dwory*, 129; Kofler, "Jewish Manors," 65.

6 Siewiński, "Pamiętniki," 17–20.

7 Ibid., 21–22.

8 Ibid., 20–23.

9 Ibid., 24–28.

10 Ibid., 28–34.

11 Ibid., 34–35, 37–38.

12 Ibid., 38–39.

13 Ibid., 39–40; Kofler, *Żydowski dwory*, 254–55; Kofler, "Jewish Manors," 143–44.

14 Kofler, *Żydowski dwory*, 256–57; Kofler, "Jewish Manors," 144–45; Siewiński, "Pamiętniki," 40–45.

15 Siewiński, "Pamiętniki," 45–48. Russian and Austrian accounts note that after fierce fighting with Austrian hussars and artillery, elements of General Pavlov's 2nd Kuban Cossack Division, followed by the bulk of General Aleksei Brusilov's 8th Army, captured Buczacz on August 25, 1914. But General Pavlov's initial attempt to seize the town of Monasterzyska ten miles to the west was beaten back by the Austrian 35th Infantry Division. The fighting cost the Kuban Division alone some 250 men, and the countryside surrounding Buczacz was strewn with Russian and Austrian corpses. *Österreich-Ungarns letzter Krieg*, 2:206–8, 211–12; Tsentralnyi derzhavnyi istorychnyi arkhiv Ukrainy, m. Kyiv (Central State Historical Archives of Ukraine in Kiev, hereafter TsDIAK), fond 363, op. 1, spr. 2, p. 51.

16 Siewiński, "Pamiętniki," 50–55.

17 Ibid., 57–59.

18 Idib., 60, 64–65; Kofler, *Żydowski dwory*, 257–59; Kofler, "Jewish Manors," 145–46.

19 Siewiński, "Pamiętniki," 62, 66–67.

20 Ibid., 67–72, 153–54.

21 Ibid., 154.

22 Ibid., 81–84, 86–87; E. Lohr, "The Russian Army and the Jews," *The Russian Review* 60 (2001): 412–14.

23 Siewiński, "Pamiętniki," 91–97.

24 Ibid., 114–17, 124–25, 128–29, 154–60.

25 Kofler, *Żydowski dwory*, 184–90, 259–65; Kofler, "Jewish Manors," 100–104, 147–50.

26 Siewiński, "Pamiętniki," 160–68. The joint German-Austrian counteroffensive, begun on May 1, 1915, in which Buczacz was liberated, cost the Austro-Hungarian forces 500,000 casualties and the Russians well over a million. *Encyclopaedia Britannica* (hereafter *EB*), 12th ed. (London, 1922), 31:863–68, 901–3, 907; 32:296–97, 598; *Österreich-Ungarns letzter Krieg*, 2:465–67, 493–94, 613–18, 728–29; *Österreich-Ungarns letzter Krieg*, vol. 3: *Das Kriegsjahr 1915*, pt. 2 (Vienna, 1932), 66–68, 71–73, 97–107, 131–32, 171–75, 526–27, 556, 558–59; *Österreich-Ungarns letzter Krieg*, vol. 4: *Das Kriegsjahr 1916*, pt. 1 (Vienna, 1933), 13–15, 19–21, 729–30; AT-OeSt, Kriegsarchiv (War Archive, hereafter KA), Neue Feldakten (new operational documents, hereafter NFA), 36 Infantry Division (hereafter I. D.), Opus (series, hereafter Op.) Nr. 449/14, Karton (box, hereafter K.) 2124.

27 Siewiński, "Pamiętniki," 169–70.

28 Ibid., 170, 176–77; D. J. Penslar, *Jews and the Military* (Princeton, 2013), 157; M. L. Rozenblit, *Reconstructing a National Identity* (New York, 2001), 54; I. Deák, *Jewish Soldiers in Austro-Hungarian Society* (New York, 1990), 24–25; I. Deák, *Beyond Nationalism* (New York, 1990), 56–58; E. A. Schmidl, *Juden in der k. (u.) k. Armee* (Eisenstadt, Austria, 1989), 5. On Austrian Army fears of spies after reoccupying Buczacz, see ÖSA, KA, NFA, 36 I. D., Op. 432/37, K. 2123; Op. 802/58, K. 2124.

29 The second Russian invasion swelled the number of refugees to 200,000 by late 1917. Even in 1921 Galicia had 20 percent fewer

Jewish inhabitants than in 1910. Lohr, "Russian Army," 404–19; E. Lohr, "1915 and the War Pogrom Paradigm in the Russian Empire," and P. Holquist, "The Role of Personality in the First (1914–1915) Russian Occupation of Galicia and Bukovina," in *Anti-Jewish Violence*, ed. J. Deckel-Chen et al. (Bloomington, IN, 2011), 41–51 and 52–73, respectively; P. Holquist, "Violent Russia, Deadly Marxism?," *Kritika* 4/3 (2003): 637–68; AT-OeSt, Archiv der Republik (Archive of the Republic, hereafter AdR), Kriegsflüchtlinge (war refugees, hereafter KFL), numerous documents in K. 15–18 for 1915–18 on refuges from Galicia and Bukovina, including Buczacz.; E. Ederer, "The Jews of Vienna in Buczacz," in *Sefer Buczacz*, 188–91; Heller, "My Memories," in *Sefer Buczacz*, 158. See also Rozenblit, *Reconstructing a National Identity*, 66; P. Wróbel, "The Jews of Galicia under Austrian-Polish Rule, 1869–1918," *Austrian History Yearbook* 24 (1994): 133–35; A. V. Prusin, *Nationalizing a Borderland* (Tuscaloosa, AL, 2005).

30 AT-OeSt, Haus-, Hof-und Staatsarchiv, Politisches Archiv I, Krieg 3 R, Haltung Russlands 1915, K. 830, #507, "Telegramm des 1. Armeekommandos an das AOK." Buczacz was given 10,000 crowns on October 20, 1915, to support reconstruction. AT-OeSt, Allgemeines Verwaltungsarchiv (hereafter AVA), Ministerium des Innern (hereafter MdI), Allgemeine Reihe (hereafter Allg.), Signatur (series, hereafter Sig.) 18, K. 2233, "Elementarschäden . . . Galizien, 1914–15, 1916": "Subventionen in Buczacz (10.000 K)."

31 AT-OeSt, AVA, MdI, Präsidium, Sig. 22, K. 2115, "Galizien, 1912–1913," P. 9283/1911; K. 2119, "Galizien, 1918," P. 17387/1918: Pniaczek Marian aus Buczacz." On allegations of Jewish espionage under Russian occupation, as well as accounts of anti-Jewish Russian violence, including the rape of forty Jewish women in Buczacz, see S. An-Sky, *The Destruction of the Jews in Poland, Galicia, and Bukovina*, trans. from Yiddish to Hebrew by S. L. Zitron, 2 vols. (Tel Aviv, 1936[?]), vol. 1, pt. 1: 7–13, 99; pt. 2: 108, 111–13, 117; S. An-Sky, *1915 diary of S. An-Sky*, ed. and trans. P. Zavadivker (Bloomington, IN, 2016), 67, 169 (n. 53), 74. For an abridged English translation

see S. Ansky, *The Enemy at His Pleasure*, trans. and ed. J. Neugroschel (New York, 2002).

32 Siewiński, "Pamiętniki," 179–86, 194–202.

33 *EB*, 12th ed., 30:908–10; *Österreich-Ungarns letzter Krieg*, vol. 5: *Das Kriegsjahr 1916*, pt. 2 (Vienna, 1934), 218; *Österreich-Ungarns letzter Krieg*, vol. 6: *Das Kriegsjahr 1917* (Vienna, 1936), 46. T. C. Dowling, *The Brusilov Offensive* (Bloomington, IN, 2008), 160–2, 173, concludes: "The massive losses" of the Russian Army "undoubtedly lowered the morale of the troops even further, and by autumn the 'disease' of revolution was beginning to infect the front," with increasing numbers of frontline units refusing to fight. Additionally, the loyal noblemen who had originally made up the officer corps were decimated and replaced by recruits who were "increasingly poisoned by propaganda," coming as they did from a home front where "disaffection with the war had long been a problem." At the same time, the offensive also "put an end to whatever slim hopes of victory, or even survival, the Habsburg leadership might have had," since "the Austro-Hungarian military had, for all intents and purposes, ceased to exist," and "the mood of the populace, already doubtful, now took a turn for the worse as war-weariness turned to defeatism."

34 *Österreich-Ungarns letzter Krieg*, 4:426–35, 465.

35 A. Lev, "The Devastation of Galician Jewry in the Bloody World War: Excerpt from a Diary," trans. from Yiddish to Russian by B. Aizenberg, in *Jewish Chronicle*, ed. L. M. Klyachko et al. (Leningrad, 1924), 3:169–76, citation on 173–74. See also P. M. Zavadivker, "Blood and Ink" (PhD diss., University of California, Santa Cruz, 2013), 9, 85, 112; An-Sky, *Destruction*, vol. 1, pt. 2: 126–27.

36 Lev, "Devastation," 174–75.

37 Ibid., 173–76; An-Sky, *Destruction*, vol. 2, pt. 4: 349–52, 384–85, 400–406. Lev was inspired by Ansky and by the historian Simon Dubnow, whom he met in St. Petersburg just before the Brusilov Offensive. After the Revolution he worked for the Evsektsiia (the Jewish Section of the Communist Party); in World War II he joined the Jewish Anti-Fascist Committee, which collected evidence on the Holocaust.

Zavadivker, "Blood and Ink," 85–86. See also L. Jockusch, *Collect and Record!* (New York, 2012), 21–22; Z. Y. Gitelman, *Jewish Nationality and Soviet Politics* (Princeton, 1972), 292–303, citing A. Lev, *Religie un klaikoidesh in kamf kegn der idisher arbeter-bavegung* (Moscow, 1923); M. Altshuler et al., "Were There Two Black Books about the Holocaust in the Soviet Union?," *Jews and Jewish Topics in the Soviet Union and Eastern Europe* 1/17 (1992): 37–55.

38 *EB*, 12th ed., 30:911–13; *Österreich-Ungarns letzter Krieg*, 6:303–12, 409.

39 AT-OeSt, AVA, MdI, Allg., Sig. 18, K. 2235, "Elementarschäden . . . Galizien, 1917"; "Ostgalizien, Hilfsaktion, October 3, 1917; AT-OeSt, AVA, MdI, Allg., Sig. 18, K. 2235, "Elementarschäden . . . Galizien, 1918"; "Galizien, wirtschafl. Wiederaufrichtung der Stadt Buczacz," October 3, 1918; AT-OeSt, AdR, KFL, K. 16, 1918, "Heimkehr der Flüchtlinge nach Galizien," Vienna, March 29, 1918, p. 3; Archiwum Główne Akt Dawnych (Central Archives of Historical Records, Warsaw, hereafter AGAD), *zespół* (fond, record group, hereafter zesp.) 311, sygn. 250, k.k. Ministerium für öffentliche Arbeiten, November 16 and 19, 1917, January 12, 1918: "Heranziehung der Zivilbevölkerung . . . zum Straßenbau"; TsDIAL, fond 146, op. 48, spr. 31–32, "Ekspozytura budowlana, c.k. Namiestnictwa (C. O. G.) w Buczaczu," June 4 and July 4, 1918.

40 Siewiński, "Pamiętniki," 205, 224–25.

41 Ibid., 250–55. Archiwum akt nowych (Central Archives of Modern Records, Warsaw, hereafter AAN), Kolekcja opracowań i odpisów dokumentów dot. stosunków Polski z Łotwą, Ukrainą, etc. (Collection of documents concerning relations between Poland and Latvia, Ukraine, etc., hereafter KOOD), 55: report by Ukrainian National Council in Buczacz County, November 7, 1918, pp. 14–17. Bochurkiv's mid-1930s Polish police file (under his Polish name, Ilarjon Bociurków) reports, "Former Ukrainian Commissioner, carried out the internment of the Polish intelligentsia in the Buczacz District. Fierce enemy of the Poles. Intelligent and previously very influential." Derzhavnyi arkhiv Ternopilskoi oblasti (State Archive of Ternopil oblast, hereafter

DATO), fond 274, op. 4, spr. 78, p. 11. Siewiński also refers to him as Bociurko.

42 Siewiński, "Pamiętniki," 257–65; AAN, KOOD, 55, pp. 128–29, Report to the Ukrainian National Council in Lwów on the elections to the Buczacz County Council, November 8, 1918.

43 Siewiński, "Pamiętniki," 267–70, 272–80, 300; Centralne Archiwum Wojskowe (Central Archives of the Polish Armed Forces, Warsaw, hereafter CAW), I:400.1554: Testimonies from the Polish-Ukrainian War, pp. 27–42; Ukrainian Violence against Polish Civilians in Buczacz Country, pp. 28–29, 33.

44 Siewiński, "Pamiętniki," 275–80. Up to five hundred Poles were incarcerated in Jazłowiec, and numerous cases of violence and murder by Ukrainian troops and peasants in the region were reported. Released in late January 1919, Siewiński discovered that his house had been ransacked: "Everyone acted on their own initiative, did whatever they wanted, and no one obeyed anyone else" (288–90, 305, 309–17).

45 Siewiński, "Pamiętniki," 327–36.

46 Ibid., 336–37, 340–61; CAW, I:400.2213, Testimonies from the Polish-Ukrainian War, p. 5; CAW, I:400.1554, pp. 27–28, 33–35, 41; *The History of the Ukrainian Army* (Lviv, 1936, in Ukrainian), 504; *Encyklopedja Wojskowa*, ed. O. Laskowski (Warsaw, 1932), 2:87.

47 Siewiński, "Pamiętniki," 361–62, 370–77; *Encyklopedja Wojskowa*, 2:88; *History of the Ukrainian Army*, 509; CAW, I:400.1554, 2 (28), 7–10 (33–36), 14 (40), and throughout, 1–16 (27–42). See also testimonies about beating and looting of Poles by Ukrainian soldiers in the Buczacz area: AAN-Ministerstwo Spraw Zagranicznych (Ministry of Foreign Affairs, hereafter MSZ), 5341a, pp. 227, 233–34; CAW, I:400.2213, testimonies from the Polish-Ukrainian War 1918–19, 5; CAW, I: 301.9.6, "Naczelne Dowództwo W. P. 1766/III, Komunikat operacyjny frontu wschodniego z dn. 7 Lipca 19 r.," and "W. P. 1747 /III, Komunikat . . . z dn. 8.7.19"; W. Laudyn, *Bój pod Jazłowcem, 11–13.VII 1919* (Warsaw, 1932), 4–9; S. Wierżyński, *Zarys historii wojennej 14-go Pułku Piechoty* (Warsaw, 1929), 10–12; W. Hupert, *Zajęcie Małopolski Wschodniej i Wołynia w roku 1919* (Lwów, 1928),

102; Prusin, *Nationalizing a Borderland*, 102–4; Subtelny, *Ukraine*, 370–71; P. R. Magocsi, *A History of Ukraine*, 2nd ed. (Toronto, 2010), 548–51. The worst pogrom occurred in Lwów in November 1918, when 150 Jews were killed and 400 wounded. W. W. Hagen, "The Moral Economy of Popular Violence," in *Antisemitism and Its Opponents in Modern Poland*, ed. R. Blobaum (Ithaca, NY, 2005), 129. See also D. Engel, "Lwów, 1918," in *Contested Memories*, ed. J. D. Zimmerman (New Brunswick, NJ, 2003), 32–44. The author Isaac Deutscher wrote, "I lived through three pogroms during the very first week of reborn Poland. This is how the dawn of Polish independence greeted us." *The Non-Jewish Jew and Other Essays* (Boston, 1982), 11.

48 Siewiński, "Pamiętniki," 379–80.

49 BOss., manuscript department, sygn. 13502/II: Papiery różne związane ze działalnością Komitetu Obrony Narodowej we Lwowie z lat 1919–20, pp. 5, 7, 9; CAW 332.46.1, sector command Buczacz, 1919–20: "Pow. Dow. Etapowe w Buczaczu, Rozkaz Nr. 1," July 20, 1919; CAW 332.46.1, letter to the editor (name of newspaper not mentioned), signed Chairman Józef Wolgner, August 10, 1919. Another speech was delivered by Second Lieutenant Chlebek, likely the old gymnasium professor's son; CAW 332.46.1, "Do Dowództwa Okręgu Etapowego we Lwowie, Raport sytuacyjny, 30.8.1919," Major Wolgner. See also *Leuchs Adressbuch aller Länder der Erde*, vol. 19b: *Galizien u. Bukowina*, 10th ed. (Nuremberg, 1907–13), 117, http://genealo gyindexer.org/view/190713Leuchs19b/190713Leuchs19b%20-%20 0133.pdf (accessed September 22, 2016), showing Wolgner as a landowner in Komarówka, near Monasterzyska in the Buczacz district, and as a partner in the lime-producing firm Wolgner & Co.

50 CAW 332.46.1, "Powiatowe Dowództwo Etapowe Buczacz," situation report, October 25, 1919; November 1, 1919; November 15, 1919.

51 CAW I:400.2213, 5–6; Subtelny, *Ukraine*, 363, 372–75; Magocsi, *History of Ukraine*, 2nd ed., 537; I. M. Cherikover (Elias Tcherikower), *The Pogroms in Ukraine in 1919* (New York, 1965, in Yiddish), and review by E. Schulman, *The Jewish Quarterly Review* 57/2 (October 1966): 159–66, citing N. Gergel, "The Pogroms in Ukraine

in 1918–1921" (in Yiddish), *Yivo Shriftn far Ekonomik un Statistik*, vol. 1 (Berlin, 1928), estimating a total of 100,000 Jewish victims. On the battles around Buczacz and Bolshevik rule in the area, see M. Tarczyński, ed., *Bitwa Lwowska 25 VII–18 X 1920*, pt. 1 (Warsaw, 2002), 315, 378, 412, 445, 468, 516, 662, 870–71, 896; P. Shandruk, ed., *The Ukrainian-Muscovite War* (Warsaw, 1933, in Ukrainian), 122, 129–30, 134–35, 137, 139–41, 144–47, 149–50, 216–17, 225, 227; I. K. Rybalka, ed., *The Civil War in Ukraine, 1918–1920* (Kiev, 1967, in Russian), 337–38; "Miscellanea Archiwalne," *Wojskowy Przegląd Historyczny* 39/1–2 (1994): 160–63, 176–77; M. Klimecki, *Galicyjska Socjalistyczna Republika Rad* (Toruń, Poland, 2006), 183; B. I. Tyshchyk, *The Galician Soviet Socialist Republic of 1920* (Lviv, 1970, in Ukrainian), 64, 84, 92–93, 95, 102, 106.

52 Siewiński, "Pamiętniki," 380–81, 435–37. On prosecutions of Polish teachers suspected of collaborating with the Bolsheviks, see TsDIAL, fond 205, op. 1, spr. 822: "Prokuratura sądu apelacyjnego we Lwowie," January 1921, pp. 35–39.

53 Text of the treaty in *The Consolidated Treaty Series*, ed. C. Perry (New York, 1919), 225:412–24D. See also "The League and the Minority Treaties," *Bulletin of International News* 5/18 (1929): 3–10.

54 See also C. Fink, "Minority Rights as an International Question," *Contemporary European History* 9/3 (2000): 385–400; M. Mazower, "Minorities and the League of Nations in Interwar Europe," *Daedalus* 126/2 (1997): 47–63; D. Engel, "Perceptions of Power: Poland and World Jewry," and M. Levene, "Resurrecting Poland," *Jahrbuch des Simon-Dubnow-Instituts* (hereafter JBDI) 1 (2002): 18–19 and 29–40, respectively. On the two commissions of inquiry established to investigate the situation of the Jews of Poland, see National Polish Committee of America, *The Jews in Poland: Official Reports of the American and British Investigating Missions* (Chicago, n.d.), 7, 14, 16–17, http://www.archive.org/stream/cu31924028644783/cu31924028644783_djvu.txt (accessed September 23, 2016). See also A. Kapiszewski, "Controversial Reports on the Situation of Jews in Poland in the Aftermath of World War I," *Studia Judaica* 7/2 (2004): 286, 293–94; I.

Zangwill, *The Voice of Jerusalem* (London, 1920); N. Davies, "Great Britain and the Jews, 1918–20," *Journal of Contemporary History* 8/2 (1973): 129; W. W. Hagen, "Before the 'Final Solution,'" *Journal of Modern History* 68/2 (1996): 351–81; J. Michlic-Coren, "Anti-Jewish Violence in Poland," in *Polin*, vol. 13: *Focusing on the Holocaust and its Aftermath*, ed. A. Polonsky (London, 2000), 34–61.

55 Copy of memorandum by American Legation in Warsaw, sent by the British legation to the Foreign Office, September 6, 1919: The National Archives (hereafter TNA): Public Record Office (hereafter PRO), Foreign Office (hereafter FO) 688/1/15, pp. 173, 178–83.

56 Report by Whitehead to Sir Horace Rumbold, British Legation, Warsaw, April 2, 1920, TNA: PRO, FO 688/2/3/, pp. 1–3 (295–97). See also the hilarious account of a discussion between Rumbold and Papal Nuncio Monsignor Ratti, later Pope Pius XI, in Warsaw in 1920, in C. Malaparte, *Coup d'état*, trans. S. Saunders (New York, 1932), 248–50.

57 *New York Times*, May 22, 1915, reproduced with slight alterations in V. Stepanovsky, *The Russian Plot to Seize Galicia*, 2nd ed. (Jersey City, NJ, 1915), 51–55; L. Wasilewski, *Die Ostprovinzen des alten Polenreichs* (Kraków, 1916), 265–68.

58 Whitehead to Sir Horace Rumbold, 4–5 (298–99). See also M. Carynnyk, "Foes of Our Rebirth," *Nationalities Papers* 39/3 (2011): 315–25; P. A. Rudling, "The OUN, the UPA and the Holocaust," in *The Carl Beck Papers in Russian & East European Studies* 2107 (Pittsburgh, 2011), 1–72.

59 M. Lozinsky, "The Problem of Eastern Galicia before the Peace Conference," in *Congressional Series Set: 66th Congress, First Session, May 19–November 19, 1919: Senate Documents* (Washington, 1919), 19:728–33; "Deutsche Gesandtschaft in Warschau an das Auswärtige Amt, Berlin, March 28, 1922: 1; "Die allgemeine Lage der ukrainischen Bevölkerung in Ostgalizien," Politisches Archiv des Auswärtigen Amts (Political Archive of the Foreign Ministry, Berlin, hereafter PAAA), Deutsche Botschaft Warschau, 1921–39, Karton 42; *League of Nations, Treaty Series* (London, 1923), 15:398, "Decision Taken by the Conference of Ambassadors regarding the Eastern Frontiers of Poland.

Paris, March 15, 1923," pp. 260–61. See also "American-Ukrainians Protest Poland's Mandate of East Galicia," *New York Times*, January 16, 1920; Ukrainian National Council, *The Case for the Independence of Eastern Galicia* (London, 1922), 5–7; S. Skrzypek, *The Problem of Eastern Galicia* (London, 1948), 4–5; M. Palij, *The Ukrainian-Polish Defensive Alliance* (Alberta, 1995), 55–56; Subtelny, *Ukraine*, 371, 425–28.

60 *Polish Atrocities in Ukrainian Galicia* (New York, 1919), 3–16. See also Y. Petrushevych, *L'Ukraine Occidentale* (1921), in PAAA, "Politik 1: Polen/Galizien, 1921–1939," R 81428; Ukrainian National Council, *The Case for the Independence of Eastern Galicia.*

61 "Report on Ukrainian Cruelties Committed on the Polish Population of Eastern Galicia," August 1919, Department of Information, AAN-MSZ, zesp. 322, sygn. 9412a, 1–4.

62 Ibid., 5–15.

63 Ibid., 16. A. Cieszynski et al., *Galicie Orientale en chiffres et en graphiques* (Warsaw, 1921), 19, 25–26, writes that in 1912–13 the University of Lwów had 3,386 Polish, 1,275 Ruthenian, and 664 Jewish students; over half of the land of Galicia, almost two-thirds of municipal property, and almost all large estates were in Polish (but actually also Jewish) hands; 92 percent of Ruthenians were peasants, compared to 45.5 percent Poles; only 6.5 percent of Ruthenians worked in industry and commerce and 2.5 percent in the liberal professions, compared to 39 and 17.5 percent of Poles, respectively (again lumping in Jews as well). PAAA, Politik 1: Polen/Galizien, 1921–39, R 81429.

Chapter 3: TOGETHER AND APART

1 Heller, "My Memories," in *Sefer Buczacz*, 146–47, 158.

2 Ibid., 159–60; M. Karniely, "My Brother Shmuel," in *Sefer Buczacz*, 223–24; Y. Beilin, *Israel* (New York, 1992), 30.

3 Heller, "My Memories," and M. Held, "The *Chalutz* Federation in Buczacz," both in *Sefer Buczacz*, 160–62 and 179–80, respectively. See also R. Yona, "Let's All Be Pioneers" (PhD diss., Tel Aviv University,

2014, in Hebrew); E. Mendelsohn, *Zionism in Poland* (New Haven, CT, 1981), 170–71, 237–40, 328–29.

4 TsDIAL, fond 339, op. 1, spr. 22, "Keren Kayemet LeYisrael (Jewish National Fund, hereafter KKL) Central Bureau for Eastern Lesser Poland," February 11, 1930, pp. 5–6; April 2, 1930, p. 81; December 11, 1932, p. 20 (all in Hebrew); Held, "The *Chalutz* Federation in Buczacz," in *Sefer Buczacz*, 180. The Fourth *Aliya* (1924–28) brought an estimated eighty thousand Jews to Palestine; twenty thousand left soon thereafter because of the economic recession (Beilin, *Israel*, 34–35).

5 Masuah Archive, Institute for Shoah Studies, Tel-Yitzhak, Israel (hereafter MAISS), AR-T-025-32/10294, D. Cymand, "The 'Zionist Youth' Movement in Galicia, 1926–1933," 1–4; oral testimony by Cymand, February 21, 1966, Hebrew University, Harman Institute of Contemporary Jewry, http://www.youtube.com/watch?v=LEQcJiGX89c (accessed September 25, 2016); M. Dagan, *On a Mission* (Tel Aviv, 1972, in Hebrew). For complaints about delayed immigration certificates and the inability to bring along older family members, see U.S. Holocaust Memorial Museum (hereafter USHMM), Record Group (hereafter RG) 31.043M (fond 342-microfilm): Records of "Ahva"; TsDIAL, fond 342, "Achwa," 1926–39, op. 1, spr. 101, 1933–35; spr. 117, 1935; spr. 27, 1932–36, p. 47; fond 337, op. 1, spr. 49, 1934, "Hanoar Hacijoni," 1929–39, pp. 32–34.

6 TsDIAL, fond 342, op. 1, spr. 27, "Achwa," 1926–39, December 16, 1935; February 19, 1935; October 26, 1936, pp. 82–83, 87, 160, respectively. Achwa's fundraising for the "Undertaking for Fortification and Security," TsDIAL, fond 342, op. 1, spr. 27, p. 159. Heller, "My Memories," in *Sefer Buczacz*, 163; MAISS, AR-T-003-17/1254/8511, M. Shif, "Achwa in Eastern Galicia"; USHMM, RG 31.043M (fond 342-microfilm): Records of "Ahva"; TsDIAL, fond 342, "Achwa," 1926–39, op. 1, spr. 101, 1933–35; spr. 117, 1935; spr. 27, 1932–36, p. 21. Achwa was banned by the Soviets in 1939.

7 One of the names on the list was Izrael Schimmer, a Polish-German variation of my maternal grandfather's name. By 1935 the shekel was paid by as many as 1,177 people, but my grandfather's name was no longer

on the list; he had meanwhile procured an immigration certificate and taken his family to Palestine. USHMM RG31.041M, Shekel Commission, Lwów, 1922–39, microfilm: correspondence with "Shekel" Commission, Buczacz branch, 1929–35, from TsDIAL, fond 336, op. 1, spr. 32, pp. 1–81. The 1935 list mentions attorney Artur Nacht, Fabius Nacht's third son. An earlier list includes Regina Schojmer, likely my maternal grandmother, aka Rina Schimmer (Szimer) or Regina Bergmann.

8 TsDIAL, fond 338, op. 1, spr. 240, The Jewish Federation in Buczacz, the Local Committee, 1925–November 1939, pp. 1–3, 24; letter of January 19, 1939, p. 65. In February the Buczacz General Zionists formed the United Jewish Bloc of all Zionist parties, reflecting their sense of urgency and isolation (66).

9 YIVO, leaflet, RG 28, May 5, 1921; An-Sky, *Destruction*, vol. 2, pt. 4, 406, wondered why "the destruction of the cemetery was perceived" by the old Jew who reported it to him "as a greater tragedy than the destruction of the city."

10 Joint Distribution Committee Archives online, microfilm 142, letter from Solomon Stern, Talmud Torah Association, Buczacz, to Jacob Schiff, New York, March 26, 1920. (Thanks to Natalia Aleksiun for this document.) See also N. W. Cohen, *Jacob H. Schiff* (Hanover, NH, 1999).

11 Biuro Sekczyi, Nakładem Centralnego Komitetu Krajowego Opieki nad Żyd. Sierotami Wojennemu w Galicyi, *Centralny Komitet Kraj. Opieki nad żydowskiemu sierotami woj. w Galicyi, sekcya Lwów: Sprawozdanie za czas od 1. stycznia 1918 do 30. czerwca 1921* (Lwów, n.d.), 14–15, 36. The committee included Mrs. Pauli Meerengel, Mrs. Cecilia Ausschnitz (or Ausschnitt), and Mrs. Gusty Kaminer, along with Dr. David Silberschein and Dr. Zygmunt Kok.

12 M. Guter, *Honoring One's Mother*, ed. A. Shenhar (Haifa, 1969, in Hebrew), 8–13. See also *Sprawozdanie Centralnego Komitetu Opieki nad Żydowskimi Sierotami w Lwowie, za lata 1923–1926* (Lwów, n.d.), 25–38, 63; A. Roll, "The Jewish Health Association," in *Sefer Buczacz*, 187.

13 Heller, "My Memories," and Pepa Anderman-Neuberg, "The Orphanage in Buczacz," in *Sefer Buczacz*, 165 and 184–85, respectively.

14 *Słowo Żydowskie*, Nr. 1 (Tarnopol, March 4, 1927): 4, in Biblioteka

Uniwersytecka we Warszawie (Warsaw University Library). Palek taught German and mathematics, as well as an extracurricular class on Jewish religion, at the state gymnasium before 1914. *Sprawozdanie dyrekcyi Gimnazyum w Buczaczu, 1914*, 25–28.

15 *Spis Nauczycieli*, ed. Z. Zagórowski (Lwów, 1924), 333; *Szkoły Rzeczypospolitej Polskiej w roku szkolnym 1930/31*, ed. M. Falski (Warsaw, 1933), 449, 542; BJ, Mf. 11712, *Sprawozdanie Dyrekcja Państwowego Gimnazjum w Buczaczu za rok szkolny 1932–1933* (Buczacz, 1933), i–iii, xxx, 1–42; *Sprawozdanie . . . za rok szkolny 1935–1936* (Buczacz, 1936), 3–5, 49. See also M. Jarecka-Żyluk et al., "From History to the Present: Faces of Gender in Poland," in *Education and Gender*, ed. O. Holz et al. (Münster, 2013), esp. 123. Viktor Petrykevych (see below) is listed on the gymnasium teachers' roll for 1933; Antoni Siewiński is listed as retired from the local four-grade school in 1925: *Spis szkół i nauczycieli w okręgu szkolnym lwowskim*, ed. S. Lehnert (Lwów, 1926), 213–14.

16 Kowalski, *Powiat Buczacki*, 68–79, also citing Ostapowicz's memoir.

17 Ibid., 79–80. See also K. Steffen, *Jüdische Polonität* (Göttingen, 2004); K. Steffen, "Das Eigene durch das Andere," *JBDI* 3 (2004): 89–111.

18 Kowalski, *Powiat Buczacki*, 81–84.

19 *Sprawozdanie: Dyrekcji państwowego gimnazjum w Buczaczu za rok szkolny 1936–1937* (Buczacz, 1937): Class lists include the future priest Ludwik Rutyna (see below); interview with Y. Bauer, Ramat Aviv, Israel, 2003 (hereafter Bauer 2003). Among his Jewish teachers Bauer remembered the former Piłsudski legionnaire Weingarten and his Latin and homeroom teacher Kornblüth, a convert to Catholicism. Thanks to Bauer's daughter Ela for introducing me to him. See also E. Bauer, *Between Poles and Jews* (Jerusalem, 2005, in Hebrew).

20 DATO, fond 231, op. 1, spr. 2017, January 29, 1933, pp. 66–67, 72, 80, also noting that the right-wing Revisionist Party gained 7 percent of the Jewish vote and had "influence especially on the Jewish youth," while manifesting a "completely correct" attitude toward the state (28). For statute and official recognition of the Economic Bloc see DATO, fond 8, op. 1, spr. 15, February 17, 1931, pp. 1, 5, 8; Heller, "My Memories," in *Sefer Buczacz*, 16.

21 DATO, fond 231, op. 1, spr. 1910, July 11, 1932.

22 DATO, fond 231, op. 1c, spr. 1703, pp. 9, 90; op. 6, spr. 982, September 15, 1932, p. 18; spr. 2034, April 22, 1933, p. 37; spr. 2049, 1935, pp. 1–14; op. 1, spr. 2325, June 24, 1935, p. 126; spr. 3372, 1937, pp. 19–21; fond 8, op. 1, spr. 289, May 24, 1939, p. 4; TsDIAL, fond 338, op. 1, spr. 218, October 23, 1934, pp. 17–18; C. Roll, "WIZO," in *Sefer Buczacz*, 186–87; *Drugi powszechny spis ludności z dn. 9.XII 1931 r. (Województwo Tarnopolskie)* (Warsaw, 1938), 30; Maurice Wolfthal private collection, Phoenix, Arizona (hereafter MWC), Directorship of Jewish Community in Buczacz to United Buczaczer Ladies Auxiliary in the Bronx, New York, February 4, 1937. My mother too attended the Polish public school and consequently did not know any Hebrew when she arrived in Palestine in 1935. *Thanks to Mr. Wolfthal for sharing his father's documents with me in 2006. Izrael Wolfthal and his future wife, Tyla Falik, attended the state gymnasium and the Talmud Torah afterschool in Buczacz; they were also members of Hashomer Hatza'ir, and Izrael was associated with the communists. They fled from Buczacz to the Soviet Union in 1941. The documents had previously belonged to Izrael's acquaintance, Abram Sommer, secretary of the Buczaczer Ladies Auxiliary in New York City.*

23 Roll, "The Hospital," and Y. P., "Dr. M. Hirschhorn," in *Sefer Buczacz*, 182–84 and 220, respectively; DATO, fond 8, op. 1, spr. 62, August 10, 1934, pp. 1–3; spr. 96, February 25 and March 22, 1935, pp. 4–5; spr. 94, pp. 2–7; spr. 180, September 9, 1937, pp. 1, 21; spr. 245, May 16, 1938, pp. 3–4; spr. 249, June, August, and September 1938, 1–9; spr. 287, February 20, 1939, p. 6; spr. 250, pp. 1–2; spr. 288, March 2, 1939, p. 4. Makabi had 40,000 members in Poland in 1936, Hapoel 5,600, and Beitar 40,000. J. Shavit, *Jabotinsky and the Revisionist Movement* (New York, 1988), 55; D. Blecking, "Jews and Sports in Poland before the Second World War," in *Jews and the Sporting Life*, ed. E. Mendelsohn et al. (New York, 2008), 21–22; *Encyclopaedia Judaica*, 2nd ed. (Farmington Hill, MI, 2007), 1:499.

24 MWC, letter by Mendel Reich on behalf of the Talmud Torah Association, Buczacz, February 26, 1936. See also Heller, "My Memories," in *Sefer Buczacz*, 163. Reich is citing Psalms 121 and Deuteronomy

32:25. See also W. Melzer, *No Way Out* (Cincinnati, 1997), 39–52, 131–53; D. Ofer, *Escaping the Holocaust* (New York, 1990), 3–20; R. Breitman and Alan M. Kraut, *American Refugee Policy and European Jewry* (Bloomington, IN, 1987), 11–111.

25 MWC, letter by directorate of the Talmud Torah Association, Buczacz, December 2, 1937; letter by Mendel Reich, president, and Chaim Kofler, headmaster of the Talmud Torah Association, Buczacz, December 8, 1937; letter by Mendel Reich to Abraham Sommer, December 21, 1937.

26 MWC, letter by Jacob Shapira to Abraham Sommer, March 30, 1939.

27 DATO, fond 274, op. 4, spr. 78, p. 36. The other two men were Izaak Witzinger and Samuel Hecht. See also Heller, "My Memories," in *Sefer Buczacz*, 164–65. Subsequent members included egg-factory worker Juda Reich, trade assistant Juda Waldfogel, wage earner Leon Buchbaum, and gymnasium graduate Marja Englender. A second group included Izak Bein, Moritz Scharf, Dawid (Ducio) Friedlender, and nineteen-year-old Natan (Nadje) Dunajer. The last two led resistance groups under the German occupation and were killed shortly before the liberation. A final group included former yeshiva student Fischel Gaster, age twenty-four; his younger sister, gymnasium graduate Chana Gaster; gymnasium graduate Oskar Neuberger, twenty-three; Jechiel Buchwald, twenty-seven; Munio Braunstein; and Dreszer. AAN, zesp. 982, sygn. 9, February 1929, p. 199; DATO, fond 231, op. 1, spr. 2325, February 15, 1935, p. 27, March 16, 1935, p. 34, May 1, 1935, p. 67, June 25, 1935, p. 97, July 26, 1935, p. 135; spr. 1802, March 18, 1933, p. 88; spr. 1990, January 9, 1934, pp. 1, 9–8; fond 274, op. 4, spr. 292, pp. 11–13, 21, 27–30, 36–37; fond 8, op. 1, spr. 101, January 25, 1936, p. 1, June 24, 1935, p. 126; op. 1, spr. 116, January 25, 1936, p. 1, January 18, 1937, p. 5. See also J. T. Gross, *Revolution from Abroad*, revised 2nd ed. (Princeton, 2002); Carynnyk, "Foes of Our Rebirth"; Rudling, "The OUN, the UPA and the Holocaust"; H. Cimek, "Jews in the Polish Communist Movement," *Studies in Politics and Society* 9 (2012): 50–56. In 1938 Stalin dissolved the communist parties of Poland, Western Ukraine, and Belarus; their leaders were summoned to Moscow, where most were murdered. The vast majority of Polish Jews did not support

communism, but one-fourth of the Communist Polish Party (KPP) leadership, and half of its Central Committee, were of Jewish origin. M. C. Steinlauf, *Bondage to the Dead* (Syracuse, NY, 1997), 35–36.

28 United Ukrainian Organizations of Chicago and Vicinity, *Report on the Polish-Ukrainian Conflict in Eastern Galicia by the Rev. James Barr, M.P., and Mr. Rhys J. Davies, M.P.*, House of Commons, September 1931 (1931), 1–4, 9–14, 119–23. See also, "Der Hilferuf der gemarterten Ukrainer," *Ostdeutsche Morgenpost*, October 28, 1930; E. Revyuk, ed., *Polish Atrocities in Ukraine* (New York, 1931), 3–6; M. Sycz, "Polish Policy toward the Ukrainian Cooperative Movement," *Harvard Ukrainian Studies* 23/1–2 (1999): 25–45.

29 TsDIAL, fond 348, op. 1, spr. 1380, May 30, 1910, March 2, 1923, April 16, 1930, May 10, 1930.

30 Branch members included treasurer Sylvester Vynnytskyi; director of the district union of cooperatives Mykola Kharkhalis; Ivan Bobyk, who served as mayor of Buczacz under the Germans; and secretary Ostap Voronka, who was arrested by the NKVD in 1941 and subsequently murdered. Thanks to his son Roman Voronka for sharing this information. TsDIAL, fond 348, op. 1, spr. 1379, Prosvita meeting minutes, February 25, 1930, April 2, 1930, and April 15, 1930; spr. 1385, March 18, 1930, pp. 1–2, 5, July 13, 1934, p. 6, and July 10, 1939, pp. 7–14; DATO, fond 8, op. 1, spr. 14, November 16, 1931, p. 40; spr. 84, November 4, 1935, p. 47; spr. 128, June 9, 1936, p. 25; spr. 220, May 5, 1938, p. 20; fond 274, op. 4, spr. 78, pp. 13, 15.

31 TsDIAL, fond 348, op. 1, spr. 1379, March 16, August 25, September 4, October 8, 26, 28, 29, 1931; September 11, 1933; February 24, 1934; October 31, 1934; March 5, 1935; DATO, fond 274, op. 4, spr. 78, p. 79.

32 Prosvita meeting minutes, May 20, 1929. The Buczacz district reading clubs network boasted 14,242 books and 3,082 readers, averaging six books per reader per year; altogether club members read on average three books per year, while Ukrainians in the district as a whole read on average one book every four years.

33 DATO, fond 231, op. 1c, spr. 1216, Buczacz, September 10, 1929,

pp. 12–24; spr. 1075, Buczacz, March 4, 1929, p. 8; spr. 1390, Tarnopol, September 24, 1930, p. 97; Buczacz, January 7, 1930, p. 79; spr. 1553, Buczacz, October 19, 1931, pp. 4–5, October, 26, 1931, pp. 9–12; spr. 2264, Buczacz, June 12, 1934, pp. 14–16, for the case of Luh's confrontation with the authorities in the village of Trościańce (Ukrainian: Trostyantsi).

34 DATO, fond 274, op. 4, spr. 78, 1935, police files of Mykhailo Baran, Bazyli Band, Sylvester Vynnytskyi, Mykhailo Hrynov, Frantek Volodymyr, Mykola Kharkhalis, Antoni Korol, Onufry Pendziy, and Volodymyr Kolcho, pp. 12, 6, 18, 27, 30, 90, 94, 44, 76, 5; Volodymyr Posatski, Yaroslav Harasevych, Yatsko Baran, Mykhailo Biloskurski, Volodymyr Levitski, Roman Lisovski, Petro Gonzalas, Mykhailo Snihurovich, pp. 33, 78, 7, 8, 56, 21, 88. For further instances of Buczacz activists, see fond 8, op. 1, spr. 79, Buczacz, March 22, 1935, p. 7; spr. 210, Buczacz May 18, 1938, p. 8; spr. 119, Buczacz, October 8, 1936, pp. 9–10; spr. 145, Buczacz, January 13, 1937, pp. 3; fond 231, op. 1c, spr. 1703, personnel overview based on 1931 census, pp. 28–31.

35 T. Zahra, "Imagined Non-Communities," *Slavic Review* (hereafter *SR*) 69 (2010): 93–119. There were also a number of Ukrainian communists in the Buczacz district, such as the KPZU branch in Jazłowiec, who also had contacts with Jewish communists in Buczacz. But very few Ukrainians appear in police reports. DATO, fond 274, op. 4, spr. 292, 1935, pp. 31, 41.

36 On the larger context, see E. D. Weitz, "From the Vienna to the Paris System," *American Historical Review* 113/2 (2008): 1313–43.

37 Ks. Piotr Mańkowski, Arcybiskup Tyt. Enejski, *Pamiętniki*, vol. 3, 1911–26, Biblioteki Naukowej (Scientific Library, Warsaw, hereafter BN), manuscript collection, sygn. IV/9781, microfilm 71320, pp. 115–28, 147–58. Subsequently published as P. Mańkowski, *Pamiętniki* (Warsaw, 2002), citations from original manuscript. See also "Biography of Bishop Piotr Mańkowski," in *Book of Remembrance*, https://biographies.library.nd.edu/catalog/biography-1212 (accessed October 2, 2016).

38 Główny Urząd Statystyczny Rzeczypospolitej Polskiej, *Skorowidz miejscowości Rzeczypospolitej Polskiej*, vol. 15: *Województwo Tarnopolskie*

(Warsaw, 1923), 6, also noting that in 1921 Tarnopol province numbered 1.4 million inhabitants: 447,000 Roman Catholics, 848,000 Greek Catholics, and 129,000 of the Jewish faith; or 642,500 Poles, 714,000 Ruthenians, and 69,000 of Jewish nationality.

39 P. Brykczynski, "Political Murder and the Victory of Ethnic Nationalism in Interwar Poland" (PhD diss., University of Michigan, 2013), 177, 181, 217–18, 228–29, 241, 245–47, 268–359.

40 M. Zatoński, "Jewish Politics in the New Poland," *Slovo* 24/1 (Spring 2012): 21–23, 37; D. Stachura, "National Identity and the Ethnic Minorities in Early Inter-War Poland," in *Poland between the Wars*, ed. P. Stachura (Basingstoke, UK, 1998), 73; DATO, fond 231, op. 1, spr. 217, November 6, 1922, pp. 25–29.

41 DATO, fond 231, op. 1, spr. 1135, p. 79; Heller, in *Sefer Buczacz*, 146; A. J. Groth, "Polish Elections, 1919–1928," *SR* 24/4 (December 1965): 653–65; *Mniejszości Narodowe w wyborach do Sejmu i Senatu w r. 1928: Opracowane przez wydział narodowościowy ministerstwa, spraw wewnętrznych* (Warsaw, 1928), 70–71, 237, 246–47. The Buczacz district had a total population in 1931 of 12,000 Roman Catholics, 5,000 Greek Catholics, and 7,000 Jews, or 13,000 Poles, 2,500 Ukrainians, 2,000 Ruthenians, and 6,000 "Hebrew-speaking [!] Jews." Notably, 20 percent of urban residents and 40 percent of villagers over ten years old were illiterate. Główny Urząd Statystyczny Rzeczypospolitej Polskiej, *Drugi powszechny spis ludności z dnia 9 grudnia 1931r* (Warsaw, 1932), 4; *Wyniki Ostateczne: Opracowania spisu ludności y dn. 9.XII 1931 r. w Postaci skróconej* (Warsaw, 1934), 4; *Drugi powszechny spis ludności 1931* (Warsaw, 1938), 30; D. Dąbrowska, A. Wein, and A. Weiss, eds., *Pinkas Hakehillot: Poland*, vol. 2: *Eastern Galicia* (Jerusalem, 1980, in Hebrew), 83. See also J. S. Kopstein et al., "Between State Loyalty and National Identity," *Polin* 24: 171–85; J. D. Zimmerman, "Józef Piłsudski and the 'Jewish Question,'" *East European Jewish Affairs* 28/1 (1998): 87–107; N. Aleksiun, "Regards from My Shtetl," *The Polish Review* 56/1–2 (2011): 57–71.

42 P. J. Wróbel, "The Rise and Fall of Parliamentary Democracy in Interwar Poland," in *The Origins of Modern Polish Democracy*, ed. M. B. B. Biskupsi, J. S. Pula, and P. J. Wróbel (Athens, OH, 2010), 148–49.

43 AAN, zesp. 982, sygn. 13, May 1930, p. 135; DATO, fond 231, op. 1, spr. 1375, May 7, 1930, pp. 17–19; spr. 1370, pp. 9–10; spr. 1450, October 7, 1930, p. 88; AAN, zesp. 982, sygn. 14, November 22, 1930, p. 154.

44 DATO, fond 231, op. 1c, spr. 1703, 1931; Perry, *Consolidated Treaty Series*, 412–24; Magocsi, *History of Ukraine*, 2nd ed., 637–38, noting Polish attempts to minimize Ukrainian demographic predominance by referring to them as Ruthenians and encouraging Carpathian subgroups such as the Lemko to develop their distinct culture and dialect. See also T. Snyder, *Sketches from a Secret War* (New Haven, CT, 2005), 68.

45 DATO, fond 231, op. 1, spr. 1913, Buczacz, January 30, 1933, pp. 7, 9; spr. 2267, Buczacz, April 20, 1934, pp. 16–17; op. 6, spr. 2030, p. 11. See also AAN, zesp. 982, sygn. 36, Tarnopol, February 8, 1933, pp. 1–2, 4, 6, 8. In 1934 the Buczacz district had 109 elementary schools, of which 49 were Polish, 49 bilingual, and 11 Ruthenian; there were only 50 Ukrainian (and 11 Jewish) teachers out of a total of 252. Most Polish teachers supported the Government Bloc, most Ukrainians the UNDO, and most Jewish teachers supported Zionism.

46 *Województwo Tarnopolskie* (Tarnopol, 1931), 83–95; Hoover Institution archives, Stanford University (hereafter HI), Poland, Ministerstwo Informacji i Dokumentacji (Ministry of Information and Documentation, hereafter MID), Records 1939–45: Reports of Polish Deportees, 1941, Box 198: Reports in Tarnopol Province: "Opis Województwa Tarnopolskiego" (undated, likely 1939 or 1940), pp. 2–3, 9, 33–35, 37, 39–41, 47–54. See also A. Krysiński, "Rozwój stosunków etnicznych w Ziemi Czerwińskiej w Polsce Odrodzonej," *Sprawy narodowościowe* (hereafter *SpNa*) 11/5–6 (1937): 387–412, 555–84; Wróbel, "Rise and Fall of Parliamentary Democracy," 150–52; D. Engle, "An Early Account of Polish Jewry under Nazi and Soviet Occupation Presented to the Polish Government-in-Exile, February 1940," *JSS* 45/1 (1983): 1–16.

47 *Księga Adresowa Małopolski: Rocznik 1935/1936* (Lwów, 1936), 1213.

48 For these and similar instances: Ministerstwo Spraw Wewnętrznych (Ministry of the Interior, hereafter MSW), W. Narodowościowy, 1251, OUN activities, 1931–32, pp. 77–78; DATO, fond 231, op. 1c, spr.

2070, Buczacz, June 23, 1933, p. 25, Buczacz, January 8, 1933, p. 27, January 1936, pp. 15–16; AAN, zesp. 982, sygn. 32, May 1937, p. 79, sygn. 29, January 1936, p. 15. See also "Żydzi: Wystąpienia antysemickie Ukraińców w Małopolsce Wschodniej," *SpNa* 7/5 (1933): 573, citing Jewish press reports on "increased anti-Semitic propaganda by Ukrainian nationalists," especially against Jews "residing in the rural areas of Eastern Lesser Poland"; "robberies of Jewish merchants, setting fire to houses, and even poisoning wells"; and cases in which "Ukrainian nationalist youngsters . . . threw stones at Jewish houses and shouted 'Heil Hitler!' and 'Death to the Jews!'"

49 DATO, fond 231, op. 1, spr. 2266, Buczacz, May 16, 1934, p. 13; spr. 2361, Buczacz, June 21, 1935, pp. 10, 12; fond 8, op. 1, spr. 99, Buczacz, May 28, 1936, p. 4; AAA, zesp. 982, sygn. 29, Tarnopol, February 1936, pp. 26, 39. Initially supportive of the government, Orthodox Jews in the Tarnopol province were alienated by the Sejm resolution of 1936 prohibiting kosher slaughter: Haluzevyi derzhavnyi arkhiv Sluzhba bezpeki Ukraïny (State Archives Department of the Security Service of Ukraine, hereafter HDA SBU), Ternopil branch, spr. 3787-II. See also Melzer, *No Way Out*, 81–90; J. M. Karlip, *The Tragedy of a Generation* (Cambridge, MA, 2013), 183; J.-P. Himka et al., "Ukrainian Radical Party," *Encyclopedia of Ukraine*, vol. 5 (1993), http://www.encyclopediaofukraine.com/display.asp?linkPath=page sUKUkrainianRadicalparty.htm (accessed October 4, 2016).

50 AAN, zesp. 982, sygn. 29, Tarnopol, March 1936, pp. 45, 47, 49–50, April 1936, pp. 65, 67, May 1936, pp. 78–79, 82, June 1936, p. 97, July 1936, pp. 117, 120, 121, August 1936, pp. 135–37; sygn. 32, Tarnopol, February 1937, pp. 23, 25, 32, March 1937, p. 43. See also J.-P. Himka, "Ethnicity and the Reporting of Mass Murder," in *Shatterzone of Empires*, ed. O. Bartov et al. (Bloomington, IN, 2013), 378–98.

51 AAN, zesp. 982, sygn. 32, March 1937, p. 53, May 1937, pp. 76–77, December 1937, p. 214; Melzer, *No Way Out*, 25–28. See also Joanna Beata Michlic, *Poland's Threatening Other* (Lincoln, NE, 2006), 87; S. Rudnicki, "Anti-Jewish Legislation in Interwar Poland," in Blobaum, *Antisemitism*, 160–61.

52 Provincial police reports could no longer identify any "signs of co-existence" between Poles and Ukrainians: AAN, zesp. 982, sygn. 32, September 1937, p. 161, October 1937, p. 175; *Svoboda* (October 10, 1937): 7. The share of Jewish university students in Poland declined from 25 percent of the student body in 1921–22 to 10 percent in 1937–38, and university authorities increasingly condoned anti-Jewish violence. Melzer, *No Way Out*, 71–80.

53 The Jews were described as "also often harmful" to the Polish state, displaying "more sympathy for the Ruthenians and generally to strangers" and providing "outstanding propagators of communist ideology" that "only they have been disseminating." AAN, zesp. 982, sygn. 35, likely 1939, pp. 1–4, 7. In 1937 the Tarnopol province registered 267 "subversive acts" resulting in eight fatalities, all attributed to the UVO-OUN; 188 suspects were arrested, of whom 118 were indicted. Most actions were directed at Poles, but proportionately Jews were more likely to be attacked. CAW VIII.800.72.1, Załącznik Nr. 5, "Zestawienie wystąpień elementów wywrotowych na tle działalności O.U.N.-U.W.O. za czas od 1.I. do 31.XII.1937 r.," p. 95. See also DATO, fond 8, op. 1, spr. 294, Buczacz, April 18, 1939, pp. 10–11; A. Krysiński, "Struktura narodowościowa miast polskich," *SpNa* 11/3 (1937): 282; AAN, zesp. 14, sygn. 414, *Instytut Badań Spraw Narodowościowych*, September 10, 1937, pp. 861–64.

54 PAAA, Polen (Poland, hereafter Pol.) V, Po 6, R 104149, Warsaw, June 21, 1938, pp. 99–103, 104–9, November 15, 1938, pp. 168–72. See also Magocsi, *Historical Atlas*, 132–33; V. Rothwell, *The Origins of the Second World War* (New York, 2001), 117–19; Melzer, *No Way Out*, 113–14, 126–27. The Moltke clan produced two imperial army chiefs of staff and an anti-Nazi activist. The ambassador joined the NSDAP in 1937 and died in 1943 as ambassador to Spain. E. Sáenz-Francés, "The Ambassadorship of Hans Adolf von Moltke (1943)," *German History* 31/1 (2013): 23–41.

55 PAAA, Pol V, Po 6, R 104149, *Bericht des DNB-Vertreters Brandt über die Ukraine*, Kattowitz, December 23, 1938, pp. 203, 208–14. On the German News Agency, see R. J. Evans, *Lying about Hitler* (New

York, 2001), 50; A. Heider, "Deutsches Nachrichtenbüro," in *Enzyklopädie des Nationalsozialismus*, ed. W. Benz et al. (Munich, 1997), 427. See also A. Statiev, *The Soviet Counterinsurgency in the Western Borderlands* (New York, 2010), 45; D. R. Marples, "Stepan Bandera," in *In the Shadow of Hitler*, ed. R. Haynes et al. (New York, 2011), 232; S. Redlich, "Jewish-Ukrainian Relations in Inter-War Poland as Reflected in Some Ukrainian Publications," in *Polin*, vol. 11: *Focusing on Aspects and Experiences of Religion*, ed. A. Polonsky (Oxford, 1998), 232–46; Y. Petrovsky-Shtern, "Reconceptualizing the Alien," *Ab Imperio* 4 (2003): 519–80.

56 PAAA, Pol V, Po 6, R 104149, Lemberg, July 27, 1939, pp. 243–49; R 104150, Lemberg, *Die Stimmung unter den Ukrainer*, August 3, 1939, pp. 67–71. Seelos was not a member of the NSDAP and was dismissed from the Foreign Service after a posting to Copenhagen in 1940–42; he rejoined the Foreign Ministry in 1953. See also Institut für Zeitgeschichte Archiv (Institute for Contemporary History, Munich), ZS-390, Dr. Seelos, Gebhard, 1287/54, *Bericht*, July 25, 1945, pp. 1–5; 5679/77, Seelos, *Erinnerungen*, March 31–August 27, 1939, evaluation by W. Jakobmeyer, May 29, 1974, pp. 6–9, and manuscript, 10–71, where Seelos notes that his last cable to Berlin on August 25, 1939, confirmed that no uprising should be expected because the UNDO had proclaimed its loyalty to the Polish regime for tactical reasons (manuscript, 54). For critical views, see *Braunbuch* (Berlin, 1968), 325, 360–61; T. Rabant, "Antypolska działalność niemieckiej służby dyplomatycznej i konsularnej w Polsce w przededniu II wojny światowej oraz jej ewakuacja i likwidacja," *Pamięć i Sprawiedliwość* 1/9 (2006): 204–5, 214.

Chapter 4: SOVIET POWER

1 V. Gekht, "The Road from Ghetto to Orphanage," in *Parallels*, Nrs. 6–7 (Moscow, 2005, in Russian), 248–74, here 248–53; V. Gekht, "Stolen Childhood," in *Korny* 23 (2004, in Russian): 137–48, here 137–39; V. Hecht, "A Long Search for Roots," http://www.buchach

.org/Buczacz/djonek.htm (in Hebrew, accessed October 23, 2016, orig. pub. in *Korny* 25 (2005, in Russian): 119–32; V. Poznanskyy, "Crushed Childhood," in *Alef* 936 (2006, in Russian), http://www.alefmagazine .com/pub549.html (accessed October 23, 2016); personal account by Hecht, courtesy of his cousin Zvi Karniel (Hirschhorn), in Hebrew, undated; J. W. Turkowa, HI, Pol., MID, Box 199, folder 5 (Buczacz), 4968, p. 11; W. Janda, Archiwum Wschodnie (Eastern Archive, Warsaw, hereafter AW), II/1561, pp. 19–20. See also E. Pytler, HI, Pol., MID, 199/5, 4507, p. 53; J. Anczarski, AW II/1224, p. 20; and J. Anczarski, *Kronikarskie zapisy z lat cierpień i grozy w Małopolsce Wschodniej* (Kraków, 1996).

2 V. Petrykevych's handwritten diary, Ivano-Frankivsk, Ukraine, in Ukrainian, transcribed and translated by S. Grachova, edited by the author, in preparation for publication. See also chapter 5.

3 S. Szymula, HI, Pol., MID, 199/5, 11240, p. 9; J. Biedroń, HI, Pol., MID, 199/5, 1564, pp. 2–3; Turkowa, HI, Pol., MID, 199/5, 4968, pp. 11–12. See also W. Antochów, *Moja Działalność w Armii Krajowej*, Wojskowe Biuro Badań Historycznych (Military Historical Research Center, Warsaw, hereafter WBBH), Zbiory specjalne Biblioteki Naukowej (Special Collections of the Scientific Library), III/49/313, pp. 1–3. In fact by late 1939 the twenty-two members of the Buczacz district committee of the Communist Party of Soviet Ukraine (KP[bU) and its executive included only three recognizably Jewish names, the rest being Ukrainian and Russian. By early 1940 there was just one identifiable Jewish member. DATO, fond R-1, op. 1, spr. 1, protocol 1, KP(b)U Tarnopol Oblast Committee meeting, December 19, 1939, p. 6, spr. 9, Protocol 6, January 15, 1940, p. 45.

4 J. Janicka, HI, Pol., MID, 199/5, 4880, p. 11; S. Pawłowski, HI, Pol., MID, 199/5, 3648, p. 4; W. Mroczkowski, HI, Pol., MID, 199/5, 7909, pp. 7–8; W. Bożek, HI, Pol., MID, 199/5, 11214, p. 6; A. Bodaj, HI, Pol., MID, 199/5, 11037, p. 5.

5 M. Bogusz, HI, Pol., MID, 199/5, pp. 63–64; J. Flondro, HI, Pol., MID, 199/5, 7987, pp. 27–28; F. Bosowski, HI, Pol., MID, 199/5, 3024, p. 27. There were many more such cases. See, e.g., M. Wołkowa,

HI, Pol., MID, 199/5, 8028, p. 50; A. Chaszczewski, HI, Pol., MID, 199/5, 5825, p. 54; B. Wojciechowski, HI, Pol., MID, 199/5, 7981, p. 25; J. Sosiak, HI, Pol., MID, 199/5, 143, p. 61; S. Milewska, HI, Pol., MID, 199/5, 8026, pp. 49–50; B. Bełz, HI, Pol., MID, 199/5, 4262, p. 24; J. Mrozikowa, Archiwum Zakładu Historii Ruchu Ludowego (Archive of the Institute for the Peasant Movement, Warsaw, hereafter AZHRL), pp. 6–7. See also W. Urban, *Droga Krzyżowa* (Wrocław, 1983), 52; N. Davies, *Europa* (Kraków, 1998), 1098. In the entire area of eastern Poland occupied by the Soviets, several thousand people were murdered by their neighbors. Most estimates of Polish victims either include the entire period of 1939–45 or focus on events after 1943. T. Snyder, *The Reconstruction of Nations* (New Haven, CT, 2003), 170, 176; H. Romański et al., *Ludobójstwo dokonane przez nacjonalistów ukraińskich na Polakach w województwie tarnopolskim 1939–1946* (Wrocław, 2004), 6.

6 Transcripts of interviews with Rutyna at his home in Buczacz in 2006 by Sofia Grachova, March 8, and Frank Grelka, June 25.

7 Transcript of interview with Hałkiewicz at his home in Lublin by Frank Grelka, April 27, 2004.

8 Transcript of interview with Kozarska-Dworska at her home in Wrocław by Frank Grelka, June 30, 2004. After the war she became a psychologist, specializing in clinical criminology. See J. Kozarska-Dworska, *Psychopatia jako problem kryminologiczny* (Warsaw, 1977).

9 Janda, AW, II/1561, pp. 8–10, 23–24.

10 Z. Fedus, "Pierwsza deportacja z województwa tarnopolskiego," *Zesłaniec* 21 (2005): 49.

11 *Za Nove Zhyttia*, January 15, 1940, p. 2.

12 *Za Nove Zhyttia*, January 15, 18, 21, 1940, pp. 2, 2, and 2, respectively.

13 *Za Nove Zhyttia*, January 28 and February 2, 1940, pp. 2 and 2, respectively. The youths were named Aspis, Rosentrauch, Nadler, and Rozenzweig, indicating that three of them were Jewish.

14 DATO, fond R-1, op. 1, spr. 6, Protocol 4, KP(b)U Tarnopol Oblast Committee meeting, January 3, 1940, pp. 7–8.

15 DATO, fond R-1, op. 1, spr. 28, Protocol 62, Appendix, December

19, 1940, pp. 143–44, spr. 27, Protocol 53, and Appendix, March 26, 1941, pp. 3, 12, 27–28.

16 Biblioteka Narodowa (National Library, Warsaw), Mf. A. 240: *Prawda Bolszewicka*, May 24, 1941, p. 1.

17 Gross, *Revolution*, 71–113; B.-C. Pinchuk, *Shtetl Jews under Soviet Rule* (Oxford, 1990), 49.

18 L. Fenerstoin, HI, Pol., MID, 199/5, 4063, p. 1; Biedroń, HI, Pol., MID, 199/5, 1564, pp. 3–4. Stefan Kowalski from Monasterzyska testified that although "after the elections there should have been celebrations all night, no one wanted to go there" (HI, Pol., MID, 199/5, 6521, p. 21). The teacher Kazimierz Sukowski remembered that "some 20 armed Soviet soldiers were positioned 300 meters from the polling station" (HI, Pol., MID, 199/5, 5655, p. 21). Paweł Januszewski, Polish Institute and Sikorski Museum Archives, London (hereafter PISM), Kol. 138/253, 10897, testified that "the elections" in Buczacz "were enforced by the armed militia." Former police official Antonin Tymiel Benjamin testified that in Monasterzyska each apartment block was assigned its own "guardian angel" charged with ensuring that all residents took part in the elections (HI, Pol., MID, 199/5, 4063, p. 1).

19 The farmer Bodaj refused to vote and went into hiding; he was later arrested: Bodaj, HI, Pol., MID, 199/5, 11037, p. 5; the farmer Józef Salomon was warned that "anyone who does not take part in the election will be deported to Russia": HI, Pol., MID, 199/5, 1445, p. 5; J. Thieberger, HI, Pol., MID, 199/5, 819, p. 6; Turkowa, HI, Pol., MID, 199/5, 4968, p. 13; T. Daniłow, HI, Pol., MID, 199/5, 5365, p. 2; W. Mriczkowski, HI, Pol., MID, 199/5, 7909, p. 8.

20 Szymula, HI, Pol., MID, 199/5, 11240, p. 10; L. Szydłowski, HI, Pol., MID, 199/5, 8973, p. 37; Wołkowa, HI, Pol., MID, 199/5, 8028, p. 51.

21 S. Siwy, HI, Pol., MID, 199/5, 9884, p. 55; S. Medyński, HI, Pol., MID, 199/5, 1009, p. 15; Flondro, HI, Pol., MID, 199/5, 7987, 28; Z. Waruszyński, HI, Pol., MID, 199/5, 5128, p. 22. The peasant Władysław Bożek observed that in Buczacz "the election committee

was made up only of Ukrainians and chaired by a Soviet functionary": Bożek, HI, Pol., MID, 199/5, 11214, p. 6. Kazimierz Siwy of Podzameczek was of the same opinion as his relative Szymin: HI, Pol., MID, 199/5, 5827, p. 54. The canon Franciszek Bosowski recalled that in Trościaniec all members of the election committee were Ukrainians. His relatives Józef and Katarzyna Bosowski, and their son, subsequently died in deportation: HI, Pol., MID, 199/5, 3024, p. 27. Membership lists of the election committees to the Supreme Soviet in the Buczacz district, published on February 10, 1940, include the former Ukrainian nationalist and future mayor of Buczacz under the Germans, Ivan Bobyk, and prewar OUN adherents and future members of the German-organized police Volodymyr Lutsiv and Vasyl Lehkyi. The vast preponderance of committee members had Ukrainian names. In December 1940, of sixty deputies elected in the district election for the local soviets in Western Ukraine, there was not a single recognizably Jewish name. *Za Nove Zhyttia*, February 2, 10, December 19, 1940, pp. 2, 2, and 1, respectively. See also Gross, *Revolution*, 109.

22 G. Hryciuk, "Victims 1939–1941," in *Shared History—Divided Memory*, ed. E. Barkan, E. Cole, and K. Struve (Göttingen, 2007), 182–83, 195; Gross, *Revolution*, xiv. See also S. Ciesielski et al., *Represje sowieckie wobec Polaków i obywateli polskich* (Warsaw, 2002). Poles made up close to 40 percent of those arrested by the Soviets in Western Ukraine and Western Belarus, Ukrainians and Jews 22 percent each; Jews were twice as likely to be arrested as Poles and three times more likely than Ukrainians. About 600 of those arrested died of torture and maltreatment in prison, 7,300 were murdered by the NKVD in spring 1940, and 1,200 executed in May–July 1941. Of the 20,000 in prison in June 1941 in Western Ukraine, 8,700 were murdered when the Germans invaded. K. Struve, *Deutsche Herrschaft, ukrainischer Nationalismus, antijüdische Gewalt* (Berlin, 2015), 216, estimates between 7,500 and 10,000 victims.

23 Hryciuk, "Victims," 182–83, 195; K. R. Jolluck, *Exile and Identity* (Pittsburgh, 2002), 13; P. Ahonen et al., *People on the Move* (New York, 2008), 124–26. See also A. V. Prusin, *The Lands Between* (New York,

2010), 142–43. According to Gross, *Revolution*, 269, Polish statistics compiled in 1944 indicated that 52 percent of deportees were ethnic Poles, 30 percent Jews, and 18 percent Ukrainians and Belarusians, suggesting that the ratio of Jewish deportees was three times higher than the proportionate Jewish population of prewar eastern Poland.

24 Fedus, "Pierwsza deportacja z województwa tarnopolskiego," 55; Janda, AW, II/1561, pp. 26–29. See also W. Janda, *Dotrwać do świtu* (Toruń, Poland, 1998).

25 Transcript of interview with B. Piotrowska-Dubik by F. Grelka in Warsaw, September 21, 2005. See also the testimony of Helena Siekierska, who was deported on the same train: AW, II/1652, pp. 1–6, and by former police officer Stanisław Pawłowski: HI, Pol., MID, 199/5, 3648, p. 4.

26 J. Bojnowski, AW, II/1115, pp. 1–31.

27 Transcript of interview with P. Pasichnyk by S. Grachova and A. Pavlyashuk at his home in Buczacz, March 3, 2006. See also "Memories of Zelena," http://history.buchach.net/spohady-zhyteliv-sela-zelena (in Ukrainian, accessed October 21, 2016). According to NKVD documents, of 1,290 inmates of the regional Czortków prison, 954 were evacuated to Novosibirsk, of whom "123 prisoner members of the OUN were shot" in the course of a "mutiny" during their march to the east; they were probably executed. Another 217 prisoners were released, and most of the remaining 119 appear to have been executed in the prison. The NKVD reported the execution of 2,464 prisoners in Lwów and 560 in Tarnopol; there were many more killings in other towns. Most, although not all, of these victims were Ukrainian political activists. I. Bilas, *The Repressive-Punitive System in Ukraine* (Kiev, 1994, in Ukrainian and Russian), 2:250–51, 262–68. For slightly different figures, see Struve, *Deutsche Herrschaft*, 252–53.

28 Transcript of interview with V. Petrykevych by S. Grachova at his home in Ivano-Frankivsk (Stanisławów), May 2006.

29 E. Worman (Bazan), Yad Vashem Archives, Jerusalem (hereafter YVA), 03/4235, 1976 (transcribed 1982, hereafter Worman 1976), pp. 1–6.

30 M. Rosner, *I Am a Witness* (Winnipeg, 1990), 13–22; E. Bauer Katz, *Our Tomorrows Never Came* (New York, 2000), 9–29.

31 A. Nir (Reinisch), YVA, 03/11147, tape 033C/5863, transcript, 1999, pp. 2–9; H. Miller, Shoah Foundation Visual History Archive, USC, Los Angeles (hereafter SFV), 47637, 1998; Gekht, "Road from Ghetto to Orphanage," 253.

32 M. Halpern, *Family and Town* (Tel Aviv, 2003, in Hebrew), 41–44; P. Anderman, *The Power of Life* (Ramat Gan, Israel, 2004, in Hebrew), 12–30.

33 G. Gross, SFV 16309, June 17, 1996 (hereafter Gross 1996); S. Tischler, YVA, 03/10229, VT-1585, transcript, 1997, pp. 2–6 (hereafter Tischler 1997).

34 Transcript of interview with J. Szechner by F. Grelka at his home in Wrocław, June 29, 2004; transcript of interview with Y. Friedlender by Eyal Ziffer, D. Friedlender's grandson, in Israel, 2004 (hereafter Friedlender 2004). See also Katz, *Our Tomorrows*, xxvii.

35 O. Bartov, "Defining Enemies, Making Victims," *AHR* 103/3 (June 1998): 771–816.

36 PISM, PRM.K.96, file 28, *Okupacja Sowiecka*, pp. 204–20, 214–16. See also J. B. Michlic, "Anti-Polish and Pro-Soviet?," in Barkan, *Shared History*, 76–77.

37 *Okupacja Sowiecka*, 217–18. The GPU had by then been renamed GUGB; it was still under the overall command of the NKVD, but was often referred to by its original name.

38 *Okupacja Sowiecka*, 218–19. Penslar, *Jews and the Military*, 207. See also B. Meirtchak, *Jewish Military Casualties in the Polish Armies in World War II* (Tel Aviv, 1994).

39 PAAA, Botschaft Moskau, Sign. 404, undated list of applications for passports by Jews in the Soviet zone of occupation in East Poland, p. 4; Chef der Sicherheitspolizei und des SD [Sicherheitsdienst, the security service of the SS], IV D 4-2, to German Embassy in Moscow, "Juden im ehem. Ostpolen, Paß- und sonstige Anträge," May 21, 1940; Schulenburg response, June 22, 1940. In August Schulenburg reported, "In recent weeks, organs of the NKVD in Lemberg have raided Jews who had fled from the [General] Government to the Soviet Union. . . . All Jews who could not provide proof of a permanent

work place were arrested and immediately brought by buses to the train in order to be transported to Kazakhstan. This action apparently entailed 20,000–25,000 Jews." Soviet sources mention the deportation of 22,000 people from Lwów, mostly Jewish *bieżeńcy* (fugitives from German-occupied Poland), on June 28–29, 1940; an NKVD report dated July 3 references 50,582 refugees deported from Lwów by the previous day, with a total of 83,207 deported from the entire Soviet zone (including 3,426 from the Tarnopol oblast), thus exceeding the generally accepted estimate of 75,000 deportees in this third wave of deportations mostly targeting Jewish refugees. PAAA, Botschaft Moskau, Sign. 495, "Rundschrift," August 5, 1940; K. T. Lewin, *Przeżyłem* (Warsaw, 2006), 40, n. 1; Bilas, *Punitive System of Repression*, 156–57; Jolluck, *Exile and Identity*, 13; Gross, *Revolution*, 269; Ahonen, *People on the Move*, 123–26.

Chapter 5: GERMAN ORDER

1 V. Petrykevych diary; B. Petrykevych interview; S. Grachova, "The Diary of Viktor Petrykevych," unpublished paper, Herder Institute, University of Marburg, Germany, 2007. The rest of the missing section, covering the first six months of the German occupation, likely depicted Petrykevych's role as director of the Buczacz District Department of People's Education under the short-lived Ukrainian nationalist administration between July and October 1941. See N. S. Myzak, *For You, Holy Ukraine* (Chernivtsi, 2004, in Ukrainian), 4:94–96.

2 See also Wehrmacht report that the Hungarians had "transported Jews by trucks from Hungary . . . and dumped them in the region." They were subsequently murdered there and in Kamieniec Podolski. Bundesarchiv (Federal Archives, Germany, hereafter BArch, here the Military Archive in Freiburg), RH 26-101/8, 24-52/3, 52/21, 26-101/2, 20-17/280, 17/277, 17/38, 17/33, 22/5, 22/187; BArch RH 162/20036, p. 797.

3 Kramarchuk served as chief of the security service; he died in the United States in 1960. While the Germans dismantled Ukrainian

self-government in the fall of 1941, they employed many Ukrainians in their own administration. Myzak, *For You, Holy Ukraine*, 4:94–96. See also Private Archive of Oleh Klymenko (hereafter PAK), in DATO, from HDA SBU, spr. 26874, vol. 1, pp. 190–93, 196.

4 The collaborationist newspaper *Buchatski Visti*, September 14, 1941, p. 3, described a much larger event on Fedor Hill on August 31, 1941, where ten thousand people commemorated the anti-Bolshevik war of 1941 and the victims of Soviet rule in 1939-41.

5 Father Antin Kaznovskyi was a prewar nationalist activist; his two other sons were killed in the war, and he "repeatedly protested . . . against the mass deportation of young Ukrainians as forced laborers to the Reich, and against the Holocaust." Arrested by the Germans but rescued by his son Volodymyr, he died shortly after his arrest by the Soviet authorities in 1958. Uliana Skalska, "Biographical Sketch," Poshuk Archive, Buczacz City Museum, making no mention of the son's wartime function.

6 These and the following accounts by Ukrainian policemen and their victims are based on: O. Klymenko and S. Tkachov, *Ukrainian Policemen in Distrikt Galizien, Kreishauptmannschaft Chortkiv* (Kharkiv, 2012, in Ukrainian), 137, 151–71, 250–58 (a list of ninety-two Ukrainian auxiliary policemen in the Buczacz district); HDA SBU, Ternopil, spr. 8540-P, pp. 13, 27; spr. 8973-P; spr. 9859-P, vol. 1, pp. 95, 133–34; vol. 2, pp. 1–3, 103–4; spr. 14050-P, 1951, pp. 122–23, 137; spr. 14320-P, pp. 17, 19–20, 44, 57, 142, 151, 159; spr. 3713, pp. 9–18; spr. 30466, 1957 indictment of Volodymyr Kaznovskyi (b. 1904, arrested 1956, sentenced to twenty-five years, hereafter Kaznovskyi indictment), appendices, vol. 1, pp. 35–36, 43–45, 53, 58–59, 192, 203–4, 222–23; vol. 2, pp. 4–5, 9, 15–16, 135–36.

7 Generally see T. Sandkühler, *"Endlösung" in Galizien* (Bonn, 1996); D. Pohl, *Judenverfolgung in Ostgalizien* (Munich, 1996).

8 The Czortków district administration was first headed by district chief Gerhard Littschwager, then, as of April 1942, by Hans Kujath. Littschwager was dismissed for corruption, described in an internal SS report as "a loser politically, professionally, and in terms of his

character," and as having driven Czortków "almost completely to rack and ruin." Behörde für die Unterlagen des Staatssicherheitsdienstes der ehemaligen Deutschen Demokratischen Republik, Ministerium für Staatssicherheit (Federal Commissioner for the Records of the State Security Service of the former German Democratic Republic, Berlin, hereafter BStU, MfS), HA XX 3047, May 14, 1943, pt. 1, pp. 19–20; BArch (Ludwigsburg Außenstelle), Personalkartei, 208 AR 611/1960; BArch ZR 572/14, pp. 1–2, 6–23 (Berlin Document Center, Series RS, hereafter BDC-RS); BArch 162/4148; Sandkühler, *Endlösung*, 78, 87, 454–55; Pohl, *Judenverfolgung*, 416–17. See also *Verwaltungsordnung für die Gemeindeverbände im Distrikt Galizien* (Lemberg, 1942), 19–28; "Material der 1. Kreishauptleutetagung des Distrikts Galizien am 2.IX.1941," Instytut Pamięci Narodowej (Institute for National Memory, Warsaw, hereafter IPN), 196 NTN-286, pp. 103, 111–13, 119, 125, 127; 196 NTN-258, p. 285.

9 See also M. Wizinger, YVA 03/3799, pp. 9, 13–14; M. Halpern, YVA M-1/E, 2310 (hereafter Halpern 1948), p. 4 (39); J. Kornblüh, Archiwum Żydowskiego Instytutu Historycznego (Archive of the Jewish Historical Institute, Warsaw, hereafter AŻIH), 301/2605 (hereafter Kornblüh 1945). The last two claim that the victims included Jews.

10 Z. Gerber, SFV 23336, November 28, 1996 (hereafter Gerber 1996); letter by M. Kleiner (in English, hereafter Kleiner 1951), Föhrenwald, April 10, 1951, in Kaznovskyi indictment; S. Rosen, YVA M-49/1935 AŻIH 03/2055 (hereafter S. Rosen 1960); Wizinger, YVA, 4–5; M. Halpern, BArch B162/5163 (hereafter Halpern 1965), pp. 436; Halpern 1948; Halpern, *Family and Town*, 45–46.

11 Kornblüh 1945; S. Rosental, AŻIH 301/2086; Wizinger, YVA, 7–8; Halpern 1948; I. Szwarc, USHMM RG-15.084M, Acc. 1997.A.0125, reel 5, AŻIH 301/327 (hereafter Szwarc 1945); I. Gelbart, YVA 033/640, E/640, E/21-1-8 (hereafter Gelbart 1948); Katz, *Our Tomorrows*, 34. See also the account of "six weeks of lawless hooliganism" with "scores of Jewish victims" by Zelig Heiss, YVA, M1Q/51, March 10, 1948.

12 S. Rosen interview with author, Tel Aviv, March 12, 2002 (hereafter S. Rosen 2002); Gelbart 1948. Gelbart later wrote that Bobyk "did all

he could to express his good relationship with the Jews" and that "any Jew could turn to him during the German rule without any difficulty." I. Gelbart, "Fourth Testimony," in *Sefer Buczacz*, 275–76. Worman 1976 described Bobyk as "rather a liberal man" who "even helped Jews on some occasions." Wizinger, YVA, 8; Kornblüh 1945. See the list of Ukrainian and Polish physicians in German-ruled Buczacz, which includes Wladimir Hamerskyj (Volodymyr Hamerskyi), Alexius Banach, and Witold Ratayski: APK zesp. 228, p. 1; 235, pp. 55, 57.

13 Wizinger, YVA, 8–9; Halpern, *Family and Town*, 46; Gross 1996; A. Appleman-Jurman, interview with author, October 19, 2005; "Letter from Dr. Max Anderman" and S. Rosental, "Second Testimony," in *Sefer Buczacz*, 236; 258, 262–64, respectively. See also MWC, account by Elie Berger: "58 Torah scrolls that were hidden by the monks of the Basilian Monastery were returned and taken to Czernowitz." May 18, 1947.

14 Wizinger, YVA, 14–15.

15 Y. Shikhor (I. Szwarc), "First Testimony," in *Sefer Buczacz*, 237–38, 273–74; DATO, fond R-174, op. 1,- od., zb. 1283, 3.9.31; letter by Arye Leib (Leon) Slutzky of the Institut für Judaistik, University of Vienna, enclosing copy of Szwarc's original account, to Simon Wiesenthal, January 25, 1978, Wiesenthal Archive in Vienna, Buczacz folder (hereafter WA/B). See also an account of the killing of three hundred Hungarian Jews near Buczacz in 1942 in H. Komański et al., "Ludobójstwo i czystki etniczne," *Na Rubieży* 4 (1995): 4–25, here 5–6.

16 Shikhor (Szwarc), "First Testimony," in *Sefer Buczacz*, 238, 266; Szwarc 1945. Similar accusations were made by Wizinger, YVA, 15, S. Rosen 1960, and Eliasz Chalfen, YVA, M1/E 1559 (hereafter E. Chalfen 1947). For conditions in these labor camps, see Gerber 1996; Mosze Ginsberg, BArch B162/5166, Tel Aviv, September 30, 1964, pp. 1219–20 (hereafter Ginsberg 1964); Gross 1996; Leon Schmetterling, SFV 2659, May 21, 1995 (hereafter Schmetterling 1995); Michael (Samuel, Shmuel) Suhl, SFV 12558, March 1, 1996; Icchak Miller, BArch B162-6081, p. 48; Staatsanwaltschaft (state attorney, hereafter StA) Oldenburg, Rep 946 Akz. 133, vol. 14: 135–37; vol. 15: 60–61, 68–70, 117–18, 119–26, 128–29, 240–43, 251; vol. 16:

74, 212–15; vol. 17: 74; StA Amberg, vol. 1506/2: 223–29, 416–17; vol. 1506/3: 23, 184; vol. 1506/5, no page numbers.

17 S. Rosen 1960; Rosental, AŻIH; letter by Bernhard Seifer, June 5, 1946, MWC (hereafter Seifer 1946); E. Bazan (Worman), "The Resistance in Buczacz," in *Sefer Buczacz*, 286; Worman 1976 and 208 AR-Z 239/59, StA Saarbrücken, vol. 3 (hereafter Gelbart 1965), p. 1007, note that the third Judenrat chairman, Dr. Engelberg, escaped after being warned by Landkommissar Walter Hoffer. Gelbart, "Fourth Testimony," in *Sefer Buczacz*, 273, and 276, where he comments that Kramer and Seifer "appealed to the Germans" on behalf of the Jews at least "until the fall of 1942." A German translation of Gelbart's account is in a letter from Simon Wiesenthal to public prosecutor Wilhelm Angelberger in Mannheim, September 3, 1965, "Bericht Polizei Israel," WA/B; Anonymous, YVA M-1/E, 1726 (hereafter Anonymous 1948); further in Michael Margules, BArch 162/5163, Saarbrücken, 1960, p. 164 (hereafter Margules 1960).

18 Halpern 1948; S. Rosen 1960; Wizinger, YVA, 23–24.

19 Gerhard von Jordan, a former German official in nearby Kołomyja (Ukrainian: Kolomyya), described a similar situation there: "On the fingers of the Gestapo commissars one could see large glittering diamonds; their wives acquired elegant underwear and good clothing materials from Jewish provisions. Furs and leather goods were acquired in large quantities. . . . From this bribery business developed a nauseating friendship between Jews and Gestapo leaders. . . . Jewish coachmen, Jewish maids, Jewish workmen and Jewish merchants went in and out of the homes of the Gestapo. To be sure this did not prevent the Gestapo from bestially murdering their good friends at the very first opportunity." BArch (Außenstelle Bayreuth), Ost-Dok. 13/236, "Erlebnisbericht über meine Tätigkeit im ehem. Generalgouvernement," November 29, 1956; G. von Jordan, *Polnische Jahre* (Bad Rappenau-Heinsheim, 1986); "Es war oft auch recht lustig," *Der Spiegel* 42 (1995): 92–101, http://mag azin.spiegel.de/EpubDelivery/spiegel/pdf/9222612; T. Kleine-Brockhoff, "Raub ohne Zeugen," *Die Zeit* 44 (1995), http://www.zeit.de/1995/44/ Raub_ohne_Zeugen (both accessed November 17, 2016).

20 Shortly after the war Abraham Chalfen wrote to Palestine that the Buczacz Judenrat had "supervised the implementation" of German orders and "the Jewish police carried them out"; the Jews "could not tell who was crueler: the Judenrat or the Gestapo." Shmuel Rosen recalled that the Judenrat adamantly refused to help a Jewish army veteran Jankiel Zuler purchase weapons, and later "threatened to denounce" Rosen's own resistance group "to the Germans if we continued"; especially Kramer, Seifer, and Berko Hersas—the only other Judenrat member who survived—"were emphatically opposed." Only the Judenrat member and former deputy mayor Emanuel Meerengel helped the resistance, as also confirmed by resistance leader Worman. Izaak Szwarc noted that a group of armed Jews deported to Buczacz from Tłumacz "troubled the Judenrat" because of "the general opinion . . . that they were not afraid of the Germans and the Ukrainians." Yehoshua Friedlender believed that Seifer "saw the poor as human dust meant to satiate the German beast and save those 'worthy of rescue' until the bad times passed." "Letter from Dr. Abraham, Łódź, January 1, 1946," in *Sefer Buczacz*, 233–35; S. Rosen 1960; S. Rosen, interview with author, Tel Aviv, March 12, 2002 (hereafter Rosen 2002); Worman 1976; Szwarc 1945; YVA M1Q/53, Samuel Hersas, "Questionnaire," October 15, 1947; Friedlender 2004.

21 Seifer 1946; Wizinger, YVA, 49; Worman 1976; S. Rosen 1960; Gelbart 1965; Kornblüh 1945; J. Kornblüh, USHMM RG-15.084M, reel 35, 301/3279, and 301/3283, January 13 and 19, 1948 (hereafter Kornblüh 1948); Rosental, AŻIH; Anonymous 1948; S. Rosen 2002. *Sefer Buczacz*, 301, cites *Haaretz* correspondent Yitzhak Bornstein writing from Warsaw in September 1949 that "the members of the Jewish council . . . stood up" to the Germans "with dignity and pride" and "did not fulfill all the Hitlerite demands. The Jews said to themselves: It is better to die with dignity than to die in disgrace." See also the detailed but false description of the Judenrat in *Gazeta Żydowska*, one of two official mouthpieces of the Jews under German occupation, May 29 and July 1, 1942.

22 Wizinger, YVA, 47; Worman 1976 (naming him Edelstein). Sala Anderman saw Munio (Menachem) Landau betray the bunker; Ebenstein then fled and was shot by the gendarme Peter Pahl. Erna Klanfer also testified that Pahl shot Ebenstein. Landau survived and testified in Haifa on November 4, 1965, that he "knew the gendarme Pahl at the time well." S. Anderman, BArch B162/5169, p. 1974 (hereafter S. Anderman, BArch); E. Klanfer, BArch B162/5180, Netanya, Israel, September 2, 1968, pp. 5626–29 (hereafter Klanfer 1968); BArch B162/5169, pp. 1835–36, respectively.

23 Wizinger, YVA, 21, 53–54; Halpern 1948; E. Chalfen 1947: this line is omitted from E. Chalfen, "Third Testimony," in *Sefer Buczacz*, 265; Gelbart, "Fourth Testimony," in *Sefer Buczacz*, 273; see also *Sefer Buczacz*, 295–96, for a reprint of a report from Paris in *Haaretz* of January 1947 on a chance encounter between a survivor and a former OD member from Buczacz.

24 Rosental, AŻIH; reference to axes expunged from Rosental, "Second Testimony," in *Sefer Buczacz*, 260; S. Rosen 1960.

25 Sala Anderman, a nurse at the hospital at the time, witnessed similar killings by the gendarme Peter Pahl and others (S. Anderman, BArch). Halpern recalled that during the second action OD men did not collaborate "as much as in the first roundup, because some of their members had also been deported." Hindzia Miller (Hilda Weitz) testified that during the fourth roundup, of April 1943, OD chief Wolcio Wattenberg, who knew her family, "fell on his knees and begged the Germans and the Ukrainians, 'Please take me, but don't take them.'" This likely led to his removal and murder. Izaak Szwarc recalled that during the same action the OD man Janek Anderman "shot a Ukrainian policeman and injured a German." The Germans then "beat him until he lost consciousness, dragged him to town," and "in front of the city hall poured gasoline on him and burned him alive." Halpern 1948; H. Weitz, SFV 47637, November 4, 1998; Szwarc 1945; Shikhor (Szwarc), First Testimony," in *Sefer Buczacz*, 246–47. See also Worman 1976; Bazan (Worman), "The Resistance in Buczacz," in *Sefer Buczacz*; Gekht, "Stolen Childhood."

26 If this was Natan (Nadje) Dunajer's mother, this account would indicate that the former communist and future resistance leader was also an OD member. For witness testimonies on Pal, see Benzion Schor, Bogotá, Colombia, November 21, 1967, BArch B/5176, pp. 4596–602; Abraham Bilgoraj, Beit Dagon, Israel, April 22, 1965, BArch B/5166, pp. 1238–45.

27 BArch B162/5182, vol. 20, January 10, 1968, pp. 6212–19 (hereafter Bauer 1968). Gelbart, "Fourth Testimony," in *Sefer Buczacz*, 282–83, notes that in June 1943 "a small group of surviving youths were hiding in the forests of Buczacz: the two Bauer brothers, List, the son of the baker, Friedlender, Fritz, and others—several dozen boys aged 17 to 22." Fritz was also a former OD member. Erna Klanfer testified that "the Jewish Ordnungsdienst knew well the terrain of Buczacz and the bunkers in which the Jews hid"; she encountered Bauer in Tel Aviv after the war and recognized him as a former policeman. Klanfer 1968. Beno Wechsler testified in Israel, "Izi Bauer was in the Jewish police that used to catch the Jews, he lives here." YVA 03/9078, September 4, 1995 (hereafter Wechsler 1995). Worman 1976, who turned down a request from the Judenrat to command the Jewish police, ended up organizing a resistance group in Buczacz. But as he testified, "one cannot say that there was one heroic battle" or "great acts of courage. . . . The best reward was that we survived." Worman claimed that as communists, Dunajer's and Friedlender's resistance groups rejected "the nationalist character of our organization"; he also accused Wizinger of joining a Polish resistance group that "attacked Jews and carried out many murderous actions and terrified everyone." Wizinger's version completely contradicts this claim. Shlomo Gutkowski (Munio Weitz), SFV 46271, August 16, 1998, gives a critical account of Worman's group (hereafter Gutkowski 1998).

28 Bazan (Worman), "The Resistance in Buczacz," in *Sefer Buczacz*, 288; Worman 1976; E. Chalfen 1947; Rosental, AŻIH; S. Rosen 1960; Gelbart 1965; AAN, zesp. 1326, 203/XV/28, May 5, 1944, p. 123.

29 *Buchatski Visti*, September 21, 1941, p. 2: "The offices of the district leadership of the OUN-M [the more moderate faction of OUN led

by Andriy Melnyk] are located at the Prosvita House (formerly the 'Sokół') under the name 'Sich.'" Kaznovskyi's deputy, Vasyl Kit, commanded the ten-man Buczacz city police force throughout the occupation; Kit's deputy Dankovych became chief of police in Barysz in 1942. There were eleven Ukrainian police outposts in the Buczacz district; each included a German gendarme. These approximately sixty men, most of them older adherents of OUN-M, were an integral component of German genocidal policies. The younger members of Bandera's more radical OUN-B went underground. Halpern, *Family and Town*, 46, writes, "Dr. Fuchs's wife was arrested." Kornblüh 1945 notes that "Mrs. Fuks, the wife of a physician who had been arrested before," was among the victims. The only Jewish witness who testified at the postwar Soviet investigation, twenty-year-old Bernard Kramer, saw "about 450 people" being led "in a column guarded by the Ukrainian district police" toward the killing site. There were three women in the first row, including "my aunt, Liuba Weisser." Another witness saw "four or five women," including "one named Fuchs." See also n. 6.

30 Shikhor (Szwarc), "First Testimony"; Rosental, "Second Testimony"; Chalfen, "Third Testimony"; Gelbart, "Fourth Testimony"; and Bazan (Worman), "The Resistance in Buczacz," all in *Sefer Buczacz*, 238, 260, 265, 274, and 285, respectively. Gelbart 1948, 1965; Szwarc 1945; E. Chalfen 1947; Rosental, AŻIH; Worman 1976; Filip Czarski, BArch B162/20035, September 26, 1967, pp. 712–13; Gerber 1996.

31 Kornblüh 1945; Kleiner 1951; Szwarc 1945; Wizinger, YVA, 20; Jakub Hornreich, BArch B1672/20035, Akko, Israel, February 2, 1966, pp. 453–56.

32 Wizinger, YVA, 1–20; Kleiner 1951; Leslie Gordon, *The Trial of Adolf Eichmann*, June 1, 1961, Session 62, part 5, *Nizkor Project*, http://www.nizkor.org/hweb/people/e/eichmann-adolf/transcripts/Sessions/Session-062-05.html (accessed November 17, 2016); S. Rosen 1960.

33 S. Rosen 1960; Bazan (Worman), "The Resistance in Buczacz," in *Sefer Buczacz*, 285; Fabian Strauber, YVA, M-1/E, 1529, Stuttgart, July 28, 1947 (hereafter Strauber 1947); DATO, fond 274, op. 4, spr. 78, p. 44; David Munczer, YVA 03/6183, October 26, 1990, pp. 3–4; Yisrael

Munczer, YVA 03/642, April 23, 1961, p. 4, and YVA 03/5878, April 27, 1990, pp. 7–8; Y. Munczer, *A Holocaust Survivor from Buczacz* (Jerusalem, 1990, in Hebrew), pp. 12–15; David Seiler, account to the Soviet Extraordinary Commission (hereafter SEC), November 5, 1944, USHMM RG-22-002m, Reel 17, folder 371.

34 The outpost reported to the SS- und Polizeiführer (SS and Police Leader, SSPF) of Distrikt Galizien in Lemberg, SS-Brigadier General Friedrich Katzmann, who reported in turn to the Höherer SS- und Polizeiführer (higher SS and police leader, HSSPF) of the General Government, Friedrich-Wilhelm Krüger, in Kraków. At the top of the hierarchy was the Reichssicherheitshauptamt (Reich Security Main Office, RSHA) in Berlin under Reinhard Heydrich (Ernst Kaltenbrunner after January 1943), whose direct boss was Reichsführer (Reich Leader) of the SS and chief of the German police Heinrich Himmler. Justiz und NS-Verbrechen (*Nazi Crimes on Trial*, *J.u.NS-V*), vol. 18, pp. 659–60. See StA Dortmund 45 Js 11/65, 4690, Arnsberg, April 2, 1968, pp. 196–204; 4692, pp. 81–83 for a personnel list of the Czortków Sipo, noting five chiefs, ten Gestapo officials, a dozen guards and administrative staff, and SS men Richard Pal and Paul Thomanek. Kurt Köllner listed about forty men in the outpost, including "criminal officials of German, Ukrainian, and Polish nationality": StA Hagen, vol. 5, April 21, 1959, p. 152; BArch B162/5164, December 1, 1964, pp. 1–10. The establishment figure for the "non-German police for 1943" in Czortków indicated 302 Ukrainian policemen and officers (3,674 for Galicia as a whole), raised to 305 (4,133) on July 1, 1943, and remaining at this level on January 1, 1944. USHMM RG-31.003M Reel 1 (1992.A.0069), from YVA M-37, March 17, July 4, and December 22, 1943, pp. 19–21, 35–39.

35 The first outpost chief was a World War I and Freikorps veteran and Nazi Party member, Detective Sergeant Fritz-Ernst Blome. Appointed in September 1941 but dismissed shortly thereafter for being "too weak," he was replaced by Detective Superintendent Karl Hildemann, who was in turn transferred in November 1942. The next chief,

Detective Sergeant Hans Velde, died from spotted fever in March 1943 and was replaced by Detective Sergeant Heinrich Peckmann, deputy chief of the outpost since late 1942. Finally, in October 1943, Detective Superintendent Werner Eisel, a lawyer and Nazi Party member, took over until the outpost was dismantled in early 1944. Of these men, only Peckmann was indicted but acquitted after the war; Blome and Eisel died in 1948 before trial proceedings could begin. *J.u.NS-V*, vol. 18, p. 659; BArch (Außenstelle Ludwigsburg) DP3/1645, indictment, Kurt Willi, Otto Köllner and Heinrich Peckmann, Saarbrücken, June 12, 1961; USHMM RG-31.003M Reel 1, BDC-RS/BArch (Berlin); Werner Eisel, Generallandesarchiv Karlsruhe (hereafter GLA-K) 309. Zug. 2001-42/881, Landesgericht (State Court, hereafter LG) Mannheim, S.B. 40; IPN Warsaw 375/33, pp. 1, 3–7; BArch ZB827 /2; BArch B162/20037, December 27, 1961, pp. 94–100; 5164, December 1, 1964, pp. 698–707; Sandkühler, *Endlösung*, 154, 440; Pohl, *Judenverfolgung*, 411–12.

36 This account is based on *J.u.NS-V*, vol. 18, pp. 655–80; BArch (Außenstelle Ludwigsburg), DP3/1645, pp. 7–23. Officially Köllner's position was at times referred to as "Judensachbearbeiter."

37 A. Angrick, "Annihilation and Labor," in *The Shoah in Ukraine*, ed. R. Brandon and W. Lower (Bloomington, IN, 2008), 190–223.

38 Among other crimes, Köllner was accused of shooting twelve patients, including three women and several children, in their beds at the Buczacz ghetto hospital in early 1943. BArch (Außenstelle Ludwigsburg), 208 AR-Z 239/59, vol. 1, pp. 17–19.

39 This account is based on *J.u.NS-V*, 18: 658-9, 677-79, 682; BArch (Außenstelle Ludwigsburg) DP3/1645, pp. 9–10, 23–24, 27–28. See also the questionnaire filled out by Peckmann on April 18, 1939, in Cologne: GLA-K 309 Zug. 2001-42/881. See further in StA Dortmund 45 Js 11/65, 4688, M. Weisinger [Wizinger], Tel Aviv, August 18, 1963, pp. 40–43; Dr. I. Schorr, Tel Aviv, September 5, 1963, p. 46; summary of accusation, May 3, 1965, pp. 161–63; 4689, J. Kohn, Beit Dagon, October 21, 1965, pp. 130–35; W. F. Müller, Ansbach, January 11, 1966, pp. 148–55; A. D. Schweiger, Haifa, July 14, 1965,

pp. 167–69; S. Elizur, Tel Aviv, June 14, 1965, pp. 175–79; 4690, Peckmann interrogation, Euskirchen, March 2, 1966, p. 8; summary and dismissal, August 24, 1966, pp. 127–49. See also N. Rosenberg, BArch B162/5163, Tel Aviv, March 3, 1960, p. 80; Schorr, 1961, pp. 403–12; Sandkühler, *Endlösung*, 442.

40 This account is based on BArch B162/5175, October 24, 1967, pp. 4253–58. Dov Rachelson described Rosenow as "a degenerate with an especially trained dog that would respond to the call 'Jude' by attacking Jews, biting and tearing off pieces of flesh. He was the ghetto's nightmare and it was enough for someone to say 'Rosenow is coming' for everyone to hide." BArch B162/5175, vol. 81, pp. 97–100. Richard Pal claimed that Hildemann was "shot by the Germans in the Baltics, because . . . just as in Czortków, he did not agree with the Jewish actions." BArch B162/5175, October 30, 1967, p. 4272. Józef Rabinowicz described "the 'executioner trio' made up of Brettschneider, Martin, and Rosenow—the latter always accompanied by a dog," and said that Brettschneider "was considered a dangerous murderer by the inhabitants of Buczacz . . . especially . . . when he was drunk." 208 AR-Z 239/59, vol. 3, Tel Aviv, October 23, 1964, pp. 935–37.

41 This account is based on *J.u.NS-V*, vol. 16, pp. 727–72. See also StA Hagen, 11 Ks 1/57, vol. 1, July 20, 1955, pp. 128–37, and references below. On labor camps in the Tarnopol area, see also Case Nr. 63, Andere Massenvernichtungsverbrechen: LG Stuttgart, 15.07.1966, Ks 7/64, Bundesgerichtshof (German Federal Supreme Court, BGH), 1 StR 601/67, May 7, 1968.

42 StA Hagen, 11 Ks 1/57, vol. 5, April 21, 1959, pp. 154, 156. Margules 1960: "Rux was very close friends with Thomanek. Both were also friends with Pahl" (likely referring to Richard Pal), p. 139.

43 BArch B162/5176, p. 66 (2); StA Hagen, 11 Ks 1/57, vol. 5, April 21, 1959, p. 157.

44 208 AR-Z 239/59, vol. 3, StA Saarbrücken, March 26, 1965, pp. 764–67; testimony by Albert Wachinger: BArch B162/5180, November 12, 1968, pp. 5669–71. See also testimony by Franz Rauscher, 5178, July 24, 1968, p. 5213. Rosental, AŻIH, witnessed several other

killings of Jews, including his two daughters, by Thomanek. S. Rosen witnessed the killing by Thomanek of Dawid Aba Stern, his wife, and two daughters at the Judenrat building. StA Hagen, 11 Ks 1/57, vol. 5, January 12, 1958, p. 14; vol. 10, May 18, 1960, p. 56.

45 In early 1943 Thomanek shot two young women point-blank in the head as they begged for their lives on their knees in front of the assembled workers at the Nagórzanka-Jagielnica camp, as punishment for visiting a nearby camp. In June that year he shot the elderly Rosen couple at the Jezierzany labor camp, presumably as unfit for work. Rosental witnessed the liquidation of the camp in Jagielnica: "I watched the Jews . . . being arrayed next to a pit of manure at the farm, surrounded by Ukrainian militia, then stepping individually on a board and being shot one after the other by Thomanek, and falling dead from the board into the pit." StA Hagen, 11 Ks 1/57, vol. 5, p. 14. Elsewhere the killing of the Rosens is attributed to Köllner during the June 8–10, 1943, action in Buczacz: 208 AR-Z 239/59, vol. 2, p. 523.

46 Thomanek was released from prison in 1979 and passed away at age eighty-nine in 1998. StA Hagen 11 Ks 1/57, vol. 13, June 12 and 28, 2001, pp. 317–18.

47 This account is based on BArch B162/5171, December 16, 1966, pp. 3444–84; 5173, May 8–22, 1967, pp. 3737–67; 5187, September 3, 1970, pp. 7587–742; 5188, September 25, 1971, and January 25, 1973; GLA-K 309 Zug. 2001-42/881, pp. 9–24. The German investigation determined that Brettschneider "had no racist or any other prejudices against Jews in Lithuania. Some of his friends were Jews and originally he even wanted to marry a Jewish woman called Markson."

48 This account is based on BArch 162/5176, March 5, 1968, pp. 4795–806.

49 This account is based on StA Mannheim 208 AR-Z 239/59, vol. 6, October 7, 1965, pp. 1672–76; BArch B162/5169, January 10, 1966, pp. 1854–55; 5167, May 6, 1966; 5171, December 16, 1966; 5173, May 29–June 5, 1967, pp. 3822–56, November 20, 1967, pp. 4592–95; 5187, September 3, 1970, August 11, 1971. See also DATO, fond

R-279, op. 1, spr. 1 (1941); GLA-K 309 Zug. 2002-42/866 (1944); BArch ZM 967/11, November 3, 1943; IPN, Warsaw, WOI/8A; April 1, 1944, p. 116; Pohl, *Judenverfolgung*, 250, n. 229.

50 S. Rosen testified that Pahl "was a drinker and could be bribed. He had several mistresses, including a Jewish woman. . . . He was known as a dangerous murderer and a sadist. People were terrified of him." Rosen saw him executing the brothers Sokolecki in summer 1943 at the Jewish cemetery. 208 AR-Z 239/59, StA Mannheim, vol. 6, December 9, 1965, pp. 1686–90; vol. 3, Beit Dagon, Israel, March 16, 1965, pp. 934–38. Ginsberg 1964, p. 1220, witnessed Pahl killing two Jewish girls in spring 1944: "He was a terrible person, he was more dreadful than any SS-man." Worman 1976 described Pahl as "a sadist and a murderer."

51 Ignacy Rabinowicz described Pahl as "a sadist"; his brother Józef Rabinowicz saw that he "personally shot Jews" in the actions of February and April 1943; Adam Steizer (Steiger), BArch B162/5169, Haifa, Israel, November 10, 1965, pp. 1829–34; 5166, Bytom, Poland, June 18, 1965, p. 1287; 5163, Tel Aviv, Israel, November 14, 1961, pp. 481–83; November 6, 1968, pp. 6817–23; Beit Dagon, Israel, on October 10, 1965; 5168, pp. 1702–5; vol. 1, pp. 79–111.

52 DATO, R-279, op. 1, spr. 1; 208 AR-Z 239/59; StA Mannheim, vol. 19, January 28, 1969, pp. 6014–21.

53 This account is based on DATO, R-279, op. 1, spr. 1; 208 AR-Z 239/59, StA Mannheim, vol. 15, April 25, 1968, pp. 5103–112; vol. 16, September 5, 1968, pp. 5330–31, 5335–36, 5340–54; GLA-K 309 Zug. 2001-42/880, StA Mannheim, 32 Js 78/66, December 20, 1968. Barg was described in 1940 as "sober, reliable, loyal and obedient," "imbued with the ideological content of National Socialism," prepared to "fully commit himself to the Reich at any time," and displaying "an impeccable attitude and conduct toward Poles and Jews." Still in police service, he was killed trying to make an arrest in 1946 and granted posthumous promotion as "a shining example of dedication to service and sense of duty." His widow received a generous death benefit. GLA-K 309, Zug. 2001-42/880.

54 This account is based on 208 AR-Z 239/59, vol. 8, pp. 3137–46.

Knaack was described in August 1943 as "a fearless gendarme" who had "distinguished himself by his courage, prudence, and determination." GLA-K 309 Zug. 2001-42/802; DATO, fond R-279, op. 1, spr. 1. Kardasz moved to the United States in 1951. BArch B162/5177, May 15, 1968, pp. 4971–74.

55 This account is based on AAN, Warsaw, III/0 Karta: AiB, 842, p. 342; BArch B1621/4148; BArch (Ludwigsburg Außenstelle) Personalkartei, 211 AR-Z 137/62, vol. 2, p. 124; Zentralkartei, Ortskartei, Buczacz, 2 AR-Z 267/60; 208 AR 76/61, vol. 8, p. 1401; AR-Z 239/59, StA Saarbrücken and Dortmund, vol. 4, June 24, 1965, pp. 1153–64; StA Mannheim, vol. 18, November 26, 1968, pp. 5695–99; vol. 21, April 23, 1969, pp. 6672–708. Lissberg's replacement as Buczacz Landkommissar was the thirty-five-year-old career civil servant Walter Hoffer, who similarly first denied any knowledge of anti-Jewish violence and then conceded having witnessed it but asserted that he never had any personal involvement. Neither man was ever indicted. See 208 AR-Z 239/59, vol. 1, March 31, 1960, pp. 252–55; vol. 3, April 7, 1965, pp. 843–55; BArch (Personalkartei) 2 AR-Z 76/61; AR-Z 267/60; StA Lübeck 2 Js 753/65, July 22, 1965, pp. 820ff; IPN, 196 NTN, 267, p. 244; IPN, 94/2425, pp. 1–3; BArch R 52 II/118-19, 149.

56 V. Petrykevych diary.

57 Henriette also remembered her husband's secretary Julia Rabinowicz as a "black-haired woman" who had studied "to be a pediatrician in Lemberg" and "spoke very good German." Julia, wife of the former Ordnungsdienst chief Józef Rabinowicz, testified that she had no knowledge of Lissberg participating in roundups or killing Jews, recalling, "One day he said to me that he was going hunting in order not to be present at a roundup. At the same time he gave me to understand that he could help neither me nor my parents, because, as he put it, he was only 'a little cog' [*ein kleines Figürchen*]." BArch 162/5163, November 15, 1961, pp. 487–90.

58 The Lissbergs also befriended the Peckmanns in Czortków, which proved useful in helping their friend, former Ukrainian district superintendent Mykhailo Chaikivskyi, when the Gestapo arrested him

in the fall of 1943. Henriette was also close to Dr. Hamerskyi and his wife, insisting that he "was a very good man with a lot of character, who was very positively inclined toward us Germans," even though "he also condemned much of what the Germans did" and "had a positive attitude toward the Jews." She dismissed as a "blatant lie" allegations that "Hamerskyi admitted Jews into the district hospital, took their valuables and then called the police." But Dr. Max Anderman and his wife, Sala, testified that in spring 1942 Hamerskyi reported the presence of a Jewish couple in the hospital, who were then shot on the spot by Pahl. S. Anderman, BArch, pp. 1972–78.

59 This account is based on 208 AR-Z 239/59, StA Mannheim, vol. 21, May 7, 1969, pp. 6743–56; May 9, 1969, pp. 6743–56 (investigations of Ewald and Berta Herzig).

60 See esp. accounts by Johannes Dech, 208 AR-Z 239/59, vol. 3, StA Saarbrücken, March 26, 1965, pp. 756–70; vol. 8, StA Mannheim, February 17, 1966, pp. 1998–2002; vol. 15, May 28, 1968, pp. 4975–84; Julius Wilcke, BArch B162/5169, March 2, 1969, pp. 2069–74; Wilhelm Weippert, AR-Z 239/59, StA Saarbrücken/Dortmund, vol. 4, June 1, 1965, pp. 1198–204; StA Mannheim, vol. 16, July 23, 1968, pp. 5189–197; vol. 18, November 10, 1968, pp. 5787–88; Franz Rauscher, BArch B162/5178, July 24, 1968, pp. 5210–23; Max Bücherl, 208 AR-Z 239/59, StA Mannheim, vol. 16, July 30, 1968, pp. 5271–78; Albert Wachinger, BArch B162/5180, November 12, 1968, pp. 5668–80; Gustav Hein, 208 AR-Z 239/59, vol. 3, April 27, 1965, pp. 1062–66; BArch B162/5178, August 13, 1968, pp. 5324–28; Rolf Lebach, BArch B162/5183, April 28, 1969, pp. 6631–34.

61 This account is based on BArch B162/5178, July 31, 1968, pp. 5254–62.

62 O. Bartov, *The "Jew" in Cinema* (Bloomington, IN, 2005), 89.

63 This account is based on BArch B162/20034, October 28, 1963, pp. 317–21.

64 For a description of the murder of several Jews near Potok Złoty by Pahl and others on September 6, 1943, see BArch B162/5185, Josef Staub, New York, August 11, 1969, pp. 7117–18. Wiesław Antochów

remembered, "The Nazis brought more than 300 young Jews from Czortków to the courtyard of the prison and shot them all there. The Jews were shot like ducks. It all happened in front of everybody's eyes. People were standing on the walls of the prison. I watched it from the windows of the Courtroom. It was terrible." IPN Kraków, S 37/03/zn, vol. 3, July 5, 1990, p. 452.

65 E. Chalfen 1947; Rosental, AŻIH; *Sefer Buczacz*, 237–94; Mosze Bider, YVA, M-1/E, 796/659, December 22, 1946; Giza Ferber, USHMM, RG-15.084M, reel 27 (AŻIH 301/2528), Bytom, July 12, 1947; 208 AR-Z 239/59, StA Mannheim, vol. 1, "Überstücke," pp. 79–111; BArch (Außenstelle Ludwigsburg) 110 AR 850/71, pp. 4–5, 13–16; "Judenwohbezirken," IPN Warsaw 196/333, pp. 276–79; "Juden-wohnbezirken," USHMM RG-31.003M Reel 1, Acc. 1992.A.0069, and YVA M-37; Jakub Wołkowicz, USHMM RG-15.084M Reel 29 (1997.A.0125, AŻIH 301/2653), Opole, July 11, 1947; "Galicia Trans-port Lists," *Aktion Reinhard Camps*, http://www.deathcamps.org/belzec /galiciatransportlist.html (accessed November 17, 2016). Over 250,000 Galician Jews were gassed in Bełżec; the camp was dismantled at the end of 1942. Galicia was declared Judenfrei on June 30, 1943; SS-controlled camps were liquidated in July 1943; only Jews employed on agricultural farms were spared. *J.u.NS-V*, vol. 18, pp. 559–60; vol. 24, pp. 10–24.

66 *Akademie-Report* (Tutzing, Germany), Nr. 3/2005, p. 31. See also W. Dressen, "The Investigation of Nazi Criminals in Western Germany," *Encyclopaedia Judaica Year Book* (1987): 132–38; D. O. Pendas, *The Frankfurt Auschwitz Trial* (New York, 2006); R. Wittmann, *Beyond Justice* (Cambridge, MA, 2005); A. Rückerl, *The Investigation of Nazi Crimes* (Hamden, CT, 1980); H. Friedlander et al., eds., *Nazi Crimes and the Law* (New York, 2008).

Chapter 6: THE DAILY LIFE OF GENOCIDE

1 Communication from Professor Linda Rosenman, University of Queensland, Australia, August–September 2015; her father, Dr. David Rosenman, worked in the Jewish hospital in Buczacz and emigrated to

Australia in the late 1930s. Leon Rosen was his uncle. Leon's two sons went to Palestine in the late 1930s; one became a professor of medicine.

2 BArch (Außenstelle Ludwigsburg), 81/301, pp. 112–18.

3 A. Klonicki-Klonymus, *The Diary of Adam's Father* (Jerusalem, 1969, in Hebrew); English trans. by A. Tomaschoff (Jerusalem, 1973).

4 Gisela Kleiner's maiden name was Kriegel; Sofia (Fish) and Hella (or Helga Bauer) Kriegel, possibly her sisters, survived. Sofia was also a nurse at the hospital, and both she and Gisela may be featured on page 211, a wartime photograph of the hospital staff. Hella did "various jobs mainly for the German army." Both women "didn't look Jewish" and apparently passed as Christians.

5 E. Skamene, SFV 37896, February 3, 1998. Menachem Kriegel, Sofia's younger brother, recalled, "After the first action she acquired false Polish papers and moved to the city of Lwów, where she worked for the last two years of the German occupation." Z. Karniel (Hirschhorn), "Grandfather Menachem Kriegel tells about the roots of the family," undated private document courtesy of the late Mr. Karniel.

6 Lucy Gertner, handed over by her mother to a convent as a small child, was baptized and fell gravely ill with tuberculosis; eventually mother and daughter were reunited. Shoshana Kleiner was hidden with peasants in a nearby village. Six-year-old Rachel Held was the only survivor of her family. Barbara Schechter, born in Buczacz in 1941, was taken by her mother to an Austrian village on false papers and reunited with the father at a DP (displaced persons) camp. In 1946 they emigrated to the United States. Interview with J. Neufeld, July 19, 2002, and subsequent email communications; interview with Regina Gertner, July 31, 2002, and communications with her daughter Lucy Gertner, June 9, 2010; correspondence with S. (Kleiner) Ages and her daughter Deena Ages, January 17, 2007, May 11–12 and September 14, 2009; R. Halpern, YVS M-1/E, 2309 (2283), June 16, 1948; Halpern, *Family and Town*, 30–31, 38, 72, 78; "Barbara Schechter Cohen interview, 2002," Voice/Vision Holocaust Survivor Oral History Archive, http://holocaust.umd.umich.edu/cohenb (accessed December 9, 2016).

7 A. Karl, SFV 9899, December 10, 1995; email exchanges, July 5 and

18, and telephone interview, July 25, 2002. The family emigrated to Peru. See M. Karl, *Escape a la Vida* (Lima, 1989).

8 R. Zurof (Tabak), SFV 6138, August 31, 1995. Zbigniew Posadowski, IPN Kraków, S 37/03/zn, vol. 2, September 25, 2002 (hereafter Posadowski 2002), p. 399, notes that in June 1944 "a Bandera member was caught" in Czortków and "admitted to having murdered 27 Poles." He "was condemned to death by hanging and the execution was carried out publicly in the market square. . . . The corpse was left hanging for three days." Romaniia Kazanovich, also born in 1936, survived in Buczacz with her grandparents, Hersh and Cyla Heller. After the war Hersh became a school director in Buczacz, and Romaniia married a local Ukrainian; later in life she considered moving to Israel. "I really love this country," she said about Ukraine. "But for some reason I never felt myself quite at home here." She thought it was time they "tell us where the Jews were buried . . . because it saddens me to think that we are all just walking on their corpses. . . . I think that people should know." R. Kazanovich, SFV 30282, April 10, 1997. In spring and summer 1944 she was cared for by the Russian Anna Skvartsova, whose Jewish husband was denounced by a Ukrainian acquaintance and killed; their daughter Gizela, born in Moscow in 1923, later "married a Jewish man named Fisher who came back from the war and they had two children." Gizela left Buczacz in 2005 to join her daughter in Israel; she was the last Jew in the city. A. Polec, *Zapomniani* (Olszanica, Poland, 2006), unpaginated.

9 G. Weksler, USHMM, RG-15.084 Acc. 1997 A.0125, Reel 19, 1865; AŻIH 301/1865 and a slightly later testimony in Yiddish, Towa Weksler, YVA, M-1/E, 2162.

10 Six years older, Aliza's sister Dvorah (Diamant) was deeply traumatized by the experience of hiding in bunkers: "I feel this fear to this day. I often wake up in the middle of the night . . . paralyzed by the fear, a fear that you cannot describe. . . . The older you get, the more difficult it is. . . . You are never liberated." A. Rosenwasser, YVS 03-10402, VT-1612, July 17, 1997; D. Diamant, YVS 03-10269, VT-1614, July 20, 1997.

11 In 2005 the Zarivny family was recognized by Yad Vashem as "Righteous among the Nations," under the Polish rendition of the name,

Zarowny: http://www.yadvashem.org/yv/pdf-drupal/poland.pdf (accessed December 27, 2016).

12 Gekht, "Road from Ghetto to Orphanage"; Gekht, "Stolen Childhood," 137–39; Hecht, "A Long Search for Roots"; V. Poznanskyy, "Crushed Childhood"; Hecht, personal account to his cousin Z. Karniel (Hirschhorn). Rutyna (interview, 2006) said that Zarivny was his brother-in-law: "They hid several Jews in Wojciechówka." For the case of Menachem Kriegel, another orphan adopted by the Red Army, see SFV 28634, April 13, 1997; Emanuel Kriegel, YVA, M-49/196, Kraków, May 28, 1945; Karniel, "Grandfather Kriegel." For David Ashkenaze, who ended up as a high-ranking Soviet officer, see SFV 38119, 1997. See also S. Kovalchuk, "He Was Shot Three Times," *Puls* (regional weekly of the Khmelnytskyi region), Nr. 24 (June 21, 2001, in Ukrainian); author's personal communication with Ashkenaze from Slavuta, Ukraine, March 8, 2004.

13 A. Resnick (Resnik, Herzog), SFV 5226, August 6, 1995; telephone interview with Dr. A. H. Resnik in 2002. There are some discrepancies between the two.

14 R. Brecher, YVA, 033/765 E/32-3-3, Czernowitz, late 1944 or early 1945; AŻIH 301/4911, Bucharest, May 20, 1945.

15 A. Nir (Reinisch), YVA 03/11147, March 9, 1999.

16 Elaine Flitman (E. Spielberg), SFV 1622, March 14, 1995.

17 Z. Heiss, YVA; J. Heiss, interview with the author, New York, October 10, 2002.

18 A. Appleman-Jurman, SFV 11552, January 29, 1996; telephone interview with author, October 19, 2005; and memoir, *Alicia* (Toronto, 1988).

19 Fannie Kupitz (Feldman), SFV 2177, April 25, 1994; interview with author, New York City, October 10, 2002.

20 For another version of Janek Anderman's death, see chapter 5. Elsewhere Anderman commented that these armed Jews "were, may history forgive me, bandits, they were no partisans, but they fought for their existence." Z. Anderman, interview with author, Tel Aviv, March 12, 2002 (hereafter Anderman 2002). On other armed Jews in the forest, see Aaron Silber, SFV 20764, October 23, 1996. Other accounts of February

1943 are in Benjamin Herzog, "The Scene at the Mass Graves after the Action," YVA M-1/E, 2322, no date, likely late 1940s, and Bernard Kramer, BArch, B162/5167, Beit-Dagon, Israel, May 12, 1966, 4 pages.

21 Anderman 2002; Ze'ev Anderman, SFV 36290, December 16, 1997.

22 S. Rosen, USHMM, reel 20, 1935 (AŻIH 301/1935), Kraków, August 6, 1946, and YVA, M-49/1935 (03/2055), Tel Aviv, December 20, 1960; Rosen, 2002. See also A. W. Kaczorowski, "Gdy grób był domem," *Biuletyn Instytutu Pamięci Narodowej* 3/98 (March 2009): 66–68; M. Paldiel, *The Path of the Righteous* (Hoboken, NJ, 1992), 191–93.

23 Wizinger, YVA. He previously worked in the tunnel reconstruction site. Another tunnel worker, Beno Wechsler, also survived; helped by Polish villagers until spring 1944, he then joined the Red Army. YVA 03/9078, Netanya, Israel, February 22 and July 2, 1968; Wechsler 1995. Henryk Rosen described Świerszczak as "a good Christian" who told them, "If I turn you in, then my kids, my grandkids, and their grandchildren will have to pay for my sin." H. Rosen, SFV 35502, November 10, 1997. The Armia Krajowa (Polish Home Army, AK) commander of the Buczacz district in 1939–43 was Mieczysław Lipa: WBBH, III/49/289, pp. 1–4.

24 Bauer 2003. Simcha Tischler had a similar opinion about his Ukrainian friends in Nagórzanka: "You could say that a brother wouldn't do more for me than they did." Tischler 1997. Schmetterling 1995 credited Ukrainians in the same village with saving him: "That's why I survived; they helped me. Not all of them . . . killed." See also Gross 1996; Rachel Schwechter, Fortunoff Video Archive for Holocaust Testimonies, Yale University Library (hereafter FA), HVT-986. On Jewish resisters and forest family camps, see also "The Jewish Gang of Buczacz (Galicia)," YVA M-1/E, 1725, January 18, 1948; Gutkowski 1998. The AK reported that Soviet "partisans displayed a dislike for Jews." AAN, AK, zesp. 1326, 203/XV/26, July 14, 1943, pp. 7–10.

25 Posadowski 2002, p. 398, testified that in March 1944 the Soviets "caught a Pole named Wolff, a German citizen or ethnic German, who had collaborated with the Gestapo, put him in the Czortków prison,

and conducted a show trial, in which he was condemned to death by hanging. The sentence was carried out at the bus terminal."

26 R. Dobrecka, AŻIH 301/2274; S. Dobrecki, AŻIH 301/3611. Both recorded in Łódź, likely in 1946.

27 Kornblüh 1948.

28 USHMM, RG-15.084M, reel 38, 1997.A.0125; AŻIH 301/197. See also Samuel Eizen, YIVO, RG 1187, Series 2, No. 1187, Box 1, folder 19.

29 M. Szpigiel, AŻIH 301/3492, Łódź, March 10, 1948; E. Grintal (Nachtigal), SFV 34780, Netanya, Israel, September 21, 1997. Nusia Wacher reported that "around the town of Tłuste, there were five Wehrmacht labor camps and all young people from the entire area who had survived worked in them until the Russians liberated us in March 1944." She recalled, "In March 1944 (Purim) the goyim murdered 42 Jews with knives in the camp of Hołowczyńce at night while they were sleeping." Private correspondence with author, Caracas, Venezuela, November 1, 2003, March 12, 2004, October 12, 2004. See also on these camps, "Vathie" or "Vati," and the German air raid on Tłuste in Szwarc 1945; Nusia Mützel, BArch (Außenstelle Ludwigsburg), 301aa5, vol. 81, pp. 121–23, 124–29; AŻIH 964/817 and 2335/2383; Bernhard Seidenfeld, YVA 033/324, Haifa, Israel; Margules 1960; Zvi Fenster, BArch (Außenstelle Ludwigsburg) 301aa5, vol. 81, May 20, 1968, pp. 95–111: "Camps in the Czortków District"; H. (Hersch, Zvi) Fenster, AŻIH 301/1310. See also Z. Fenster, "Bericht über die Vernichtung" (July 1941–April 1944), August 2, 1968: International Tracing Service archives, Bad Arolsen, Germany (ITS), 821 88099-0-1. Komański, "Ludobójstwo i czystki etniczne," 14, on the murder of Jews by Ukrainians wielding "axes and other sharp tools" in Jezierzany, July 1941.

Chapter 7: NEIGHBORS

1 V. Petrykevych diary.

2 Tsentalnyi derzhavnyi arkhiv vyshchykh orhaniv vlady ta upravlinnia (Central State Archives of the Supreme Bodies of Power and

Government of Ukraine, Kiev, hereafter TsDAVO), fond 3833, op. 1, spr. 134, December 15, 1943, pp. 76–79.

3 G. Motyka, "Der Krieg im östlichen Galizien," *Karta* 1 (2000): 36–37. See also M. Terles, *Ethnic Cleansing of Poles in Volhynia and Eastern Galicia, 1942–1946* (Toronto, 1993); K. Stadnik, "Ukrainian-Polish Population Transfers, 1944–46," in *Warland*, ed. P. Gatrell et al. (London, 2009), 165–87. On Buczacz, see N. Davies, *Europe: A History* (New York, 1996), 1034–35; Urban, *Droga Krzyżowa*, 52–55. See also "Kartotek zbrodni ukraińskich w Małopolsce Wschodnie w latach 1939–1945," BOss., 166629/I, vol. 1, pp. 319, 329–31, 337, 353, 356, 378, 390, 464, 476; "Informacja Wschodnia," BS, P. 349 Cim., 1943–44: September 1943, pp. 22–26; December 1943, pp. 97–99; March 1944, pp. 162–63, describing the Germans as "indifferent to the Ukrainian anti-Polish campaign."

4 V. Petrykevych diary; W. Wołkowski, AZHRL, Lublin, 1958, pp. 1–25, concluding that 835 Poles were killed in "mass murders carried out by Ukrainian murderers" in eighteen towns and villages in the Buczacz district. For numerous additional eyewitness accounts from the surrounding districts, see J. Wołczański, *Eksterminacja* (Kraków, 2006), 2:22–27, 92–94, 98–99, 105–7, 111–12, 116–17, 126, 128, 130, 141, 244, 248–49, 398–401, 428–30, claiming that "one could always come to an understanding with the Germans," since among Poles they found "civilized people who spoke German," but that "the so-called Banderites" accomplished "the extermination of the Polish nation" in Galicia.

5 Rutyna interviews in March and June 2006; Studium Polski Podziemnej (Polish Underground Trust, London), Lol 5/11o, April 30, 1943, pp. 90–96, 99, 104–7. While stressing "the colossal loss of the Polish population," the report added, "The loss of the Jewish population remains beyond comment." M. Sobków, "Völker am Scheideweg," *Karta* 1 (2000): 77.

6 V. Petrykevych diary. Soviet reconnaissance units reached Buczacz the day before, March 23. On the massacre in Korościatyn, see also Sobków, "Völker am Scheideweg," 77, claiming that 160 Poles were butchered there.

7 Sobków, "Völker am Scheideweg," 78; BOss., 16599/II, "Ilu na jest Polaków," p. 242.

8 Transcript of interview with S. Kubasiewicz by Frank Grelka in 2005, and written reminiscences he provided. See also "Repatriacja," *Luszpiński*, http://www.luszpinski.pl/doc (accessed October 21, 2016).

9 TsDAVO, fond 3833, op. 1, spr. 134, March 23, 1944, pp. 1–4; May 27, 1944, pp. 65–66; Sobków, "Völker am Scheideweg," 82, 85. See also Edward Hładkiewicz, YVA 06/337, Milewski, pp. 3–4: "Krupa from the hamlet of Kizia" near Koropiec "murdered his wife, since she was Polish," and describing the massacre in Korościatyn; Wołczański, *Eksterminacja*, 1:141; H. Komański et al., eds., *Ludobójstwo dokonane przez nacjonalistów ukraińskich na Polakach w województwie tarnopolskim 1939–1946* (Wrocław, 2004), 170–71, 651–53, 664–68, 673–74. Father Kazimierz Slupski saved several Jews in Puźniki, including the gymnasium teacher Adolf Korngut and the Judenrat member Bernhard Seifer. See W. Bartoszewski et al., eds., *Righteous among Nations* (London, 1969), 337–39; W. Tannenzapf et al., *Memories from the Abyss* (Toronto, 2009), 113–16. For an account of a massacre in February 1945 in the mixed village of Zaleszczyki Małe (Ukrainian: Mali Zaleshchyky), see Franciszek Kowalski, AW, II/1339, esp. pp. 1–8, 15–37. The AK reported the killing of over one hundred Poles, "mostly women, old people and children," in Burakówka (Ukrainian: Buryakivka), Zaleszczyki county, on December 17–18, 1944, as well as in various villages in Buczacz and Czortków Counties, with the result that "the number of those registered for departure to the West has greatly increased." PAK, DATO, Report No. 5, January 1, 1945, single page. Other atrocities in IPN Kraków, S 37/03/zn, vol. 3, November 22, 2002, pp. 412–13; Komański, "Ludobójstwo i czystki etniczne," 14–15, 22–25; Józef Kroczak, AZHRL.

10 BOss. 16721/I, Stanisławów PKO (Polski Komitet Opiekuńczy, Hilfskomitee, Polish Welfare Committee) to Kraków RGO (Rada Główna Opiekuńcza, Main Welfare Council), June 8, 1944, pp. 325, 331, 333; V. Petrykevych diary. See also Polish analysis of UPA and local self-defense groups, spring 1944, AAN, zesp. 1325, DRK (Delegatura

Rządu na Kraj, the Polish government in exile's underground delegation to Poland), 202/III-126, p. 14.

11 See n. 3 above.

12 BOss. 16721/I, October 1–15, 1944, pp. 138–49.

13 See also district chief Hans Kujath's report on evacuating the Czortków
district: BArch R52 III/2, March 20, 1944, pp. 5–8; and account of the
visit to Buczacz by Galicia's governor Otto Wächter on April 8, 1944,
soon after its recapture, mentioning the presence of "about 1,000 Jews,
who had hidden in the area," and for whom the retreating "Bolshevik
troops had no time": BArch R52 III/2, April 9, 1944, pp. 60–65.

14 DATO, fond P-69, op. 1, spr. 8. An undated report for the Ternopil
oblast cites 7,000 civilians shot and 1,839 deported to Germany: fond
R-274, op. 1, spr. 123, p. 17.

15 BArch Baden-Württemberg, GLA-K, 309 Zug. 2001-42/868, Sonderband
32, exhumation protocols, interrogation transcripts, and reports, trans.
from Russian into German for the trial of Brettschneider et al., pp. 11–18.

16 Among the early commission members were Abram Eber, Markus
Kleiner, Józef Kornblüh, and Samuel Rosental; testimonies were given
by Samuel Horowitz, Alicja Jurman, and David Seiler. Later the commission included Abba Reiner; chief of the district health department
Brandwein; and the doctors Anderman and Chalfen. SEC, HDA
SBU, m. Ternopil, spr. 14050-P, p. 151. See also M. Sorokina, "People
and Procedures," *Kritika* 6/4 (2005): 797–831.

17 The 14th SS Volunteer Division "Galicia," whose creation was announced in April 1943, brought eighteen thousand Ukrainians into
the ranks of the Waffen-SS. Many of them died in a futile battle with
the Red Army the following year; numerous survivors joined the UPA,
alongside thousands of deserting Ukrainian policemen. D. R. Marples,
Heroes and Villains (New York, 2007), 183–93. Sipo concluded that
"the Ukrainian population perceives the authorization of a Ukrainian
military formation as expressing the will of the Reich to make positive
use of Ukrainians for the construction of the East, to some extent in
preference to the Poles": Meldungen aus dem GG [Generalgouver-
nement, General Government], 1–31.5.1943, BArch R58/7743, p. 9.

Father Yevtemyi Bobretskyi of the Basilian monastery in Buczacz became divisional chaplain; he later died in Siberia. Myzak, *For You, Holy Ukraine*, 4:10–14. *Lvivski Visti*'s lead article, May 8, 1943, reported, "The first day of recruiting volunteers . . . was conducted in a good atmosphere and numerous applicants were registered." The July 8 issue describes a May 1 recruitment launch assembly on Fedor Hill led by Landkommissar Hoffer, Kreishauptmann Kujath, and Ukrainian district committee chair Mykhailo Rosliak, with fifteen thousand people and six hundred horsemen. Biblioteka Uniwersytecka we Wrocławiu (University Library in Wrocław), 3842 IV, microfilms 101, 102, 116, 126, 151. See also *Krakivski Visti*, May 29, 1943, issue 113, p. 3: Ossolineum Wrocław, 295.897 II.

18 V. Petrykevych diary. The German Security Police reported at the time, "The situation on the Eastern Front . . . has further exacerbated the anxiety of the Ukrainians about the Bolsheviks. . . . The Ukrainian intelligentsia, which works especially closely with the German administration, is already trying to find out from German officials, what will become of it in case of a Bolshevik victory." BArch R70 Polen/204, pp. 8, 11.

19 M. Khvostenko, reminiscences collected by M. Kozak, March 27, 2003.

20 J. Trembach, recollections recorded by R. Kryvenchuk, collected by Mykola Kozak, 2003. See also Halpern, *Family and Town*, 89. The Polish Izabela Kocik testified that in spring or summer 1943 "I saw my classmate Marysia, whose surname was probably Aszkinazy, at the head of an eight-person column" on the main street of Czortków, "surrounded by a group of armed German gendarmes and Ukrainian policemen. Marysia, a very good and polite girl, gave me such a desperate look, that I will never forget her gaze to my last day. I knew she was going to her death." IPN Kraków, S 37/03/zn, vol. 2, September 6, 2002, p. 389.

21 Hałkiewicz interview, 2004; Rutyna interviews in March and June 2006.

22 M. Szczyrba, USHMM RG-15.084 M Reel 38 (1997.A.0125) UC (AŻIH 301/3684), Warsaw, May 7, 1945, pp. 1–20.

23 M. Boczar, Minkowice Oławskie, August 1, 1947, AŻIH 303/VIII/222, pp. 49–50. The five Jews included Basia and Sara Strauber of Potok Złoty, likely relatives of Fabian and Josef Strauber of the same town. See

Strauber 1947; J. Strauber, deposition, New York, August 11, 1969, BArch B162/5185, pp. 7117–18.

24 E. Czechowicz, Szczecin, October 2, 1947, AŻIH 303/VIII/223, pp. 70–72. See also J. B. Michlic, "Rescuer-Rescuee Relationships in the Light of Postwar Correspondence in Poland, 1945–1949," *Yad Vashem Studies* 39 /2 (2011): 169–207. On Altschüler, who was also a member of the Jewish police, see BArch B162/5181, December 5, 1968, pp. 5892–97; BArch (Bayreuth, Lastenausgleicharchiv), ZLA 1/220643600, M1.3/173/2/5, pp. 22–23, 32–34, 37–38, 49–50; AŻIH 313/3, March 21, 1947.

25 DATO, fond R-1, op. 1, spr. 101, August 1, 1944, pp. 103–6.

26 DATO, fond R-1, op. 1, spr. 101, September 6, 1944, pp. 130–42.

27 Bilas, *Punitive System of Repression*, 2:478–82, 514–17.

28 DATO, fond P-69, op. 1, spr. 32, p. 4; op. 11, spr. 22, pp. 1–2, 12–13.

29 DATO, fond P-69, op. 11, spr. 22, pp. 1–2; spr. 31, September 25, 1946, pp. 35–37; November 17, 1946, p. 30.

30 DATO, fond R-1, op. 1, spr. 561, January 31, 1947, p. 150; spr. 871, April 1–July 1, 1947, pp. 93–96; September 20, 1947, pp. 97–98; fond P-69, op. 1, spr. 31, January 1, 1947, pp. 38–40; spr. 54, pp. 66–67.

31 DATO, fond P-69, op. 1, spr. 65, pp. 19–34; spr. 47, pp. 10–11; fond R-1, op. 1, spr. 871, October 25, 1947, pp. 100–101; October 23, 1947, pp. 102–3; "Memorial" society, Buczacz branch, estimate based on local primary sources and secondary works. For Soviet reports of crimes by their own troops and officials, see DATO, fond P-10, op. 1, spr. 1, p. 105; spr. 6, p. 13; spr. 10, pp. 61, 75; spr. 31, pp. 15, 55; spr. 713, p. 122; fond P-19, op. 1, spr. 23, p. 2; spr. 146, p. 117; fond P-69, op. 1, spr. 11, p. 14; spr. 33, pp. 53–54; spr. 35, pp. 1–2; spr. 61, pp. 15, 20; spr. 64, p. 52; spr. 65, p. 37; spr. 87, p. 11. See also V. Serhiichuk, *Ten Tumultuous Years* (Kiev, 1998, in Ukrainian and Russian), 425–26.

32 DATO, fond P-69, op. 1, spr. 65, pp. 19–34; spr. 284, April 19, 1945, pp. 2–3, 13–14, 29 (likely September–October 1945); spr. 608, June 20, 1945, pp. 5–6.

33 On November 1, 1947, the Ternopil region reported taking in 35,106 Ukrainian immigrant families from Poland, for a total of 155,621 people. Of those, 1,575 families with 7,105 persons were settled in the Buczacz

district in 1,575 houses that had formerly belonged to relocated Poles, to deported families of OUN-UPA members, or to murdered Jews. These "young citizens of Soviet Ukraine, along with other working people," were now "happily and tirelessly working in order to reach the goals of Stalin's postwar 5-year plan." DATO, fond R-1833, op. 2, spr. 101, pp. 1–7.

AFTERMATH

1 Pasichnyk interview, 2006.

2 I. Duda, *Buczacz* (Lviv, 1985, in Ukrainian).

3 Pasichnyk interview, 2006; O. Synenka, *For the Homeland, for My People* (Ternopil, 2002, in Ukrainian), 151–55.

4 Ivan Yosypovych Synenkyi, PA, October 29, 2004; transcript of interview with O. Synenka and I. Senekyi by Sofia Grachova and Andriy Pavlyashuk, Buczacz, March 2, 2006.

5 Synenka and Senekyi interview, 2006; K. Sapir Weitz, "The Landscape of Their Childhood: Ruhama Albag's Journey in the Footsteps of Great Hebrew Writers" (in Hebrew), *Maariv*, February 16, 2015, http://www.maariv.co.il/culture/literature/Article-463561 (accessed August 26, 2016); R. Albag, *To the Place: Following the Booksteps* (Tel Aviv, 2015, in Hebrew); R. Albag, "It's the 'Synagoga,' Not Something Else," *Haaretz*, September 28, 2001, B13.

6 T. Pavlyshyn, "The Holocaust in Buczacz," *Nova Doba* 48 (December 1, 2000, in Ukrainian).

7 O. Chorniy, "The Front in Buczacz," *Nova Doba* 45 (November 10, 2000, in Ukrainian).

8 Duda, *Buczacz*; PA, Buczacz City Museum: this record contains many more similar cases. The collaborationist *Lvivski Visti* reported on February 29, 1943, on an anti-Bolshevik meeting of "497 representatives of the Ukrainian population of the Buczacz district" in protest of "the Bolshevik policy of conquest," asserting "that communism is alien to us" and vowing to "fight against Bolshevism" and "work together with Greater Germany" in order "to bring about the final victory." BUW, 3842 IV, microfilm 43.

Index

About the Author

Omer Bartov is the John P. Birkelund Distinguished Professor of European History at Brown University. Born and raised in Israel, he is the author of several well-respected books on war, genocide, and the Holocaust, including *Hitler's Army, Murder in Our Midst, Mirrors of Destruction*, and *Germany's War and the Holocaust*. His most recent book, *Erased: Vanishing Traces of Jewish Galicia in Present-Day Ukraine,* investigates interethnic relations in the borderlands of Eastern Europe and the contemporary politics of memory in that region. He has written for the *New Republic*, the *Wall Street Journal*, the *Nation*, and *The New York Times Book Review*, and is currently directing the project "Israel-Palestine: Lands and Peoples," at the Watson Institute for International and Public Affairs at Brown University. He lives in Cambridge, Massachusetts.

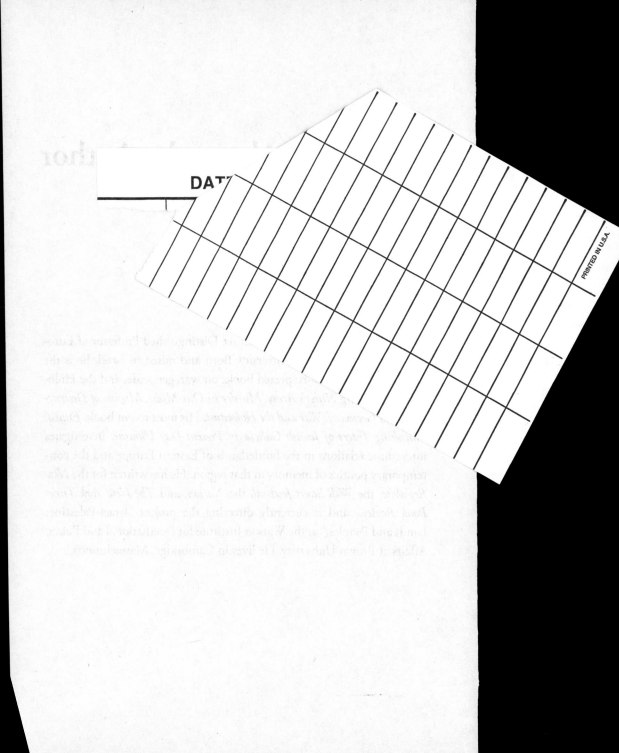